Contemporary
Quotations

Contemporary Quotations

Compiled by

James B. Simpson

Thomas Y. Crowell Company

New York   *Established 1834*

To the memory of
Ann Gillis Slocum

and for *Dick, Jane, Joe, Mary, Matt, Jimmy,* and *Angela,*
      whose generation will voice
      the contemporary quotations of the future

Preface

This book celebrates our articulate age, an age of incredibly swift communication when a succinct phrase may be flashed around the world and quoted in a dozen languages before the end of the day on which it is spoken.

The pronouncements of the world's political and cultural leaders sometimes constitute the very essence of the news; the words of lesser figures, perhaps not as momentous but often more incisive, are also an integral part of the story of our times. Our era boasts eloquent spokesmen from every level of society, and I believe their words should not be buried in the formidable and sometimes inaccessible files of newspapers and magazines.

Most of the quotations in this book gained attention the moment they were written or spoken. More than a few are bright threads in the fabric of modern history. Some will become more important in the perspective of time. A goodly number already echo back and forth across the seas and across the years.

My work on this book has stretched over more than a decade. It is an avocation that seemed to be waiting just around a corner almost as soon as I had put undergraduate days behind me. In its pursuit I have read eight daily newspapers, ten weekly magazines, from twelve to fifteen monthly magazines, and as many specialized journals as I could cover. This basic reading was augmented with selections from new books and offerings from the lecture platform, the pulpit, the theater, radio and television. Sometimes a burden, but never a bore, the compilation has given direction to my days and a *raison d'être* for reading anything, anywhere, anytime.

While my choice of quotations has been directed by what I like to regard as a fairly catholic curiosity, this is nevertheless one man's collection. Another's scrapbook would bear *his* distinctive stamp. The reader may judge how successfully I have differentiated between the significant and the inconsequential, between what is for the moment and what is likely to have enduring interest.

I am especially indebted to television, for it was while serving as editorial consultant for one of NBC's first panel programs that I became convinced of the lasting interest of some of the material I gathered. The idea persisted and became a reality in *Best Quotes of '54, '55, '56* (published also by the Thomas Y. Crowell Company), part of which is incorporated in this volume.

The late Ann Gillis Slocum, brilliant producer of *Who Said That?* gave me the opportunity to do the initial research and I shall always be grateful to her. Many others have also contributed to this book, especially the journalists here and abroad who first recorded so much of the material. My long-time friend and associate, Edward M Story, has been of invaluable help in the preparation and editing of the manuscript. Even while studying at Berkeley Divinity School, New Haven, for ordination to the Episcopal priesthood, he has given his time without limit to the careful indexing of sources and subjects. Mrs. John Samuel Ruef of New Haven also helped in indexing. Miss Louella D. Everett of Boston, Mass., that gallant, incomparable lady and scholar who edited three editions of *Bartlett's Familiar Quotations*, also gave me generous counsel. Like Mr. Story, she occasionally sent what she gleaned from her own careful reading. Miss Patricia L. Brueckner made important contributions to the organization and general structure of the book. My secretary, Miss Viola Ann Terradista, has been a valuable helper with correspondence, particularly in the verification of some quotations.

In addition, I am eager to thank Mr. Gilbert Cam and the New York Public Library for the use of the Frederick Lewis Allen Memorial Room. For me it has been a haven of peace, an island of solitude, a monk's cell of quietness in the middle of Manhattan, and it has served my research well.

Interest and encouragement is unusually important in carrying out a prolonged project and in that respect I am indebted to my family and to numerous friends, including Phyllis Battelle, Don Benjamin, Ruth Berkeley, Fred Bray, Gorton Carruth, Eleanor Early, Lucy Freeman, Murray Gartner, Bill Guthman, Jacqueline James, Howard Johnson, Eleanor Jordan, H. V. Kaltenborn, Julie King, Bernard Kinzer, Patricia Ludorf, Charles P. McCurdy, Jr., Beverly Reitz, Elsa Russell, Henry Sell, Alice Boyd Stockdale, Amy Vanderbilt, George Whipple, and the Bishop of Springfield, the Right Reverend Albert A. Chambers.

All who seek to understand our times will be indebted to the men and women who are quoted in these pages.

James B. Simpson

New York
May 18, 1964

Contents

The Nation

The World

Man

Communications and the Arts

American Government

Whatever the outcome of the appeal, I do not intend to turn my back on Alger Hiss.

> DEAN ACHESON, Secretary of State, on a former aide's conviction for perjury, *Time*, Feb. 6, 1950.

For me, there is very little doubt about these standards or these principles. They were stated for us a very long time ago . . . on the Mount of Olives.

> DEAN ACHESON, *ibid*.

I will undoubtedly have to seek what is happily known as gainful employment, which I am glad to say does not describe holding public office.

> DEAN ACHESON, on leaving his position as Secretary of State, *Time*, Dec. 22, 1952.

We are not the bosses of taxpayers; they are ours.

> T. COLEMAN ANDREWS, on changing name of his department from Internal Revenue Bureau to Internal Revenue Service, news reports of Oct. 24, 1955.

There is something wrong with any law that causes that many people to have to take a whole day off from their jobs to find out how to comply.

> T. COLEMAN ANDREWS, report that 12 million taxpayers in 1954 sought help from Internal Revenue Service in filling out income tax forms, *ibid*.

We're not advocating the plowing under of every fourth farmer.

> EZRA TAFT BENSON, Secretary of Agriculture, defending presidential recommendation that so-called marginal farmers should turn to other work, news reports of Feb. 2, 1954.

1

They have a passion for anonymity.

> LOUIS BROWNLOW, who, as chairman of President Roosevelt's Committee on Administrative Management in 1936–37, originated the phrase "passion for anonymity" (that eventually became a cliché) in speaking of FDR's advisers such as Harry Hopkins and Felix Frankfurter; recalled on his death, Sept. 28, 1963.

I was offered the ambassadorship of Liberia once, when that post was earmarked for a Negro. I told them I wouldn't take a Jim Crow job.

> RALPH BUNCHE, after becoming UN Under Secretary, *Think*, Jan., 1961.

There is one difference between a tax collector and a taxidermist—the taxidermist leaves the hide.

> MORTIMER CAPLAN, Director, Internal Revenue Service, *Time*, Feb. 1, 1963.

When the history of this Republic shall be written, Woodrow Wilson's titanic figure will tower above the puny pygmies who now bark at his memory as Pike's Peak towers above the fog of an Arkansas swamp.

> TOM CONNALLY, U.S. Representative, 1916–28, U.S. Senator, 1928–52; called "Tawl Tawm from Texas," he was noted for flamboyant oratory and this statement, urging that the UN be given support denied the League of Nations, was recalled on his death, Oct. 28, 1963.

We cannot put the face of a person on a stamp unless said person is deceased. My suggestion, therefore, is that you drop dead.

> JAMES EDWARD DAY, Postmaster General, letter dictated but not mailed to a petitioner who wanted himself portrayed on a postage stamp, *New York Times*, March 7, 1962.

Local defense must be reinforced by the further deterrent of massive retaliatory power.

> JOHN FOSTER DULLES, Secretary of State, address to Council on Foreign Relations, Jan. 12, 1954, establishing "massive retaliation" as a reference closely associated with the Dulles era.

2

There is only one defense—a defense compounded of eternal vigilance, sound policies, and high courage.

> JOHN FOSTER DULLES, news reports of March 30, 1954.

You have to take chances for peace, just as you must take chances in war. . . . The ability to get to the verge without getting into the war is the necessary art. If you try to run away from it, if you are scared to go to the brink, you are lost. We've had to look it square in the face—on the question of enlarging the Korean war, on the question of getting into the Indochina war, on the question of Formosa. We walked to the brink and we looked it in the face. We took strong action.

> JOHN FOSTER DULLES, "How Dulles Averted War," by James Shepley, *Life*, Jan. 16, 1956. The catch phrase, "brinksmanship," was afterwards linked with Dulles' policies.

First we just gave them these surpluses. Next we agreed to pay freight on transportation to ports. Then we agreed to mill the grain and package it. The next thing we'll be asked to cook and serve it.

> SENATOR ALLEN ELLENDER, on complaints of relief and charitable agencies against food given them by U.S. Government, April 1, 1956.

An "egghead" is one who stands firmly on both feet in mid-air on both sides of an issue.

> SENATOR HOMER FERGUSON, on "egghead" intellectuals in government, news summaries of May 28, 1954.

We have the power to do any damn fool thing we want to do, and we seem to do it about every ten minutes.

> SENATOR WILLIAM FULBRIGHT, on Senate's right to change its mind, *Time*, Feb. 4, 1952.

Conferences at the top level are always courteous. Name-calling is left to the foreign ministers.

> AVERELL HARRIMAN, former ambassador to Russia, news summaries of Aug. 1, 1955.

3

If ignorance paid dividends, most Americans could make a fortune out of what they don't know about economics.

> LUTHER HODGES, Secretary of Commerce, *Wall Street Journal*, March 14, 1962.

Thirty years ago we used to believe there were only two occasions in which the American people would respect the privacy of the President—in prayer and fishing. I now detect you have lost the second part of this. . . . That is one of the degenerations of the last thirty years.

> HERBERT HOOVER, while vacationing at Fraser, Colorado, with President Eisenhower, news reports of Sept. 2, 1954.

I was in favor of giving former Presidents a seat in the Senate until I passed 75 years. Since then I have less taste for sitting on hard-bottomed chairs during long addresses.

> HERBERT HOOVER, *This Week*, Feb. 7, 1960.

The 49th star twinkles. The Senate can make it gleam.

> *Houston Press*, May 29, 1958, editorial urging Alaska's admission as a state.

You can't set a hen in one morning and have chicken salad for lunch.

> GEORGE HUMPHREY, Secretary of the Treasury, on the impossibility of quick economic change, *Time*, Jan. 26, 1953.

It's a terribly hard job to spend a billion dollars and get your money's worth.

> GEORGE HUMPHREY, *Look*, Feb. 23, 1954.

I don't think you can spend yourself rich.

> GEORGE HUMPHREY, on compensatory spending during business declines, news summaries of Jan. 28, 1957.

Democracy does not necessarily result from majority rule, but rather from the forged compromise of the majority with the minority . . . The philosophy of the Constitution . . . is not simply to grant the majority

4

the power to rule but is also to set out limitation after limitation upon that power . . .

> SENATOR DANIEL KEN INOUYE of Hawaii, in a debate on Senate rules, 1963.

The decision before us directly . . . is the power of the minority to reflect a proportional share of their view upon the legislative result.

> SENATOR DANIEL KEN INOUYE, *ibid.*

The Negro says, "Now." Others say, "Never." The voice of responsible Americans . . . says, "Together." There is no other way. Until justice is blind to color, until education is unaware of race, until opportunity is unconcerned with the color of men's skins, emancipation will be a proclamation but not a fact.

> LYNDON JOHNSON, Vice President, Memorial Day address, Gettysburg, Pa., May 30, 1963.

Too often our Washington reflex is to discover a problem and then throw money at it, hoping it will somehow go away.

> SENATOR KENNETH B. KEATING, *New York Times*, Dec. 24, 1961.

I was well acquainted with the gag that if you looked like your passport picture, you needed a trip. I was unprepared for the preponderance of thug-like pictures which I found in the course of processing passports.

> FRANCES KNIGHT, State Dept. Passport Division Chief, ruling that it is all right for Americans to smile in passport photo, *New York Herald Tribune*, Feb. 21, 1957.

I expect to fight that proposition until hell freezes over. Then I propose to start fighting on the ice.

> SENATOR RUSSELL LONG of Louisiana, on President Kennedy's request for a cutoff of funds to areas practicing segregation, *New York Times*, July 14, 1963.

It's like getting a shave and having your appendix out at the same time.

> ROBERT LOVETT, on exigencies of being Secretary of Defense, *Saturday Evening Post*, May 28, 1960.

5

When an Italian talks with an American he's inclined to feel a twinge of inferiority. America is rich and strong. Italy is poor. But when he talks to me, he's more at ease. I still represent a big, strong nation but I am a woman—and he's a man.

> CLARE BOOTHE LUCE, ambassador to Italy, news reports of May 4, 1954.

I am grateful for the overwhelming vote of confirmation in the Senate. We must now wait until the dirt settles. My difficulties, of course, go some years back when Senator Wayne Morse was kicked in the head by a horse.

> CLARE BOOTHE LUCE, statement to newsmen a half hour after Senate confirmed her nomination as ambassador to Brazil; her comment on the Oregon Senator touched off another controversy and she resigned the post within 48 hours, news reports of April 29, 1959.

I have in my hand 57 cases of individuals who would appear to be either card-carrying members or certainly loyal to the Communist party, but who, nevertheless, are helping to shape our foreign policy.

> SENATOR JOSEPH McCARTHY, speech which began his investigations and the era of McCarthyism, news reports of Feb. 9, 1950.

He sought to make U.S. policies understandable at the rice-roots level.

> Newsweek, Feb. 19, 1962, on Attorney General Robert Kennedy's visit to Japan.

Sound the sirens, close the schools and get going.

> WILLIAM QUINN, Governor of Hawaii, message shouted into overseas telephone wire from Washington to Honolulu seconds after Hawaii became 50th state, New York Times, March 13, 1959.

That's one wrong impression I can correct for you right away. I have been a bricklayer and housepainter. I think I had just as much connection with the working class as you have. I'm a country boy.

> JAMES RIDDLEBERGER, ambassador to Russia, reply to Nikita Khrushchev, news reports of May 29, 1955.

No form letters are sent out from this office. No husband was ever Section Three, Paragraph II-a, to his wife.

> ANNA ROSENBERG, Assistant Secretary of Defense, Newsweek, Feb. 27, 1951.

Let me say with a Georgia accent that we cannot solve this problem if it requires a diplomatic passport to claim the rights of an American citizen.

> DEAN RUSK, Secretary of State, commenting that the government should not commend restaurants which admit darkskinned diplomats while banning American Negroes, *Life*, International Edition, Jan. 1, 1962.

We're eye-ball to eye-ball and the other fellow just blinked.

> DEAN RUSK, on crisis with Cuba, *Saturday Evening Post*, Dec. 8, 1962.

Our voice is muted, our friends are embarrassed, our enemies are gleeful . . . We are running this race with one of our legs in a cast.

> DEAN RUSK, warning of racial strife's crippling effects on U.S. foreign policy, *New York Herald Tribune*, May 28, 1963.

. . . If we can now take even this one step along a new course, then frail and fearful mankind may find another step and another until confidence replaces terror and hope takes over from despair.

> DEAN RUSK, asking Senate ratification of nuclear test ban treaty with Russia, *New York Times*, Aug. 13, 1963.

The pace of events is moving so fast that unless we can find some way to keep our sights on tomorrow, we cannot expect to be in touch with today.

> DEAN RUSK, *Time*, Dec. 6, 1963.

. . . Continuity does not rule out fresh approaches to fresh situations.

> DEAN RUSK, on foreign policy following President Kennedy's assassination, *ibid*.

. . . The Constitution . . . speaks not only of the freedom of speech but also of trial by jury instead of trial by accusation.

> SENATOR MARGARET CHASE SMITH, one of the first denunciations of Senator Joseph McCarthy and his charges of Communists in high places, *Newsweek*, June 12, 1950.

In the White House, the future rapidly becomes the past; and delay is itself a decision.

> THEODORE SORENSEN, special counsel to President Kennedy, *Nation's Business*, June, 1963.

7

America today stands poised on a pinnacle of wealth and power, yet we live in a land of vanishing beauty, of increasing ugliness, of shrinking open space, and of an over-all environment that is diminished daily by pollution and noise and blight. This, in brief, is the quiet conservation crisis of the 1960's.

> STEWART UDALL, Secretary of the Interior, explaining title of his book, *The Quiet Crisis*, Holt, Rinehart and Winston, 1963.

At a time when American blood is again being shed to preserve our dream of freedom, we are constrained fearlessly and frankly to call the charges . . . what they truly are: a fraud and a hoax perpetrated on the Senate of the United States and the American people. They represent perhaps the most nefarious campaign of half-truths and untruths in the history of this republic.

> U.S. Senate Sub-Committee Democratic majority report on Senator Joseph McCarthy's charges of Communist infiltration, *Time*, July 24, 1950.

Until this moment, Senator, I think I never really gauged your cruelty or your recklessness. . . . If it were in my power to forgive you for your reckless cruelty, I would do so. I like to think I'm a gentle man, but your forgiveness will have to come from someone other than me.

> JOSEPH NYE WELCH, Army counsel, to Senator Joseph McCarthy, June 9, 1954, a high point in Senate Army-McCarthy hearings, deploring McCarthy's charge an aide of Welch's law firm had belonged to a Communist front group, *New York Times*, June 10, 1954.

Let us not assassinate this lad further, Senator. You've done enough. Have you no sense of decency, sir? At long last, have you left no sense of decency?

> JOSEPH NYE WELCH, *ibid.*

. . . What is good for the country is good for General Motors, and vice versa.

> CHARLES E. WILSON, President of General Motors, when asked by Chairman Richard Russell of Senate Armed Services Committee if, as Secretary of Defense, "Would you make a decision adverse to General Motors?" news reports of Jan. 23, 1953.

8

. . . But I have always liked bird dogs better than kennel-fed dogs myself —you know, one that will get out and hunt for food rather than sit on his fanny and yell.

> CHARLES E. WILSON, Secretary of Defense, on unemployment, a comment that became known as "Secretary Wilson's bird dog statement," news reports of Oct. 11, 1954.

I somehow feel there's a boomerang loose in the room.

> CHARLES E. WILSON, on ducking questions at a news conference, *New York Times*, Mar. 25, 1957.

Presidents

The second office of this government is honorable and easy, the first is but a splendid misery.
>THOMAS JEFFERSON, May 13, 1797, inspiration for title of Jack Bell's *The Splendid Misery*, Doubleday, 1960.

Harry S. Truman

As we move forward into the second half of the twentieth century, we must always bear in mind the central purpose of our national life. . . . We work for a better life for all, so that men may put to good use the great gifts with which they have been endowed by their Creator.
>PRESIDENT TRUMAN, State of the Union address, 1950.

The attack upon Korea makes it plain beyond all doubt that Communism has passed beyond the use of subversion to conquer independent nations and will now use armed invasion and war.
>PRESIDENT TRUMAN, broadcast announcing American intervention after North Korean troops had crossed 38th parallel border line, *Time*, July 3, 1950.

A President has to expect those things.
>PRESIDENT TRUMAN, on assassination attempt, Nov. 1, 1950.

The only thing you have to worry about is bad luck. I never have bad luck.
>PRESIDENT TRUMAN, *ibid.*

When I was a little boy I read about a fairy princess. And there she is.
>PRESIDENT TRUMAN, welcoming Princess Elizabeth on her first visit to Washington, *Time*, Nov. 12, 1951.

Men of the armed forces in Korea, you will go down in history as the first army to fight under a flag of a world organization in the defense of human freedom. . . . Victory may be in your hands, but you are winning a greater thing than military victory, for you are vindicating the idea of freedom under international law.

> PRESIDENT TRUMAN, address shortly after Korean War entered its second year, *Time*, July 16, 1951.

I have tried my best to give the nation everything I had in me. There are probably a million people who could have done the job better than I did it, but I had the job and I always quote an epitaph on a tombstone in a cemetery in Tombstone, Arizona: "Here lies Jack Williams. He done his damndest."

> PRESIDENT TRUMAN, at his first news conference after announcing that he would not seek a third term as President, *Time*, April 28, 1952.

If I'd known how much packing I'd have to do, I'd have run again.

> PRESIDENT TRUMAN, on leaving White House, *Time*, Jan. 26, 1953.

I don't care what people call me. I've been called everything. But I instructed the White House staff always to call Mr. Hoover "Mr. President" and I did myself. . . .

> MR. TRUMAN, in an interview with etiquette writer Amy Vanderbilt, news summaries of Jan. 23, 1955.

Any man who has had the job I've had and didn't have a sense of humor wouldn't still be here.

> MR. TRUMAN, news reports of April 19, 1955.

I'm glad to be rid of it. One really can't enjoy being President of the greatest republic in the history of the world. It's just too big a job for any one man to control it.

> MR. TRUMAN, when asked if he missed being President, news reports of July 12, 1955.

I felt as if I had lived five lifetimes in my first five days as President.*

> MR. TRUMAN, *Years of Decision*, autobiography, Doubleday, 1955.

---

* On Mr. Truman's 75th birthday, May 8, 1959, Eleanor Roosevelt (recalling the moment in the White House when she told him, "Harry, the President is dead") said:

11

It is a terrible—and I mean terrible—nuisance to be kin to the President of the United States.

> MR. TRUMAN, letter to his mother and sister a few weeks after becoming President, *ibid.*

I always considered statesmen to be more expendable than soldiers.

> MR. TRUMAN, *ibid.*

There is the big white jail.

> MR. TRUMAN, viewing the White House on a pre-breakfast walk in Washington, *New York Herald Tribune*, April 14, 1958.

It can't be done because I've tried it and it doesn't work. Whenever you put a man on the Supreme Court, he ceases to be your friend. I'm sure of that.

> MR. TRUMAN, *New York Herald Tribune*, April 29, 1959.

Most of the visitors come here to see if the animal is still alive. But I fool 'em; I stay in my office most of the time.

> MR. TRUMAN, on visitors to Truman Library, Independence, Mo., *Quote*, Sept. 13, 1959.

These tearjerkers, these fellows who are always saying what oughta been done and they weren't there and they don't know a damn thing about it . . . They keep crying their eyes out about those people who were killed by those bombs. I haven't heard any of them crying about those boys who were in those upside-down battleships in Pearl Harbor.

> MR. TRUMAN, when asked if he had any regrets about ordering atomic bombing of Hiroshima and Nagasaki, *Time*, Sept. 22, 1961.

"The character of my friend was proved on that terrible day. He was frightened—as he should have been. For no man had ever been placed so abruptly in such a seat of responsibility. And yet there was never in him the slightest hint that he would try to evade what fate had thrust upon him. I knew then he was a good man. Later I thrilled to watch him grow to greatness. With every decision he grew, until to the entire world he was a towering figure. The decisions he made then shaped the very world we live in today."

12

It seems like there is always somebody for supper.

> Mr. Truman, on life in the White House, *The Good New Days*, by Merriman Smith, Bobbs-Merrill, 1962.

Dwight David Eisenhower

. . . Whatever America hopes to bring to pass in the world must first come to pass in the heart of America. More than escape from death, it is a way of life. More than a haven for the weary, it is a hope for the brave. This is the hope that beckons us onward in this century of trial. . . .

> President Eisenhower, concluding his Inaugural Address, *Time*, Jan. 26, 1953.

I feel almost like bawling on my own shoulder.

> President Eisenhower, on first anniversary of his election, *New York World Telegram and Sun*, Nov. 5, 1953.

. . . From behind the Iron Curtain, there are signs that tyranny is in trouble and reminders that its structure is as brittle as its surface is hard.

> President Eisenhower, State of the Union message, Jan. 7, 1954.

. . . That precious intangible, the initiative, is becoming ours.

> President Eisenhower, *ibid*.

From this day forward, the millions of our school children will daily proclaim in every city and town, every village and rural school house, the dedication of our nation and our people to the Almighty.

> President Eisenhower, on signing law for inclusion of the words "under God" in the pledge of allegiance to the flag, June 14, 1954.

. . . For any American who had the great and priceless privilege of being raised in a small town there always remains with him nostalgic memories of those days. And the older he grows the more he senses what he owed

13

to the simple honesty and neighborliness, the integrity that he saw all around him in those days. . . .

> PRESIDENT EISENHOWER, address to National Editorial Association, June 22, 1954.

It is only governments that are stupid, not the masses of people.

> PRESIDENT EISENHOWER, address to World Christian Endeavor Community, July 25, 1954.

As quickly as you start spending federal money in large amounts, it looks like free money.

> PRESIDENT EISENHOWER, Feb. 9, 1955.

. . . Do not try to say, "They are going to attack me today, therefore I shall attack them yesterday. . . ."

> PRESIDENT EISENHOWER, on over-preparedness, March 30, 1955.

. . . The last thing I would ever ask any man that I appoint to a high office is what are going to be his decisions in specific cases.

> PRESIDENT EISENHOWER, on his appointees, *ibid*.

They have a freedom I would personally dearly love.

> PRESIDENT EISENHOWER, on White House squirrels, *ibid*.

There will never be a child in the United States denied this emergency protection for want of ability to pay.

> PRESIDENT EISENHOWER, on anti-polio vaccine, May 4, 1955.

There are a number of things wrong with Washington. One of them is that everyone has been too long away from home.

> PRESIDENT EISENHOWER, news conference of May 11, 1955.

I have one yardstick by which I test every major problem—and that yardstick is: Is it good for America?

> PRESIDENT EISENHOWER, national address on his farm bill veto, April 16, 1956.

14

Worry is a word that I don't allow myself to use.

PRESIDENT EISENHOWER, news conference, Sept. 12, 1956.

. . . I come today to pay my respects to the plow. Ever since I had the invitation to this meeting, I have been trying to think in my mind of some instrument invented by man that has meant more to him than the plow. I can think of none. In fact, the plow has become the symbol of peace. . . . I think, therefore, that no group of American citizens can feel closer to peace, feel closer to the need for peace, than does the great agricultural community.

PRESIDENT EISENHOWER, address at Newton, Iowa, Sept. 21, 1956.

Farming looks mighty easy when your plow is a pencil, and you're a thousand miles from the corn field.

PRESIDENT EISENHOWER, on "synthetic farmer" experts in Washington, address at Peoria, Ill., Sept. 25, 1956.

The history of free men is never really written by chance but by choice —their choice.

PRESIDENT EISENHOWER, address at Pittsburgh, Oct. 9, 1956.

. . . Leadership is a word and a concept that has been more argued than almost any other I know. . . . I would far rather get behind and recognizing the frailties and the requirements of human nature, I would rather try to persuade a man to go along, because once I have persuaded him he will stick. If I scare him, he will stay just as long as he is scared, and then he is gone.

PRESIDENT EISENHOWER, on working with members of Congress, Nov. 15, 1956.

Before all else, we seek, upon our common labor as a nation, the favor of Almighty God. And the hopes in our hearts fashion the deepest prayers of our people:

May we pursue the right—without self-righteousness.

May we know unity—without conformity.

May we grow in strength—without pride of self.

15

May we, in our dealings with all peoples of the earth, ever speak truth and serve justice.

> PRESIDENT EISENHOWER, beginning his second Inaugural Address, Jan. 20, 1957.

. . . The role of a Vice President in an administration is exactly what the President makes it. I happen to have very positive and particular views about the thing. I believe that it is almost showing indifference to the welfare of the American people, unless you keep the Vice President aware of everything that is going on. Even if Mr. Nixon and I were not good friends, I would still have him in every important conference of government, so that if the Grim Reaper would find it time to take, remove me from this scene, he is ready to step in without any interruption, and certainly, without being completely unaware of what is going on in Government.

> PRESIDENT EISENHOWER, on the broadening role of the vice presidency, news conference of Feb. 6, 1957.

We succeed only as we identify in life, or in war, or in anything else, a single overriding objective, and make all other considerations bend to that one objective.

> PRESIDENT EISENHOWER, on necessity of high taxes to maintain world peace, address to Advertising Council, April 2, 1957.

But this money is not charity. In his daily work, out of his regular wages, your husband earned the monthly checks which will be coming to you now while your children are growing to maturity. You can accept them proudly.

> PRESIDENT EISENHOWER, message to Mrs. Jane Gavin, ten-millionth beneficiary of Social Security, news reports of June 7, 1957.

. . . I refer you to the second term of President Washington . . . when I compare the weak, inconsequential things they say about me, compared to what they say about the man who I think is the greatest human the English-speaking race has produced, then I can be quite philosophical about it.

> PRESIDENT EISENHOWER, on accepting criticism, Aug. 7, 1957.

16

Well, it's hard for a mere man to believe that woman doesn't have equal rights.
> PRESIDENT EISENHOWER, when asked about discrimination based on sex, *ibid.*

To make this talk I have come to the President's Office in the White House. I could have spoken from Rhode Island where I have been staying recently. But I felt that, in speaking from the house of Lincoln, of Jackson and of Wilson, my words would better convey both the sadness I feel in the action I was compelled today to make, and the firmness with which I intend to pursue this course until the orders of the Federal Court at Little Rock can be executed without unlawful interference.
> PRESIDENT EISENHOWER, on sending troops to enforce order during Little Rock integration crises; address to the nation, Sept. 24, 1957.

. . . We are getting to the point where we know that a great many of our secrets are known to the enemy, but they are still secret from our friends, which seems to be a rather anomalous situation.
> PRESIDENT EISENHOWER, on needed revision of security laws, news conference of Oct. 30, 1957.

. . . I find it a bit wearing, but I find it endurable, if you have got the faith in America that I have.
> PRESIDENT EISENHOWER, on responsibilities of presidency, *ibid.*

Accomplishment will prove to be a journey, not a destination.
> PRESIDENT EISENHOWER, address to opening session of North Atlantic Council, Paris, Dec. 16, 1957.

Our real problem is not our strength today; it is the vital necessity of action today to ensure our strength tomorrow.
> PRESIDENT EISENHOWER, State of the Union message to Congress, Jan. 9, 1958.

If our history teaches us anything, it is this lesson: So far as the economic potential of our nation is concerned, the believers in the future of America have always been the realists. I count myself as one of this company.
> PRESIDENT EISENHOWER, *ibid.*

17

I propose that we agree that outer space should be used only for peaceful purposes. We face a decisive moment in history in relation to this matter. Both the Soviet Union and the United States are now using outer space for the testing of missiles designed for military purposes. The time to stop is now.

> PRESIDENT EISENHOWER, to USSR, Jan. 12, 1958.

This desk of mine is one at which a man may die, but from which he cannot resign.

> PRESIDENT EISENHOWER, quoted by friends, *Parade*, Feb. 2, 1958.

I don't think that a person, just sitting in this post, will be doing his job best if he sits in Washington . . . I do not believe that any individual, whether he is running General Motors or the United States of America, his phase of it, can do the best job by just sitting at a desk and putting his face in a bunch of papers.

> PRESIDENT EISENHOWER, April 30, 1958.

Emphatically, our economy is not the Federal Reserve System, or the Treasury, or the Congress, or the White House. This nation of 43,000,000 families, 174,000,000 people, is what we all think and what we do; that is our economy. Our economy is the result of millions of decisions we all make every day about producing, earning, saving, investing and spending.

> PRESIDENT EISENHOWER, address to economic mobilization conference of American Management Association, May 20, 1958.

There can be no such thing as Fortress America. If ever we were reduced to the isolation implied by that term we would occupy a prison, not a fortress.

> PRESIDENT EISENHOWER, State of the Union message, Jan. 9, 1959.

Look at the hand. Each finger is not of itself a very good instrument for either defense or offense. But close it in a fist and it can become a very formidable weapon to defense. And so our job was to make each finger stronger, sturdier, so as to get a fist that could defy anyone that would think of aggression against the free world and the values that it is still defending as it was then defending.

> PRESIDENT EISENHOWER, address to North Atlantic Council meeting, April 2, 1959, recalling NATO's early days.

What we call foreign affairs is no longer foreign affairs. It's a local affair. Whatever happens in Indonesia is important to Indiana. Whatever happens in any corner of the world has some effect on the farmer in Dickinson County, Kansas, or on a worker in a factory.

> PRESIDENT EISENHOWER, address to graduating class of Foreign Service Institute, June 12, 1959.

Oh, that lovely title, ex-President . . .

> PRESIDENT EISENHOWER, *New York Post*, Oct. 26, 1959.

Personally I do not feel that any amount can properly be called a surplus as long as the nation is in debt. I prefer to think of such an item as a reduction on our children's inherited mortgage.

> PRESIDENT EISENHOWER, State of the Union address, Jan. 7, 1960.

We live . . . in a sea of semantic disorder in which old labels no longer faithfully describe. Police states are called "people's democracies." Armed conquest of free people is called "liberation." Such slippery slogans make more difficult the problems of communicating true faith, facts and beliefs . . . We must use language to enlighten the mind, not as the instrument of the studied innuendo and distorter of truth. And we must live by what we say.

> PRESIDENT EISENHOWER, State of the Union message, Jan. 7, 1960.

Today, flying here through five time zones, across about 3,500 miles, at a little less than the speed of sound, over fertile fields and prosperous cities —the trip is an index to American growth in my own lifetime.

> PRESIDENT EISENHOWER, on arriving in Anchorage on first visit after Alaska became a state, June 12, 1960.

You are no longer an Arctic frontier. You constitute a bridge to the continent of Asia and all its people.

> PRESIDENT EISENHOWER, *ibid.*

We believe profoundly that constant and unnecessary governmental meddling in our economy leads to a standardized, weakened and tasteless society that encourages dull mediocrity, whereas private enterprise, dependent upon the vigor of healthful competition, leads to individual responsibility, pride of accomplishment and, above all, national strength.

> PRESIDENT EISENHOWER, address to Republican National Convention, July 26, 1960.

I believe it's a tradition in baseball that when a pitcher has a no-hitter going, no one reminds him of it.

> PRESIDENT EISENHOWER at news conference of Sept. 7, 1960, on being told that his birthday, Oct. 4, would make him the oldest President to serve in office.

I feel like the fellow in jail who is watching his scaffold being built.

> PRESIDENT EISENHOWER, on construction of reviewing stands for President-elect John F. Kennedy's inauguration, *New York Times*, Dec. 6, 1960.

There is a limit to what the United States in self-respect can endure. That limit has now been reached.

> PRESIDENT EISENHOWER, announcing break of diplomatic relations with Cuba, Jan. 2, 1961.

Progress implies both new and continuing problems and, unlike Presidential administrations, problems rarely have terminal dates.

> PRESIDENT EISENHOWER, State of the Union message, Jan. 12, 1961, a few days before leaving office.

Each of us has his portion of ego. At least one night I dreamed that the 22nd Amendment [limiting a President to two terms] had been repealed —and it wasn't wholly a nightmare.

> MR. EISENHOWER, when asked if he would like to be back in the White House, *New York Times*, May 13, 1962.

John Fitzgerald Kennedy

. . . I carry with me from this state to that high and lonely office to which I now succeed more than fond memories and firm friendships. The enduring qualities of Massachusetts—the common threads woven by the Pilgrim and the Puritan, the fisherman and the farmer, the Yankee and the immigrant—will not be and could not be forgotten in this nation's executive mansion. They are an indelible part of my life, my conviction, my view of the past, and my hopes in the future.

> PRESIDENT-ELECT KENNEDY, address to Massachusetts Legislature, *New York Times*, Jan. 10, 1961.

. . . Of those to whom much is given, much is required. And when at some future date the high court of history sits in judgment on each one of us—recording whether in our brief span of service we fulfilled our responsibilities to the state—our success or failure, in whatever office we may hold, will be measured by the answers to four questions—were we truly men of courage . . . were we truly men of judgment . . . were we truly men of integrity . . . were we truly men of dedication?

> PRESIDENT-ELECT KENNEDY, *ibid.*

We observe today, not a victory of party but a celebration of freedom—symbolizing an end as well as a beginning—signifying renewal as well as change.

> PRESIDENT KENNEDY, beginning his Inaugural Address, Jan. 20, 1961.*

Let the word go forth from this time and place, to friend and foe alike, that the torch has been passed to a new generation of Americans—born in this century, tempered by war, disciplined by a hard and bitter peace, proud of our ancient heritage—and unwilling to witness or permit the slow undoing of those human rights to which this nation has always been committed, and to which we are committed today at home and around the world.

> PRESIDENT KENNEDY, *ibid.*

Let every nation know, whether it wishes us well or ill, that we shall pay any price, bear any burden, meet any hardship, support any friend, oppose any foe to assure the survival and the success of liberty.

> PRESIDENT KENNEDY, *ibid.*

---

* President Kennedy's Inaugural Address was incorporated in his funeral tribute given by the Auxiliary Bishop of Washington, the Most Reverend Philip Hannan, at St. Matthew's Cathedral, Washington, Nov. 25, 1963.

To those peoples in the huts and villages of half the globe struggling to break the bonds of mass misery, we pledge our best efforts to help them help themselves, for whatever period is required—not because the Communists may be doing it, not because we seek their votes, but because it is right. If a free society cannot help the many who are poor, it cannot save the few who are rich.
PRESIDENT KENNEDY, *ibid*.

So let us begin anew—remembering on both sides that civility is not a sign of weakness, and sincerity is always subject to proof. Let us never negotiate out of fear. But let us never fear to negotiate.
PRESIDENT KENNEDY, *ibid*.

Let both sides seek to invoke the wonders of science instead of its terrors. Together let us explore the stars, conquer the deserts, eradicate disease, tap the ocean depths and encourage the arts and commerce.
PRESIDENT KENNEDY, *ibid*.

Now the trumpet summons us again—not as a call to bear arms, though arms we need—not as a call to battle, though embattled we are—but a call to bear the burden of a long twilight struggle year in and year out, "rejoicing in hope, patient in tribulation"—a struggle against the common enemies of man: tyranny, poverty, disease and war itself.
PRESIDENT KENNEDY, *ibid*.

In the long history of the world, only a few generations have been granted the role of defending freedom in its hour of maximum danger. I do not shrink from this responsibility—I welcome it. I do not believe that any of us would exchange places with any other people or any other generation. The energy, the faith, the devotion which we bring to this endeavor will light our country and all who serve it—and the glow from that fire can truly light the world.
PRESIDENT KENNEDY, *ibid*.

And so, my fellow Americans: ask not what your country can do for you—ask what you can do for your country.
PRESIDENT KENNEDY, *ibid*.

22

My fellow citizens of the world: ask not what your country can do for you—ask what you can do for the freedom of man.
> PRESIDENT KENNEDY, *ibid.*

Finally, whether you are citizens of America or citizens of the world, ask of us here the same high standards of strength and sacrifice which we ask of you. With a good conscience our only sure reward, with history the final judge of our deeds, let us go forth to lead the land we love, asking His blessing and His help, but knowing that here on earth God's work must truly be our own.
> PRESIDENT KENNEDY, conclusion of Inaugural Address, *ibid.*

To state the facts frankly is not to despair the future nor indict the past. The prudent heir takes careful inventory of his legacies, and gives a faithful accounting to those whom he owes an obligation of trust.
> PRESIDENT KENNEDY, on the outgoing administration, State of the Union message, Jan. 31, 1961.

My God, in this job he's got the nerve of a burglar.
> PRESIDENT KENNEDY, on Adlai Stevenson as UN Ambassador, *Time*, Feb. 24, 1961.

Geography has made us neighbors. History has made us friends. Economics has made us partners; and necessity has made us allies.
> PRESIDENT KENNEDY, May 17, 1961, address to Canadian Parliament.

Tell him, if he doesn't mind, we'll shake hands.
> PRESIDENT KENNEDY, to interpreter, on meeting Premier Khrushchev for the first time, Vienna, June 4, 1961.

I hear it said that West Berlin is militarily untenable—and so was Bastogne, and so, in fact, was Stalingrad. Any danger spot is tenable if men—brave men—will make it so.
> PRESIDENT KENNEDY, address to the nation, July 25, 1961.

23

. . . the freedom of the city is not negotiable. We cannot negotiate with those who say, "What's mine is mine and what's yours is negotiable."
PRESIDENT KENNEDY, *ibid.*

You have offered to trade us an apple for an orchard. We do not do that in this country.
PRESIDENT KENNEDY, on Berlin, to Soviet Foreign Minister Andrei Gromyko, Oct. 6, 1961.

Khrushchev reminds me of the tiger hunter who has picked a place on the wall to hang the tiger's skin long before he has caught the tiger. This tiger has other ideas.
PRESIDENT KENNEDY, *New York Times*, Dec. 24, 1961.

A strong America depends on its cities—America's glory and sometimes America's shame.
PRESIDENT KENNEDY, State of the Union address, Jan. 11, 1962.

The day before my inauguration President Eisenhower told me, "You'll find that no *easy* problems ever come to the President of the United States. If they are easy to solve, somebody else has solved them." I found that hard to believe, but now I know it is true.
PRESIDENT KENNEDY, *Parade*, April 8, 1962.

To paraphrase the old saying, "Good news is no news." So the kind of news a President usually gets is bad. But it is important that there is a lot of good news, too, which does not immediately cross the President's desk. One must remember to keep a balance, to maintain a broad perspective and to refuse to be overwhelmed by bad news.
PRESIDENT KENNEDY, *ibid.*

. . . The American people will find it hard, as I do, to accept a situation in which a tiny handful of steel executives whose pursuit of private power and profit exceeds their sense of public responsibility, can show such utter contempt for the interest of 185 million Americans.

PRESIDENT KENNEDY, on increase in price of steel, April 11, 1962.*

I know that when things don't go well they like to blame the Presidents, and that is one of the things which Presidents are paid for . . .

PRESIDENT KENNEDY, news conference of June 14, 1962.

The path we have chosen for the present is full of hazards, as all paths are. But it is the one most consistent with our character and courage as a nation and our commitments around the world. The cost of freedom is always high, but Americans have always paid it. And one path we shall never choose, and that is the path of surrender, or submission.

PRESIDENT KENNEDY, address to the nation announcing blockade of Cuba to stop delivery of Russian missiles and other armaments, Oct. 22, 1962.

The mere absence of war is not peace. The mere absence of recession is not growth.

PRESIDENT KENNEDY, State of the Union message, Jan. 14, 1963.

. . . I can report that the State of this old but youthful Union, in the 175th year of its life, is good.

PRESIDENT KENNEDY, *ibid*.

In the dark days and darker nights when England stood alone—and most men save Englishmen despaired of England's life—he mobilized the English language and sent it into battle. The incandescent quality of his words illuminated the courage of his countrymen.

PRESIDENT KENNEDY, on conferring honorary citizenship on Winston Churchill, April 9, 1963.†

---

* It was the surprise increase in the price of steel which caused President Kennedy to remark to his associates: "My father always told me they were sons of bitches, but I never really believed him until now." Questioned at his news conference, May 9, 1962, Mr. Kennedy said: "The statement . . . quotes my father as having expressed himself strongly to me, and in this I quoted what he said, and indicated that he had not been on many other occasions wholly wrong."

† A *New York Times* editorial added: "Sir Winston Churchill said of himself that he was half American and all English. Now he is all American and all English." (For

. . . His stately ship of life, having weathered the severest storms of a troubled century, is anchored in tranquil waters, proof that courage and faith and zest for freedom are truly indestructible. The record of his triumphant passage will inspire free hearts all over the globe.
PRESIDENT KENNEDY, *ibid.*

. . . Everything changes but change itself.
PRESIDENT KENNEDY, on the nature of the present age, address on 90th anniversary of Vanderbilt University, May 19, 1963.

Equality of opportunity does not mean equality of responsibility.
PRESIDENT KENNEDY, on duty of educated citizens to help safeguard rights of all Americans, *ibid.*

We are confronted primarily with a moral issue. It is as old as the Scriptures and is as clear as the American Constitution.
PRESIDENT KENNEDY, asking nation's support in enforcing civil rights; his telecast followed admission of two Negroes to the University of Alabama, June 11, 1963.

Events of recent weeks have again underlined how deeply our Negro citizens resent the injustice of being arbitrarily denied equal access to those facilities and accommodations which are otherwise open to the general public. That is a daily insult which has no place in a country proud of its heritage—the heritage of the melting pot, of equal rights, of one nation and one people.
PRESIDENT KENNEDY, message to Congress on proposed Civil Rights Act, June 19, 1963.

No one has been barred on account of his race from fighting or dying for America—there are no "white" or "colored" signs on the foxholes or graveyards of battle.
PRESIDENT KENNEDY, *ibid.*

text of Sir Winston's message to Mr. Kennedy, see section on Foreign Governments: Great Britain.)

. . . It should not be necessary for any American citizen to demonstrate in the streets for the opportunity to stop at a hotel, or to eat at a lunch counter in the very department store in which he is shopping, or to enter a motion picture house, on the same terms as any other customer.

PRESIDENT KENNEDY, *ibid.*

I . . . ask every member of Congress to set aside sectional and political ties, and to look at this issue from the viewpoint of the nation. I ask you to look into your hearts—not in search of charity, for the Negro neither wants nor needs condescension—but for the one plain, proud and priceless quality that unites us all as Americans: a sense of justice. In this year of the Emancipation centennial, justice requires us to insure the blessings of liberty for all Americans and their posterity—not merely for reasons of economic efficiency, world diplomacy and domestic tranquility—but, above all, because it is right.

PRESIDENT KENNEDY, conclusion of address, *ibid.*

. . . We are all idealists. We are all visionaries. Let it not be said of this Atlantic generation that we left ideals and visions to the past, nor purpose and determination to our adversaries. We have come too far, we have sacrificed too much, to disdain the future now.

PRESIDENT KENNEDY, address to West German Parliament, Frankfurt, June 25, 1963.

There are many people in the world who really don't understand—or say they don't—what is the great issue between the free world and the Communist world. . . . There are some who say that Communism is the wave of the future. . . . And there are some who say in Europe and elsewhere "we can work with the Communists." . . . And there are even a few who say that it's true that Communism is an evil system but it permits us to make economic progress. Let them come to Berlin!

PRESIDENT KENNEDY, address at City Hall, West Berlin, June 26, 1963.

You live in a defended island of freedom, but your life is part of the main. So let me ask you . . . to lift your eyes beyond the dangers of today to the hopes of tomorrow, beyond the freedom merely of this city of Berlin and all your country of Germany to the advance of freedom everywhere, beyond the wall to the day of peace with justice, beyond yourselves and ourselves to all mankind.

PRESIDENT KENNEDY, *ibid.*

All free men, wherever they may live, are citizens of Berlin. And therefore, as a free man, I take pride in the words *"Ich bin ein Berliner"* [I am a Berliner].

PRESIDENT KENNEDY, *ibid*

Ireland is moving in the mainstream of current world events. . . . Your future is as promising as your past is proud and your destiny lies not as a peaceful island in a sea of trouble but as a maker and a shaper of world peace.

PRESIDENT KENNEDY, address to Irish Parliament, Dublin, June 28, 1963.*

The supreme reality of our time is our indivisibility as children of God and the common vulnerability of this planet.

PRESIDENT KENNEDY, *ibid.*

The greatest art of the world was the work of little nations. The most enduring literature of the world came from little nations. The heroic deeds that thrill humanity through generations were the deeds of little nations fighting for their freedom and, yes, the salvation of mankind came through a little nation.

PRESIDENT KENNEDY, *ibid.*

In its first two decades, the age of nuclear energy has been full of fear, yet never empty of hope. Today the fear is a little less and the hope a little greater. For the first time, we have been able to reach an agreement which can limit the dangers of this age.

PRESIDENT KENNEDY, on ratifying treaty to limit nuclear testing, Oct. 7, 1963.

---

* Said *The Irish Independent*, as quoted by *The National Observer*, July 1, 1963: "After three generations, a young man of fully Irish stock has reached the last point of integration into American life—the chief executive post of the nation."

If this treaty fails, it will not be our doing, and even if it fails we shall not regret that we have made this clear and honorable national commitment to the cause of man's survival.

> PRESIDENT KENNEDY, *ibid.*

EDITOR'S NOTE: *During the days immediately following President Kennedy's assassination, his words were quoted everywhere, along with tributes and reminiscences. Especially notable were portions of his last speech and comments by his closest friend in the Church; his wife; a newspaper columnist; a dramatist; an archbishop; and an ambassador:*

We in this country, in this generation, are—by destiny rather than choice —the watchmen on the walls of world freedom. We ask, therefore, that we may be worthy of our power and responsibility—that we may exercise our strength with wisdom and restraint—and that we may achieve in our time and for all time the ancient vision of peace on earth, goodwill toward men. That must always be our goal—and the righteousness of our cause must always underlie our strength. For as was written long ago: "Except the Lord keep the city, the watchman waketh but in vain."

> PRESIDENT KENNEDY, conclusion of address prepared for Dallas luncheon to which he was en route when assassinated, Nov. 22, 1963.

In the decade that lies ahead—the challenging, revolutionary Sixties—the American Presidency will demand . . . that the President place himself in the very thick of the fight, that he care passionately about the fate of the people he leads, that he be willing to serve them at the risk of incurring their momentary displeasure.

> PRESIDENT KENNEDY, on the office of the President; statement was among those most frequently recalled following his assassination.

. . . a youthful Lincoln, who in his time and in his sacrifice, has made more sturdy the hopes of this nation and its people.

> RICHARD CARDINAL CUSHING, Archbishop of Boston, *New York Herald Tribune*, Nov. 25, 1963.

May the angels, dear Jack, lead you into Paradise.

> CARDINAL CUSHING, interpolation in ancient prayer at end of funeral Mass, Nov. 25, 1963.

Dear God, please take care of your servant John Fitzgerald Kennedy.

> JACQUELINE BOUVIER KENNEDY, inscription for prayer cards at funeral.

When Jack quoted something, it was usually classical, but I'm so ashamed of myself—all I keep thinking of is this line from a musical comedy. At night, before we'd go to sleep, Jack liked to play some records; and the song he loved most came at the very end of this record. The lines he loved to hear were: "Don't let it be forgot, that once there was a spot, for one brief shining moment that was known as Camelot."

> JACQUELINE BOUVIER KENNEDY, quoted by Theodore H. White in "For President Kennedy, An Epilogue," *Life*, Dec. 6, 1963, © 1963, Time, Inc. Her reference is to the Broadway hit *Camelot*, book and lyrics by Alan Jay Lerner, which opened Dec. 4, 1960.

There'll be great Presidents again—and the Johnsons are wonderful, they've been wonderful to me—but there'll never be another Camelot again.

> JACQUELINE BOUVIER KENNEDY, *ibid.*

For a while I thought history was something that bitter old men wrote. But then I realized history made Jack what he was. You must think of him as this little boy, sick so much of the time, reading in bed, reading history, reading the Knights of the Round Table, reading Marlborough. For Jack, history was full of heroes. And if it made him this way—if it made him see the heroes—maybe other little boys will see. Men are such a combination of good and bad. Jack had this hero idea of history, the idealistic view.

> JACQUELINE BOUVIER KENNEDY, *ibid.*

I'm *never* going to live in Europe. I'm not going to "travel extensively abroad." That's a desecration. I'm going to live in the places I lived with Jack. In Georgetown, and with the Kennedys at the Cape. They're my family. I'm going to bring up my children. I want John to grow up to be a good boy.

> JACQUELINE BOUVIER KENNEDY, *ibid.*

Whenever you drive across the bridge from Washington into Virginia, you see the Lee Mansion on the side of the hill in the distance. When Caroline was very little, the mansion was one of the first things she learned to recognize. Now, at night you can see his flame beneath the mansion for miles away.

> JACQUELINE BOUVIER KENNEDY, on the plot near Robert E. Lee's home, in Arlington, Va., selected for her husband's grave and "eternal flame," *ibid.*

30

He was a young lion, treading his way with a proud grace until a murderous hate stopped him in his path, and after that there was darkness.
> MAX LERNER, columnist, *New York Post*, Nov. 24, 1963.

What a terrible thing has happened to us all! To you there, to us here, to all everywhere. Peace who was becoming bright-eyed, now sits in the shadow of death; her handsome champion has been killed as he walked by her very side. Her gallant boy is dead. What a cruel, foul, and most unnatural murder! We mourn here with you, poor, sad American people.
> SEAN O'CASEY, letter to Mrs. Rose Russell, leader of New York City Teachers Union, *New York Times*, Nov. 27, 1963.

Thinking of him, we all see so vividly what we admire in a human life, and what are the great causes we care about. The impact of his example will help and inspire men and women for time yet to come.
> ARTHUR MICHAEL RAMSEY, Archbishop of Canterbury, at memorial service in St. Paul's Cathedral, London, *New York Times*, Dec. 2, 1963.

President Kennedy was so contemporary a man—so involved in our world—so immersed in our times—so responsive to its challenges—so intense a participant in the great events and great decisions of our day, that he seemed the very symbol of the vitality and exuberance that is the essence of life itself.
> ADLAI STEVENSON, reply in UN General Assembly to tributes to the late President Kennedy, *New York Times*, Nov. 27, 1963.

Lyndon Baines Johnson

I will do my best. That is all I can do. I ask for your help—and God's.
> PRESIDENT LYNDON JOHNSON, statement on reaching Andrews Air Force Base, Md., on flight from Dallas, scene of President Kennedy's assassination, Nov. 22, 1963.

I'd rather give my life than be afraid to give it.
> PRESIDENT JOHNSON, rejecting Secret Service's advice that he ride rather than walk in Mr. Kennedy's funeral procession, Nov. 25, 1963.

All I have I would have given gladly not to be standing here today.
> PRESIDENT JOHNSON, beginning his first address to joint session of Congress, Nov. 27, 1963, two days after President Kennedy's burial.

The greatest leader of our time has been struck down by the foulest deed of our time. . . . No words are sad enough to express our sense of loss. No words are strong enough to express our determination to continue the forward thrust of America that he began.

PRESIDENT JOHNSON, *ibid.*

This nation will keep its commitments from South Vietnam to West Berlin. We will be unceasing in the search for peace, resourceful in our pursuit of areas of agreement even with those with whom we differ, and generous and loyal to those who join with us in common cause.

PRESIDENT JOHNSON, *ibid.*

In this age when there can be no losers in peace and no victors in war—we must recognize the obligation to match national strength with national restraint—we must be prepared at one and the same time for both the confrontation of power and the limitation of power—we must be ready to defend the national interest and to negotiate the common interest.

PRESIDENT JOHNSON, *ibid.*

We will serve all of the nation, not one section or one sector, or one group, but all Americans. These are the *United* States—a united people with a united purpose.

PRESIDENT JOHNSON, *ibid.*

An assassin's bullet has thrust upon me the awesome burden of the Presidency. I am here today to say I need your help. I cannot bear this burden alone. I need the help of all Americans, in all America.

PRESIDENT JOHNSON, *ibid.*

This is our challenge—not to hesitate, not to pause, not to turn about and linger over this evil moment, but to continue on our course so that we may fulfill the destiny that history has set for us. Our most immediate tasks are here on this Hill.

PRESIDENT JOHNSON, *ibid.*

We have talked long enough in this country about equal rights. We have talked for 100 years or more. It is time now to write the next chapter—and to write it in the books of law.

PRESIDENT JOHNSON, *ibid.*

All of us have lived through seven days that none of us will ever forget. We're not given the divine wisdom to answer why this has been, but we are given the human duty of determining what is to be—what is to be for America, for the world, for the cause we lead, for all the hopes that live in our hearts.

> PRESIDENT JOHNSON, Thanksgiving Day address to the nation, Nov. 28, 1963.

Yesterday is not ours to recover, but tomorrow is ours to win or to lose. I am resolved that we shall win the tomorrows before us. So I ask you to join me in that resolve, determined that from this midnight of tragedy we shall move toward a new American greatness.

> PRESIDENT JOHNSON, *ibid.*

. . . We know tonight that our system is strong—strong and secure. A deed that was meant to tear us apart has bound us together.

> PRESIDENT JOHNSON, *ibid.*

. . . In these days, the fate of this office is the fate of us all.

> PRESIDENT JOHNSON, *ibid.*

I'm always pressed for time. An hour late and a dollar short.

> PRESIDENT JOHNSON, interview with Stewart Alsop, *Saturday Evening Post*, Dec. 14, 1963.

Unfortunately many Americans live on the outskirts of hope—some because of their poverty, some because of their color, and all too many because of both. Our task is to help replace their despair with opportunity.

> PRESIDENT JOHNSON, in his first State of the Union message, Jan. 8, 1964, opening "war on poverty" that became a major objective of his Administration.

While I have been lavishly praised by some . . . lavishly criticized by some . . . generally speaking, the American nation has conducted itself as you would expect it to in a crisis, and would get very good grades.

> PRESIDENT JOHNSON, on his first hundred days in office; news conference, Feb. 29, 1964.

33

Politics

Vote for the man who promises least; he'll be the least disappointing.
> BERNARD BARUCH, quoted in *Meyer Berger's New York*, Random House, 1960.

In any assembly the simplest way to stop the transacting of business and split the ranks is to appeal to a principle.
> JACQUES BARZUN, Dean of Faculties, Columbia University, *The House of Intellect*, Harper & Row, 1959.

With all the confidence of a man dialing his own telephone number. . . .
> JACK BELL, of the Associated Press, description of Robert A. Taft's manner in handling political crises, *The Splendid Misery*, Doubleday, 1960.

I like Ike.
> IRVING BERLIN, title of song written for 1952 Eisenhower campaign, adapted by Mr. Berlin from an earlier song, *They Like Ike*, written in 1950 for his Broadway musical, *Call Me Madam*.

This is the first Convention of the space age—where a candidate can promise the moon and mean it.
> DAVID BRINKLEY, NBC commentator, on the 1960 presidential nominations, quoted in *Newsweek*, March 13, 1961.

Nowhere are prejudices more mistaken for truth, passion for reason, and invective for documentation than in politics. That is a realm, peopled only

34

by villains or heroes, in which everything is black or white and gray is a forbidden color.

> JOHN MASON BROWN, *Through These Men*, Harper & Row, 1956.

The more I observed Washington, the more frequently I visited it, and the more people I interviewed there, the more I understood how prophetic L'Enfant was when he laid it out as a city that goes around in circles.

> JOHN MASON BROWN, *ibid.*

Physician extraordinary to the body politic, skilled in diagnosis, bold in prognosis, forthright in prescription, buoyant of bedside manner and articulate in professional discourse; a scholarly statesman who, like Demosthenes of old in an age not dissimilar to our own, speaks eloquently of the noble purpose of democracy and the urgency of unity in the great cause of peace.

> COLUMBIA UNIVERSITY, on conferring Doctorate of Laws on Adlai Stevenson, October 31, 1954.

A distinguished member since 1948 of the "most exclusive gentlemen's club in the world," Senator Smith reaffirms the growing realization, wisely recognized by her astute constituents, that ability and proven performance, rather than sex, provide the reasonable standards for political selection.

> COLUMBIA UNIVERSITY, on conferring Doctorate of Laws on Senator Margaret Chase Smith of Maine, June 1, 1955.

I have come to the conclusion that politics are too serious a matter to be left to the politicians.

> GENERAL CHARLES DE GAULLE, letter quoted in *Twilight of Empire: Memoirs of Prime Minister Clement Attlee*, A. S. Barnes Co., 1962.

. . . My decision on this matter is as certain and final as death and the staggering New Deal taxes.

> THOMAS E. DEWEY, letter to his 1948 campaign manager announcing he would never again seek the presidency, *Time*, Jan. 2, 1950.

. . . I have found out in later years we were very poor, but the glory of America is that we didn't know it then.

> DWIGHT EISENHOWER, speaking of his childhood, on laying cornerstone of Eisenhower Museum, Abilene, Kansas, and opening his campaign for presidential nomination, *Time*, June 16, 1952.

35

Free government is the political expression of a deeply felt religious faith.
DWIGHT EISENHOWER, *ibid.*

Our aims are clear: to sweep from office an Administration which has fastened on every one of us the wastefulness, the arrogance and corruption in high places, the heavy burdens and the anxieties which are the bitter fruit of a party too long in power.
DWIGHT EISENHOWER, accepting nomination as Republican candidate for presidency, *Time*, July 21, 1952.

Neither a wise man nor a brave man lies down on the tracks of history to wait for the train of the future to run over him.
DWIGHT EISENHOWER, campaign speech, *Time*, Oct. 6, 1952.

That job [ending the war] requires a personal trip to Korea. I shall make that trip. I shall go to Korea.
DWIGHT EISENHOWER, in final address during 1952 presidential campaign. The single sentence caught the nation's imagination during stalemated "police action" in Korea and was credited with helping Eisenhower win election.

It is high time that we had real and positive policies in the world that we understand. . . . We are tired of aristocratic explanations in Harvard words.
DWIGHT EISENHOWER, in a 1952 campaign speech, recalled after more than a dozen Harvard men were named to the higher echelons of his administration, *Time*, Jan. 26, 1953.

There was a man from the United States, a political figure—and I am not going to name him because he is still alive—we had just cleaned up North Africa, and this man came to me and said he hoped I knew that no American general could have a success of that scope and kind and fail to be considered for the presidency. I kicked him out of the office.
PRESIDENT EISENHOWER, story related at news conference, Jan. 13, 1955.

I have my own ideas, as everyone else does, of what is a proper sphere of activity for the President of the United States. One of them . . . is that he doesn't go out barnstorming for himself under any condition. . . .
PRESIDENT EISENHOWER, news conference of Feb. 8, 1956.

I believe when you are in any contest you should work like there is—to the very last minute—a chance to lose it. This is battle, this is politics, this is anything.

> PRESIDENT EISENHOWER, on presidential elections, Sept. 27, 1956.

. . . These calculations overlook the decisive element: what counts is not necessarily the size of the dog in the fight—it's the size of the fight in the dog.

> PRESIDENT EISENHOWER, on relative strength of political parties, address to Republican National Committee, Jan. 31, 1958.

The worst mistake I made was in not working to elect the man I thought should be my successor.

> DWIGHT EISENHOWER, statement nearly two years after Richard Nixon's unsuccessful campaign for presidency, *Quote*, Aug. 5, 1962.

I don't think the United States needs super-patriots. We need patriotism, honestly practiced by all of us, and we don't need these people that are more patriotic than you or anybody else.

> DWIGHT EISENHOWER, on extremist political activity in the U.S., *New York Times*, Nov. 24, 1962.

I'm for each and against none.

> DWIGHT EISENHOWER, on potential 1964 Republican candidates for the presidency, *New York Herald Tribune*, July 12, 1963.

This is what I mean to people—sense and honesty and fairness and a decent amount of progress. I don't think the people want to be listening to a Roosevelt, sounding as if he were one of the Apostles, or the partisan yipping of Truman . . . So there's no use my making compromises with the truth, supposedly for the party, because if I were caught in one falsehood, and what I stand for in people's eyes got tarnished, then not just me but the whole Republican gang would be finished.

> PRESIDENT EISENHOWER, *The Ordeal of Power*, by Emmet John Hughes, Atheneum, 1963.

I despise all adjectives that try to describe people as liberal or conservative, rightist or leftist, as long as they stay in the useful part of the road. [Even

37

more, I despise people who] go to the gutter on either the right or the left, and hurl rocks at those in the center.

>DWIGHT EISENHOWER, *Time*, Oct. 25, 1963.

I thought it completely absurd to mention my name in the same breath as the Presidency.

>DWIGHT EISENHOWER, recalling his initial reaction to suggestions that he run for office, *Mandate for Change*, Doubleday, 1963.

That log house did me more good in politics than anything I ever said in a speech.

>JOHN NANCE GARNER, twice U.S. Vice President, on receiving a birthday cake in shape of log cabin in which he was born, *New York Journal-American*, Nov. 24, 1959.

. . . Minority groups now speak much more loudly than do majority groups which I classify as the forgotten American, the man who pays his taxes, prays, behaves himself, stays out of trouble and works for his government.

>SENATOR BARRY GOLDWATER, CBS-TV, Jan. 26, 1961.

Rules for Visiting the Kennedys: Prepare yourself by reading the *Congressional Record, U.S. News & World Report, Time, Newsweek, Fortune, How to Play Sneaky Tennis*, and the *Democratic Digest*. Memorize at least three jokes. Anticipate that each Kennedy will ask you what you think of another Kennedy's (a) dress, (b) hairdo, (c) back-hand, (d) latest public achievement. Be sure to answer, "Terrific." This should get you through dinner. Now for the football field. It's "touch" but it's murder. If you don't want to play, don't come. If you do come, play, or you'll be fed in the kitchen and nobody will speak to you. Don't let the girls fool you. Even pregnant, they can make you look silly. If Harvard played touch, they'd be on the varsity . . .

>DAVE HACKETT, a Kennedy family friend, quoted by Joe McCarthy in *The Remarkable Kennedys*, Dial, 1960.

It was then that he really faced the sheer, God-awful boredom of not being President.

>JAMES HAGERTY, White House press secretary, on President Eisenhower's decision to seek a second term, quoted seven years later by another presidential assistant, Emmet John Hughes, in his book, *The Ordeal of Power*, Atheneum, 1963.

When it comes to facing up to serious problems, each candidate will pledge to appoint a committee. And what is a committee? A group of the unwilling, picked from the unfit, to do the unnecessary. But it all sounds great in a campaign speech.

> RICHARD HARKNESS, news commentator, *New York Herald Tribune,* June 15, 1960.

Once upon a time my political opponents honored me as possessing the fabulous intellectual and economic power by which I created a world-wide depression all by myself.

> HERBERT HOOVER, on depression days, *Chicago Sun-Times,* Feb. 28, 1958.

. . . Tough as boiled owls.

> SENATOR HUBERT H. HUMPHREY, on his opponents for Democratic presidential nomination, *Time,* May 9, 1960.

What is politics but persuading the public to vote for this and support that and endure these for the promise of those?

> GILBERT HIGHET, "The Art of Persuasion," *Vogue,* Jan., 1951.

. . . A high-level persuader will begin by hints, and rich stimulating morsels, and tantalizing glimpses into the Luminous Void. Slowly, slowly, almost reluctantly, he will lead his Sanchos farther into the Impossible. Soon they will be pushing bravely ahead, jumping the chasms between the Inexplicables, swinging freely across the ravines of the Incomprehensible, glissading upwards on the slopes of the Unutterable. Sometimes, dizzy with the thin air, they will pull their master gaily ahead into the unknown, and even if he tries to restrain them they will link arms and swing him out over the edge of sanity. Yet even then, the adventure of persuasion began slowly, slowly, patiently, quietly, slowly.

> GILBERT HIGHET, *ibid.*

Idealism is the noble toga that political gentlemen drape over their will to power.

> ALDOUS HUXLEY, essayist and philosopher, recalled at his death, *New York Herald Tribune,* Nov. 24, 1963.

39

They've been peddling eyewash about themselves and hogwash about Democrats. What they need is a good mouthwash.

> SENATOR LYNDON B. JOHNSON, candidate for Vice President, charging Republicans with slurring Senator Kennedy's patriotism, *Quote*, Oct. 23, 1960.

I am a free man, an American, a United States Senator and a Democrat in that order. I am also a liberal, a conservative, a Texan, a taxpayer, a rancher, a businessman, a consumer, a parent, a voter, and not as young as I used to be nor as old as I expect to be—and I am all these things in no fixed order.

> SENATOR LYNDON JOHNSON, on seeking Democratic Presidential nomination of 1960; recalled when he became President, Nov. 22, 1963.*

I am not able—nor even the least interested in trying—to define my political philosophy by the choice of a one-word or two-word label. . . . At the heart of my own beliefs is a rebellion against this very process of classifying, labeling, and filing Americans under headings: regional, economic, occupational, religious, racial, or otherwise. I bridle at the very casualness with which we have come to ask each other, "What is your political philosophy?"

> SENATOR LYNDON JOHNSON, *ibid.*

Yet government is an expression of philosophy, and active governments are inevitably guided by philosophers. As I see it, the mandate of our system—and, perhaps, the ultimate genius of it—is that the American people should be the true philosophers of the American Government within the limits upon governmental powers set by our Constitution.

> SENATOR LYNDON JOHNSON, *ibid.*

The tenets of my own beliefs. . . .

First, I believe every American has something to say and, under our system, a right to an audience.

Second, I believe there is always a national answer to each national problem, and, believing this, I do not believe that there are necessarily two sides to every question.

Third, I regard achievement of the full potential of our resources—

---

* First published in *Texas Quarterly*, University of Texas, 1958; reprinted, *Christian Science Monitor*, Nov. 27, 1963.

physical, human, and otherwise—to be the highest purpose of the governmental policies next to the protection of those rights we regard as inalienable.

Fourth, I regard waste as the continuing enemy of our society and the prevention of waste—waste of resources, waste of lives, or waste of opportunity—to be the most dynamic of the responsibilities of our government.

> SENATOR LYNDON JOHNSON, *ibid.*

A newspaper reported that I spend $30,000 a year buying Paris clothes and that women hate me for it. I couldn't spend that much unless I wore sable underwear.

> JACQUELINE KENNEDY, answering charges that she was an overly chic candidate for First Lady, *New York Times*, Sept. 15, 1960.

To exclude from positions of trust and command all those below the age of 44 would have kept Jefferson from writing the Declaration of Independence, Washington from commanding the Continental Army, Madison from fathering the Constitution, Hamilton from serving as Secretary of the Treasury, Clay from being elected Speaker of the House, and Christopher Columbus from discovering America.

> SENATOR JOHN F. KENNEDY, replying to ex-President Harry S. Truman's assertion that he might not be mature or experienced enough for presidency, *New York Times*, July 5, 1960.

We stand today on the edge of a new frontier—the frontier of the 1960's —a frontier of unknown opportunities and perils—a frontier of unfulfilled hopes and threats.*

> SENATOR KENNEDY, speech accepting presidential nomination, *New York Times*, July 16, 1960.

. . . the new frontier of which I speak is not a set of promises—it is a set of challenges. It sums up not what I intend to offer the American people, but what I intend to ask of them. It appeals to their pride, not their

---

* Columnist David Wise, *New York Herald Tribune*, March 5, 1961, credited Walt W. Rostow, economic historian, Massachusetts Institute of Technology, with suggesting the phrase "new frontier" to Mr. Kennedy during a Boston cocktail party, June 16, 1960.

pocketbook—it holds out the promise of more sacrifice instead of more security.
> SENATOR KENNEDY, *ibid.*

I hope that no American, considering the really critical issues facing this country, will waste his franchise and throw away his vote by voting either for me or against me solely on account of my religious affiliation. It is not relevant.
> SENATOR KENNEDY, on his Roman Catholicism, *Time*, July 25, 1960.

I believe in an America where the separation of church and state is absolute—where no Catholic prelate would tell the President, should he be a Catholic, how to act, and no Protestant minister would tell his parishioners for whom to vote—where no church or church school is granted any public funds or political preference—and where no man is denied public office merely because his religion differs from the President who might appoint him or the people who might elect him.
> SENATOR KENNEDY, address to Protestant ministers, Houston, Sept. 12, 1960.

I believe in an America where religious intolerance will someday end— where all men and all churches are treated as equal—where every man has the same right to attend or not to attend the church of his choice—where there is no Catholic vote, no anti-Catholic vote . . . and where Catholics, Protestants, and Jews . . . will refrain from those attitudes of disdain and division which have so often marred their works in the past, and promote instead the American ideal of brotherhood.
> SENATOR KENNEDY, *ibid.*

I really don't think there's anything I could say to President Truman that's going to cause him, at the age of 76, to change his particular speaking manner. Perhaps Mrs. Truman can, but I don't think I can.
> SENATOR KENNEDY, comment on Mr. Truman's blunt remarks, in third television debate with Vice President Richard M. Nixon, Oct. 13, 1960.

Politicians are the same all over. They promise to build a bridge even where there is no river.
> NIKITA KHRUSHCHEV, Soviet premier, *New York Herald Tribune*, Aug. 22, 1963.

The Democrats have been hogging the administration at Washington for 20 years, and it's about time the people began to squeal.

> HENRY B. KRAJEWSKI, Secaucus, N.J., explaining why he chose the pig as the symbol of his perennial presidential candidacy, *Time*, March 17, 1952.

From defending the common man we pass on to exalting him and we find ourselves beginning to imply not merely that he is as good as anybody else but that he is actually better. Instead of demanding only that the common man be given an opportunity to become as uncommon as possible, we make his commonness a virtue and, even in the case of candidates for high office, we sometimes praise them for being nearly indistinguishable from the average man in the street.

> JOSEPH WOOD KRUTCH, essay in *Is the Common Man Too Common?* University of Oklahoma Press, 1954.

Secretly, no doubt, we hope that they are somehow superior, but we feel at the same time that a kind of decency requires them to conceal the fact as completely as possible.

> JOSEPH WOOD KRUTCH and others, *ibid.*

New York has total depth in every area. Washington has only politics; after that, the second biggest thing is white marble.

> REPRESENTATIVE JOHN LINDSAY of New York, *Vogue*, Aug. 1, 1963.

An important maxim to remember is "don't be an amateur." The job of being a professional politician, in spite of the odium which some persons have falsely attached to it, is a high and difficult one.

> HENRY CABOT LODGE, JR., on his role as unofficial campaign manager for presidential nomination of Dwight Eisenhower, *Time*, Dec. 17, 1951.

I have the experience to be Governor. I know how to play craps. I know how to play poker. I know how to get in and out of the Baptist Church and ride horses. I know the oil and gas business. I know both sides of the streets.

> GOVERNOR EARL LONG of Louisiana, speech in the Legislature, news reports of May 31, 1959.

43

They are troubadours of trouble and crooners of catastrophe.
> CLARE BOOTHE LUCE, on Democrats, *Newsweek*, Jan. 24, 1955.

After years of living with the coldest realities I still believe that one reaps what one sows and that to sow kindness is the best of all investments.
> JOSEPH W. MARTIN, JR., *My First Fifty Years in Politics*, McGraw-Hill, 1960.

Although I myself do not drink, I always make a point of shaking hands with bartenders whenever I come across them, because their recommendations, voiced at that moment when men's minds are highly receptive to ideas, carry much weight in a community.
> JOSEPH W. MARTIN, JR., *ibid.*

On the New Frontier in Washington the biggest crime for a girl to commit is to be ugly. For a man it's not to assert his masculinity. It's exactly like a medieval court.
> JONATHAN MILLER, in satirical British review, *Beyond the Fringe*, quoted in *Life*, Aug. 16, 1963.

The electric smile which is requisite for all American public figures never faded; the note of deep earnestness for which Americans ceaselessly crave, infused all his oratory.
> MALCOLM MUGGERIDGE, British journalist, on Franklin D. Roosevelt's campaigns, "The Titans: United States of America," BBC-TV, Jan. 16, 1962.

Politics is the diversion of trivial men who, when they succeed at it, become important in the eyes of more trivial men.
> GEORGE JEAN NATHAN, news summaries, July 9, 1954.

If a community is not sufficiently eager to accept a political handout, the arms of local leaders are twisted until they holler "Uncle Sam" and take the money.
> EDWIN NEILAN, president, U.S. Chamber of Commerce, address on federal spending, Los Angeles, Sept. 6, 1963.

. . . Pat doesn't have a mink coat. But she does have a respectable Republican cloth coat. And I always tell her she'd look good in anything.
> RICHARD M. NIXON, television speech, Sept. 23, 1952, denying use of "slush fund" from California backers and offering to resign as vice presidential candidate.

. . . We did get something—a gift. . . . It was a little cocker spaniel dog in a crate . . . sent all the way from Texas. Black and white spotted. And our little girl, Tricia, the six-year-old—named it Checkers. And you know the kids love that dog and I just want to say this right now, that regardless of what they say about it, we're going to keep it.
> RICHARD M. NIXON, *ibid*.

I have a theory that in the United States those who seek the Presidency never win it. Circumstances rather than a man's ambition determine the result. If he is the right man for the right time, he will be chosen.
> RICHARD M. NIXON, on state visit to La Paz, Bolivia, as Vice President of U.S., news summaries of May 11, 1958.

Religion will be in this campaign to the extent that the candidates of either side talk about it. I shall never talk about it and we'll start right now.
> RICHARD M. NIXON, beginning campaign against John F. Kennedy, Chicago news conference, July 29, 1960.

I can only say tonight to you that I believe in the American dream because I have seen it come true in my own life.
> RICHARD M. NIXON, accepting nomination for the presidency, *New York Times*, July 30, 1960.

. . . I hope that . . . television, radio, and the press first recognize the great responsibility they have to report all the news and second recognize that they have a right and a responsibility if they are against a candidate to give him the shaft but also recognize if they give the shaft, [to] put one lonely reporter on the campaign who will report what the candidate says now and then.
> RICHARD M. NIXON, widely quoted reprimand to the press after unsuccessful race for governorship of California, *Time*, Nov. 16, 1962.

Heu vatum ignarae mentes! quid vota repulsum, quid promissa iuvant? tua quid praesagia, Gallup? (The seers saw not defeat, poor souls, vain prayers, vain promises, vain Gallup poll.)

> Oxford University's citation conferring honorary Doctorate of Civil Law on former President Truman ("to Harricum Truman, Doctoris in Iure Civili"), June 20, 1956.

Harricum! Harricum! Give 'em hell, Harricum!

> Oxford University student cheer for former President Truman, *ibid.*

It is a period described in North America as one when politicians go around shooting from the lip. It therefore behooves outsiders, even though friendly to all parties involved, to avoid not only participating in the shooting but keeping out of the line of fire.

> Lester Pearson, advice to visitors to British Isles during national elections, news reports of May 17, 1955.

People only leave by way of the box—ballot or coffin.

> Senator Claiborne Pell, on life in Washington, *Vogue*, Aug. 1, 1963.

. . . There is a vast difference between being against a man because of his religion or race and being against him because one believes that his religious or other convictions affect his fitness for high office. I am not prejudiced against Christian Scientists, but I would not want to see one become a federal health official. . . . Quakers are fine, but I would not want to see a thorough-going Quaker become our Secretary of Defense.

> Rt. Rev. James Pike, Episcopal Bishop of California, "Should A Catholic Be President?" *Life*, Dec. 21, 1959.

I am here tonight as a delegate to this convention because without prefix, without suffix and without apology, I am a Democrat.

> Sam Rayburn, Speaker, House of Representatives, address as permanent chairman of Democratic National Convention, Aug. 15, 1956.

You will feel that you are no longer clothing yourself; you are dressing a public monument.

> Eleanor Roosevelt, advice for wives of U.S. Presidents, *New York Herald Tribune*, Oct. 27, 1960.

Always be on time. Do as little talking as humanly possible. Remember to lean back in the parade car so everybody can see the President. Be sure not to get too fat, because you'll have to sit three in the back seat.

> ELEANOR ROOSEVELT, on campaign behavior for wives, *New York Times*, Nov. 11, 1962.

If one man offers you democracy and another offers you a bag of grain, at what stage of starvation will you prefer the grain to the vote?

> BERTRAND RUSSELL, *Silhouettes in Satire*, edited by Robert E. Egner, New American Library, 1958.

Republicans sleep in twin beds—some even in separate rooms. That is why there are more Democrats.

> WILL STANTON, "How to Tell a Democrat From a Republican," *Ladies' Home Journal*, Nov., 1962.

Let's talk sense to the American people.

> ADLAI STEVENSON, in speech accepting nomination for the presidency at Democratic convention in Chicago, new reports of July 26, 1952.

I would not seek your nomination for the presidency because the burdens of that office stagger the imagination. Its potential for good or evil now, and in the years of our lives, smothers exultation and converts vanity to prayer.

> ADLAI STEVENSON, accepting Democratic nomination for President, *Time*, Aug. 4, 1952.

I venture to suggest that partiotism is not a short and frenzied outburst of emotion but the tranquil and steady dedication of a lifetime.

> ADLAI STEVENSON, address to American Legion Convention, news summaries of Aug. 30, 1952.

When an American says he loves his country, he means not only that he loves the New England hills, the prairies glistening in the sun or the wide rising plains, the mountains and the seas. He means that he loves an inner air, an inner light in which freedom lives and in which a man can draw the breath of self-respect.

> ADLAI STEVENSON, campaign address, *Time*, Sept. 8, 1952.

As to their platform, well, nobody can stand on a bushel of eels.
> ADLAI STEVENSON, comment on Republican platform, *ibid.*

The people know what has been done and now they want to know what will be done. A party cannot live on laurel leaves.
> ADLAI STEVENSON, on Democratic record, *ibid.*

Some, perhaps, find it politically profitable to cultivate the vineyards of anxiety. I would warn them lest they reap the grapes of wrath.
> ADLAI STEVENSON, campaign address, *Time*, Oct. 20, 1952.

It is a tragedy that the Old Guard has succeeded in doing what Hitler's best general never could do: they have captured Eisenhower.
> ADLAI STEVENSON, campaign address, *Time*, Nov. 3, 1952.

Someone asked me . . . how I felt and I was reminded of a story that a fellow townsman of ours used to tell—Abraham Lincoln. They asked him how he felt once after an unsuccessful election. He said he felt like a little boy who has stubbed his toe in the dark. He said that he was too old to cry, but it hurt too much to laugh.
> ADLAI STEVENSON, commenting on his defeat by General Eisenhower in the presidential election of 1952, news reports of Nov. 5, 1952.

Come in and have some fried post-mortems on toast.
> ADLAI STEVENSON, on opening his door to reporters the morning after he was defeated for presidency, *Time*, Nov. 17, 1952.

He who slings mud generally loses ground.
> ADLAI STEVENSON, news summaries, Jan. 11, 1954.

The idea that you can merchandise candidates for high office like breakfast cereal—that you can gather votes like box tops—is, I think, the ultimate indignity to the democratic process.
> ADLAI STEVENSON, accepting nomination for presidency, news reports, Aug. 18, 1956.

. . . There is a New America every morning when we wake up. It is upon us whether we will it or not. The New America is the sum of many small changes—a new subdivision here, a new school there, a new industry where there had been swampland—changes that add up to a broad transformation of our lives. Our task is to guide these changes. For, though change is inevitable, change for the better is a full-time job.

> ADLAI STEVENSON, presidential campaign address, Miami, Florida, news reports of Sept. 26, 1956.

Every Republican candidate for President since 1936 has been nominated by the Chase National Bank.

> ROBERT A. TAFT, after his defeat at 1952 Republican convention.

Congress can no more change the laws for qualification of voters than it can change the boiling point of water.

> SENATOR HERMAN TALMADGE, CBS-TV, April 26, 1962.

County judge, chairman of a committee, President of the U.S.; they are all the same kind of jobs. It is the business of dealing with people.

> HARRY TRUMAN, quoted by Jonathan Daniels, *The Man of Independence*, Lippincott, 1950.

I was very well assured if I could see enough people, I could be elected. That is what I did and this is the way it came out.

> HARRY TRUMAN, recalling his 1948 election, CBS-TV, May 27, 1955.

I never give them hell. I just tell the truth, and they think it is hell.

> HARRY TRUMAN, on campaign technique, *Look*, April 3, 1956.

A politician is a man who understands government, and it takes a politician to run a government. A statesman is a politician who's been dead 10 or 15 years.

> HARRY TRUMAN, to Reciprocity Club of Washington, *New York World-Telegram & Sun*, April 12, 1958.

You don't set a fox to watching the chickens just because he has a lot of experience in the hen house.

> HARRY TRUMAN, on Vice President Nixon's candidacy for the presidency, *Quote*, Oct. 30, 1960.

Whenever a fellow tells me he's bipartisan, I know he's going to vote against me.

> HARRY TRUMAN, *Quote*, Jan. 21, 1962.

Women have been in everything else—why not in politics? There's no reason why a woman shouldn't be in the White House as President, if she wants to be. But she'll be sorry when she gets there.

> HARRY TRUMAN, *McCall's*, Sept., 1962.

It's all so solemn. Somebody will get up and say: "I thank the gentleman for his contribution," when all the guy did was belch or gargle. Now I'm all for back-scratching, but I'd like to see a wink once in a while.

> REPRESENTATIVE JAMES TUMULTY, of New Jersey, comment after his first year in House of Representatives, news reports of July 30, 1955.

Law

One might risk establishing the following mathematical formula for bribery, namely $OG = PLR \times AEB$: The opportunity for graft equals the plethora of legal requirements multiplied by the number of architects, engineers and builders.

> HAROLD BIRNS, New York Buildings Commissioner, on confusion of housing and building laws, *New York Times*, Oct. 2, 1963.

My view is, without deviation, without exception, without any ifs, buts, or whereases, that freedom of speech means that you shall not do something to people either for the views they have, or the views they express, or the words they speak or write.

> HUGO BLACK, Associate Justice, U.S. Supreme Court, on "absolutes" of the Bill of Rights, *One Man's Stand For Freedom*, edited by Irving Dilliard, Knopf, 1963.

Fraud is the homage that force pays to reason.

> CHARLES P. CURTIS, lawyer, *A Commonplace Book*, Simon & Schuster, 1957.

There are only two ways to be quite unprejudiced and impartial. One is to be completely ignorant. The other is to be completely indifferent. Bias and prejudice are attitudes to be kept in hand, not attitudes to be avoided.

> CHARLES P. CURTIS, *ibid.*

We are about to make motherhood a crime. No civilized government in the history of mankind has ever done this.

> ADRIAN DUPLANTIER, Louisiana State Senator, on a bill making criminal the act of bearing more than one illegitimate child. Measure passed, 21–16. *New York Herald Tribune*, June 15, 1960.

The clearest way to show what the rule of law means to us in everyday life is to recall what has happened when there is no rule of law. The dread knock on the door in the middle of the night . . .

> PRESIDENT EISENHOWER, address marking first U.S. Law Day, news summaries of May 5, 1958.

. . . I deplore the need or the use of troops anywhere to get American citizens to obey the orders of constituted courts; but I want to point this one thing out: there is no person in this room whose basic rights are not involved in any successful defiance to the carrying out of court orders.

> PRESIDENT EISENHOWER, on Arkansas's defiance of Supreme Court school desegregation order, news conference of May 14, 1958.

. . . Laws governing business are not really written in Congress, but in the Courts, and what five members of the Supreme Court say the law is, may be something vastly different from what Congress intended the law to be. . . . If we persist in that kind of a system of law—and if we enforce it impartially against all offenders—virtually every business in America, big and small, is going to have to be run from Atlanta, Sing Sing, Leavenworth, or Alcatraz.

> BENJAMIN FAIRLESS, President, U.S. Steel, "Guilty Before Trial," address at Boston, May 18, 1950.

To pierce the curtain of the future, to give shape and visage to mysteries still in the womb of time, is the gift of the imagination. It requires poetic sensibilities with which judges are rarely endowed and which their education does not normally develop. These judges must have something of the creative artist in them; they must have antennae registering feeling and judgment beyond logical, let alone quantitative, proof.

> FELIX FRANKFURTER, New York Times, Nov. 28, 1954.

Fragile as reason is and limited as law is as the expression of the institutionalized medium of reason, that's all we have standing between us and the tyranny of mere will and the cruelty of unbridled, unprincipled, undisciplined feeling.

> FELIX FRANKFURTER, on his dedication to law, quoted in report of his retirement after 23 years on U.S. Supreme Court, New York Herald Tribune, Aug. 30, 1961.

The aim of law is the maximum gratification of the nervous system of man.

> LEARNED HAND, former Judge, U.S. Court of Appeals, *Time*, May 5, 1958.

A self-made man may prefer a self-made name.

> LEARNED HAND, on granting permission for Samuel Goldfish to change his name to Samuel Goldwyn, *The Lion's Share*, by Bosley Crowther, Dutton, 1957.

The spirit of liberty is the spirit which is not too sure that it is right.

The spirit of liberty is the spirit which seeks to understand the minds of other men and women. The spirit of liberty is the spirit which weighs their interests alongside its own bias.

The spirit of liberty remembers that not even a sparrow falls to earth unheeded.

The spirit of liberty is the spirit of Him who, nearly 2,000 years ago, taught mankind a lesson that it has never learned, but has never quite forgotten: that there may be a kingdom where the least shall be heard and considered side by side with the greatest.

> LEARNED HAND, recalled on his death at 89, *New York Herald Tribune*, Aug. 19, 1961.

. . . If a beachhead of cooperation may push back the jungles of suspicion, let both sides join in creating a new endeavor—not a new balance of power, but a new world of law, where the strong are just and the weak secure and the peace preserved.

> PRESIDENT KENNEDY, Inaugural Address, Jan. 20, 1961.

It may be true that the law cannot make a man love me, but it can keep him from lynching me, and I think that's pretty important . . .

> REV. MARTIN LUTHER KING, JR., Negro clergyman, *Wall Street Journal*, Nov. 13, 1962.

. . . In the South . . . the Sheriff is the man. I don't care what people write in books, it's the Sheriff who has contact with the jury list, with the taxes and assessments, and all the legal and illegal activities going on in the county. He can make a person's life miserable by harassment—I mean white or black.

> James Nabrit, Jr., President, Howard University, *New York Herald Tribune*, May 1, 1963.

. . . To the Negro in these counties in the South the image of America is the image of the Sheriff.

> James Nabrit, Jr., *ibid.*

. . . The importance that this Southern Negro sees in the elections in the United States is not who is elected President, all he wants to know is who's going to be Sheriff. That's the person who's going to be on his back. I'm not talking about Negroes in the universities, I'm talking about the ordinary Negro whose life is just one risk after another.

> James Nabrit, Jr., *ibid.*

A criminal lawyer, like a trapeze performer, is seldom more than one slip from an awful fall, and because he must swing rascals away from the clutches of the law to get top billing, he is eternally pinned in the hot arc-light of controversy. If he drops his client in mid-air, he is damned for clumsiness. If he slides the sinner down a guy-wire near the exits, he is absolutely certain to be booed by those in the audience who feel the miscreant will get home ahead of them and steal the silverware. If he grows reckless in his zeal to win, he may learn, too late, that no splints yet invented will heal a lawyer's broken reputation.

> Paul O'Neil, staff writer for *Life*, June 22, 1959, in an article on the prominent attorney, Edward Bennett Williams, © 1959, Time, Inc.

The law is the highest inheritance the sovereign people has, for without the law there would be no sovereign people and no inheritance.

> Roscoe Pound, Dean Emeritus, Harvard Law School, address for first U.S. Law Day, *Time*, May 5, 1958.

Law is experience developed by reason and applied continually to further experience.

> Roscoe Pound, interview in *Christian Science Monitor*, April 24, 1963.

If you have two people doing business with each other, they have got to have something in common.

> Roscoe Pound, on international law, *ibid.*

What we lawyers want to do is to substitute courts for carnage, dockets for rockets, briefs for bombs, warrants for warheads, mandates for missiles . . .

CHARLES RHYNE, chairman, World Conference on World Peace Through Law, *Wall Street Journal*, June 27, 1963.

Obscenity is whatever happens to shock some elderly and ignorant magistrate.

BERTRAND RUSSELL, *Look*, Feb. 23, 1954.

Fairness is what justice really is.

POTTER STEWART, Associate Justice, U.S. Supreme Court, *Time*, Oct. 20, 1958.

A trial is still an ordeal by battle. For the broadsword there is the weight of evidence; for the battle-axe the force of logic; for the sharp spear, the blazing gleam of truth; for the rapier, the quick and flashing knife of wit.

LLOYD PAUL STRYKER, noted trial lawyer, quoted in reports of his death, June 22, 1955.

Trying a case the second time is like eating yesterday morning's oatmeal.

LLOYD PAUL STRYKER, *ibid*.

Late every night in Connecticut, lights go out in the cities and towns, and citizens by tens of thousands proceed zestfully to break the law. . . . And, of course, there is always a witness to the crime—but as though to make the law completely unenforceable, Connecticut forbids spouses from testifying against one another.

TIME, March 10, 1961, on Connecticut laws against contraceptives.

In civilized life, law floats in a sea of ethics.

EARL WARREN, Chief Justice, U.S. Supreme Court, *New York Times*, Nov. 12, 1962.

Distrust all mothers-in-law. They are completely unscrupulous in what they say in court. The wife's mother is always more prejudiced against the husband than even the most ill-treated wife. If I had my way, I am afraid I would abolish mothers-in-law entirely.

> SIR GEOFFREY WRANGHAM, British High Court Justice and specialist in divorce cases, *Boston Herald*, Oct. 10, 1960.

Court Opinions

Sex and obscenity are not synonymous. Obscene material is material which deals with sex in a manner appealing to prurient interest.

> WILLIAM BRENNAN, JR., U.S. Supreme Court, in ruling, June 24, 1957, that established a new legal standard for obscenity.

Sex, a great and mysterious motive force in human life, has indisputably been a subject of absorbing interest to mankind through the ages.

> WILLIAM BRENNAN, JR., *ibid.*

In the relationship between man and religion, the state is firmly committed to a position of neutrality.

> TOM C. CLARK, U.S. Supreme Court, majority opinion holding that religious exercises in public schools are unconstitutional, *New York Herald Tribune*, June 18, 1963.

Time and experience have forcefully taught that the power to inspect dwelling places, either as a matter of systematic area-by-area search or, as here, to treat a specific problem, is of indispensable importance in the maintenance of community health; a power that would be greatly hobbled by the blanked requirement of the safeguards necessary for a search of evidence of criminal acts.

> FELIX FRANKFURTER, U.S. Supreme Court, majority opinion, May 5, 1959, holding that health inspectors may enter a private home without a search warrant.

. . . Ours is an accusatorial and not an inquisitorial system—a system in which the state must establish guilt by evidence independently and freely secured and may not by coercion prove its charge against an accused out of his own mouth.

> FELIX FRANKFURTER, in majority opinion that confessions extracted by police coercion may not be used in evidence, March 26, 1961.

The basic guarantees of our Constitution are warrants for the here and now and unless there is an overwhelmingly compelling reason, they are to be promptly fulfilled.

> ARTHUR GOLDBERG, U.S. Supreme Court, unanimous opinion holding that Memphis, Tenn., must desegregate all recreational facilities at once, without delay or gradualism, *New York Times*, May 27, 1963.

. . . The concept of neutrality can lead to . . . a brooding and pervasive devotion to the secular and a passive, or even active, hostility to the religious. Such results are not only not compelled by the Constitution, but, it seems to me, are prohibited by it.

> ARTHUR GOLDBERG, in an opinion agreeing with but partially mitigating Supreme Court ruling on unconstitutionality of religious exercises in public schools, June 17, 1963.

Slovenliness is no part of my religion, nor is it conducive to rest. Scripture commands cleanliness.

> JAMES B. M. McNALLY, Justice, New York Supreme Court Appellate Division, in unanimous opinion holding it is legal to use a coin-operated, self-service laundry on Sunday, *New York Times*, June 19, 1959.

What is obscenity to one person is but a subject of scientific inquiry to another.

> EDMUND PALMIERI, Federal Judge, in ruling on controversial materials imported by Kinsey Institute for Sex Research, *New York Times*, Jan. 3, 1958.

The Fourth Amendment and the personal rights it secures have a long history. At the very core stands the right of a man to retreat into his own home and there be free from unreasonable governmental intrusion.

> POTTER STEWART, U.S. Supreme Court, author of unanimous decision that Constitution bars police from mechanical eavesdropping, *New York Times*, March 6, 1961.

We come then to the question presented: Does segregation of children in public schools solely on the basis of race, even though the physical facilities and other "tangible" factors may be equal, deprive the children of the minority group of equal education opportunities? We believe that it does. . . . We conclude that in the field of public education the doctrine of "separate but equal" has no place.

> U.S. SUPREME COURT unanimous decision (written by Chief Justice Warren) outlawing Negro segregation in public schools, May 17, 1954.

Manifestly, state boundaries cannot extend beyond the national boundary. By annexing Texas, the U.S. certainly did not commit itself to relinquish what has been a fundamental cornerstone of its world policy. That would mean in effect that Texas was not annexed to the U.S., but that the U.S. was annexed to Texas.

> U.S. SUPREME COURT, ruling that Texas, Louisiana and other Gulf states reach only three miles out, not three leagues (10½ miles) as claimed, and therefore owed some 100-million dollars in oil revenues, *Time*, May 26, 1958.

It generates a feeling of inferiority as to their status in the community that may affect their hearts and minds in a way unlikely ever to be undone.

> EARL WARREN, Chief Justice, on the segregation of Negro students, May 24, 1954.

Criminology

It's not the people in prison who worry me. It's the people who aren't.

> EARL OF ARRAN (Arthur Gore), London columnist, *New York Times*, Jan. 7, 1962.

"Payola" is the year's new word. It doesn't sound as ugly as "bribe," but it means the same thing. It was first coined to describe the money that disc jockeys took to plug certain records. Now the word is being applied to almost any shady deal involving a payoff.

> WILLIAM ATTWOOD, "The Age of Payola," *Look*, March 29, 1960.

The California executioner keeps banker's hours. He never kills before 10 o'clock in the morning, never after 4 in the afternoon.

> CARYL CHESSMAN, whose innocence or guilt was at the center of a long controversy, in letter written on eve of his execution at San Quentin Prison, *New York Post*, May 3, 1960.

When you read this, he will have killed me. I will have exchanged oblivion for an unprecedented 12-year nightmare.
> CARYL CHESSMAN, *ibid.*

The first need of the youthful probationer is immersion in a tepid bath of human acceptance and goodwill.
> IRVING BEN COOPER, Federal Judge, on men newly admitted to probation, *New York Times*, March 20, 1962.

Alcatraz, the Federal prison with a name like the blare of a trombone . . .
A black molar in the jawbone of the nation's prison system . . .
> THOMAS GADDIS, *Birdman of Alcatraz*, Random House, 1955.

Banks are an almost irresistible attraction for that element of our society which seeks unearned money.
> J. EDGAR HOOVER, Director, Federal Bureau of Investigation, news reports of April 7, 1955.

We are a fact-gathering organization only. We don't clear anybody. We don't condemn anybody. Just the minute the FBI begins making recommendations on what should be done with its information, it becomes a Gestapo.
> J. EDGAR HOOVER, *Look*, June 14, 1956.

I am devoted to detective novels. They make such a nice change from my work. I particularly like your American ones, where the hero is invariably amorous, alcoholic and practically indestructible. But unfortunately, my dear, crime is solved not by single masterminds . . .
> RICHARD LEOFRIC JACKSON of Scotland Yard, President of Interpol (International Criminal Police Organization), *Saturday Evening Post*, Oct. 28, 1961.

A policeman's gun is his cross, and he carries it always.
> STEPHEN KENNEDY, New York Police Commissioner, *Saturday Evening Post*, Sept. 8, 1956.

The main reason why the unlighted streets were not turned into a dark and steaming jungle was the reaction of the community. . . . In the dark all men were the same color. In the dark our fellow man was seen more clearly than in the normal light of a New York night.

> STEPHEN KENNEDY, on the unexpected "zero" crime rate when a power failure plunged into blackness a five-mile area of Manhattan with a population of 500,000, *Time*, Aug. 31, 1959.

I hate this "crime doesn't pay" stuff. Crime in the U.S. is perhaps one of the biggest businesses in the world today.

> DR. PAUL KIRK, Professor of Criminalistics, University of California, *Wall Street Journal*, Feb. 26, 1960.

. . . I defended about 140 people for murder in this country and I think in all of the cases I received just one Christmas card, from all of these defendants . . .

> SAMUEL LEIBOWITZ, Judge, Kings County Court, Brooklyn, CBS-TV, May 28, 1954.

A burglar has a right to burglarize my home just as well as anybody else's. I'm no better than anyone else. At 102 Coleridge Street, I'm just Citizen Leibowitz.

> SAMUEL LEIBOWITZ, on a Brooklyn burglar who removed the Judge's trousers from his bedroom and took $72, *New York Herald Tribune*, Jan. 18, 1959.

The thought that I had cut off an innocent young life and the knowledge of the grief I had caused both his family and mine has been present in my consciousness every day of every year for the past quarter century. It is not, gentlemen, an easy thought to live with. At any time in the past 25 years, I would have welcomed joyously the chance to take Bobby Franks' place—to lay down my life if it would restore his.

> NATHAN LEOPOLD, letter to Illinois State Parole Board, news reports of March 18, 1955.

It was just one long gob of nothing. Complete monotony. The same thing every day. Weaving fiber chair bottoms. Drudgery. No hope, reward or advancement. Spiritually it was as bleak and empty as it is possible to imagine.

> NATHAN LEOPOLD, on prison life, "Murder on His Conscience," by John Bartlow Martin, *Saturday Evening Post*, April 2–23, 1955.

Ever since I can remember, I have heard how bright I was.
> NATHAN LEOPOLD, on his IQ of 206 to 210, *ibid*.

Thousands of prisoners, especially long-term prisoners, look to me to vindicate the rehabilitation theory of imprisonment. I will do my best not to fail in that trust.
> NATHAN LEOPOLD, on winning parole after serving more than 33 years of a life prison sentence, news reports of Feb. 21, 1958.

What a rotten writer of detective stories life is!
> NATHAN LEOPOLD, *Life Plus 99 Years*, Doubleday, 1958.

We have reason to believe you have committed an offense.
> LONDON POLICE ticket for overtime parking, quoted by columnist John Crosby, *New York Herald Tribune*, Nov. 4, 1963.

A woman has a much better chance than a man of acquittal on a murder charge. Of course, if she happens to be a blonde, her chances rise about 45%. With attractive women, whose chances are much better again, juries sometimes have to be restrained from handing them a medal for their crimes.
> DR. JOHN MCGEORGE, Australian psychiatrist, *Quote*, March 12, 1960.

[There is] the persistent failure of the law to distinguish between crime as an accident, incidental explosive event, crime as a behavior pattern expressive of chronic unutterable rage and frustration, crime as a business or elected way of life.
> DR. KARL MENNINGER, quoted in "Criminals Are People," editorial in *Christian Science Monitor*, Aug. 4, 1959.

One thing I can't understand is why the newspapers labeled me the Mad Bomber. That was unkind.
> GEORGE METESKY, comment to newsmen after his arrest for placing 20 bombs in public places over a 17-year period, *New York Journal-American*, Jan. 22, 1957.

A questing, thrusting, restless, credulous, oddly innocent people, who fell for charlatans as readily as they did for authentic ideas and idealism (and) whose sometimes sanctimonious attitudes switched suddenly to violence and bloodshed. Flowers for Mother's Day and flowers for a gangster's funeral. The insistent beat of the jazz orchestras and the new syncopation —the rat-tat-tat of the sawn-off machine gun.

> MALCOLM MUGGERIDGE, "The Titans: United States of America," BBC-TV, Jan. 16, 1962.

Gangsters and their murderous feuds, dramatised in innumerable stories, films and plays, became an integral part of the often misleading image of America projected throughout the world. What provided the gangsters with their great opportunity was Prohibition, introduced in a burst of collective righteousness. With the same whole-heartedness that they embarked upon Prohibition, they set themselves to evade it.

> MALCOLM MUGGERIDGE, *ibid.*

Juvenile delinquency starts in the high chair and ends in the death chair.

> JAMES D. C. MURRAY, veteran defense lawyer, *New York World-Telegram & Sun*, Sept. 8, 1956.

A woman will almost never tell you the truth, while most men defendants will. Women have a furtive, concealing nature, and to some extent they're pathological liars who can conceive of situations that never existed.

> JAMES D. C. MURRAY, *ibid.*

Crime is a logical extension of the sort of behavior that is often considered perfectly respectable in legitimate business.

> ROBERT RICE, *The Business of Crime*, Farrar, Straus and Cudahy, 1956.

A man may be disconcerted because of unconscious wants. For instance, Americans need rest, but do not know it. I believe this to be a large part of the explanation of the crime wave in the United States.

> BERTRAND RUSSELL, quoted by Alan Wood, *Bertrand Russell: The Passionate Skeptic*, Simon & Schuster, 1958.

Nathan Leopold walked out of Stateville Prison Thursday into the wonderful world of free men. He promptly got sick.

> JOHN JUSTIN SMITH, prize-winning lead on release of Nathan Leopold after more than 33 years in prison, *Chicago Daily News*, March 13, 1958.

. . . There was the South Ozone National Bank looking as though it had been waiting for me.

> WILLIE SUTTON, *I, Willie Sutton* ("The Personal Story of the Most Daring Bank Robber and Jail Breaker of Our Time") by Quentin Reynolds, Farrar, Straus & Company, 1953.

It is a rather pleasant experience to be alone in a bank at night. . . .

> WILLIE SUTTON, *ibid.*

In the circle in which I travel, a dumb man is more dangerous than a hundred rats.

> JOE VALACHI, convicted murderer and racketeer, expressing confidence in his ability to testify to U.S. Senate subcommittee, *New York Herald Tribune*, Sept. 27, 1963.

You live by the gun and knife, and die by the gun and knife.

> JOE VALACHI, on the secret code of crime syndicate known as Cosa Nostra, testimony to U.S. Senate subcommittee, *New York Herald Tribune*, Oct. 2, 1963.

Armed Forces

I am convinced that the best service a retired general can perform is to turn in his tongue along with his suit, and to mothball his opinions.
> GENERAL OMAR BRADLEY, Armed Forces Day address, *New York Times*, May 17, 1959.

The major deterrent [to war] is in a man's mind. The major deterrent in the future is going to be not only what we have, but what we do, what we are willing to do, what they think we will do. Stamina, guts, standing up for the things that we say—those are deterrents.
> ADMIRAL ARLEIGH BURKE, *U.S. News & World Report*, Oct. 3, 1960.

More than three million square miles of territory to protect, ten thousand miles of border to guard, and a fence to build ten, 11 or 12 miles high . . . It is better to have less thunder in the mouth and more lightning in the hand.
> GENERAL BEN CHIDLAW, Commander, Continental Air Defense, *Time*, Dec. 20, 1954.

I return with feelings of misgiving from my third war—I was the first American commander to put his signature to a paper ending a war when we did not win it.
> GENERAL MARK CLARK, retiring UN Far Eastern commander, *New York Herald Tribune*, Oct. 21, 1953.

When you put on a uniform, there are certain inhibitions that you accept.
> GENERAL DWIGHT EISENHOWER, on learning that President Truman had relieved General Douglas MacArthur of command, April 11, 1951.

The most terrible job in warfare is to be a second lieutenant leading a platoon when you are on the battlefield.
PRESIDENT EISENHOWER, March 17, 1954.

. . . That was not the biggest battle that ever was, but for me it always typified one thing—the dash, the ingenuity, the readiness at the first opportunity that characterizes the American soldier.
PRESIDENT EISENHOWER, on the tenth anniversary of Battle of the Remagen Bridgehead, March 8, 1955.

The purpose is clear. It is safety with solvency. The country is entitled to both.
PRESIDENT EISENHOWER, urging unification of ground, sea, and air commands, April 17, 1958.

I am quite sure that the American people feel it is far more important to be able to hit the target than it is to haggle over who makes a weapon or who pulls a trigger.
PRESIDENT EISENHOWER, *ibid*.

We're battling bastards of Bataan
No mama, no papa, no Uncle Sam;
No aunts, no uncles, no cousins, no nieces;
No pills, no planes, no artillery pieces.
. . . And nobody gives a damn.
GI song lyrics written during ill-fated defense of Bataan early in World War II, quoted by Louis Morton, *The Fall of the Philippines*, Department of the Army, 1953.

That monkey meat is all right until the animal's hands turn up on your plate.
GI saying, *ibid*.

Make no mistake about it. The first man who will walk on the moon has already been born. I hope in America.
LIEUTENANT GENERAL JAMES GAVIN, former Army research chief, *Quote*, March 23, 1958.

The Academy's long-range mission will be to train generals, not second lieutenants.

> GENERAL HUBERT HARMON, first Commander, Air Force Academy, *Newsweek*, June 6, 1955.

When we know as much about people as hog specialists know about hogs, we'll be better off.

> MAJOR GENERAL LEWIS HERSHEY, Selective Service Director, news reports of June 18, 1956.

The field of combat was a long, narrow, green-baize covered table. The weapons were words.

> ADMIRAL TURNER JOY, after a full year of truce talks in Korea, news summaries of Dec. 31, 1952.

There is always inequity in life. Some men are killed in a war, and some men are wounded, and some men are stationed in the Antarctic and some are stationed in San Francisco. It's very hard in military or personal life to assure complete equality. Life is unfair.

> PRESIDENT KENNEDY, to Reservists anxious to be released from active duty, March 21, 1962.

As the bomb fell over Hiroshima and exploded, we saw an entire city disappear. I wrote in my log the words: "My God, what have we done?"

> CAPTAIN ROBERT LEWIS, co-pilot of the B-29, *Enola Gay*, NBC-TV, May 19, 1955.

The world has turned over many times since I took the oath on the plain at West Point, and the hopes and dreams have long since vanished; but I still remember the refrain of one of the most popular barracks ballads of that day which proclaimed most proudly that old soldiers never die; they just fade away. And like the old soldier in that ballad, I now close my military career and just fade away, an old soldier who tried to do his duty as God gave him the sight to see that duty.

> GENERAL DOUGLAS MACARTHUR, address to Congress after being relieved of duties by President Truman, April 19, 1951.

I have one criticism [about] Negro troops who fought under my command in the Korean War. They didn't send me enough of them.

> GENERAL MACARTHUR, denying report he was a "white supremacist," *Time*, June 11, 1951.

Expect only five per cent of an intelligence report to be accurate. The trick of a good commander is to isolate the five per cent.

> GENERAL MACARTHUR, quoted in *MacArthur: His Rendezvous With History*, by Major General Courtney Whitney, Knopf, 1956.

In war, when a commander becomes so bereft of reason and perspective that he fails to understand the dependence of arms on Divine guidance, he no longer deserves victory.

> GENERAL MACARTHUR, *ibid.*

No honor I have ever received moves me more deeply. Perhaps this is because I can recall no parallel in history where a great nation recently at war has so distinguished its former enemy commander.

> GENERAL MACARTHUR, on receiving one of Japan's highest decorations, *New York Times*, June 22, 1960.

Duty, honor, country: Those three hallowed words reverently dictate what you ought to be, what you can be, what you will be. They are your rallying point to build courage when courage seems to fail, to regain faith when there seems to be little cause for faith, to create hope when hope becomes forlorn.

> GENERAL MACARTHUR, "Duty, Honor, Country," an address at West Point on receiving Sylvanus Thayer Award for service to his nation, May 12, 1962; full text in *National Observer*, May 20, 1962, and March 11, 1963.

. . . In memory's eye I could see those staggering columns of the first World War, bending under soggy packs on many a weary march, from dripping dusk to drizzling dawn, slogging ankle deep through mire of shell-pocked roads to form grimly for the attack, blue-lipped, covered with sludge and mud, chilled by the wind and rain, driving home to their objective, and for many, to the judgment seat of God.

> GENERAL MACARTHUR, on World War I, *ibid.*

. . . Twenty years after, on the other side of the globe, again the filth of murky foxholes, the stench of ghostly trenches, the slime of dripping dugouts, those boiling suns of the relentless heat, those torrential rains of devastating storms, the loneliness and utter desolation of jungle trails, the

bitterness of long separation from those they loved and cherished, the deadly pestilence of tropical disease, the horror of stricken areas of war.
GENERAL MACARTHUR, on World War II, *ibid.*

In my dreams I hear again the crash of guns, the rattle of musketry, the strange, mournful mutter of the battlefield. But in the evening of my memory always I come back to West Point. Always there echoes and re echoes. Duty, honor, country.
GENERAL MACARTHUR, nearing conclusion of his address, *ibid.*

Decision—calmness in action and decision in the crisis. . . . I would say that is essential not only in generals and military leaders, but also in political life. Decisions! And a General, a Commander-in-Chief who has not got the quality of decision, then he is no good.
FIELD MARSHAL MONTGOMERY, CBS-TV, April 28, 1959.

In Europe, the ubiquitous G.I., with his camera like a third eye, created wherever he went a little America, air-conditioned, steam-heated and neon-lighted. In American eyes, he was a liberator and defender of freedom. In other eyes he often seemed part of an American army of occupation. To all he symbolized Europe's enfeeblement, and the shift of world power and wealth across the Atlantic.
MALCOLM MUGGERIDGE, British journalist, "The Titans: United States of America," BBC-TV, Jan. 16, 1962.

War is like a giant pack rat. It takes something from you, and it leaves something behind in its stead. It burned me out in some ways, so that now I feel like an old man, but still sometimes act like a dumb kid. It made me grow up too fast.
AUDIE MURPHY, most decorated soldier of World War II, *New York Journal-American*, Aug. 30, 1955.

A decision is the action an executive must take when he has information so incomplete that the answer does not suggest itself.
ADMIRAL ARTHUR WILLIAM RADFORD, Chairman, U.S. Joint Chiefs of Staff, *Time*, Feb. 25, 1957.

One of the most wonderful things that happened in our *Nautilus* program was that everybody knew it was going to fail—so they let us completely alone so we were able to do the job.

> ADMIRAL HYMAN G. RICKOVER, testimony to Senate committee, *Reader's Digest*, July, 1958.

We fight any enemy the President designates. We don't just keep talking Communism, Communism, Communism. You might build up hate against one enemy and find yourself fighting another.

> GENERAL DAVID MONROE SHOUP, interviewed a month before his retirement as Commandant, U.S. Marine Corps, *Forbes*, Dec. 1, 1963.

. . . The Marine Corps is the Navy's police force and as long as I am President that is what it will remain. They have a propaganda machine that is almost equal to Stalin's. . . .

> PRESIDENT TRUMAN, rejecting suggestion that Marine Corps should be represented on Joint Chiefs of Staff. The statement caused wide dismay and Mr. Truman later apologized. *Time*, Sept. 18, 1950.

If our air forces are never used, they have achieved their finest goal.

> GENERAL NATHAN TWINING, Air Force Chief of Staff, quoted by International News Service, news summaries of March 31, 1956.

Sir, a doolie is that insignificant whose rank is measured in negative units, one whose potential for learning is unlimited.

> U.S. AIR FORCE ACADEMY, self-description of first-year men, referred to as "doolies," *Time*, Jan. 19, 1962.

Babies satisfactorily born.

> U.S. ARMY code message (to Big Three's Potsdam Conference) on successful test of atomic bomb at Alamogordo, N.M., an event which set in motion Allied plans for attack on Hiroshima; quoted by Winston Churchill, *Triumph and Tragedy*, Houghton Mifflin, 1953.

I rose by sheer military ability to the rank of Corporal.

> THORNTON WILDER, novelist and playwright, on World War I army service, news summaries of Jan. 12, 1953.

69

Business

Management is now where the medical profession was when it decided that working in a drug store was not sufficient training to become a doctor.
>LAWRENCE APPLEY, president, American Management Association, *Men at the Top,* by Osborn Elliott, Harper & Row, 1959.

The Engineering of Consent.
>EDWARD BERNAYS, title for book on public relations profession in which he pioneered, University of Oklahoma Press, 1955.

. . . Closer together than the hands of a clock at twenty minutes of eight.
>ROBERT BEDINGFIELD, financial writer, on the brothers John and Clint Murchison, Jr., *New York Times,* Jan. 15, 1961.

A good manager is a man who isn't worried about his own career but rather the careers of those who work for him. My advice: Don't worry about yourself. Take care of those who work for you and you'll float to greatness on their achievements.
>H. S. M. BURNS, president, Shell Oil Co., *Men at the Top,* by Osborn Elliott, Harper & Row, 1959.

The ideas I stand for are not mine. I borrowed them from Socrates. I swiped them from Chesterfield. I stole them from Jesus. And I put them in a book. If you don't like their rules, whose would you use?
>DALE CARNEGIE, on his book, *How to Win Friends and Influence People,* quoted in *Newsweek,* Aug. 8, 1955.

I can remember senior officials without a smile on their faces saying, "Well, Minister, we have studied the contract with great care and we see no way in which we can get out of it." They do not grasp that in business a reputation for keeping absolutely to the letter and spirit of an agreement, even when it is unfavorable, is the most precious of assets, although it is not entered in the balance sheet.

> LORD CHANDOS (Oliver Lyttelton, 1st Viscount), international banking and metals executive who served in Churchill cabinet and also headed Britain's Board of Trade, *Memoirs of Lord Chandos: An Unexpected View From the Summit*, New American Library, 1963.

I have heard speakers . . . use the phrase, "I can say without fear of contradiction. . . ." Anyone who says this in a modern democracy, or to the shareholders of a modern company, should see the doctor.

> LORD CHANDOS, *ibid.*

When I've had a rough day, before I go to sleep I ask myself if there's anything more I can do right now. If there isn't, I sleep sound.

> L. L. COLBERT, president, Chrysler Corporation, *Newsweek*, Aug. 22, 1955.

Money itself isn't the primary factor in what one does. A person does things for the sake of accomplishing something. Money generally follows.

> COLONEL HENRY CROWN, owner of the Empire State Building, *New York Times*, Feb. 21, 1960.

Owing money has never concerned me so long as I know where it could be repaid.

> COLONEL HENRY CROWN, *ibid.*

A birthday is a big event in everybody's life. It should be a holiday—with pay.

> MICHAEL DARLING, Chicago labor leader, endorsing movement to extend holidays to include birthdays, news summaries of Jan. 18, 1954.

Bigness taxes the ability to manage intelligently . . . The growth of bigness has resulted in ruthless sacrifices of human values. The disappearance of free enterprise has submerged the individual in the impersonal corporation. When a nation of shopkeepers is transformed into a nation of clerks, enormous spiritual sacrifices are made.

> WILLIAM O. DOUGLAS, Associate Justice, U.S. Supreme Court, to an audience of business men, *New York Post*, Aug. 11, 1963.

71

In the tiny space of twenty years, we have bred a whole generation of working Americans who take it for granted that they will never be out of a job or go a single year without a salary increase.

> K. K. DuVall, president, Chicago Merchandise National Bank, *Time*, Sept. 10, 1956.

I wanted to focus some public attention on the country's forgotten man— the corporation executive paid around $10,000 a year. After taxes and educating his children and perhaps one major illness, he reaches the age of 55 without saving a penny. There's something wrong with the system when a man who does everything he should do ends up in that spot.

> John Ekblom, Hupp Corporation board chairman, on rejecting a $110,000 bonus, *New York Herald Tribune*, June 26, 1959.

I'll try to be the salesman of shares in America.

> Keith Funston, at age 40 on leaving the presidency of Trinity College, Hartford, Conn., to become president of New York Stock Exchange, *Time*, June 4, 1951.

One of the greatest pieces of economic wisdom is to know what you do not know.

> John Kenneth Galbraith, economic adviser to President Kennedy, *Time*, March 3, 1961.

I have no complex about wealth. I have worked hard for my money, producing things people need. I believe that the able industrial leader who creates wealth and employment is more worthy of historical notice than politicians or soldiers.

> John Paul Getty, American multi-millionaire, *Time*, Feb. 24, 1958.

I have often maintained that I possess a rare talent and strong inclination to be a beachcomber. . . . If it were not for the demands made upon me by my business, I would provide living proof that a man can live quite happily for decades without ever doing any work.

> John Paul Getty, *My Life and Fortunes*, Duell, Sloan & Pearce, 1963.

The best investment on *earth* is earth.

> Louis Glickman, New York real estate owner, *New York Post*, Sept. 3, 1957.

Practically all problems in the realm of judgment, in the realm of operating a business involving men and women, in the realm of government, whether executive, legislative or judicial, can be handled more efficiently by a man and wife, in our estimation. The American people, in our judgment, if they had sense, would elect a man president and a wife as vice-president.

> BRUCE AND BEATRICE GOULD, statement to *Wall Street Journal*, June 17, 1955, on their twenty years of joint editorship of the *Ladies' Home Journal*.

Once upon a time there was a little girl who *always* said "Thank you" at birthday parties; who called friends of the family "Aunt" Helen and "Uncle" Jim; and who passed out free cookies *the day* her lemonade stand opened. When this little girl grew up she didn't go to heaven. She went into public relations. And learned that what to her had always been unconscious art is now classified as a science—"the engineering of consent" —worth a hundred a week to her and millions in good will to her clients.

> MARY ANNE GUITAR, "The Million Dollar Science," *Mademoiselle*, Sept., 1956.

There is nothing like the ticker tape except a woman—nothing that promises, hour after hour, day after day, such sudden developments; nothing that disappoints so often or occasionally fulfills with such unbelievable, passionate magnificence.

> WALTER KNOWLETON GUTMAN, economist, *Coronet*, March, 1960.

. . . A corporation prefers to offer a job to a man who already has one, or doesn't immediately need one. The company accepts you if you are already accepted. To obtain entry into paradise, in terms of employment, you should be in a full state of grace.

> ALAN HARRINGTON, on executive hiring practices, *Life In the Crystal Palace*, Knopf, 1959.

We are all, it seems, saving ourselves for the Senior Prom. But many of us forget that somewhere along the way we must learn to dance.

> ALAN HARRINGTON, on preparation to enjoy retirement, *ibid*.

I have found it to be the craft of arranging truths so that people will like you. Public-relations specialists make flower arrangements of the facts, placing them so that the wilted and less attractive petals are hidden by sturdy blooms.

> ALAN HARRINGTON, on public relations, *ibid.*

In the old days we used to say that when the United States economy sneezed the rest of the world went to bed with pneumonia. Now when the United States economy sneezes the other countries say "Gesundheit."

> WALTER HELLER, chairman, President's Council of Economic Advisers, *New York Times*, May 8, 1961.

The woman who climbs to a high post and then wants everybody to know how important she is, is the worst enemy of her own sex.

> MRS. CLAIRE GIANNINI HOFFMAN, only woman director of the Bank of America, news reports of July 7, 1954.

The dinosaur's eloquent lesson is that if some bigness is good, an overabundance of bigness is not necessarily better.

> ERIC JOHNSTON, four-times president, U.S. Chamber of Commerce, warning against trend to bigness in American business, *Quote*, Feb. 23, 1958.

The Bell System is like a damn big dragon. You kick it in the tail, and two years later, it feels it in its head.

> FREDERICK KAPPEL, chairman, American Telephone and Telegraph Co., "The Surprising Story of Ma Bell," by J. Robert Moskin, *Look*, Aug. 28, 1962.

You can delegate authority, but you can never delegate responsibility for delegating a task to someone else. If you picked the right man, fine, but if you picked the wrong man, the responsibility is yours—not his.

> RICHARD E. KRAFVE, president, Raytheon Company, *Boston Sunday Globe*, May 22, 1960.*

Like the wheel—which we have learned to make stronger and more cheaply, but which remains unaltered in concept—the book, we may hope, is a unique and lasting invention.

> DAN LACY, managing director, American Book Publishers Council, *Newsweek*, Nov. 14, 1960.

---

* A similar thought was expressed by Vice Admiral Hyman Rickover, *New York Times*, Oct. 7, 1963, in regard to his construction program for nuclear submarines: "A project manager can delegate authority but not responsibility. Responsibility is indivisible. When something goes wrong and you cannot find the specific individual to put your finger on, then you have never really had responsibility."

American capitalism has been both overpraised and overindicted . . . it is neither the Plumed Knight nor the monstrous Robber Baron.

> MAX LERNER, *America as a Civilization*, Simon & Schuster, 1958.

Every day I have matutinal indisposition that emanates from the nauseous effluvia of that oppressive slave statute.

> JOHN L. LEWIS, comment on Taft-Hartley Act, news reports of May 10, 1954.

All forms of government fall when it comes up to the question of bread—bread for the family, something to eat. Bread to a man with a hungry family comes first—before his union, before his citizenship, before his church affiliation. Bread!

> JOHN L. LEWIS, on the dangers of unemployment, *Saturday Evening Post*, Oct. 12, 1963.

Business more than any other occupation is a continual dealing with the future; it is a continual calculation, an instinctive exercise in foresight.

> HENRY R. LUCE, speech quoted in *Fortune* promotional material, Oct., 1960.

Success is that old ABC—ability, breaks and courage.

> CHARLES LUCKMAN, manufacturing executive and architect, *New York Mirror*, Sept. 19, 1955.

This is an industry of ideas and imagination, and what we are selling is hope.

> STEVE MAYHAM, executive of Toilet Goods Association, *Time*, June 16, 1958.

The business executive is by profession a decision maker. Uncertainty is his opponent. Overcoming it is his mission. Whether the outcome is a consequence of luck or of wisdom, the moment of decision is without doubt the most creative and critical event in the life of the executive.

> JOHN MCDONALD, "How Businessmen Make Decisions," *Fortune*, Aug., 1955.

Anybody who has any doubt about the ingenuity or the resourcefulness of a plumber never got a bill from one.

> GEORGE MEANY, president, American Federation of Labor, himself a former plumber, CBS-TV, Jan. 8, 1954.

75

The American people would rather give away some of their rice, wheat, butter, textiles and medicines to the needy people in Communist China, Cuba and elsewhere behind the Iron Curtain than to sell these goods for gold mined by slave labor.

> GEORGE MEANY, *New York Times*, April 1, 1962.

When white-collar people get jobs, they sell not only their time and energy, but their personalities as well. They sell by the week, or month, their smiles and their kindly gestures, and they must practice that prompt repression of resentment and aggression.

> C. WRIGHT MILLS, *White Collar*, Oxford University Press, New York, 1956.

The language of economics is seldom limpid, but in H Street they usually manage to remove from it the very last flickering colophon of charm.*

> JAMES MORRIS, on the World Bank at 1818 H Street, Washington, *The Road to Huddersfield: A Journey to Five Continents*, Pantheon, 1963.

The phenomenon I refer to . . . is the tidal wave of craving for convenience that is sweeping over America. Today convenience is the success factor of just about every type of produce and service that is showing steady growth.

> CHARLES MORTIMER, president, General Foods Corporation, address to American Marketing Association, *New York Herald Tribune*, May 14, 1959.

. . . The creeping notion that additives are badditives.

> CHARLES MORTIMER, calling for campaign against ban on food coloring, *Wall Street Journal*, Dec. 29, 1960.

Money is like manure. If you spread it around, it does a lot of good. But if you pile it up in one place, it stinks like hell.

> CLINT MURCHISON, JR., Texas financier, quoting his father's advice, *Time*, June 16, 1961.

---

* Examples of bankers' jargon: positive-income elasticity of demand, developmental situations in which utilization of resources has not reached an optimum, projects being organizationally related to infrastructure investment, end-use visits, debt-equity ratios, pay-out analyses, acquaintance missions, and credit-worthiness.

Today's public opinion, though it may appear as light as air, may become tomorrow's legislation—for better or for worse.

> EARL NEWSOM, public relations counselor, quoted in American Petroleum Institute newsletter, Winter, 1963.

Happiness is just a thing called change.

> NEWSWEEK, Feb. 27, 1961, on the 100,000 executives who change jobs annually.

We have gone completely overboard on security. Everything has to be secured, jobs, wages, hours—although the ultimate in security is jail, the slave labor camp and the salt mine.

> COLA PARKER, president, National Association of Manufacturers, news reports of Dec. 9, 1955.

Many minor executives prefer a generous expense account to a raise in salary which would be heavily taxed and more soberly spent. It is they who support the so-called "expense account restaurants," places of exotic décor where patrons lunch in a darkness which is all but complete. They cannot see to read the prices on the menu, but these, in the special circumstances, are irrelevant.

> C. NORTHCOTE PARKINSON, "Parkinson's Second Law," *The Law and the Profits*, Houghton Mifflin, 1960.

Perfection of planning is a symptom of decay. During a period of exciting discovery or progress, there is no time to plan the perfect headquarters. The time for that comes later, when all the important work has been done.

> C. NORTHCOTE PARKINSON, *ibid*.

Public Relations is the management function which evaluates public attitudes, identifies the policies and procedures of an individual or an organization with the public interest, and executes a program of action to earn public understanding and acceptance.

> PUBLIC RELATIONS NEWS, New York City, definition printed on cards distributed to the public relations profession, 1954.

I don't meet competition. I crush it.

> CHARLES REVSON, founder of Revlon, Inc., *Time*, June 16, 1958.

We have got to understand women the way they do each other. We must learn to use a woman's inconsistency as the key to approaching her.
>   CHARLES REVSON, *Sales Management*, March 3, 1961.

The leader must know, must know that he knows, and must be able to make it abundantly clear to those about him that he knows.
>   CLARENCE B. RANDALL, retired chairman, Inland Steel Company, *Making Good in Management*, McGraw-Hill, 1964.

Facts, as such, never settled anything. They are working tools only. It is the implications that can be drawn from facts that count, and to evaluate these requires wisdom and judgment that are unrelated to the computer approach to life.
>   CLARENCE B. RANDALL, *ibid.*

I was born into it and there was nothing I could do about it. It was there, like air or food or any other element . . . The only question with wealth is what you do with it.
>   JOHN D. ROCKEFELLER, JR., *Time*, Sept. 24, 1956.

Giving is the secret of a healthy life. Not necessarily money, but whatever a man has of encouragement and sympathy and understanding.
>   JOHN D. ROCKEFELLER, JR., *ibid.*

Well, yes, you could say we have independent means.
>   JOHN D. ROCKEFELLER, III, reply to an Indianapolis newspaper reporter who asked, "Are you a multimillionaire?" news summaries of Oct. 24, 1955.

Father taught us that opportunity and responsibility go hand in hand. I think we all act on that principle; on the basic human impulse that makes a man want to make the best of what's in him and what's been given him.
>   LAURENCE ROCKEFELLER, on objectives of the Rockefeller brothers, "From Riches to Success," *U.S. News & World Report*, Feb. 1, 1960.

I can't help from making money, that is all.
>   HELENA RUBENSTEIN, on cosmetic business which made her worth more than $100,000,000, *New York Journal-American*, March 12, 1958.

Next to the dog, the wastebasket is man's best friend.

> SAN FRANCISCO EXECUTIVE, commenting on the vast amount of reading required of businessmen, "The Flood That Drowns the Boss," *Business Week*, Aug. 18, 1956.

He called me during the Depression . . . and said he wanted to buy a large building. I asked him if the Empire State would do.

> JOSEPHINE SCHAEFER, New York real estate broker, on how she sold the Hotel Pierre to John Paul Getty, *New York Times*, May 8, 1963.

Most women would be better off if they paid less attention to their investments, not more . . . And the women could continue to do what they do best—be women.

> ALBERT SCHWABACHER, JR., "Women and Money," *Vogue*, April 1, 1963.

What self-respecting woman wants anything common around if she can buy something preferred? . . . Women like quality-brand.

> ALBERT SCHWABACHER, JR., *ibid*.

It was management by crony, on a horse-trading basis . . .

> ALFRED P. SLOAN, JR., on William Durant and early days of automotive industry, "My Years With General Motors," *Fortune*, Sept., 1963.

He banged the door on the way out, and out of that bang came eventually the Chrysler corporation.

> ALFRED P. SLOAN, JR., on Walter Chrysler's departure from General Motors, *ibid*.

. . . Even for the neurotic executive—as for everyone else—work has great therapeutic value; it is generally his last refuge, and deterioration there marks the final collapse of the man; his marriage, his social life, and the outside interests—all have suffered beforehand.

> RICHARD AUSTIN SMITH, "The Executive Crack-up," *Fortune*, May, 1955.

The true influence of work in the crack-up of an executive comes down to this: a neurotic individual encounters in his work a special stress (or a series of stresses) that at some point unbearably intensifies the conflicts in his own personality; then he goes to pieces . . . though success can be the result of a strong neurotic drive, the neurosis will eventually make trouble for the individual.

> RICHARD AUSTIN SMITH, *ibid*.

Some of these men come to me to have a bridge built. I build cantilever extensions into prosperity.

> BENJAMIN SONNENBERG, public relations counsel, on making executives into "business statesmen," *Men At the Top*, by Osborn Elliott, Harper & Row, 1959.

Whenever I think, I make a mistake.

> ROGER STEVENS, New York real estate and theatre executive, "How Businessmen Make Decisions," *Fortune*, Aug., 1955.

There is nothing as universal in this world as human thirst. . . . Our market is as big as the world and the people in it.

> LEE TALLEY, on being elected president of Coca-Cola, *Newsweek*, May 19, 1958.

The Chinese laundry doesn't have to compete; it's competed against.

> C. M. TAN, Chinese Consolidated Benevolent Association, *New York Herald Tribune*, Oct. 23, 1960.

The instability of the economy is equaled only by the instability of economists.

> JOHN H. WILLIAMS, Harvard University professor, *New York Times*, June 2, 1956.

The rush of power to the head is not as becoming as a new hat.

> HELEN VAN SLYKE, only woman president of an American perfume company, counsel for female executives, *New York Times*, Aug. 28, 1963.

80

I really believe that more harm is done by old men who cling to their influence than by young men who anticipate it.

> OWEN D. YOUNG, retired chairman of General Electric and adviser to six U.S. presidents, *New York Herald Tribune*, July 12, 1962.

Beware of inherited wealth. The job of getting is better than spending. I have often marveled at the fact that so many large Eastern businesses are headed by Western boys. Is it because the son of the well-to-do Eastern family is exposed to social temptations which sap his energies and dull his perceptions, thus causing him to be outrun in life's race despite his heritage of accomplishment and family connections? A debutante party is certainly not a fitting prelude to a busy day, nor is a night at the Stork Club. The Western boy at work in New York, bolstered, perhaps, by a little quiet homework, keen and fresh each morning, has proved himself tough competition for the man who wears the club tie. This business of how a young man spends his evenings is a part of that thin area between success and failure. . . .

> ROBERT R. YOUNG, chairman, New York Central Railroad, address to the graduating class of Culver Military Academy, *Newsweek*, June 20, 1955.

They come from all over the country to New York. The executive's wife decides they will move to New York. She says, "John, you're the boss now. I've been doing the laundry and raising the kids all my life. It's time we enjoyed opening nights in New York." So the company packs up and moves to New York.

> WILLIAM ZECKENDORF, president, Webb & Knapp, predicting continuance of office construction boom, "A Newer New York," *Life*, Aug. 10, 1959.

Madison Avenue

The faults of advertising are only those common to all human institutions. If advertising speaks to a thousand in order to influence one, so does the church. And if it encourages people to live beyond their means, so does matrimony. Good times, bad times, there will always be advertising. In good times, people want to advertise; in bad times, they have to.

> BRUCE BARTON, chairman, Batten, Barton, Durstine & Osborn, *Town & Country*, Feb., 1955.

Advertising did not invent the products or services which called forth jobs, nor inspire the pioneering courage that built factories and machinery to produce them. What advertising did was to stimulate ambition and desire—the craving to possess, which is the strongest incentive to produce. To satisfy this craving the factory was impelled to turn itself into a growing factory; and then, by the pressure of mass demand, into many factories. Mass production made possible mass economies, reflected in declining prices, until the product that began as the luxury of the rich became the possession of every family that was willing to work.

> Bruce Barton, *Reader's Digest*, April, 1955 (the first issue of the *Digest* to carry advertisements).

Advertising is of the very essence of democracy. An election goes on every minute of the business day across the counters of hundreds of thousands of stores and shops where the customers state their preferences and determine which manufacturer and which product shall be the leader today, and which shall lead tomorrow.

> Bruce Barton, *ibid.*

In advertising there is a saying that if you can keep your head while all those around you are losing theirs—then you just don't understand the problem.

> Hugh M. Beville, Jr., director of Research and Planning, NBC, corporate brochure, Nov. 18, 1954.

Doing business without advertising is like winking at a girl in the dark. You know what you are doing, but nobody else does.

> Steuart Henderson Britt, advertising consultant, *New York Herald Tribune*, Oct. 30, 1956.

When you try to formalize or socialize creative activity, the only sure result is commercial constipation. . . . The good ideas are all hammered out in agony by individuals, not spewed out by groups.

> Charles Brower, president, Batten, Barton, Durstine & Osborn, *Editor & Publisher*, Dec. 7, 1957.

Writers are sensitive people. To do their job well, they have to be. . . . But after a while these writing fellows sometimes try to take on a more extroverted look than anyone else in the agency. They'll come into your office, throw copy down on your desk, and proclaim, "This is only great —merely great, Charlie!" They want you to think they are hard-shelled, but all the time I know they aren't. They must be treated gently, explained to others.

CHARLES BROWER, *ibid*.

There is no such thing as "soft sell" and "hard sell." There is only "smart sell" and "stupid sell."

CHARLES BROWER, to National Sales Executives Convention, news reports of May 20, 1958.

This is the great era of the goof-off, the age of the half-done job. The land from coast to coast has been enjoying a stampede away from responsibility. It is populated with laundry men who won't iron shirts, with waiters who won't serve, with carpenters who will come around some day maybe, with executives whose mind is on the golf course, with teachers who demand a single salary scale so that achievement cannot be rewarded, with students who take cinch courses. . . .

CHARLES BROWER, *ibid*.

A new idea is delicate. It can be killed by a sneer or a yawn; it can be stabbed to death by a quip and worried to death by a frown on the right man's brow.

CHARLES BROWER, to Association of National Advertisers, *Advertising Age*, Aug. 10, 1959.

After all the meetings are over, the phones have stopped ringing and the vocalizing has died down, somebody finally has to get out an ad, often after hours. Somebody has to stare at a blank piece of paper. This is probably the very height of lonesomeness. Out of the recesses of his mind must come words which interest, words which persuade, words which inspire, words which sell. Magic words. I regard him as the man of the hour in our business today.

LEO BURNETT, agency chairman, address to American Association of Advertising Agencies, news reports of Oct. 19, 1955.

One man's brain plus one other will produce about one half as many ideas as one man would have produced alone. These two plus two more will produce half again as many ideas. These four plus four more begin to represent a creative meeting, and the ratio changes to one quarter as many. . . .

ANTHONY CHEVINS, vice-president, Cunningham & Walsh, "The Positive Power of Lonethink," *Advertising Age*, April 27, 1959.

Advertising is what you do when you can't go see somebody. That's all it is.

> FAIRFAX CONE, agency partner, *Christian Science Monitor*, March 20, 1963.

A man who is hungry need never be told of his need for food. If he is inspired by his appetite, he is immune to the influence of Messrs. Batten, Barton, Durstine & Osborn. The latter are effective only with those who are so far removed from physical want that they do not already know what they want.

> JOHN KENNETH GALBRAITH, Professor of Economics, Harvard University, *The Affluent Society*, Houghton Mifflin, 1958.

Advertising is found in societies which have passed the point of satisfying the basic animal needs.

> MARION HARPER, JR., president, McCann-Erickson, *New York Herald Tribune*, Sept. 16, 1960.

The advertising man in the typical case needs the challenge and the thrill of the numbers game as much as he needs his salary. Advertising is selling, and the great satisfaction of selling is closing the sale. The advertising man never can close a sale; in fact, he can never be certain that it was his effort which made the sale possible. Worst of all, he works in black anonymity. Everybody in America may know his ad, but not one citizen in a thousand will know so much as the name of the agency which prepared the ad, and within the agency only a handful of people will know that this individual advertising man had anything to do with the ad.

> MARTIN MAYER, "The Advertising Man: Habitat, Functions and History," *Madison Avenue, U.S.A.*, Harper & Row, 1958.

If I had to sum it all up, I'd say there are three breeds of account executives: the play-it-safe-and-by-the-rule-book transmitting agent; the neutralist, who's never quite sure from one day to the next of his role in the agency-client relationship; and the truly creative account man, who may never write a line of copy in his life, but who, in his own way, is every bit as creative as the finest copywriter in the business.

> EMIL MOGUL, advertising executive, *anny*, Oct. 21, 1960.

. . . The greatest barrier to creativity in some agencies is the fact that management is having more fun playing businessman than working at advertising.

> ERNEST A. JONES, president, MacManus, John & Adams, Inc., *Sales Management*, June 20, 1958.

Creativity is our single product. And heaven help the agency management that does not recognize that fact of life. They may wind up as unemployed as Zeppelin pilots.

> ERNEST A. JONES, *Advertising Age*, Jan. 16, 1961.

Not until people decide that they want to have meek spirits and contrite hearts will advertising stress plain living and high thinking. And when that time comes, I suspect we'll advertise that we have the best spirit-humbler there is.

> LAWRENCE C. LOCKLEY, Columbia University Graduate School of Business, *Saturday Review*, July 16, 1960.

The Hidden Persuaders

> VANCE PACKARD, title of book on the unseen influences of advertising and public relations, McKay, 1955.

The Pyramid Builders

> VANCE PACKARD, title of book on the structure of American businesses, McKay, 1961.

The consumer is not a moron. She is your wife.

> DAVID OGILVY, advice to advertising copywriters, *New York Herald Tribune*, Aug. 29, 1956.

It has taken more than a hundred scientists two years to find out how to make the product . . . I have been given thirty days to create its personality and plan its launching. If I do my job well, I shall contribute as much as the hundred scientists to the success of this product.

> DAVID OGILVY, *Confessions Of An Advertising Man*, Atheneum, 1963.

The only thing that matters is caring, deep caring. . . . The way to make your plans and your products and your themes and your campaigns and your shows and your letters and your programs more solid, more effective, is to go back to Main Street, your Main Street, your memory source of the things that are deepest and truest and greatest. Be the man or the woman you have it in you to be—and you won't be false to Main Street.

> JEAN RINDLAUB, vice-president, Batten, Barton, Durstine & Osborn, "Main Street—And How to Find Your Way Back," address to Advertising Federation of America, June 8, 1959.

AMERICAN ADVERTISERS AND AMERICAN FREE ENTERPRISE WILL INCREASE RESPECT FOR THEM[SELVES] WITH AMERICAN PUBLIC IF THEY WILL MODIFY SENSATIONAL HARD-SELL COMMERCIALS ABOUT TRIVIALITIES ON NEWS BROADCASTS AT THIS TIME OF WORLD CRISIS. THEY WILL ALSO INCREASE RESPECT FOR AMERICA FROM FOREIGNERS WHO LISTEN TO SUCH BROADCASTS. AND THEY MIGHT EVEN SELL MORE GOODS.

> RAYMOND RUBICAM, retired founder of Young & Rubicam, Inc., telegram at time of Lebanon crisis, *Advertising Age*, July 21, 1958.

To dare every day to be irreverent and bold. To dare to preserve the randomness of mind which in children produces strange and wonderful new thoughts and forms. To continually scramble the familiar and bring the old into new juxtaposition.

> GORDON WEBBER, vice-president of television production, Benton & Bowles, Inc., recommendations to women in business, *Advertising Age*, Oct. 31, 1960.

Their dedication is to competitive creativity—a deep desire within the consciousness of each man to create something better today than yesterday's best.

> JOHN ORR YOUNG, pioneer advertising executive, on what makes an advertising agency great, *New York Times*, Sept. 29, 1960.

Memorable Advertising

American Home has an edifice complex.

> AMERICAN HOME MAGAZINE, advertisement on residential construction, *Advertising Age*, Sept. 18, 1961.

No bottles to break—just hearts.

> ARPÈGE, for its perfume-mist in plastic containers, *New Yorker*, Dec. 16, 1961.

Promise her anything, but give her Arpège.
>ARPÈGE slogan used throughout the 1950's and 60's, coined in 1946 by Edouard L. Cournand, president of Lanvin Parfums, Inc.

Next to myself, I like BVD best.
>BVD (Bradley, Voorhees and Day), famous advertisement for men's underwear, quoted in report of sale of trademark, *Time*, Aug. 13, 1951.

Does she . . . or doesn't she?
>CLAIROL, INC., largest U.S. hair-coloring manufacturer, *Newsweek*, Aug. 19, 1963.

Getting there is half the fun.
>CUNARD STEAMSHIP COMPANY, LTD., advertising slogan used throughout the 1950's.

Diamonds are forever . . .
>DE BEER CONSOLIDATED MINES LTD., slogan used in magazine advertising in 1950 and ensuing years.

If your friendly neighborhood grocer doesn't have a jar—knock something off a shelf on the way out.
>DILLY BEANS, quoted in *Advertising Age*, Oct. 31, 1960.

Pajamas are a cloak for man and his dreams. They are retreat, sanctuary, shelter. Pajamas are tranquility, a gateway to privacy. They are illusionary, for pleasures unguessable.
>EXCELLO PAJAMAS, *New York Times*, Nov. 12, 1961.

America's most gifted whiskey.
>FOUR ROSES' Christmas ad, cited for sales effectiveness, *Printers' Ink*, Dec. 23, 1960.

. . . A shop for after-dark (clothing) when a husband changes from company man to a man who wants company.
>FRANKLIN SIMON, announcing opening of After-Dark Shop, *New York Times*, Oct. 30, 1960.

Is it true that English women make better wives? Decidedly yes—say English husbands.
> GORDON'S DRY GIN LTD., *Vogue*, April 1, 1963.

It sits as lightly on a heavy meal as it does on your conscience.
> GENERAL FOODS, television commercial for Jello, Nov. 3, 1963.

Good, excellent, superior, above par, nice, fine, choice, rare, priceless, unparagoned, unparalleled, superfine, superexcellent, of the first water, crack, prime, tip-top, gilt-edged, first-class, capital, cardinal, *couleur de rose*, peerless, matchless, inestimable, precious as the apple of the eye; satisfactory, fair, fresh, unspoiled, sound; GKN: over 80 companies making steel and steel products.
> GUEST, KEEN & NETTLEFOLDS, LTD., advertisement in London underground trains, Jan., 1962, "with acknowledgments to Rogét."

IBM cards: working paper . . . not paper work.
> INTERNATIONAL BUSINESS MACHINES CORP., inscription on tabulating cards, 1960.

May you have the health of a salmon—a strong heart and a wet mouth.
> TOAST FOR IRISH HIGHBALL, publicized by Irish Export Board, quoted in Robert Alden's advertising news column, *New York Times*, Dec. 16, 1960.

Health and long life to you. The wife of your choice to you. Land free of rent to you, from this day forth.
> TOAST FOR IRISH COFFEE, *ibid.*

Take a bath in the dark tonight and let the water make love to your skin.
> LANVIN PERFUMES AND SOAPS, *New Yorker*, June 3, 1961.

The city, a synonym for people, for paradox, for life itself, a whole world just outside your window. Before your very eyes it changes. And snow-clad streets burst into bloom. And the stillness of the night turns to the roar of day. And people pass. A party-bound tot, a gyrating jaywalker, a lone man against the restless man of traffic, and women, graceful even

jackknifing, long-legged, into a car. All this passing by one window in the city.
> LIFE, advertisement in *New York Times*, March 5, 1958.

The beer that made Milwaukee jealous . . .
> MEXICAN BREWERY ADVERTISEMENT, quoted by Dave Garroway, *Good Housekeeping*, Feb., 1957.

Good coffee is like friendship: rich and warm and strong.
> PAN-AMERICAN COFFEE BUREAU, *Life*, July 28, 1961.

The Rendez-vous is so romantic . . . it's downright dangerous.
> THE PLAZA HOTEL, *New Yorker*, Oct. 22, 1960.

Women are quite unlike men. Women have higher voices, longer hair, smaller waistlines, daintier feet and prettier hands. They also invariably have the upper hand.
> STEPHEN POTTER, "Womanship: The Art of Understanding Women Without Actually Doing So," advertisement of *Ladies' Home Journal*, newspapers of Sept. 17, 1957.

Womanship, of course, is the art of Not Letting Them Know It, the art of remaining one-up while seeming, or seeming to desire to seem, one-down. For example, it is almost impossible to know what a woman is thinking about. But a man who is accomplished in the art of Womanship will never let on that he doesn't know what a woman is thinking about.
> STEPHEN POTTER, *ibid*.

The greatest tragedy is indifference.
> RED CROSS, Greater New York Area, theme of 1961 fund-raising campaign prepared by Young & Rubicam as volunteer agency, *New York Times*, Feb. 9, 1961.

At sixty miles an hour the loudest noise in the new Rolls-Royce comes from the electric clock.
> ROLLS-ROYCE advertisement, regarded by David Ogilvy as the best advertising "headline" he ever devised, *Confessions Of An Advertising Man*, Atheneum, 1963.

Dryest gin in town. Ask any Martini.
> SEAGRAM'S GIN, *New Yorker*, March 11, 1961.

Elegance is the goal that daring talent sometimes attempts but seldom achieves. It is the difference between good works and honored master-pieces. Elegance may be found in a jewel or a gesture. Sometimes, but not often, it is found in products of the market place . . .
> SCHENLEY WHISKEY, *Chicago Sun-Times*, April 22, 1958

A child is an island of curiosity surrounded by a sea of question marks.
> SHELL OIL COMPANY, *Time*, Jan. 20, 1961.

There are dancing rooms and dining rooms; listening rooms and talking rooms. . . . Big rooms, small rooms, banquet rooms, ballrooms. . . . Pink rooms, red rooms, blue rooms, bedrooms. . . . Fun rooms, sun rooms, old rooms, new rooms; altogether, six hundred and two rooms.
> ST. REGIS HOTEL, New York, *Town & Country*, Sept., 1963.

Mas Tiempo para el Amor. (Translation: More Time for Love.)
> ADVERTISING SLOGAN credited with swift sale of washing machines in Spain, news reports of April 29, 1956.

Adam and Eve ate the first vitamins, including the package.
> E. R. SQUIBB, advertisement advocating balanced diet rather than re-liance on vitamin pills; first-place winner in Sixth Annual Advertising Awards of *Saturday Review*, April 19, 1958.

Tired of getting junk mail from someone you don't know? Try getting junk mail from someone you do know.
> SURPRISE CLUB, New York mail-order gift club, cited in *Newsweek*, Feb. 27, 1961.

When I Grow Up: Sharp and clear the dreams of the young—and always framed in gold . . . Vision, the projected power of the mind, builds a better world for each generation.
> TENNESSEE GAS TRANSMISSION COMPANY, *Time*, May 12, 1958.

Friendly Americans win American friends.

> U.S. TRAVEL SERVICE, slogan for promoting the nation as a world tourist attraction, *New York Journal-American*, July 10, 1963.

In some advertising, the selling message ends with a period. In other advertising, the selling message ends with a sale. In either event, it costs the advertiser just as much to run a poor ad—as it does to run a good one.

> YOUNG & RUBICAM, INC., advertising agency, *Advertising Agency Magazine*, Feb. 14, 1958.

Polishing the client's apple is no way to improve his advertising. Polishing a good idea is. And polishing. And polishing. And polishing. Until good becomes better. And better becomes best.

> YOUNG & RUBICAM, INC., *Printers' Ink*, Jan. 6, 1961.

Secure the shadow 'ere the substance fade,
Let Nature imitate what Nature made!

> ADVERTISEMENT OF 1839–1860 PERIOD of "tin-types," the first practical method of taking photographs, quoted in *The Daguerreotype in America*, Duell, Sloan & Pearce, Inc., 1961.

Americana

Relations between the sexes are so complicated that the only way you can tell if members of the set are "going together" is if they're married. Then, almost certainly, they are not.

CLEVELAND AMORY, *Who Killed Society?*, Harper and Row, 1960.

. . . The modern American suburb demands a new kind of piety. It demands quick Masses, else the parking lot becomes a most unholy jam.

APRIL OURSLER ARMSTRONG, *Water In the Wine*, McGraw-Hill, 1963.

Except the American woman, nothing interests the eye of American man more than the automobile, or seems so important to him as an object of esthetic appreciation.

A. H. BARR, JR., director of museum collection, Museum of Modern Art, on displaying "pop art" that incorporated pieces of old automobiles, 1963.

Symphonies in bars and cabs, classical drama on television any day of the week, highbrow paperbacks in mountainous profusion (easier to buy than to read), "art seminars in the home," capsule operas . . . this cornucopia thrust at the inexperienced and pouring out its contents over us all deadens attention and keeps taste still-born, like any form of gross feeding.

JACQUES BARZUN, Dean of Faculties, Columbia University, writing in the British monthly *Encounter*, quoted in *Time*, Sept. 29, 1961.

Culture: what a monstrous and much-abused word it is! And what distance lies between the dusty American image of culture in which Mrs. X imported two stone lions from Florence to be placed on her Baltimore lawn, and this image, tonight, of a nationwide, gay, relaxed audience, happily responding to a symphonic satire! We have come a long way.

> LEONARD BERNSTEIN, on opening fund-raising drive for National Culture Center in Washington, *New York Times*, Nov. 30, 1962.

The South may have lost the war, but it appears to be winning the centennial.

> KARL S. BETTS, executive director, Civil War Centennial Commission, *Newsweek*, Dec. 12, 1960.

We expect to eat and stay thin, to be constantly on the move and ever more neighborly . . . to revere God and be God.

> DANIEL BOORSTIN, professor of history, University of Chicago, on contradictions of American life, *Newsweek*, Feb. 26, 1962.

So many citizens of the world have lost their children to wars, but we lost our daughter to something far more worthwhile. That is peace.

> PAUL BOYD, Martinez, California, on death of his 20-year-old daughter, Nancy, a Peace Corps volunteer teacher, in crash of a Philippine plane, *New York Post*, March 5, 1963.

This four-year tragedy [the Civil War] . . . is the Hamlet and King Lear of the American past. . . . And the strange thing is that it does not leave us depressed, disheartened, or discouraged. It is precisely through the great tragedies that we get our most significant and uplifting experience.

> BRUCE CATTON, author, on Civil War's fascination to Americans, *Newsweek*, Dec. 12, 1960.

. . . Made by General Motors, on order from Sears Roebuck.

> RICHARD CONDON, author, on American cities, *Newsweek*, Feb. 11, 1963.

. . . Cocktail music he accepts as audible wallpaper.

> ALISTAIR COOKE, "The Innocent American," *Holiday*, July, 1962.

The Upsons lived the way every family in America wants to live—not rich, but well-to-do. They had two of everything: two addresses, the flat on Park and a house in Connecticut; two cars, a Buick sedan, and a Ford station wagon; two children, a boy and a girl; two servants, man and maid; two clubs, town and country; and two interests, money and position. Mrs. Upson had two fur coats and two chins. Mr. Upson had two chins, two passions—golf and business—and two aversions, Roosevelt and Jews.

> PATRICK DENNIS (Edward Everett Tanner), in his novel, *Auntie Mame*, Vanguard, 1955.

Like a city in dreams, the great white capital stretches along the placid river from Georgetown on the west to Anacostia on the east. It is a city of temporaries, a city of just-arriveds and only-visitings, built on the shifting sands of politics, filled with people passing through.

> ALLEN DRURY, on Washington, D.C., scene of his Pulitzer Prize novel on U.S. Senate, *Advise and Consent*, Doubleday, 1959.

A good many of us today are content to be fat, dumb and happy. With a polyunsaturated diet of the coming 35-hour week, the fly-now-pay-later vacation, and fringe benefits, many of us live in a chromium-plated world where the major enemy we face is crab-grass.

> JOHN H. GLENN, JR., Marine officer, who thrice orbited the earth, address to annual luncheon of The Associated Press, *New York Times*, April 23, 1963.

The spielers on the bandstand reminded the hometowners of a pleasant truth—here, near the breast of the land, they were living the kind of life the founding fathers had in mind. In small towns everywhere, it was a day of community self-congratulations. Half a century later, it is a day consecrated to the itch to be elsewhere.

> LESLIE HANSCOM, on the Fourth of July, "Smalltown USA," *Newsweek*, July 8, 1963.

What ever happened to Saturday night?

> LESLIE HANSCOM, *ibid.*

You cannot gauge the intelligence of an American by talking with him; you must work with him. The American polishes and refines his way of doing things—even the most commonplace—the way the French of the seventeenth century polished their maxims.

> ERIC HOFFER, philosopher and writer, *Forbes*, Dec. 1, 1963.

94

Jacqueline Bouvier Kennedy leaves a shining gift of beauty in this historic house. At every turn we are freshly conscious of our heritage. The most knowledgeable expert as well as the busloads of school children who visit will always know that a young and radiant First Lady lived here. We know her better than ever before and hold her close to our hearts with inexpressible pride.

> LADY BIRD JOHNSON, after Mrs. Kennedy had moved from the White House, *New York Herald Tribune*, Dec. 7, 1963.

Science and time and necessity have propelled us, the United States, to be the general store for the world, dealers in everything. Most of all, merchants for a better way of life.

> LADY BIRD JOHNSON, recalling an old wooden sign (T. J. Taylor—Dealer in Everything) on her father's store in Karnack, Texas, *Newsweek*, Dec. 9, 1963.

Americans . . . are not only hospitable in emergency but radiant: The most lavishly helpful people in the world, accepting the burden of nuisances as if they were bunches of hothouse flowers, all the more delightful because unexpected.

> PAMELA HANSFORD JOHNSON, describing the feelings of a professor from England, in her novel, *Night and Silence Who Is Here?*, Scribners, 1963.

I felt like a moth hanging on the windowpane.

> JACQUELINE KENNEDY, on her first night in the White House, *Newsweek*, Jan. 1, 1961.

. . . The shades you pull down at night—they are enormous and they have pulleys and ropes. You're like a sailor taking in a sail. I'm afraid it will always be a little impossible for the people who live there. It's an office building.

> JACQUELINE KENNEDY, *ibid.*

It is only in the upper-class level that each husband sits next to the other man's wife.

> LOUIS KRONENBERGER, *Company Manners*, Bobbs-Merrill, 1954.

The moving van is a symbol of more than our restlessness; it is the most conclusive evidence possible of our progress.

LOUIS KRONENBERGER, *ibid.*

Ladies bathed before noon, after their three-o'clock naps, and by nightfall were like soft teacakes with frostings of sweat and sweet talcum.

HARPER LEE, describing a hot summer day in a Southern town, *To Kill A Mockingbird*, Lippincott, 1960.

. . . Prosperity would seem more soundly shored if, by a saving grace, more of us had the grace to save.

LIFE editorial, "Is Thrift Un-American?" May 7, 1956.

The American's conversation is much like his courtship. . . . He gives an inkling and watches for a reaction; if the weather looks fair, he inkles a little more. Wishing neither to intrude nor be intruded upon, he advances by stages of acceptance, by levels of agreement, by steps of concurrence.

DONALD LLOYD, professor and Peace Corps counselor, "The Quietmouth American," *Harper's*, Sept., 1963.

. . . Somehow the gangster's demise rejuvenated my friends, it reassured them, and one of them, a gentle little lady, said, "Thank heavens, there'll always be a Chicago."

JOHN BARTLOW MARTIN, "To Chicago with Love," *Saturday Evening Post*, Oct. 15, 1960.

. . . The city roared with life, traffic sped up the Outer Drive, trucks rumbled down Western Avenue, and elevated trains roared by overhead on the wondrous El, reared against the sky. Randolph Street in the theatrical district blazed with light nightlong . . . And always there was the wonderful lake, a limitless inland sea. It was all rather innocent foolishness. Today the El no longer seems romantic to me, just an obsolete nuisance. The slums are not picturesque, just appalling; Randolph Street and Rush Street not glamorous, just tinsel cheap; gangsterism not exciting, just dreary and dangerous. But this change is in me, not in the city, and I have no doubt that only yesterday some other young man got off a train from Indiana, longing for excitement and opportunity, and found it here.

JOHN BARTLOW MARTIN, *ibid.*

"Map of Ireland!" they say of a young Gael, meaning you'd know him for Irish anywhere by the light in his eyes and the set of his jaw. Nobody says, "Map of America!" of any of us—not even of the slender girls with the long legs and the fine ankles. . . . People know us well enough. They know us everywhere. They know what we are and where we come from. But nobody thinks "The map of America!" when we go by. You don't talk about continents that way.
     ARCHIBALD MACLEISH, "Sweet Land of Liberty," *Collier's*, July 8, 1955.

The map of America is a map of endlessness, of opening out, of forever and ever. No man's face would make you think of it but his hope might, his courage might.
     ARCHIBALD MACLEISH, *ibid*.

Spring has many American faces. There are cities where it will come and go in a day and counties where it hangs around and never quite gets there. . . . Summer is drawn blinds in Louisiana, long winds in Wyoming, shade of elms and maples in New England. . . . Autumn is the American season. In Europe the leaves turn yellow or brown, and fall. Here they take fire on the trees and hang there flaming. We think this frost-fire is a portent somehow: a promise that the continent has given us. Life, too, we think, is capable of taking fire in this country; of creating beauty never seen.
     ARCHIBALD MACLEISH, *ibid*.

To our neighbors, East and West, the symbols of the Republic are enormous chimneys leaking their pink smoke into the clean, blue sky, or huge derricks wading into the sea itself for oil, or deserted mining towns where gold and silver were once dug. But we ourselves—what do we think of the world's talk? . . . Do steel and oil alone explain it? Is it only metal that speaks here and an ooze pumped out of muck? Or have the minds of men imagined these tall towers?
     ARCHIBALD MACLEISH, *ibid*.

. . . We live in a cocktail culture whose unlovely symbol is the ring on the best mahogany.
     ELSA MAXWELL, *How To Do It*, Little, Brown, 1957.

97

The Communist pie is nothing but crust. In America we have an upper crust and a lower crust, but it's what's between—the middle class—that gives the real flavor.

> Mrs. Virginia L. McCleary, housewife, Luling, Texas, who sent a pie (mistaken for a bomb) to Premier Khrushchev during his visit to the U.S., *New York Times,* Oct. 2, 1960.

You find it driving to work, alongside all those other people, but alone with your thoughts. The car has become a secular sanctuary for the individual, his shrine to the self, his mobile Walden Pond.

> Edward McDonagh, sociologist, on privacy in a mass society, *Time,* May 10, 1963.

If you are already secured in your shelter and others try to break in, they may be treated as unjust aggressors and repelled with whatever means will effectively deter their assault.

> L. C. McHugh, S. J., "Ethics At the Shelter Doorway," in *America,* Sept. 30, 1961. A widespread controversy was set off by his assertion that one probably had no "grave obligation" to admit less prudent neighbors to a private fallout shelter.

In the old days, everything was private. There were private houses and private parties and private balls and private yachts and private railroad cars and private everything. Now everything is public—even one's private life.

> Mrs. G. Alexander McKinlock of Chicago and Palm Beach, *Who Killed Society?* by Cleveland Amory, Harper & Row, 1960.

The capacity for friendship usually goes with highly developed civilization. The ability to cultivate people differs by culture and class but on the whole educated people have more ways to make friends . . . In England, for instance, you find everyone in your class has read the same books. Here people grope for something in common—like a newly engaged girl who came to me and said, "It's absolutely wonderful! His uncle and my cousin were on the same football team."

> Margaret Mead, *Life,* Sept. 14, 1959.

Those tragic comedians, the Chamber of Commerce red hunters, the Women's Christian Temperance Union smellers, the censors of books, the Klan regulators, the Methodist prowlers, the Baptist guardians of sacred vessels—we have the national mentality of a police lieutenant.

> H. L. MENCKEN, typical of the remarks that caused the *New York Herald Tribune* to call him "a specialist in sentences that could lacerate millions at a time"; quoted in reports of his death, Jan. 29, 1956.

The townspeople are morons, yokels, peasants and genus homo boobiensis . . . surrounded by gaping primates from the upland valleys.

> H. L. MENCKEN, after covering Scopes evolution trial at Dayton, Tennessee, *ibid.*

O death where is thy sting? O grave, where is thy victory? Where, indeed? Many a badly stung survivor, faced with the aftermath of some relative's funeral, has ruefully conceded that the victory has been won hands down by a funeral establishment—in disastrously unequal battle.

> JESSICA MITFORD, *The American Way of Death*, Simon & Schuster, 1963, a book which caused a sensation among funeral directors and gave a boost to organizations for low-cost burial.

It was, they told themselves, the American century. And so it was, in the sense that what they had all mankind wanted. Along the wide turnpike roads their cars endlessly processed; the appurtenances of affluence poured in a quenchless stream from industry's bountiful conveyor-belt. Madison Avenue experts easily persuaded them to want more, and to consume more. Television screens held up to them the image of their own well-being. Their way of life was the blueprint on which all other ways of life, including the Communists, were based. They were rich, and if wealth was power, then they were powerful indeed. But was it?

> MALCOLM MUGGERIDGE, British journalist, "The Titans: United States of America," BBC-TV, Jan. 16, 1962.

. . . The pursuit of happiness to which Americans are nationally dedicated.

> MALCOLM MUGGERIDGE, *ibid.*

A great variety of collective activities provided substitute pageantry to a society which had eschewed kings, nobility and courts. What Americans called "togetherness" was part of their mystique. Rooted in vehement and intransigent individualism, they became more than any other Western people, a collectivity.

> MALCOLM MUGGERIDGE, on the Masons, Elks, and similar groups, in the 1920's and '30's, *ibid.*

Our national flower is the concrete cloverleaf.

> LEWIS MUMFORD, city planner and architect, deploring loss of some national shrines to new highways, *Quote*, Oct. 8, 1961.

. . . The bidet to the average American is still a mystery unplumbed. . . . [its] real usage is obscured in the daily monsoon of showers and tubs whereby Americans suppose themselves to be properly abluted.

> NEWSWEEK, April 22, 1963, on upsurge of interest in bidets because of increased American travel in Europe.

. . . Something like wearing a three-cornered hat with an Ivy League suit.

> NEW YORK HERALD TRIBUNE, on President and Mrs. Kennedy's state dinner at Mt. Vernon, July 13, 1961.

. . . Where the used-car lots succeed one another like a string of past lives.

> SEAN O'FAOLAIN, on areas ringing Chicago's Loop, *Holiday*, Dec., 1960.

You can't tell a millionaire's son from a billionaire's.

> VANCE PACKARD, on democracy of preparatory schools, *The Status Seekers*, David McKay, 1959.

The status seekers . . . are people who are continually straining to surround themselves with visible evidence of the superior rank they are claiming.

> VANCE PACKARD, *ibid.*

. . . Status seekers are altering our society by their preoccupation, in the midst of plenty, with acquiring evidences of status. The people of this country have become increasingly preoccupied with status primarily because of the impact on their lives of big housing developments, big advertisers, big trade-unions, and big corporate hierarchies. As a result, democracy is still more of an ideal than a reality.

> VANCE PACKARD, *ibid.*

One couldn't get homesick for the White House. One might miss the beauty of the White House because, of course, it has wonderful proportions and is a lovely house. But one couldn't be homesick for the White House.

> ELEANOR ROOSEVELT, CBS-TV, 1954.

. . . If Chicago is one of the Seven Wonders, then the eighth is that a city should be so pointlessly huge. . . . It goes on and on, over and over, a Walt Whitman storehouse of democracy come alive, a Sears catalogue of people and occupations endlessly varied in repetitive similitudes. . . . Why so much, so many, so indiscernibly all-alike-and-different? Who needs all these dry goods stores, groceries, factories, railroad yards, sidings, lamp posts, funeral parlors? Would the world collapse if there were just one less?

> ISAAC ROSENFELD, "Life In Chicago," *Commentary*, June, 1957.

The Yankees may have outfought us, but we're going to outlive them.

> JOHN SALLING, at 110, one of three surviving Confederate veterans, on hearing of the death of Albert Woolson, 109, last remaining Union veteran; news summaries of Aug. 20, 1956.

Not often in the story of mankind does a man arrive on earth who is both steel and velvet, who is as hard as rock and soft as drifting fog, who holds in his heart and mind the paradox of terrible storm and peace unspeakable and perfect.

> CARL SANDBURG, opening sentence in address to joint session of Congress marking 150th anniversary of Abraham Lincoln's birth, news reports of Feb. 13, 1959.

Always the path of American destiny has been into the unknown. Always there arose enough of reserves of strength, balances of sanity, portions of wisdom to carry the nation through to a fresh start with ever-renewing vitality.

> CARL SANDBURG at Gettysburg, Pa., on 96th anniversary of Lincoln's Gettysburg Address, *New York Times*, Nov. 20, 1959.

Boston is a moral and intellectual nursery always busy applying first principles to trifles.

> GEORGE SANTAYANA, philosopher, *Santayana: The Later Years*, edited by Daniel Cory, Braziller, 1963.

(America is) that "producer's economy" . . . which first creates articles and then attempts to create a demand for them; an economy that has flooded the country with breakfast foods, shaving soaps, poets, and professors of philosophy.
GEORGE SANTAYANA, *ibid.*

. . . Young people are just as bad as servants. They deserve each other.
ELEONORA SEARS, Boston spinster, *Vogue*, Feb. 15, 1963.

The name of the subspecies, then, is Exurbanite; its habitat, the Exurbs. The exurb is generally further from New York than the suburb on the same railway line. Its houses are more widely spaced and generally more various and more expensive. The town center tends to quaintness and class, rather than modernity and glass, and the further one lives from the station the better.
A. C. SPECTORSKY, *The Exurbanites*, Lippincott, 1955.

The trouble is that hardly anybody in America goes to bed angry at night.
GEORGE STIGLER, Chicago economist, on U.S. complacency, *Time*, May 10, 1963.

With progress in roads came more cars, more roads for the cars, and more cars for the roads that had been built to accommodate more cars.
TIME, Oct. 6, 1961, "One For the Roads," report on U.S. highways and superhighways.

The "servant problem" has long been a staple of female conversation among those who could afford the problem, but never, as today, have so many talked about so few.
TIME, Sept. 21, 1962.

Air-conditioning has bequeathed America a new—some say even better —reading season. People with brains spend the summer in their non-sweat, air-conditioned cars, offices, and homes, reaching for a good book instead of a hot beer, leaving the delights of ant-ridden picnics . . . to those who would rather burn their skins than illuminate their minds.
LON TINKLE, book editor, *Dallas News*, *Saturday Review*, April 12, 1958.

102

Breakfast is the one meal at which it is perfectly good manners to read the paper. . . .

>AMY VANDERBILT, *Amy Vanderbilt's Complete Book of Etiquette,* Doubleday, 1954.

The granddaughter of the girl who wouldn't show her instep now shows her step-ins.

>ALICE VAN RENSSELAER, on why old-fashioned flirting is extinct, *The Last Resorts,* by Cleveland Amory, Harper and Row, 1952.

Why don't you come right out and say it? You mean am I some kind of nut, or something. Yes. I'm a Civil War nut and I love to shoot off an old musket. And all of these other guys are nuts, too. We love it that way.

>ARTHUR ZIPPLER, a Philadelphia resident who joined 3,500 Civil War "buffs" in re-creating Battle of Bull Run, *New York Herald Tribune,* July 20, 1961.

New York City

After 20 annual visits, I am still surprised each time I return to see this giant asparagus bed of alabaster and rose and green skyscrapers.

>CECIL BEATON, *It Gives Me Great Pleasure,* John Day, 1955.

. . . I regard it as a curiosity: I don't let myself get caught in the wheels.

>LUDWIG BEMELMANS, on enjoying life in Manhattan, *Time,* July 2, 1951.

. . . A real page-four-of-the-*Daily News* neighborhood.

>JIMMY BRESLIN, sports writer, on the rugged area of Manhattan in which he grew up, *Newsweek,* May 6, 1963.

. . . The food of the city's most celebrated dining salons, with one or perhaps two exceptions, is neither predictably elegant nor superb. More often than not it is predictably commonplace.

>CRAIG CLAIBORNE, food editor, *New York Times,* Sept. 1, 1963.

103

In this country, success is commonly regarded as an exclusively American product, and it is advertised on matchbook covers and in the back pages of adventure magazines, accessible by way of a high-school education or a new truss. It is thought by some to have a distinctly bitter taste, not unlike a mouthful of dimes. But its smell is generally conceded to be sweet.
> STEPHEN BIRMINGHAM, "Young Men of Manhattan," *Holiday*, March, 1961.

A great many people go after success simply for the shiny prizes it brings. . . . More men pursue it than women. And nowhere is it pursued more ardently than in the city of New York.
> STEPHEN BIRMINGHAM, *ibid.*

Snobography
> BURT BOYAR, on obtaining the *right* seat in the *right* restaurant, *Esquire*, Jan., 1962.

She shows definite promise of becoming the greatest free-loader in town.
> ROGER BROWNE, New York purchase commissioner, on Lilly, baby hippopotamus at Central Park Zoo, *New York Times*, Jan. 30, 1961.

I always knew children were anti-social. But the children of the West Side—they're savage.
> MARC CONNELLY, author, after being knocked down by a wicker chair thrown from a tenement roof, news reports of May 28, 1954.

There is and has long been . . . a special bond between New York and me . . . How often, at difficult moments, I looked to New York, I listened to New York, to find out what you were thinking and feeling here, and always I found a comforting echo.
> CHARLES DE GAULLE, President of France, at luncheon honoring his arrival in New York, *New York Times*, April 27, 1960.

Those lions still are rude and wild,
For while they pose as meek and mild,
   To keep their fierceness hid,
Down from their pedestals they'd leap,

104

As soon as New York went to sleep—
  If New York ever did!

> ARTHUR GUITERMAN, poem inspired by the great stone lions in front of New York Public Library, *The New York Public Library in Fiction, Poetry, and Children's Literature*, published by the library, 1950.

. . . One of those evenings when New York seems to promise everything, and it all comes true.

> HOLIDAY, March, 1962, in an article on "The New York Career Girl."

Many times have I consulted them as one consults an oracle. If we are to believe the ancients, the voice of the people must be taken very seriously indeed.

> SIR GLADWYN JEBB, British ambassador to UN, on Manhattan cab drivers, news reports of Feb. 24, 1954.

No other city in the United States can divest the visitor of so much money with so little enthusiasm. In Dallas, they take away with gusto; in New Orleans, with a bow; in San Francisco, with a wink and a grin. In New York, you're lucky if you get a grunt.

> FLETCHER KNEBEL, "But It's A Tough Place to Visit," *Look*, March 26, 1963.

To start with, there's the alien accent. "Tree" is the number between two and four. "Jeintz" is the name of the New York professional football team. A "fit" is a bottle measuring seven ounces less than a quart. This exotic tongue has no relationship to any of the approved languages at the United Nations, and is only slightly less difficult to master than Urdu.

> FLETCHER KNEBEL, *ibid.*

I don't like the life here. There is no greenery. It would make a stone sick.

> NIKITA S. KHRUSHCHEV, on visit to New York, *Time*, Oct. 10, 1960.

A hundred times have I thought New York is a catastrophe and fifty times: It is a beautiful catastrophe.

> LE CORBUSIER, *New York Herald Tribune*, Aug. 6, 1961.

If you do climb upon his knee, do it with love and remember he is a great human person. Make him happy that the children in this great city of New York want to hold his hand, touch his head and sit on his lap. For here we are today, all these 150 years later, still loving his stories.

> EVA LE GALLIENNE, on conducting a story-hour at Hans Christian Andersen statue in Central Park, *New York Herald Tribune*, Sept. 23, 1956.

. . . This capital city of high-tension activity.

> STANLEY LEVEY, defining New York, *New York Times*, Nov. 2, 1957.

New York attracts the most talented people in the world in the arts and professions. It also attracts them in other fields. Even the bums are talented.

> EDMUND LOVE, introduction to his book, *Subways Are For Sleeping*, Harcourt, Brace, 1957.

I never tire of singing my own "Manhattan Magnificat" . . . Often I look out of my sixth floor window at midnight or an early hour of the morning at the squares of gold and topaz and I pray for all the worry-weary souls behind those windows—and the glad and gay ones, too. For there is gaiety in this sprawling metropolis. You hear it in the cheep of sparrows in the park, the laughter of children in playgrounds, the banter of taxi drivers lightly insulting other motorists, and it is a truer gaiety than that which glitters in the night spots or theatres, where visitors so often seek it.

> SISTER MARYANNA, Dominican Academy, East 68th Street, *New York Daily News*, April 9, 1960.

He speaks English with the flawless imperfection of a New Yorker.

> GILBERT MILLSTEIN, on restaurant owner André Surmain, *Esquire*, Jan., 1962.

If associations like yours don't face the challenge of the times, you will before very long face constriction, decentralization, deterioriation, the geriatrician, the mortician and, finally, the archeologist. . . .

> ROBERT MOSES, former head of New York parks commission, answering the Fifth Avenue Association's criticism of his work on 1964 World's Fair, *New York Herald Tribune*, Oct. 25, 1963.

The two moments when New York seems most desirable, when the splendor falls all around about and the city looks like a girl with leaves in her hair, are just as you are leaving and must say good-bye, and just as you return and can say hello.

> NEW YORKER, Jan. 11, 1955.

I hope that his next incarnation, when his bones cease their rattling, will be amid pleasant things that would have been familiar to him, amid sounds —the sounds of a prosperous and friendly restaurant at its best hour, the sounds from the kitchen when it is busiest, and the sounds of corks being drawn from bottles and of ice being shaken and of knives and forks and of waiters' questioning voices and of customers in cheerful conversation over a good dinner, sounds that we all know and that signify perhaps the most amiable moments of our days, wherever we are, or, as we all happen to be, in the midst of life.

> NEW YORKER, Dec. 31, 1960, quoting a letter from "Our friend the long-winded lady," on some future life for deceased owner of a very small French restaurant in Manhattan's East 60's.

Poets have celebrated the wit and sonority of the names of American towns, but to our way of thinking they are not a patch on the telephone exchanges of New York. We linger over the rippling liquefaction of "SUsquehanna," the sturdiness of "MOnument," the liveliness of "SPring." We dote on forthright "CAnal" and sing of sweet "LOrraine." These are names to dial and conjure with. And what of our rich legacy from an OLder CIvilization—stirring names like "TRafalgar," "OXford," "WHitehall," "CHelsea," and "REgent"? Is this great tradition to be curtailed on behalf of intercity dialing?

> NEW YORKER, Jan. 14, 1961.*

Taxes are the death of taxidermy. The folks who used to be the backbone of our business—the Vanderbilts, Astors, Goulds and Belmonts—still shoot a tiger now and then or catch a marlin or bag a wild turkey, but, with the old estates gone, where would they find a place to hang them?

> ELMER ROWLAND, on closing a Manhattan taxidermy trade operated since 1883, *New York Times*, July 26, 1959.

---

* Attorney Melvin Belli, president of San Francisco's Anti-Digit Dialing League, promised a booklet entitled *How to Murder the Telephone Company*. He told columnist Jimmy Breslin, *New York Herald Tribune*, Oct. 11, 1963: "I am not a San Quentin convict (with a number). Yukon is a colorful name. So is Klondike and Sutter and the more lyrical Valencia. They are not going to make numbers out of my people."

Take a good deep breath of filth.
> ALAN STEEGER AND STANTON BURNETT, program on air pollution in New York, NBC-TV, Dec. 3, 1962.

This city's got the right name—New York. Nothing ever gets old around here.
> RALPH STEPHENSON, counterman at Pennsylvania Station's Saverin Restaurant, as demolition of the station was begun, *New York Times*, Oct. 29, 1963.

The pneumatic noisemaker is becoming the emblematic Sound of New York, the way the bells of Big Ben are the Sound of London.
> HORACE SUTTON, "You Can't Live in New York," *Saturday Evening Post*, March 11, 1961.

. . . New York, where 250 people die each day, and where the living dash for empty apartments . . . Where on page 29 of this morning's newspaper are pictures of the dead; on page 31 are pictures of the engaged; on page 1 are pictures of those who are running the world, enjoying the lush years before they land back on page 29.
> GAY TALESE, *New York—A Serendipiter's Journey*, Harper & Row, 1961.

. . . An office block, possibly made of pre-stressed celery.
> KENNETH TYNAN, "A Memoir of Manhattan," *Holiday*, Dec., 1960.

Coming to New York from the muted mistiness of London, as I regularly do, is like traveling from a monochrome antique shop to a Technicolor bazaar.
> KENNETH TYNAN, *ibid.*

. . . You can see in pantomime the puppets fumbling with their slips of paper (but you don't hear the rustle), see them pick up their phone (but you don't hear the ring), see the noiseless, ceaseless moving about of so many passers of pieces of paper: New York, the capital of memoranda, in touch with Calcutta, in touch with Reykjavik, and always fooling with something.
> E. B. WHITE, office windows at twilight, "Here Is New York," CBS-TV, 1958.

New York is to the nation what the white church spire is to the village—
the visible symbol of aspiration and faith, the white plume saying the way
is up!

> E. B. WHITE, quoted in *Mental Health in the Metropolis*, McGraw-
> Hill, 1962.

Who the hell looks up, in this town? Who has time?

> DAVID ZICKERMAN, New York Cabbie No. 2865, when asked if he had
> ever noticed a reproduction of Statue of Liberty atop a warehouse on
> Manhattan's West Side, *New York Times*, Oct. 2, 1960.

United Nations

All peoples have the right of self-determination.
> Afro-Asian declaration on colonialism, approved by General Assembly 89–0, U.S. and 8 other countries abstaining, *New York Times*, Dec. 15, 1960.

Inadequacy of political, economic, social or educational preparedness should never serve as a pretext for delaying independence.
> Afro-Asian declaration on colonialism, *ibid.*

The new member states which we shall shortly have the pleasure of welcoming will bring the Assembly nearer in practice to what it ideally is—an assembly fully representative of the whole human race. If, to match this accession of strength, we can bring to our work a corresponding sense of community, as dwellers on this small and threatened planet, then indeed this Assembly may deserve a noble title—the assembly of humanity.
> Frederick H. Boland of Ireland, President, General Assembly, *New York Times*, Sept. 21, 1960.

To campaign against colonialism is like barking up a tree that has already been cut down.
> Sir Andrew Cohen, British representative, UN Trustee Council, *Quote*, Feb. 23, 1958.

We do not believe in having happiness imposed upon us.
> José A. Correa, Ecuador's ambassador to UN, replying to Russian delegate, *New York Times*, July 20, 1960.

110

Whereas mankind owes to the child the best it has to give . . .

> Declaration of the Rights of the Child, opening words of resolution approved by General Assembly's Social, Humanitarian and Cultural Committee by vote of 70–0 (South Africa and Cambodia abstaining), *New York Times*, Oct. 20, 1959.

The child shall be entitled from his birth to a name and a nationality.

The child shall enjoy the benefits of social security. He shall be entitled to grow up and develop in health; to this end special care and protection shall be provided both to him and to his mother, including adequate pre-natal and post-natal care. . . . The child who is physically, mentally or socially handicapped shall be given the special treatment, education and care required by his particular condition. . . . The child is entitled to receive education, which shall be free and compulsory at least in the elementary stages. . . .

The child shall in all circumstances be among the first to receive protection and relief. . . .

The child shall be protected from practices which may foster racial, religious and any other forms of discrimination. He shall be brought up in a spirit of understanding, tolerance, friendship among peoples, peace and universal brotherhood and in the full consciousness that his energy and talents should be devoted to the service of his fellow men.

> Declaration of the Rights of the Child, *ibid.*

You can discuss, argue and talk back to the Americans, as we have discussed, argued and talked back to them during all the years of our subjugation, and since—without being slapped down or getting shot at dawn. One wonders, sometimes, what would happen to a Latvian or an Estonian or a Lithuanian who talked back to Mr. Khrushchev. We know, of course, what happened to the Hungarians who did just that.

> Francisco A. Delgado, Philippine delegate, defending U.S. colonial rule, *New York Times*, Oct. 6, 1960.

. . . The United Nations was not set up to be a reformatory. It was assumed that you would be good before you got in and not that being in would make you good.

> John Foster Dulles, Secretary of State, comment on UN Charter, news reports of July 9, 1954.

I have now come to believe that the United Nations will best serve the cause of peace if its Assembly is representative of what the world actually is and not merely representative of the parts which we like.

> JOHN FOSTER DULLES, *ibid.*

I feel impelled to speak today in a language that in a sense is new—one which I, who have spent so much of my life in the military profession, would have preferred never to use. That new language is the language of atomic warfare.

> DWIGHT EISENHOWER, address to UN to seek establishment of international atomic energy agency for peaceful uses of atomic power, Dec. 8, 1953.

. . . Let no one think that the expenditure of vast sums for weapons and systems of defense can guarantee absolute safety for the cities and citizens of any nation. The awful arithmetic of the atomic bomb does not permit of any such easy solution.

> DWIGHT EISENHOWER, *ibid.*

. . . The United States pledges . . . its determination to help solve the fearful atomic dilemma—to devote its entire heart and mind to find the way by which the miraculous inventiveness of man shall not be dedicated to his death, but consecrated to his life.

> DWIGHT EISENHOWER, conclusion of address, *ibid.*

Peace and justice are two sides of the same coin.

> DWIGHT EISENHOWER, news conference of Feb. 6, 1957.

If the United Nations once admits that international disputes can be settled by using force, then we will have destroyed the very foundation of the organization, and our best hope of establishing a world order. That would be a disaster for us all.

> DWIGHT EISENHOWER, address to the nation, Feb. 20, 1957, on Israel's invasion of Egypt.

In most communities it is illegal to cry "fire" in a crowded assembly. Should it not be considered serious international misconduct to manufacture a general war scare in an effort to achieve local political aims?

> DWIGHT EISENHOWER, address to General Assembly, on Middle East crisis, Aug. 13, 1958.

112

Any nation, seduced by glittering promises into becoming a cat's-paw for an imperialistic power, thereby undermines the United Nations and places in jeopardy the independence of itself and all others.
> DWIGHT EISENHOWER, address to General Assembly, Sept. 22, 1960.

The last sound on the worthless earth will be two human beings trying to launch a homemade space-ship and already quarreling about where they are going next.
> WILLIAM FAULKNER, author, address to UNESCO Commission meeting, *New York Times*, Oct. 3, 1959.

Greece is a sort of American vassal; the Netherlands is the country of American bases that grow like tulip bulbs; Cuba is the main sugar plantation of the American monopolies; Turkey is prepared to kow-tow before any United States pro-consul and Canada is the boring second fiddle in the American symphony.
> ANDREI GROMYKO, Russian delegate, *New York Herald Tribune*, June 30, 1953.

The UN is not just a product of do-gooders. It is harshly real. The day will come when men will see the UN and what it means clearly. Everything will be all right—you know when? When people, just people, stop thinking of the United Nations as a weird Picasso abstraction, and see it as a drawing they made themselves.
> DAG HAMMARSKJÖLD, Secretary-General, *Time*, June 27, 1955.*

Constant attention by a good nurse may be just as important as a major operation by a surgeon.
> DAG HAMMARSKJÖLD, on UN's role in keeping peace in Middle East, news summaries of March 18, 1956.

---

* Secretary-General Hammarskjöld was well described by Alistair Cooke, *New York Herald Tribune*, Oct. 5, 1957: "Who is this rare bird, perched at the eerie dead center of the world's hurricane, whom all men delight to praise? A Machiavelli with a Boy Scout's exterior? A gross flatterer? . . . A monstrous appeaser? Clean is the word for Hammarskjöld. A blond, tanned man, clean shaven, a man just out of a bath. 'Central Casting,' looking him over quickly for a feature part . . . would assign him without a second thought as the sympathetic brother of the grieving heroine; or the third Swiss guide in an Alpine rescue. . . . The secret of his good nature, his interminable patience . . . is probably that he was born in a small country that must for survival measure with a steady hand the crushing weight of the giants who stand on either side."

I have never seen difficulties that prevented leading politicians of great maturity and strong personalities from getting together when they felt it made sense.

> DAG HAMMARSKJÖLD, *ibid.*

"Freedom from fear" could be said to sum up the whole philosophy of human rights.

> DAG HAMMARSKJÖLD, on 180th anniversary of Virginia Declaration of Rights, *Quote*, May 20, 1956.

I never discuss discussions.

> DAG HAMMARSKJÖLD, after talks with Russian leaders, *Look*, Sept. 19, 1956.

. . . In the seeming void of the Room, there is something we want to say. We want to bring back the stillness which we have lost in our streets, and in our conference rooms. We want to bring back the idea of worship, devotion to something which is greater and higher than we are ourselves.

> DAG HAMMARSKJÖLD, on UN's Meditation Room, *Guideposts*, Oct., 1957.

We are at a turn of the road where our attitude will be of decisive significance, I believe, not only for the future of this organization, but also for the future of Africa. And Africa may well in present circumstances mean the world.

> DAG HAMMARSKJÖLD, as Soviet Union cast its first vote in favor of UN military force in the Congo, *Time*, Aug. 1, 1960.

The Assembly has witnessed over the last weeks how historical truth is established; once an allegation has been repeated a few times, it is no longer an allegation, it is an established fact, even if no evidence has been brought out in order to support it. However, facts are facts, and the true facts are there for whosoever cares for truth. Those who invoke history will certainly be heard by history. And they will have to accept its verdict as it will be pronounced on the basis of the facts by men free of mind and firm in their conviction that only on a scrutiny of truth can a future of peace be built.

> DAG HAMMARSKJÖLD, replying to Premier Khrushchev's attack in General Assembly, *New York Times*, Oct. 4, 1960.

I shall remain in my post during the term of my office as a servant of the organization in the interests of all those other nations, as long as they wish me to do so. In this context the representative of the Soviet Union spoke of courage. It is very easy to resign; it is not so easy to stay on. It is very easy to bow to the wish of a big power. It is another matter to resist. As is well known to all members of this Assembly, I have done so on many occasions and in many directions. If it is the wish of those nations who see [in] the organization their best protection in the present world, I shall now do so again.

> Dag Hammarskjöld, *ibid.*

You try to save a drowning man without prior authorization and even if he resists you; you do not let him go even when he tries to strangle you. I do not believe that anyone would wish the organization to follow other rules than those you apply to yourself when faced with such a situation.

> Dag Hammarskjöld, on UN actions in the Congo, *New York Times*, Oct. 18, 1960.

The end of all political effort must be the well-being of the individual in a life of safety and freedom.

> Dag Hammarskjöld, *ibid.*

. . . The real victim is the future.

> Dag Hammarskjöld, on efforts to discredit UN, *New York Times*, Feb. 19, 1961.

What has been called the Revolution of Expectation has begun, and will certainly continue. The hungry believe that they could and ought to be fed, the sick that they could and ought to be healthy, the illiterate and ignorant that they could and ought to receive a decent education.

> Sir Julian Huxley, address proposing UN agency to cope with world's rapidly rising population, *New York Times*, Nov. 20, 1959.

It is our earnest wish that the UN—in its structure and in its means—may become ever more equal to the magnitude and nobility of its tasks, and that the day may come when every human being will find therein an effective safeguard for the rights which derive directly from his dignity as a person.

JOHN XXIII, in encyclical *Pacem in Terris*, April 10, 1963.

I'll put it this way—now the prodigal has returned home after squandering a fortune. The prodigal has reformed.

TOSHIKAZU KASE, Japan's first permanent delegate, comment a few hours after Japan was elected a member, *New York World-Telegram and Sun*, Dec. 21, 1956.

. . . We prefer world law, in the age of self-determination, to world war in the age of mass extermination.

JOHN F. KENNEDY, address to General Assembly, Sept. 25, 1961.

We cannot expect that all nations will adopt like systems, for conformity is the jailer of freedom and the enemy of growth.

JOHN F. KENNEDY, *ibid*.

All the sparrows on the roof-tops are crying about the fact that the most imperialist nation that is supporting the colonial regime in the colonies is the United States of America and [the US representative] is indignant over that. What innocence, may I ask, is being played here when it is known that this virtuous damsel has already got a dozen illegitimate children?

NIKITA S. KHRUSHCHEV, Soviet Premier, speaking in General Assembly, *New York Times*, Oct. 2, 1960.

That expression "positive neutrality" is a contradiction in terms. There can be no more positive neutrality than there can be a vegetarian tiger.

V. K. KRISHNA MENON, Indian Defense Minister, address to General Assembly, *New York Times*, Oct. 18, 1960.

I shall take all the troubles of the past, all the disappointments, all the headaches, and I shall pack them in a bag and throw them in the East River.

TRYGVE LIE, on retiring from his duties as UN Secretary-General, news summaries of Dec. 31, 1953.

116

With the danger of fire, and in the absence of an organized fire department, it is only common sense for the neighbors to join in setting up their
own volunteer fire brigades.

> Trygve Lie, on the North Atlantic Treaty Organization and the Pan-
> American defense arrangement, *In the Cause of Peace*, Macmillan,
> 1954.

This organization is created to prevent you from going to hell. It isn't
created to take you to heaven.

> Henry Cabot Lodge, Jr., U.S. Ambassador to UN, on purpose of UN,
> news summaries of Jan. 28, 1954.

It has been well said that a hungry man is more interested in four sand-
wiches than four freedoms.

> Henry Cabot Lodge, Jr., appealing to Senate Appropriations Commit-
> tee for renewed support of UN technical assistance program, news re-
> ports of March 29, 1955.

We live in a welfare state which seeks to put a floor below which no one
sinks but builds no ceiling to prevent man from rising.

> Henry Cabot Lodge, Jr., at luncheon marking Premier Khrushchev's
> arrival in New York, news reports of Sept. 18, 1959.

May the United Nations ever be vigilant and potent to defeat the swallowing up of any nation, at any time, by any means—by armies with banners,
by force or by fraud, by tricks or by midnight treachery.

> Henry Cabot Lodge, Jr., at dedication of plaque honoring 37,000
> servicemen who died while fighting under UN's unified command in
> Korean War, *New York Times*, June 28, 1960.

Do not touch us; do not touch those with whom we are tied; do not seek
to extend Communist imperialism. That is very simple and ought to be
easily understood by everybody.

> Henry Cabot Lodge, Jr., to Soviet delegate in Security Council, *New
> York Times*, July 20, 1960.

My delegation cannot refrain from speaking on this question. We have had such an intimate knowledge of boxcars and of deportations to unknown destinations that we cannot be silent.

> GOLDA MEIR, Foreign Minister of Israel and head of that nation's delegation to UN, address to General Asembly on Soviet action in Hungary, news reports of Nov. 21, 1956.

It is, I believe, a simple but sometimes forgotten truth that the greatest enemy to present joy and high hopes is *the cultivation of retrospective bitterness.*

> ROBERT GORDON MENZIES, Prime Minister of Australia, address to General Assembly, *New York Times*, Oct. 6, 1960.

You can look at the UN through many eyes—the eye of faith, of hope, of charity, the eye of disillusion, the eye of mockery, the eye of fear or distaste, even the eye of poetry; but whatever your bias, vantage point or field of vision, you can hardly fail to recognize it as one of the supremely interesting sights of our time.

> JAMES MORRIS, British correspondent, *New York Times*, Oct. 2, 1960.

It would indeed be the ultimate tragedy if the history of the human race proved to be nothing more noble than the story of an ape playing with a box of matches on a petrol dump.

> DAVID ORMSBY GORE, British Minister of State, *Christian Science Monitor*, Oct. 25, 1960.

I had hoped it would be the conscience of the world and it is. I had hoped it would help erase the racial barriers and it has. . . .

> GENERAL CARLOS P. ROMULO, Philippine ambassador to U.S., writing on UN 16 years after he had addressed its founding session with the words, "Let us make this floor the last battlefield." *I Walked With Heroes*, Holt, Rinehart, and Winston, 1961.

Nations will rise and fall but equality remains the ideal. The universal aim is to achieve respect for the entire race, not for the dominant few.

> GENERAL CARLOS P. ROMULO, *ibid.*

. . . It would seem that those eminent gentlemen must know that there is nothing to spy on in the United Nations and therefore, there could be no spies. That is the obvious reason why the Soviets never fill their quota.

ELEANOR ROOSEVELT, former member of U.S. delegation, commenting on charges that UN is a nest of Communist spies, *New York World-Telegram & Sun*, March 9, 1954.

Twenty-seven years ago, as Emperor of Ethiopia, I mounted the rostrum in Geneva, Switzerland, to address to the League of Nations an appeal for relief from the destruction which had been unleashed against my defenseless nation. I spoke then both to and for the conscience of the world . . . Today, I stand before the world organization which has succeeded to the mantle discarded by its discredited predecessor. In this body is enshrined the principle of collective security which I unsuccessfully invoked at Geneva. Here, in this Assembly, reposes the best—perhaps the last—hope for the peaceful survival of mankind.

HAILE SELASSIE, Emperor of Ethiopia, address to General Assembly, Oct. 4, 1963. He became the first ruler to address both League of Nations and UN.

Africa for Africans means Africa for the Africans and not Africa as a hunting ground for alien ambitions.

ADLAI STEVENSON, U.S. ambassador to UN, *New York Times*, Feb. 19, 1961.

We must stop pulling up the roots of this fragile plant every few days to see if it is growing. That is the best way to kill the plant and, I suspect, that that may be the objective of some of these incessant attacks.

ADLAI STEVENSON, speaking in General Assembly on UN relationships with the Congo, *New York Times*, March 22, 1961.

The first principle of a free society is an untrammeled flow of words in an open forum.

ADLAI STEVENSON, *New York Times*, Jan. 19, 1962.

In the United Nations, day after day, we struggle to inject into the discourse—the often rough, fierce, intemperate dialogue of the nations—

those elements of order without which we are condemned to stand in fearful exposure on that last fatal brink that overlooks Armageddon.

ADLAI STEVENSON, address on receiving Liberties Medallion of American Jewish Committee, *New York Post*, May 26, 1963.

. . . The only worthy response to danger and failure is a renewed dedication to success; and I trust it will be written of the American people in our time, not that we refused to soil our hands with the imperfections of ourselves and of the world, but that we grew stronger, striving to overcome them.

ADLAI STEVENSON, *ibid.*

I believe in the forgiveness of sin and the redemption of ignorance.

ADLAI STEVENSON, reply to a heckler who asked him to state his beliefs in a United Nations Day address at Dallas, *Time*, Nov. 1, 1963.

I don't want to send them to jail. I want to send them to school.

ADLAI STEVENSON, on pickets who attacked him in Dallas, *ibid.*

President Johnson has directed me to affirm to this Assembly that there will be no "Johnson policy" toward the United Nations—any more than there was a "Kennedy policy." There was—and is—only a United States policy, and that, too, outlasts violence and outlives men.

ADLAI STEVENSON, address to UN General Assembly, *New York Times*, Nov. 27, 1963, after Mr. Kennedy's assassination in Dallas.

Dag Hammarskjöld was a man of learning and a poet of the breed for whom books and libraries are necessary delights.

U THANT, Acting Secretary-General, on dedication of new UN library named for late Secretary-General, *New York Times*, Nov. 17, 1961.

I don't know what I can do with such a bunch of clowns.

U THANT, criticizing Katanga President Moise Tshombe and several of his ministers for continued refusal to negotiate differences during Congo crisis, *New York Times*, July 22, 1962.

I speak not as the Secretary-General of the United Nations, not as an Asian, not as a Burmese, but as a human being, a member of that species, *Homo sapiens,* whose continued existence is in the balance.

    U THANT, beginning an address to Economic Club of New York, *Saturday Review,* March 23, 1963.

Surely with a little good will and a little give-and-take, it should not be impossible to reach an early agreement on what has become a game of arithmetic!

    U THANT, on international inspection of nuclear resources, *ibid.*

For countless ages the sun rose and set, the moon waxed and waned, the stars shone in the Milky Way, but it was only with the coming of man that these things were understood. Man has unveiled secrets which might have been thought undiscoverable. Much has been achieved in the realm of art, science, literature, and religion. Is all this to end because so few are able to think of man rather than of this or that group of men?

    U THANT, on possibility of world-wide extermination, *ibid.*

My feeling is that in the Seventies, if there are Seventies, the world will witness four big powers—the United States of America, Europe, Russia and China.

    U THANT, comment at news conference at UN, *New York Times,* June 29, 1963.

One by one, the proud, solemn black men advanced through the murmuring chamber to take their new-won seats. Carrying themselves with graven dignity, often combining ritual facial scars with impeccable European manners, they came from lands of jungle and desert whose very names were scarcely known to the West. . . . In the sweep of history, the 15th UN Assembly might be regarded as the time of the Africans.

    TIME, Oct. 3, 1960.

Our conference here in 1945 did much more than draft an international agreement among fifty nations. . . . [we] set down on paper the only principles which will enable civilized human life to continue to survive on this globe.

    HARRY TRUMAN, speaking at conference marking UN's tenth anniversary, *New York Herald Tribune,* June 25, 1955.

I am not a gentleman. I am representative of the Soviet Union here.

> SEMYON TSARAPKIN, Soviet delegate to UN, in reply to Ambassador Lodge's inquiry on why "the gentleman" was asking for the floor. Lodge replied, "The two are not necessarily mutually exclusive," news reports of June 26, 1954.

The great powers are climbing from the pedestal of greatness to the pedestal of insanity. We expect leadership from them; they give us destruction. We expect wisdom from them; they give us lack of knowledge. We expect objectivity from them; they present us with blurred vision.

> JAJA WACHUKU, Foreign Minister, Nigeria, address to General Assembly, *New York Times*, Oct. 11, 1961.

It is the same midnight brew, dipped from the same cauldron of hysteria.

> JAMES WADSWORTH, U.S. ambassador to UN, on Cuba's charges of American aggression, *New York Times*, Jan. 5, 1961.

Some of us throw bombs. I throw ideas. We have men to do the shooting but I do the shouting.

> M'HAMMED YAZID, spokesman at UN for rebel Algeria, *New York Times*, March 18, 1961.

Foreign Governments

Argentina

Without fanaticism one cannot accomplish anything.

> EVITA PERÓN, on her devotion to the dictatorship of her husband, Juan Perón, *Time*, May 21, 1951.

Australia

Immigration is an adventure not only to the migrant but to the native-born. The newcomer faces the unknown [while] the native-born is also faced with the necessity of living . . . in peace and good will, not only with his neighbor but with his fellowmen of whatever creed and whatever country.

> ALEXANDER DOWNER, immigration minister, address to Australians, *Christian Science Monitor*, Aug. 13, 1963.

Belgium

Youth is the first victim of war; the first fruit of peace. It takes 20 years or more of peace to make a man; it takes only 20 seconds of war to destroy him.

> BAUDOUIN I, address to joint session of U.S. Congress, May 12, 1959.

In Western Europe there are now only small countries—those that know it, and those that do not know it yet.

> THEO LEFEVRE, Prime Minister, *The Observer*, London, Feb. 3, 1963.

Brazil

We have turned our back on the sea and penetrated to the heartland of the nation. Now the people realize their strength.
> JUSCELINO KUBITSCHEK, President of Brazil, on $500-million new capital city, Brasilia, *Time*, April 25, 1960.

. . . There was only solitude and a jaguar screaming in the night.
> JUSCELINO KUBITSCHEK, on site chosen for Brasilia, *ibid*.

To the wrath of my enemies I leave the legacy of my death. I take the sorrow of not being able to give to the humble all that I wished.
> GETULIO VARGAS, President of Brazil, suicide note after 58 generals forced him to resign, news reports of Aug. 25, 1954.

Canada

I am not anti-American. But I am strongly pro-Canadian.
> JOHN DIEFENBAKER, Prime Minister, *New York Times*, July 13, 1958.

The situation is one something like living with your wife. Sometimes it is difficult and even irritating to live with her but it is always impossible to live without her.
> LESTER PEARSON, Secretary of State for External Affairs, defining attitude toward U.S., news summaries of March 15, 1955.

The grim fact is that we prepare for war like precocious giants and for peace like retarded pygmies.
> LESTER PEARSON, on receiving Nobel Peace Prize at Oslo, *New York Times*, Dec. 12, 1957.

To deserve success rather than to achieve it.
> LESTER PEARSON, on his "formula for life," quoted on his election as Prime Minister, *Time*, April 19, 1963.

We worry when you look hard at us, but we are also touchy about being overlooked.
> LESTER PEARSON, Commencement address at Notre Dame University, *New York Times*, June 10, 1963.

We are always watching Big Brother to see what trouble he might get us in—while at the same time protesting the fact that Big Brother is not watching us.
> LESTER PEARSON, *ibid.*

Communist China

Passivity is fatal to us. Our goal is to make the enemy passive.
> MAO TSE-TUNG, Chairman of Communist party, *Time*, Dec. 18, 1950.

Communism is not love. Communism is a hammer which we use to crush the enemy. . . .
> MAO TSE-TUNG, *ibid.*

Revolution is not a dinner party, nor an essay, nor a painting, nor a piece of embroidery; it cannot be advanced softly, gradually, carefully, considerately, respectfully, politely, plainly and modestly.
> MAO TSE-TUNG, *ibid.*

Let a hundred flowers bloom. Let a hundred schools of thought contend.
> MAO TSE-TUNG, in speech acknowledging "contradictions" within Communist society, news summaries of Dec. 29, 1957.

Despise the enemy strategically, but take him seriously tactically.
> MAO TSE-TUNG, in a handbook for revolutionaries, *Time*, March 22, 1963.

. . . Swollen in head, weak in legs, sharp in tongue but empty in belly.
> MAO TSE-TUNG's description of intellectuals, *The Wilting of the Hundred Flowers* by Mu Fu-sheng, Praeger, 1963.

125

All the experiences of the Chinese people, accumulated in the course of successive decades, tell us to carry out a people's democratic dictatorship.

> Mao Tse-tung, acknowledging charges that he is a dictator, quoted in *Classics In Political Science*, Philosophical Library, 1963.

. . . Reactionaries must be deprived of the right to voice their opinions; only the people have that right.

> Mao Tse-tung, defining "democratic dictatorship," *ibid*

Enemy advances, we retreat: enemy halts, we harass; enemy tires, we attack; enemy retreats, we pursue.

> Mao Tse-tung, on his strategy for war, quoted by Dwight Eisenhower, *Mandate for Change*, Doubleday, 1963.

Cuba

I began revolution with 82 men. If I had [to] do it again, I do it with 10 or 15 men and absolute faith. It does not matter how small you are if you have faith and plan of action.

> Fidel Castro, Premier of Cuba, on receiving tumultuous New York welcome during U.S. visit a few months after coming to power, *New York Times*, April 22, 1959.

Let us look at the case of chickens. In some places, when the supplies arrived, it was thought that chickens under the Socialist system had to be given to all persons registered as consumers. Supplies intended for 150 persons were cut up in such a way that 600 persons would receive a small piece. There were some incidents.

> Carlos Rafael Rodriguez, president, Cuban National Institute of Agrarian Reform, admitting errors in planning and distribution, *New York Times*, April 1, 1962.

Egypt

In a few years there will be only five kings in the world—the King of England and the four kings in a pack of cards.

> King Farouk, *Life*, April 10, 1950.

126

Fate does not jest and events are not a matter of chance—there is no existence out of nothing.

> GAMAL ABDEL NASSER, first President, Egyptian Republic, *Egypt's Liberation: Philosophy of the Revolution*, Public Affairs Press, 1955.

We're a sentimental people. We like a few kind words better than millions of dollars given in a humiliating way.

> GAMAL ABDEL NASSER, on his refusal of foreign economic aid from the West, *Réalités*, Jan., 1958.

Within the Arab circle there is a role wandering aimlessly in search of a hero. For some reason it seems to me that this role is beckoning to us— to move, to take up its lines, put on its costumes and give it life. Indeed, we are the only ones who can play it. The role is to spark the tremendous latent strengths in the region surrounding us to create a great power, which will then rise up to a level of dignity and undertake a positive part in building the future of mankind.

> GAMAL ABDEL NASSER, *ibid*.

France

Political thought in France is either nostalgic or utopian.

> RAYMOND ARON, *The Opium of the Intellectual*, Doubleday, 1957.

The work was killing me; they called me out of bed at all hours of the night to receive resignations of prime ministers.

> VINCENT AURIOL, on retirement as President of France, news summaries of Feb. 1, 1954.

People of France, great people! Pride! Courage! Hope!

> CHARLES DE GAULLE, exhortation proclaiming creed for Fifth French Republic four days before his inauguration as its head, *New York Times*, Jan. 4, 1959.

National interest in the nation, common interest in the community. That is what I, now as yesterday, have the duty to represent, to make valid and even to impose if the public welfare demands it. These are my obligations, and I will not fail.

> GENERAL DE GAULLE, on being invested as President, news reports of Jan. 9, 1959.*

Finally, I address myself to France. My dear and old country, here we are once again together faced with a heavy trial. By virtue of the mandate the people have given me and the national legitimacy that I have embodied for twenty years, I call on everyone to support me whatever happens.

> GENERAL DE GAULLE, on uprising in Algeria, *New York Times*, Jan. 30, 1960.

France is convinced that peace will remain precarious so long as two thousand million human beings remain in the depths of misery alongside their more fortunate brothers. She believes that there is certainly nothing more significant than the organization, cutting across differences in policy, of cooperation between those who lack nothing to help those who lack all.

> GENERAL DE GAULLE, address to British Parliament, *New York Times*, April 8, 1960.

It is quite natural to feel a nostalgia for what was the Empire, just as one can miss the mellowness of oil lamps, the splendor of sailing ships, the charm of the carriage era. But what of it? There is no valid policy outside realities.

> GENERAL DE GAULLE, *Time*, June 27, 1960.

Once upon a time there was an old country, wrapped up in habit and caution.

> GENERAL DE GAULLE, opening of nationally televised address on French domestic and foreign position in mid-1960, *New York Times*, June 15, 1960.

. . . The whole world recognizes that order and progress have once again got a chance in our country. What to do with it? Ah, to do a great deal. For we have to transform our old France into a new country and marry

---

* President René Coty's inaugural tribute to General de Gaulle was quoted in news reports of Jan. 9, 1959: "The first among Frenchmen is now the first man of France."

it to its time. France must find prosperity in this way. This must be our great national ambition.

GENERAL DE GAULLE, *ibid*.

Frenchwomen, Frenchmen, this is the ground on which we are playing our game and this is where we are going. However diverse may be our ideas or our interests, we are going there together, for the stake is the destiny of France.

GENERAL DE GAULLE, conclusion of address, *ibid*.

Old Earth, eaten away by the ages, buffeted by rains and winds, exhausted, but ever ready to produce again what life needs to go on. Old France, weighted down by History, wracked by wars and revolutions, rising and falling from grandeur to decline, yet ever renewed, from century to century, with its genius for renewal. Old man, perennial recruit of crisis, not detached from enterprise, feeling the approach of the eternal cold, but never weary of staring into the shadows watchful for the gleam of hope.

GENERAL DE GAULLE, on himself and his country, *Esquire*, April, 1961.

In the name of France I order that all means be employed . . . to bar the route of these men. I forbid . . . any soldier to execute their orders . . . Frenchwomen, Frenchmen, help me!

GENERAL DE GAULLE, radio appeal on Algerian revolt and threatened invasion of Paris, *Life*, May 5, 1961.

You start out giving your hat, then you give your coat, then your shirt, then your skin, and finally your soul.

GENERAL DE GAULLE, on Russia, *New York Herald Tribune*, Sept. 22, 1961.

Diplomats are useful only in fair weather. As soon as it rains they drown in every drop.

GENERAL DE GAULLE, quoted by a former Cabinet aide, Constantin Melnick, *Newsweek*, Oct. 1, 1962.

Since a politician never believes what he says, he is surprised when others believe him.

GENERAL DE GAULLE, *ibid*.

129

Treaties are like roses and young girls. They last while they last.
> GENERAL DE GAULLE, during talk with West German Vice Chancellor Ludwig Erhard on Franco-German treaty, *Time,* July 12, 1963.

What the French criticize [in Coca-Cola] is less the drink itself than the civilization, the style of life of which it is a sign . . . a symbol . . . red delivery trucks and walls covered with signs, placards and advertisements . . . it is a question of the whole panorama and morale of French civilization.
> LE MONDE, editorial on a bill pending in the National Assembly to ban the sale of the American soft-drink, a reaction to what had come to be called "the Coca-Colonization" of France, *Time,* March 13, 1950.

This time we won't even hear them.
> ANTOINE PINAY, Foreign Minister, on rubber-soled shoes of West German Army, news summaries of Dec. 31, 1955.

A minister of finance is a legally authorized pickpocket.
> PAUL RAMADIER, Minister of Finance, *Quote,* Oct. 7, 1956.

West Germany

We can find no better place or moment than this place or moment to say that in the new Germany, every man, no matter what nationality, race or creed, will enjoy true safety and freedom.*
> KONRAD ADENAUER, Chancellor, on his first visit since World War II to Bergen-Belsen, infamous Nazi concentration camp site, *New York Times,* Feb. 3, 1960.

---

* In the same year in which Adenauer spoke of "the new Germany," foreign correspondent William Shirer completed his monumental *The Rise and Fall of the Third Reich* (Simon and Schuster, 1960) using near the frontispiece two quotations from wartime figures: "A thousand years will pass and the guilt of Germany will not be erased—" Hans Frank, Governor General of Poland, statement before he was hanged; "Hitler was the fate of Germany and this fate could not be stayed—" Field Marshal Walther von Brauchitsch, Commander in Chief of the German Army, 1938–1941.

. . . The rare case where the conquered is very satisfied with the conqueror.

> KONRAD ADENAUER, on British-French-American occupation of Berlin, *New York Times*, March 21, 1960.

God . . . provided that the stomach would vomit out substances that were bad for it. But He overlooked the human brain.

> KONRAD ADENAUER, *Newsweek*, May 6, 1963.

Only the stupidest calves choose their own butcher.

> KONRAD ADENAUER, opposing Western wheat shipments to Russia, *New York Herald Tribune*, Oct. 6, 1963.

A solution is not possible between ourselves and other opponents alone, but only with the help of our friends—and thank God we have friends in the world again.

> KONRAD ADENAUER, on his retirement at 87 after 14 years as head of West Germany's first post-war government, *New York Herald Tribune*, Oct. 13, 1963. The occasion recalled Sir Winston Churchill's tribute to "Der Alte" (The Old Man) as "the greatest German since Bismarck."

Every German who did not spend the entire Nazi era in prison camps must feel responsible and must atone for the sins committed by the murderers in German uniforms and in the name of Germany.

> HEINRICH ALBERTZ, acting mayor of West Berlin, on 20th anniversary of the uprising in Warsaw ghetto, *New York Times*, April 19, 1963.

We Berliners know that we cannot defend Berlin with sweat and printer's ink alone. But we are proud of our right of freedom of speech, today above all when tyrants in this same city wish to strangle us into silence.

> BERLINER ILLUSTRIRTE, in special 1961 issue saluting American friendship.

Refugees—People who vote with their feet.

> BERLINER ILLUSTRIRTE, on crowds fleeing communist Germany, *ibid.*

131

The last freedom—freedom to flee.
> BERLINER ILLUSTRIRTE, *ibid.*

We do not live in the Bavarian forests. We do not live on the west bank of the Rhine. We live behind the Communist guns in this encircled city. That is a geographical fact. But we belong to the West and we will continue belonging to the West.
> WILLY BRANDT, mayor of Berlin, *New York Times,* Dec. 7, 1958.

We cannot say now that these Nazis were only a handful of Germans. They were people out of our midst, from our own blood, out of our own kind. We cannot deny this.
> OTTO DIBELIUS, Bishop, German Evangelical Church, address over West Berlin radio on the eve of the Eichmann trial, *New York Times,* April 11, 1961.

My only task is to be silent. I must feel my way back in the world.
> GRAND ADMIRAL KARL DOENITZ, Adolf Hitler's successor, on being released after serving a ten-year sentence for war crimes, Oct. 1, 1956.

We have agreed on the shell of an egg. What will be in the egg, we do not know.
> LUDWIG ERHARD, Vice Chancellor, following international conference on formula for reducing tariffs, *Newsweek,* June 3, 1963.

I am an American invention.
> LUDWIG ERHARD, who, on succeeding Konrad Adenauer in 1963 as Chancellor of West Germany, recalled that his anti-Nazi war record had attracted the confidence of the U.S. Army and gave rise to his appointment as an economic administrator, *Time,* Nov. 1, 1963.

Eighty per cent were cheering the Queen, ten per cent were cheering the horses, and ten per cent were cheering me—and those were German tourists.
> THEODOR HEUSS, President of West Germany, on state visit to Elizabeth II, in London, *Newsweek,* Nov. 3, 1958.

132

. . . The next war criminals will come from the chemical and electronics industries.

> ALFRED KRUPP, head of Krupp industries, on being asked if he would again make guns for warfare, *New York Times*, Jan. 18, 1959.

Ghana

It is very unfair—to be accused of being Communist on the basis of anti-colonialism. I think anti-colonialism was invented by the United States of America.

> KWAME NKRUMAH, President of Ghana, *New York Times*, March 9, 1961.

Great Britain

I think the British have the distinction above all other nations of being able to put new wine into old bottles without bursting them.

> CLEMENT ATTLEE, Prime Minister, on rebuilt House of Commons, *Time*, Nov. 6, 1950.

It's nice to keep in touch—besides, it's the only place in London where you can park a car.

> LORD ATTLEE, former Prime Minister, on why he attends House of Lords, *The Times*, London, Feb. 4, 1962.

Democracy means government by discussion but it is only effective if you can stop people talking.

> LORD ATTLEE, *Anatomy of Britain* by Anthony Sampson, Harper & Row, 1962.

The job of a prime minister is to get the general feeling—collect the voices. And then when everything reasonable has been said, to get on with the job and say, "Well, I think the decision of the Cabinet is this, that or the other. Any objections?" Usually there aren't.

> LORD ATTLEE, *ibid.*

People talk as if derailments were infectious. There is, in any case, no question of adopting Continental signalling systems, any more than we shall be serving zabaglione in the British dining cars.

> RICHARD BEECHING, chairman, British Transport Commission, after several railway accidents, *Punch*, Feb. 14, 1962.

The House of Lords is the British Outer Mongolia for retired politicians.

> ANTHONY WEDGWOOD BENN, Lord Stansgate, *New York Times*, Feb 11, 1962.

If you have to have an adjectival phrase, then "the persistent commoner" would be better.

> ANTHONY WEDGWOOD BENN, objection to being called "the reluctant peer" during his long and eventually successful campaign for peers to have the right to relinquish their titles, *New York Times*, Aug. 1, 1963.

It takes two to make love and two partners to make trade agreements work. Unrequited trade or unrequited exports pay no better than unrequited love.

> R. A. BUTLER, Chancellor of the Exchequer, comparison of affairs of state to affairs of the heart, news summaries of Jan. 29, 1954.

. . . Six hundred men all thinking a great deal of themselves and very little of each other.

> SIR JAMES CASSELS, retired justice, on House of Commons, *Anatomy of Britain* by Anthony Sampson, Harper & Row, 1962.

The party system is much favored by an oblong form of chamber. It is easy for an individual to move through those insensible gradations from left to right, but the act of crossing the floor [to change parties] is one which requires serious consideration. I am well-informed on this matter for I have accomplished that difficult process not only once but twice.

> WINSTON CHURCHILL, argument for retaining rectangular shape of the House of Commons in its post-war rebuilding, *Time*, Nov. 6, 1950.

During these last months the King walked with death as if death were a companion . . . whom he recognized and did not fear. In the end, death came as a friend and after a happy day of sunshine and sport, after "good-night" to those who loved him best, he fell asleep as every man and woman who strives to fear God and nothing else in the world may hope to do.

> WINSTON CHURCHILL, on death of George VI, Feb. 6, 1952.

To quell the Japanese resistance man by man and conquer the country yard by yard might well require the loss of a million American lives and half that number of British. Now all this nightmare picture had vanished. In its place was the vision—fair and bright indeed it seemed—of the end of the whole war in one or two violent shocks.

> WINSTON CHURCHILL, recalling his feelings on learning in 1945 of successful U.S. test of atomic bomb, *Triumph and Tragedy*, Houghton Mifflin, 1953.

There never was a moment's discussion. . . . There was unanimous . . . agreement around our table.

> WINSTON CHURCHILL, on swift decision of U.S. and Britain, at Potsdam, to drop atomic bomb on Japan, *ibid.*

. . . Just before dawn I awoke suddenly with a short stab of almost physical pain. A hitherto subconscious conviction that we were beaten broke forth and dominated my mind. All the pressure of great events, on which I had mentally so long maintained my "flying speed," would cease and I should fall.

> WINSTON CHURCHILL, on his post-war election defeat, *ibid.*

The honorable member must not, in his innocence, take the bread from the mouths of the Soviet secret service.

> WINSTON CHURCHILL, reply to question in Parliament on Britain's protection against atom bomb attack, news summaries of April 26, 1954.

All over the globe there has been a sense of kindly feeling and generous admiration. Even envy wore a friendly smile.

> WINSTON CHURCHILL, address asking Commons to adopt a resolution welcoming home Elizabeth II from her first tour of Commonwealth, news reports of May 18, 1954.

It was the nation and the race dwelling all 'round the globe that had the lion's heart. I had the luck to be called upon to give the lion's roar. I also hope that I sometimes suggested to the lion the right place to use his claws.

> WINSTON CHURCHILL, address on 80th birthday,* news reports of Dec. 1, 1954.

. . . It may be that we shall by a process of sublime irony have reached a stage in this story where safety will be the sturdy child of terror, and survival the twin brother of annihilation.

> WINSTON CHURCHILL, on hydrogen bomb, news reports of March 3, 1955.

I do not see any way of realizing our hopes about world organization in five or six days. Even the Almighty took seven.

> WINSTON CHURCHILL, message to President Roosevelt prior to Yalta Conference, quoted in papers made public by U.S. State Dept. in March, 1955.

No more let us falter. From Malta to Yalta. Let nobody alter.

> WINSTON CHURCHILL, message to Roosevelt on completion of plans for Malta meeting prior to Yalta Conference, *ibid.*

Never have the august duties which fall upon the British monarchy been discharged with more devotion than in the brilliant opening of Your Majesty's reign. We thank God for the gift He has bestowed upon us and vow ourselves anew to the sacred causes and wise and kindly way of life of which Your Majesty is the young, gleaming champion.

> WINSTON CHURCHILL, toast to Elizabeth II at dinner attended by the Queen at No. 10 Downing Street on eve of Churchill's resignation as Prime Minister, news reports of April 4, 1955.

This conference should not be overhung by a ponderous or rigid agenda or led into mazes of technical details, zealously contested by hordes of experts and officials drawn up in a vast cumbrous array.

> WINSTON CHURCHILL, on what a "summit conference" should not be, recalled at time of Geneva Conference, news reports of July 20, 1955.

---

* To mark Churchill's 80th year, John Masefield, poet laureate of England, wrote "On the Birthday of a Great Man":

This Man, in darkness saw, in doubtings led;
In danger did; in uttermost despair,
Shone with a Hope that made the midnight fair.
The world he saved calls blessings on his head.

It is a remarkable comment on our affairs that the former prime minister of a great sovereign state should thus be received as an honorary citizen of another. I say "great sovereign state" with design and emphasis for I reject the view that Britain and the Commonwealth should now be relegated to a tame and minor role in the world. Our past is the key to our future, which I firmly trust and believe will be no less fertile and glorious. Let no man underrate our energies, our potentialities and our abiding power for good.

> WINSTON CHURCHILL, accepting honorary U.S. citizenship conferred by act of Congress, *New York Times*, April 10, 1963.

We are, I suggest rightly, so anxious that neither the police nor the security service should pry into private lives, that there is no machinery for reporting the moral misbehavior of Ministers. . . . It is perhaps better thus, than that we should have a "police state."

> LORD DENNING (Alfred Thompson Denning), Master of the Rolls, concluding his official report on sex scandal that involved Cabinet Minister John Profumo, *Life*, Oct. 11, 1963.

The judges of England have rarely been original thinkers or great jurists. Many have been craftsmen rather than creators. They have needed the stuff of morals to be supplied to them so that out of it they could fashion the law.

> LORD PATRICK DEVLIN, Judge of the High Court, quoted by Ludovic Kennedy, "The Legal Barbarians," *Spectator*, Sept. 15, 1961.

I declare before you all that my whole life, whether it be long or short, shall be devoted to your service and the service of our great imperial family to which we all belong.

> PRINCESS ELIZABETH, address on her 21st birthday, recalled five years later on death of her father, George VI, Feb. 6, 1952.

I pray that God will help me to discharge worthily this heavy task that has been laid upon me so early in my life.

> ELIZABETH II, on succeeding to throne, news summaries of Feb. 29, 1952.

To that new conception of an equal partnership of nations and races I shall give myself, heart and soul, every day of my life.

> ELIZABETH II, in her Christmas address from Auckland, New Zealand, Dec. 25, 1953.

. . . It is my resolve that under God I shall not only rule but serve. That is not only the tradition of my family. It describes, I believe, the modern character of the British Crown.

> ELIZABETH II, speech from throne opening a session of Australian parliament, news reports of Feb. 16, 1954.

In the turbulence of this anxious and active world many people are leading uneventful, lonely lives. To them dreariness, not disaster, is the enemy. They seldom realize that on their steadfastness, on their ability to withstand the fatigue of dull repetitive work and on their courage in meeting constant small adversities depend in great measure the happiness and prosperity of the community as a whole. . . . The upward course of a nation's history is due in the long run to the soundness of heart of its average men and women.

> ELIZABETH II, Christmas broadcast from Sandringham to Commonweath, Dec. 25, 1954.

There are long periods when life seems a small, dull round, a petty business with no point, and then suddenly we are caught up in some great event which gives us a glimpse of the solid and durable foundations of our existence. I hope that tomorrow will be such an occasion.

> ELIZABETH II, on eve of becoming first reigning monarch to open Canadian parliament, news reports of Oct. 14, 1957.

In the old days the monarch led his soldiers onto the battlefield and his leadership at all times was close and personal. Today things are very different. I cannot lead you into battle. I do not give you laws or administer justice but I can do something else—I can give my heart and my devotion to these old islands and to all the peoples of our brotherhood of nations.

> ELIZABETH II, Christmas address to Commonwealth, Dec. 25, 1957; annual event was televised for first time.

Now therefore I declare my will and pleasure that while I and my children shall continue to be styled and known as the House and Family of Windsor, my descendants other than descendants enjoying the style, title or attributes of Royal Highness and the titular dignity of Prince or

Princess and female descendants who marry and their descendants who marry and their descendants, shall bear the name of Mountbatten-Windsor.

> ELIZABETH II, decree incorporating family name of her husband, issued shortly before birth of Prince Andrew whose children would be first called Mountbatten-Windsor, *New York Times*, Feb. 9, 1960.

We are fortunate to have inherited an institution [the House of Lords] which we certainly should never have had the intelligence to create. We might have been landed with something like the American Senate.

> LORD ESHER (Oliver S. B. Brett, 3rd Viscount Esher), *Wall Street Journal*, May 2, 1963.

. . . That fascinating and paradoxical association of sovereign nations known as the Commonwealth.

> GEOFFREY GODSELL, an editor of *The Christian Science Monitor*, writing on "The Commonwealth," Oct. 24, 1960.

We are proud of the stock from which we came. . . . This is no snobbery: it is not foolish pride. It is common piety that we honor our fathers and our mothers, that we praise famous men and the fathers who begat us.*

> LORD HAILSHAM (Quintin Hogg), addressing Lords during debate on peers' right to drop a title, quoted by Charles Hussey,† British editor, in article entitled, " 'Call Me Mister,' Peers Request," *New York Times*, Aug. 25, 1963.

Why employ intelligent and highly paid ambassadors and then go and do their work for them? You don't buy a canary and sing yourself. I therefore give notice that from about midsummer I shall go on strike and sit more in the control tower—just in time to avoid visiting a foreign secretary in the moon.

> LORD HOME (Alexander Frederick Douglas-Home, 14th Earl of Home), Foreign Secretary, exhausted by "this business of perambulation," *New York Times*, April 21, 1961.

---

* Within the year Lord Hailsham dropped his peerage to seek a seat in Commons and was thus quoted by *Newsweek*, Dec. 9, 1963: "If you have a name like Hogg, the first thing to establish is that you are proud of it. . . . Lord Hailsham is dead! God bless Quintin Hogg!"

† Of non-hereditary titles, Hussey wrote: "Life peers not only have no pride of noble ancestry, they also have no hope of noble posterity for their peerage dies with them. There are no coronets on their 24 male chromosomes."

. . . In spite of strong claims of several rivals, the right choice for us is the robin. . . . In addition to slight differences of plumage, the British race of the robin is also distinguished from continental races by its open and exceptionally friendly behaviour to human beings in both town and country.

> LORD HURCOMB (Cyril William Hurcomb, 1st Baron Hurcomb), chairman, British Section, International Council for Bird Preservation, announcing selection of the robin as Britain's national bird, *New York Herald Tribune*, Dec. 28, 1960.

You gave the world the guillotine
But still we don't know why the heck
You have to drop it on our neck.
We're glad of what we did to you,
At Agincourt and Waterloo.
And now the Franco-Prussian War
Is something we are strongly for.
So damn your food and damn your wines,
Your twisted loaves and twisting vines,
Your table d'hôte, your à la carte,
Your land, your history, your art.
From now on you can keep the lot.
Take every single thing you've got,
Your land, your wealth, your men, your dames,
Your dream of independent power,
And dear old Konrad Adenauer,
And stick them up your Eiffel Tower.

> ANTONY JAY, programs editor, British Broadcasting Corp., on France's rejection of Britain as a member of Common Market, *Time*, Feb. 8, 1963.

It is the day we have all been looking forward to for over 14 years. It is the last day of food rationing. I regard it as a great privilege to be the Minister of Food on this day.

> GWILYM LLOYD GEORGE, on lifting of controls on meat—the last rationed item of World War II, news reports of July 4, 1954.

He is forever poised between a cliché and an indiscretion.

> HAROLD MACMILLAN, on office of Foreign Secretary (one of his former posts), *Newsweek*, April 30, 1956.

People are so much nicer to you in other countries than they are at home. At home, you always have to be a politician; when you're abroad, you almost feel yourself a statesman.

> HAROLD MACMILLAN, Prime Minister, *Look*, April 15, 1958.

The wind of change is blowing through the continent.

> HAROLD MACMILLAN, address to South African Parliament, Feb. 4, 1960. Later *The Christian Science Monitor* observed editorially that the Prime Minister had added a durable phrase to the language of freedom—the wind of change—and recalled that statesmen had been similarly inspired as long ago as 458 B.C. when Aeschylus in his *Libation-Bearers* wrote: "Zeus at last may cause our ill wind to change."

. . . A strange, a perverted creed that has a queer attraction both for the most primitive and for the most sophisticated societies. . . . Once the bear's hug has got you, it is apt to be for keeps.

> HAROLD MACMILLAN, on Communism, *New York Herald Tribune*, Oct. 15, 1961.

Power? It's like a Dead Sea fruit. When you achieve it, there is nothing there.

> HAROLD MACMILLAN, *Parade*, July 7, 1963.

I was determined that no British government should be brought down by the action of two tarts.*

> HAROLD MACMILLAN, on withstanding demands that he resign following a sex scandal that shook Britain and caused War Minister John Profumo to leave the Cabinet, news reports of July 13, 1963.

. . . You must be like an oak tree—your branches spreading out widely so that the new saplings may grow in their shade. You must not be a beech tree, growing so straight that you give no shade to the next generation.

> HAROLD MACMILLAN, on leadership of younger men who composed majority of his Cabinet, *Newsweek*, July 22, 1963.

---

* This poem was widely quoted in Britain and the U.S. after Profumo admitted he had been false in March, 1963, in denying to Commons that there had been no truth in reports about his intimacy with Miss Christine Keeler.

What have you done? cried Christine.
You've wrecked the whole party machine.
To lie in the nude may be rude,
But to lie in the House is obscene.

Commenting on the publicity, *Time*, June 21, 1963, referred to Miss Keeler as "Britain's fastest rising fallen woman."

I have never found, in a long experience of politics, that criticism is ever inhibited by ignorance.

HAROLD MACMILLAN, *Wall Street Journal*, Aug. 13, 1963.

. . . A man of charm, charm, charm and luck, luck, luck.

LEONARD MOSLEY, describing Lord Mountbatten, *The Last Days of the British Raj*, Harcourt, Brace, 1962.

In the end it may well be that Britain will be honored by the historians more for the way she disposed of an empire than for the way in which she acquired it.

SIR DAVID ORMSBY GORE, ambassador to U.S., *New York Times*, Oct. 28, 1962.

It's no good shutting your eyes and saying "British is best" three times a day after meals and expecting it to be so. We've got to work for it by constantly criticizing and improving.

PRINCE PHILIP, DUKE OF EDINBURGH, on national complacency, *Look*, Aug. 7, 1956.

All money nowadays seems to be produced with a natural homing instinct for the Treasury.

PRINCE PHILIP, DUKE OF EDINBURGH, *Wall Street Journal*, June 6, 1963.

The House of Lords can play only the part of a constitutional obstacle to progressive legislation. I and my party are for complete abolition of this chamber.

WOGAN PHILIPPS, second Baron Milford, "maiden speech" on becoming House of Lords' first Communist member, *Time*, July 12, 1963.

The real rulers of England are not so much in the center of a solar system, as in a cluster of interlocking circles, each one largely preoccupied with its own professionalism and expertise, and touching others only at one edge. . . . They are not a single Establishment but a ring of Establishments, with slender connections.

ANTHONY SAMPSON, *Anatomy of Britain*, Harper & Row, 1962.

Lord Hailsham said the other day that the machinery of government was creaking. My Lords, it is not even moving sufficiently to emit a noise of any kind.

> LORD SANDWICH (Alexander V. E. P. Montague, 10th Earl of Sandwich), addressing House of Lords, *New York Times*, April 21, 1963.

Better "red" than dead.

> Slogan of nuclear disarmament movement in England during the 1960's.

Greater love hath no man than this, that he lay down his friends for his life.

> JEREMY THORPE, member of Parliament, on changes in the cabinet, *Wall Street Journal*, Aug. 20, 1962.

The British are a self-distrustful, diffident people, agreeing with alacrity that they are neither successful nor clever and only modestly claiming that they have a keener sense of humor, more robust common sense, and greater staying power as a nation than all the rest of the world put together.

> THE TIMES, of London, in an editorial quoted in *Fourth Leaders From The Times, 1950*, Times Publishing Co., Ltd.

We can't vote for the President of the United States, but he is the most important executive officer we possess. We can't have any voice in who is to be Secretary of State, but he is the most important diplomatic officer we possess. You didn't ask for it; we didn't ask for it; but that is the situation.

> ARNOLD TOYNBEE, on American elections, news summaries of Jan. 15, 1951.

Britain Friday withdrew the farthing from circulation as a coin of the realm because after 800 years it isn't worth a farthing any more.

> UPI dispatch, *Chicago Sun-Times*, July 30, 1960.

Fortunately for the sons of Kings, the ceremonies with which British life abounds afford a series of nursery slopes down which a diffident and inarticulate Royal apprentice may be conducted, by gentle stages, into public life at little risk to his own reputation, and without imposing too much embarrassment upon the people.

> DUKE OF WINDSOR, in his biography, *A King's Story*, Putnam, 1951.

On the single occasion that I . . . set out from the Palace on foot, the cry of wounded tradition that went up could not have been louder had I traveled third-class by train to Windsor.

> DUKE OF WINDSOR, *ibid*.

From her invincible virtue and correctness she looked out as from a fortress upon the rest of humanity with all of its tremulous uncertainties and distractions.

> DUKE OF WINDSOR, on his mother, the dowager Queen Mary, *ibid*.

India

The Population Explosion.

> CBS television program, Nov. 11, 1959, dealing with problems of India's rapidly increasing population. The title at once was adopted by advocates of birth control.

It is clear now—and this phenomenon is in itself sufficient to restore faith in the superiority of a free society—that the sacred soil of India has a concrete and potent meaning which has converted us overnight into a monolith in the face of the enemy. It is possible that nationhood requires to be tempered in the fires of war. If this is so, then we are ready now to be tested.

> B. K. NEHRU, ambassador to U.S., *New York Times*, Nov. 25, 1962, on eve of first anniversary of Communist Chinese invasion.

I am writing you about the humble broom. The normal Indian broom can be used only if one bends down to it or sits. A broom or brush with a long handle, which can be used while a person is standing, is far more effective and less tiring. All over the world these standing brooms are used. Why then do we carry on with a primitive method which is inefficient and psychologically wrong? Bending down to sweep in this way encourages subservience in mind.

> JAWAHARLAL NEHRU, Prime Minister, letter to his ministers, supporting project of Mrs. Harriet Bunker, wife of U.S. Ambassador Ellsworth Bunker, *Time*, Aug. 8, 1960.

144

All this business of Communism conquering the world. No doubt you can quote from their texts . . . [But] read the old tracts of any religion—they all wanted to conquer the world. Nevertheless they settled down after the first burst of enthusiasm. . . . When there are enough things to go around, it is far better to produce them than to break each other's heads.
> JAWAHARLAL NEHRU, in television interview, *New York Herald Tribune*, Oct. 10, 1960.

Democracy is good. I say this because other systems are worse.
> JAWAHARLAL NEHRU, *New York Times*, Jan. 25, 1961.

The very swiftness of the end showed the correctness of the Indian assessment.
> JAWAHARLAL NEHRU, on seizure of Portuguese enclaves, Goa, Dumao, and Diu, *Newsweek*, Jan. 1, 1962.

Israel

In Israel, in order to be a realist you must believe in miracles.
> DAVID BEN-GURION, Prime Minister, CBS-TV, Oct. 5, 1956.

I'm living in a house and I know I built it. I work in a workshop which was constructed by me. I speak a language which I developed. And I know I shape my life according to my desires by my own ability. I feel I am safe. I can defend myself. I am not afraid. This is the greatest happiness a man can feel—that he could be a partner with the Lord in creation. This is the real happiness of man—creative life, conquest of nature, and a great purpose.
> DAVID BEN-GURION, on new country he helped to build, NBC-TV, Sept. 22, 1957.

The real thing . . . is that people throughout the world realize what happened in our very lifetimes.
> DAVID BEN-GURION, during preparations for trial of Adolph Eichmann, *New York Journal-American*, March 16, 1961.

145

In the shadow of . . . dangers and injustices, Israel perseveres for the fifteenth year in succession in her arduous and constructive endeavors: the ingathering of the exiles, the conquest of the desert, the advancement of education and science, fraternal co-operation with new and developing states in Asia, Africa and Latin America.

> DAVID BEN-GURION, Premier, *New York Herald Tribune*, April 28, 1963.

The trebling of the population in this small and impoverished country, flowing with milk and honey but not with sufficient water, rich in rocks and sand dunes but poor in natural resources and vital raw materials, has been no easy task: indeed, practical men, with their eyes fixed upon things as they are, regarded it as an empty and insubstantial utopian dream.

> DAVID BEN-GURION, *ibid.*

Israel's economic and cultural progress is due to three things: the pioneering spirit that inspires the best of our immigrant and Israeli youth, who respond to the challenge of our desolate areas and the ingathering of the exiles; the feeling of Diaspora Jewry that they are partners in the enterprise of Israel's resurgence in the ancient homeland of the Jewish people; and the power of science and technology which Israel unceasingly—and not without success—tries to enhance.

> DAVID BEN-GURION, *ibid.*

When through the malice of fate a large part of these Jews whom we fought against are alive, I must concede that fate must have wanted it so. I always claimed that we were fighting against a foe who through thousands of years of learning and development had become superior to us.

> ADOLF EICHMANN, confessed executor of six million Jews during Nazi era, article written while awaiting trial in Israel, *Life*, Dec. 5, 1960.

I no longer remember exactly when, but it was even before Rome itself had been founded that the Jews could already write. It is very depressing for me to think of that people writing laws over 6,000 years of written history. But it tells me that they must be a people of the first magnitude, for law-givers have always been great.

> ADOLF EICHMANN, *ibid.*

146

But to sum it all up, I must say that I regret nothing. . . . I will not humble myself or repent in any way.
>ADOLF EICHMANN, *ibid.*

If someone had said to me, "Your father is a traitor"—I mean my own father is a traitor—and I had to kill him, I would have done it.
>ADOLF EICHMANN, on his devotion to duty, *New York Times*, April 22, 1961.

But what was done was not of my doing. I had the feeling of a Pontius Pilate. I felt that it was not with me that the guilt lay.
>ADOLF EICHMANN, *New York Herald Tribune*, June 27, 1961.

No one can demand that you be neutral toward the crime of genocide. If . . . there is a judge in the whole world who can be neutral toward this crime that judge is not fit to sit in judgment.
>GIDEON HAUSNER, Attorney General for Israel, defending legality of Eichmann trial, *New York Times*, April 12, 1961.

In Maidanek, Poland, there was only one place where the children were treated kindly; at the entrance to the gas chambers each one was handed a sweet.
>GIDEON HAUSNER, in indictment of Eichmann, *New York Times*, April 16, 1961.

He is responsible because of the conspiracy and the plots for all that happened to the Jewish people—from the shores of the Arctic Oceans to the Aegean Sea, from the Pyrenees to the Urals. But his criminal responsibility for oppression, for torment, for starvation, for despoliation, and for murder, derives from a legal principle which is very close to the principle of conspiracy. And that is the principle of the complicity in crime.
>GIDEON HAUSNER, summation in Eichmann trial, news summaries of Dec. 16, 1961.

My handkerchief is terribly important to me. It's the only thing in the country I can stick my nose into.
>CHAIM WEIZMANN, after retiring as the first President of Israel, *Time*, Nov. 17, 1952.

Japan

We want to open windows on to a wider world for our Crown Prince.
> VISCOUNT MATSUDAIRA, to Elizabeth Gray Vining, American who received the unprecedented invitation to tutor the Crown Prince of Japan, quoted in her book, *Windows for the Crown Prince*, Lippincott, 1952.

This afternoon at 4:15 at the Imperial Household Hospital, Her Highness the Crown Princess honorably effecting delivery, the honorable birth of a son occurred. The exalted mother and child are honorably healthy.
> JAPANESE RADIO, announcement of birth of a Prince second in line to throne, *Newsweek*, March 7, 1960.

There is a tremendous rush of voiceless voices.
> NOBUSKE KISHI, Premier, on demonstrations that caused cancellation of President Eisenhower's visit to Japan, *New York Times*, June 17, 1960.

Laos

I am a good friend to Communists abroad but I do not like them at home.
> SOUVANNA PHOUMA, Premier, defining the art of being a neutralist, *Life*, Nov. 3, 1961.

Mexico

A woman is a citizen who works for Mexico. We must not treat her differently from a man, except to honor her more.
> ADOLFO LOPEZ MATEOS, President, on the growing emancipation of women, *Time*, Oct. 12, 1959.

Netherlands

Let us all do the best we can. Leave the rest to God. He will not forsake this poor world. . . .
> QUEEN JULIANA, speech to U.S. Congress, *Time*, April 14, 1952.

Pakistan

The kingdoms and the crowns which the Moslems have lost in the course of history are far less important than the kingdom of the free and searching mind which they have lost in the process of intellectual stagnation.
MOHAMMAD AYUB KHAN, President, *New York Times*, Nov. 12, 1960.

Philippines

I have sat at the sumptuous tables of power, but I have not run away with the silverware.
DIOSDADA MACAPAGAL, President, on his career, *Time*, Nov. 24, 1961.

The tide of world affairs ebbs and flows in and out. Old empires die, new nations are born, alliances rise and vanish. But through all this vast confusion the mutual friendship of our two countries shines like a tenfold beacon in the night.
GENERAL DOUGLAS MACARTHUR, on 15th anniversary of Philippines' independence, *New York Times*, July 5, 1961.

South Africa

To remain neutral, in a situation where the laws of the land virtually criticized God for having created men of color, was the sort of thing I could not, as a Christian, tolerate.
ALBERT JOHN LUTHULI, a former Zulu chief, address on receiving Nobel Peace Prize, *Time*, Dec. 22, 1961.

Soviet Union

We will put our fingers around a glass together. We will put our hands in yours to shake in friendship. But we will not put our fingers on the ink pad.
NIKOLAI BULGANIN, Premier, condemning the fingerprinting of applicants for American visas, news reports of May 28, 1956.

149

They pay little attention to what we say and prefer to read tea leaves.
> NIKITA KHRUSHCHEV, on press interpretations of Soviet attitudes, July 5, 1955.

I know what I say at times is not very diplomatic.
> KHRUSHCHEV, at Geneva Conference, July 20, 1955.

Those who wait for that must wait until a shrimp learns to whistle.
> KHRUSHCHEV, on Russia's fidelity to Communism, Sept. 18, 1955.

Each year humanity takes a step towards Communism. Maybe not you, but at all events your grandson will surely be a Communist.
> KHRUSHCHEV, to William Hayter, British ambassador, news summaries of June 19, 1956.

Whether you like it or not, history is on our side. We will bury you!
> KHRUSHCHEV, to Western ambassadors at Kremlin reception, Nov. 17, 1956.*

If we could have the revolution over again, we would carry it out more sensibly and with smaller losses. But history does not repeat itself. The situation is favorable for us. If God existed, we would thank Him for it.
> KHRUSHCHEV, to Western ambassadors at reception at Polish Embassy, Moscow, Nov. 18, 1956.

The Communist must act like a surgeon who takes a sharp knife and operates on a man's body to cut out malignant growths and thus makes possible the further development and strengthening of the organism. This is our approach to the life of our society and to our work.
> KHRUSHCHEV, address on awarding Order of Lenin, *Pravda*, Jan. 14, 1957.

---

* Moscow later denied the remark, but when asked about it at the National Press Club in Washington, Sept. 17, 1959, Khrushchev said: "I really spoke about that, but my statement was deliberately distorted. What I meant was not physical burying of anyone at any time, but a change of the social system in the historical development of society." On Aug. 24, 1963, to Westerners in his audience at Split, Yugoslavia, the Premier remarked: "I once said, 'We will bury you,' and I got into trouble with it. Of course we will not bury you with a shovel. Your own working class will bury you."

After the liquidation of classes we have a monolithic society. Therefore, why found another party? That would be like voluntarily letting someone put a flea in your shirt.

> KHRUSHCHEV, addressing delegation of French Socialists, *Der Monat,* June, 1957.

They were black sheep in a good herd—we took the black sheep by the tail and threw them out.

> KHRUSHCHEV, on prominent Russian leaders ousted from Soviet Presidium, news reports of July 10, 1957.

We congratulated each other and went off to bed.

> KHRUSHCHEV, on launching of first earth satellite, news summaries of Nov. 1, 1957.

The outlines of its majestic bright edifice appear more and more clearly before the eyes of the people.

> KHRUSHCHEV, on emergence of Communism, address on 40th anniversary of Bolshevik Revolution, Nov. 6, 1957.

No matter how humble a man's beginnings, he achieves the stature of the office to which he is elected.

> KHRUSHCHEV, *Time,* Jan. 6, 1958.

We say the name of God, but that is only habit. We are atheists.

> KHRUSHCHEV, *ibid.*

. . . Only an idiot, pardon the word, will oppose this.

> KHRUSHCHEV, on progress that is possible in Communist countries, interview with *The Times,* London, Jan. 31, 1958.

Capitalism is at its ebb. . . . This does not mean that it is already lying down with its legs stretched out; much work has yet to be done to bring it to such a state. But this is inevitable, just as death inevitably comes to a living organism or plant after a specific stage of development.

> KHRUSHCHEV, address to Hungarian Academy of Sciences, April 9, 1958.

May she live long! I owe it all to her.
> KHRUSHCHEV, banquet toast to his wife, *Look*, April 15, 1958.

I regard Berlin as a test case, as a sort of litmus paper that will show the direction of Western intentions.
> KHRUSHCHEV, *The Observer*, London, Dec. 21, 1958.

The so-called free world constitutes the kingdom of the dollar . . .
> KHRUSHCHEV, address at 21st Congress of Communist Party, Jan. 27, 1959.

. . . Revolutions are not exportable.
> KHRUSHCHEV, declaration that Russia does not wish to impose Communism on other nations, *ibid.*

Heretofore, every peasant . . . knew only too well that when he had a horse he could manage his homestead and that without a horse he could not make his living. Now times have changed. The development of industry, the growth of the means of production: this is our powerful horse.
> KHRUSHCHEV, *ibid.*

The imperialists would like to destroy the Socialist countries as a hungry wolf would like to kill a lion, but here is the rub, his stomach is too small and the teeth, too, are not what they were—worn down, you know.
> KHRUSHCHEV, address at Leipzig trade union conference, March 7, 1959.

. . . The people are behaving toward Communism as they do toward new shoes; they are afraid that they might pinch them.
> KHRUSHCHEV, *ibid.*

Don't you have a machine that puts food into the mouth and pushes it down?
> KHRUSHCHEV, to U.S. Vice-President Nixon, on observing inventions in American model house at Moscow Fair, news reports of July 25, 1959.

152

I'm an old sparrow, so to say, and you cannot muddle me by your cries.
> KHRUSHCHEV, when heckled at dinner of Economics Club of New York, Sept. 17, 1959.

Let there be more corn and more meat and let there be no hydrogen bombs at all.
> KHRUSHCHEV, in Iowa on U.S. tour, news reports of Sept. 24, 1959.

Thank you all from the bottom of my heart for your hospitality and, as we say in Russia, for your bread and salt. Let us have more and more use for the short American word "O.K."
> KHRUSHCHEV, concluding his first visit to U.S., news reports of Sept. 28, 1959.

We do not sell ideas if they are not good. Ideas are not salami.
> KHRUSHCHEV, *New York Herald Tribune*, Feb. 11, 1960.

Figuratively speaking, our Socialist steed is full of energy and it has already graphically shown the whole world its wonderful qualities. As to the Capitalist steed which the United States is riding, as the saying goes, "There was a horse, but it is worn out," and it starts limping in both legs.
> KHRUSHCHEV, in address at New Delhi, *New York Herald Tribune*, Feb. 13, 1960.

We consider that the Monroe Doctrine has outlived its time, has outlived itself, has died, so to say, a natural death. Now the remains of this doctrine should best be buried as every dead body is so that it should not poison the air by its decay.
> KHRUSHCHEV, at Kremlin news conference, *New York Times*, July 13, 1960.

Comrades, we live at a splendid time: Communism has become the invincible force of our century. The further successes of Communism depend to an enormous degree on our will, our unity, our foresight and resolve. . . . Men of the future, Communists of the next generation, will envy us.
> KHRUSHCHEV, addressing Party conference, *Time*, April 7, 1961.

I greet you on a small piece of Soviet territory. Sometimes we drink out of a small glass but we speak with great feeling.

> KHRUSHCHEV, welcoming President Kennedy to Russian Embassy in Vienna, *New York Times,* June 13, 1961.

A mighty unifying thunderstorm, marking the springtime of mankind, is raging over the earth.

> KHRUSHCHEV, on publication of the 47,000-word "new program" of Communist Party, *Life,* Aug. 11, 1961.

Bombs do not choose. They will hit everything. I will not hesitate to give orders . . . to crush military bases of the North Atlantic bloc located in Greece. And they would not, of course, have any mercy on the olive groves or on the Acropolis, because bombs do not differentiate. . . . Perhaps someone is counting on declaring some cities to be "open" as they managed to do in the last war. . . . In the future, if nuclear weapons are unleashed there will be no front and no rear.

> KHRUSHCHEV, speaking at a "friendship rally" in Moscow, *New York Herald Tribune,* Aug. 12, 1961.

It is not a question of mooning him but of demooning him. Our national emblem is already on the moon, but we don't want to place a coffin beside it.

> KHRUSHCHEV, on landing a Soviet astronaut on moon, *New York Times,* Sept. 8, 1961.

Truly a little body often harbors a great soul.

> KHRUSHCHEV, on U.S. Communist Party, *New York Herald Tribune,* Oct. 22, 1961.

Communism must not be regarded as a table set with empty plates around which sit high-minded and fully equal peoples. To ask people to join such communism would be like inviting them to eat milk with an owl. It would be a parody of communism.

> KHRUSHCHEV, *New York Times,* March 7, 1962.

. . . No one is born a Communist. I know it from experience. In the Soviet Union farmers keep on looking in the barn for "their horses" even after they have given them to the collective.

> KHRUSHCHEV, speech in Rumania, *New York Herald Tribune,* June 21, 1962.

. . . The President of the United States is competing with the President of France in courting the old West German widow.

> KHRUSHCHEV, address in East Berlin following President Kennedy's visit to West Berlin, *New York Times*, July 3, 1963.

Russian-Chinese friendship is as firm and indestructible as the Himalayas, as deep as the Pacific, as vast as the Yangtze and the Volga.

> PRAVDA, Soviet state newspaper, *Dragon In the Kremlin* by Marvin Kalb, Dutton, 1961.

If any foreign minister begins to defend to the death a "peace conference" you can be sure his Government has already placed its orders for new battleships and airplanes.

> JOSEPH STALIN, quoted in reports of his death, March 5, 1953.

Tanganyika

Freedom to many means immediate betterment, as if by magic. . . . Unless I can meet at least some of these aspirations, my support will wane and my head will roll just as surely as the tickbird follows the rhino.

> JULIUS NYERERE, Prime Minister, *Time*, Dec. 15, 1961.

Turkey

Photographers are the only dictators in America.

> CELAL BAYAR, President, during visit to U.S., news summaries of Feb. 1, 1954.

Vietnam

Follow me if I advance! Kill me if I retreat! Revenge me if I die!

> NGO DINH DIEM, battle cry on becoming President of Vietnam in 1954, *Time*, Nov. 8, 1963.

. . . These Buddhist barbecues.

> MADAME NGO DINH NHU, referring to Buddhist monks who burned themselves to death in public protest of her family's regime that limited religious freedom. When Madame Nhu realized the expression had caused immense ill will she said it was an Americanism her daughter had learned from U.S. servicemen, *New York Herald Tribune*, Oct. 17, 1963.

They aren't interested in diplomacy but prefer to discuss the sex of angels.
MADAME NHU, on U.S. officials who would not receive her, quoted by CBS commentator Harry Reasoner, Oct. 20, 1963.

It was accidental suicide.
VIETNAM GOVERNMENT announcement contending that President Ngo Dinh Diem and his brother, Ngo Dinh Nhu, were not intentionally killed when their government was overthrown, *Time*, Nov. 15, 1963.

Education

There must be such a thing as a child with average ability, but you can't find a parent who will admit that it is his child. . . . Start a program for gifted children, and every parent demands that his child be enrolled.

> Thomas D. Bailey, Florida state superintendent of schools, *Wall Street Journal*, Dec. 17, 1962.

I am quite sure that in the hereafter she will take me by the hand and lead me to my proper seat. I always have a great reverence for teachers. For teachers, both lay and clerical, and for nurses. They are the most underpaid people in the world for what they do.

> Bernard M. Baruch, recalling one of his early teachers, news summaries of Aug. 29, 1955.

Teaching is not a lost art, but the regard for it is a lost tradition.

> Jacques Barzun, dean, Graduate School, Columbia University, *Newsweek*, Dec. 5, 1955.

The test and the use of man's education is that he finds pleasure in the exercise of his mind.

> Jacques Barzun, "Science vs. the Humanities: A Truce to the Nonsense on Both Sides," *Saturday Evening Post*, May 3, 1958.

The drums of Africa still beat in my heart. They will not let me rest while there is a single Negro boy or girl without a chance to prove his worth.

> Mary McLeod Bethune, president, Bethune-Cookman College, news reports of May 19, 1955.

Work 'em hard, play 'em hard, feed 'em up to the nines, and send 'em to bed so tired that they are asleep before their heads are on the pillow.

> FRANK BOYDEN of Deerfield Academy, on how to run a successful prep school, news summaries of Jan. 2, 1954.

I want to feel that boys can discuss things with me anytime. The problem is important now, not later. It may disappear after a good lunch, but he doesn't know that now.

> FRANK BOYDEN, *Life*, Nov. 30, 1962.

I never reprimand a boy in the evening—darkness and a troubled mind are a poor combination.

> FRANK BOYDEN, *ibid.*

If I take refuge in ambiguity, I assure you that it's quite conscious.

> KINGMAN BREWSTER, JR., interviewed on evening of his appointment as 17th president of Yale, *New York Herald Tribune*, Oct. 14, 1963.

She knows what is the best purpose of education: not to be frightened by the best but to treat it as part of daily life.

> JOHN MASON BROWN, tribute to Edith Hamilton, classical scholar and author, *Publishers' Weekly*, March 17, 1958.

Remember, you have been spared the unintentional cruelty of that kind of progressive education which misleads the young into believing that they will always be free to do what they want to do, at the moment and in the way they want to do it. The reality of life is quite different. Most people spend most of their days doing what they do not want to do in order to earn the right, at times, to do what they may desire.

> JOHN MASON BROWN, graduation address at Groton, *Esquire*, April, 1960.

The shrewd guess, the fertile hypothesis, the courageous leap to a tentative conclusion—these are the most valuable coin of the thinker at work. But in most schools guessing is heavily penalized and is associated somehow with laziness.

> JEROME S. BRUNER, psychologist, *The Process of Education*, Harvard University Press, 1960.

When her last child is off to school, we don't want the talented woman wasting her time in work far below her capacity. We want her to come out running.

> MARY BUNTING, president, Radcliffe College, on establishing an institute for independent study for gifted women, *Life*, Jan. 13, 1961.

Four-fifths of our undergraduates feel inferior for life.

> SIR ALEXANDER CARR-SAUNDERS, London School of Economics, on social chasm between quasi-aristocratic Oxford and Cambridge vs provincial universities, *The Anatomy of Britain*, by Anthony Sampson, Harper & Row, 1962.

The library is not a shrine for the worship of books. It is not a temple where literary incense must be burned or where one's devotion to the bound book is expressed in ritual. A library, to modify the famous metaphor of Socrates, should be the delivery room for the birth of ideas—a place where history comes to life.

> NORMAN COUSINS, *American Library Association Bulletin*, Oct., 1954.

The man who reads only for improvement is beyond the hope of much improvement before he begins.

> JONATHAN DANIELS, *Three Presidents and Their Books*, University of Illinois Press, 1956.

The American male at the peak of his physical powers and appetites, driving a hundred and sixty big white horses across the scenes of an increasingly open society, with week-end money in his pocket and with little prior exposure to trouble and tragedy, personifies "an accident going out to happen." He is not always a college undergraduate, and not all undergraduates are trouble-prone, but I am sure that any close observer of the campus will agree that there is no more vulnerable human combination than an undergraduate.

> JOHN SLOAN DICKEY, president, Dartmouth College, "Conscience and the Undergraduate," *Atlantic*, April, 1955.

The college undergraduate is a lot of things—many of them as familiar, predictable, and responsible as the bounce of a basketball, and others as startling (and occasionally as disastrous) as the bounce of a football.

> JOHN SLOAN DICKEY, *ibid.*

Philanthropy is an American habit and the modern foundation is an American invention. To make human beings healthier, happier, wiser, more conscious of the rich possibilities of human existence and more capable of realizing them. . . .

> CHARLES DOLLARD, president, Carnegie Corporation, reply to a Congressional committee investigating alleged subversive activities by tax-free foundations, news summaries of Dec. 28, 1954.

I wouldn't attach too much importance to these student riots. I remember when I was a student at the Sorbonne in Paris I used to go out and riot occasionally.

> JOHN FOSTER DULLES, Secretary of State, on student riots at U.S. Embassy in Indonesia, news summaries of April 15, 1958.

. . . Anyone who solemnly announces in the year 1962 that he will be guided in matters of English usage by a dictionary published in 1934 is talking ignorant and pretentious nonsense.

> BERGEN EVANS, professor of English, Northwestern University, *Atlantic*, May, 1962, in defense of *Webster's Third New International Dictionary*.

A school free to concentrate on those services that only schools can give is in a position to do more effective teaching than one that must be all things to all children and to their parents, too.

> JOHN H. FISCHER, dean, Teachers College, Columbia University, *Saturday Review*, Sept. 17, 1960.

The teaching of reading—all over the United States, in all the schools, in all the text books—is totally wrong and flies in the face of all logic and common sense. Johnny couldn't read . . . for the simple reason that nobody ever showed him how. Johnny's only problem was that he was unfortunately exposed to an ordinary American school.

> RUDOLF FLESCH, *Why Johnny Can't Read*, Harper & Row, 1955, a book that called for new standards for the teaching of reading.

Of dictionaries, as of newspapers, it might be said that the bad ones are too bad to exist, the good ones too good not to be better.

> WILSON FOLLETT, author and editor, beginning a review of *Webster's Third New International Dictionary* in *Atlantic*, January, 1962.

Webster III, behind its front of passionless objectivity, is in truth a fighting document. And the enemy it is out to destroy is every obstinate vestige of linguistic punctilio, every surviving influence that makes for the upholding of standards, every criterion for distinguishing between better usages and worse. In other words, it has gone bodily to the school that construes traditions as enslaving, the rudimentary principles of syntax as crippling, and taste as irrelevant.

WILSON FOLLETT, *ibid.*

They go forth [into the world] with well-developed bodies, fairly developed minds and undeveloped hearts. An undeveloped heart—not a cold one. The difference is important . . .

E. M. FORSTER, novelist, on British public school boys, quoted in article on Winchester College, *Life*, April 2, 1951.

As long as learning is connected with earning, as long as certain jobs can only be reached through exams, so long must we take the examination system seriously. If another ladder to employment was contrived, much so-called education would disappear, and no one would be a penny the stupider.

E. M. FORSTER, *New York Times*, Nov. 24, 1963.

Education is the ability to listen to almost anything without losing your temper or your self-confidence.

ROBERT FROST, *Reader's Digest*, April, 1960.

Education doesn't change life much. It just lifts trouble to a higher plane of regard. . . . College is a refuge from hasty judgment.

ROBERT FROST, *Quote*, July 9, 1961.

. . . Hanging around until you've caught on.

ROBERT FROST, defining a college education, *Philadelphia Inquirer*, Jan. 30, 1963.

. . . I was still learning when I taught my last class.

CLAUDE FUESS, on retirement after 40 years as teacher and head of Phillips Andover Academy, *Independent Schoolmaster*, Atlantic-Little, Brown, 1952.

161

The exchange program is the thing that reconciles me to all the difficulties of political life. It's the one activity that gives me some hope that the human race won't commit suicide, though I still wouldn't count on it.
> SENATOR J. WILLIAM FULBRIGHT, on Fulbright Fellowships, *New Yorker*, May 10, 1958.

. . . I was resolved to sustain and preserve in my college the bite of the mind, the chance to stand face to face with truth, the good life lived in a small, various, highly articulate and democratic society.
> VIRGINIA GILDERSLEEVE, dean emeritus, Barnard College, in autobiography, *Many a Good Crusade*, Macmillan, 1954.

The ability to think straight, some knowledge of the past, some vision of the future, some skill to do useful service, some urge to fit that service into the well-being of the community—these are the most vital things education must try to produce. If we can achieve them in the citizens of our land, then, given the right to knowledge and the free use thereof, we shall have brought to America the wisdom and the courage to match her destiny.
> VIRGINIA GILDERSLEEVE, concluding autobiography, *ibid*.

If you feel that you have both feet planted on level ground, then the university has failed you.
> ROBERT GOHEEN, president, Princeton University, baccalaureate address, *Time*, June 23, 1961.

The commencement speaker represents the continuation of a barbaric custom that has no basis in logic. If the state of oratory that inundates our educational institutions during the month of June could be transformed into rain for Southern California, we should all be happy awash or waterlogged.
> SAMUEL GOULD, chancellor, University of California, *Time*, June 27, 1960.

The responsibility of a dictionary is to record the language, not set its style.
> PHILIP GOVE, editor-in-chief of *Webster's Third New International Dictionary*, letter to *Life*, Nov. 17, 1961.

I've got my diploma and it's filled in with my name, Ernest Green. And I feel awful good about it.

> ERNEST GREEN, first Negro to be graduated from Central High School, Little Rock, Ark., *Christian Science Monitor*, May 28, 1958.

There she sits, a figure of learning, a Queen Victoria with brains, vast, booted, bosomy, comprised of elements which are intellectual, emotional, comfortable, romantic, olfactory, personal, universal.

> GEOFFREY GRIGSON, description of British Museum Reading Room on its hundredth anniversary, *The Observer*, London, May 19, 1957.

A Socrates in every classroom.

> WHITNEY GRISWOLD, president, Yale University, on his ambitious standard for building a Yale faculty, *Time*, June 11, 1951.

Year after year these congregations hear the same exhortations, the same appeals to youth to sally forth, knight-errant, and slay the same old dragons in the same old sinful world. Yet these dragons, unlike their mortal cousins the dinosaurs, have managed to keep well ahead of the game. If Darwin himself had picked them as favorites in the cosmic sweepstakes, they could not have run a better race.

> WHITNEY GRISWOLD, baccalaureate address, June 10, 1956.

Could Hamlet have been written by a committee, or the Mona Lisa painted by a club? Could the New Testament have been composed as a conference report? Creative ideas do not spring from groups. They spring from individuals. The divine spark leaps from the finger of God to the finger of Adam . . .

> WHITNEY GRISWOLD, baccalaureate address, June 8, 1957.

There is no lack of opportunity for learning among us. What is lacking is a respect for it . . . an honest respect such as we now have for technical competence or business success . . . We honor learning, but do not believe in it. We reward it with lengthy obituaries and a wretched living wage. Rather than submit to it ourselves, we hire substitutes; rather than cultivate our own brains, we pick theirs. We spend as much time and energy on short-cuts to learning and imitations of learning as we do on learning itself.

> WHITNEY GRISWOLD, address to American Academy and National Institute of Arts and Letters, *New York Times*, May 22, 1958.

163

Books won't stay banned. They won't burn. Ideas won't go to jail. In the long run of history, the censor and the inquisitor have always lost. The only sure weapon against bad ideas is better ideas.
> WHITNEY GRISWOLD, *New York Times*, Feb. 24, 1959.

It is a jumble of English for script writers, and radio English and TV English, and everything but English English—almost.
> WHITNEY GRISWOLD, on teaching of English in public secondary schools, *Christian Science Monitor*, Dec. 28, 1960.

A college education is a taste for knowledge, a taste for philosophy, a capacity to explore, question and perceive relationships between fields of knowledge and experience.
> WHITNEY GRISWOLD, on revising Yale's curriculum; remark recalled in report of his death at 56, *New York Times*, April 20, 1963.

The world is always upside down to a baccalaureate speaker. . . . Things have got to be wrong in order that they may be deplored.
> WHITNEY GRISWOLD, *ibid.*

The presidency of a large university is an anachronism. The public demands that the president be everywhere at all times. He is thought to be omniscient, omnipresent, and Mr. Chips all rolled into one.
> WHITNEY GRISWOLD, in an interview in 1955 with a student reporter from *Yale Daily News;* recalled in *New York Herald Tribune*, Oct. 13, 1963.

But the day when the president can play the role of "Prexy" is gone. . . . He is like a fireman who sees six fires from the window, dashes out to extinguish one, and hopes somebody else will get the other five. This is not a complaint. It's a plain statement of fact.
> WHITNEY GRISWOLD, *ibid.*

Every citizen of this country, whether he pounds nails, raises corn, designs rockets or writes poetry, should be taught to know and love his American heritage; to use the language well; to understand the physical universe, and to enjoy the arts. The dollars he gains in the absence of enlightenment like this will be earned in drudgery and spent in ignorance.

> Calvin Gross, first address after becoming superintendent of New York City public schools, *New York Times*, April 27, 1963.

To be able to be caught up into the world of thought—that is educated.

> Edith Hamilton, *Saturday Evening Post*, Sept. 27, 1958.

Education is a difficult enough process under any condition because educational effort is primarily an expression of hope on the part of the student . . . The Negro pupil is obliged to be more hopeful than the white student. He is asked to have faith and confidence which at the moment he is in school seems unreasonable and unjustifiable.

> Carl Hansen, superintendent of schools, Washington, D.C., *Fortune*, Sept., 1963.

What's the point in any writer's trying to compose clear and graceful prose, to avoid solecisms, to maintain a sense of decorum and continuity in that magnificent instrument, the English language, if that peerless authority, Webster's Unabridged, surrenders abjectly to the permissive school of speech? . . . Relativism is the reigning philosophy of our day, in all fields. Not merely in language, but in ethics, in politics, in every field of human behavior. There is no right or wrong—it is all merely custom and superstition to believe so. If the majority behave a certain way, that is the way to behave. Popularity gives sanction to everything.

> Sydney J. Harris, columnist, *Chicago Daily News*, Oct. 20, 1961, on *Webster's Third New International Dictionary*.

The end product of education, yours and mine and everybody's, is the total pattern of reactions and possible reactions we have inside ourselves.

> S. I. Hayakawa, semantics authority, "How Words Change Our Lives," *Saturday Evening Post*, Dec. 27, 1958.

There is a danger of adding to our lexicon the term "guilt by *un*association," which might be defined as the practice of one zealot's suspecting another who is not as noisy as he is.

> Henry Heald, president, Ford Foundation, *New York Times*, Sept. 30, 1956.

What, precisely, is the role of America's foundations in today's world? They must take the risks that governments, individuals and other institutions cannot assume. They must seek and support new ways of attacking basic human problems. They must invest in experiment, innovation and demonstration. They must be a source not merely of money for worthy causes but of the "venture capital" essential to human progress.
> HENRY HEALD, *New York Times*, March 18, 1962.

Professional jargon is unpleasant. Translating it into English is a bore. I narrow-mindedly outlawed the word "unique." Practically every press release contains it. Practically nothing ever is.
> FRED HECHINGER, on resigning as education editor, *New York Herald Tribune*, Aug. 5, 1956.

The invention of I.Q. did a great disservice to creativity in education. . . . Individuality, personality, originality, are too precious to be meddled with by amateur psychiatrists whose patterns for a "wholesome personality" are inevitably their own.
> JOEL HILDEBRAND, professor emeritus of chemistry, University of California, address to national conference on "Education for Creativity in the Sciences," *New York Times*, June 16, 1963.

No greater nor more affectionate honor can be conferred on an American than to have a public school named after him.
> HERBERT HOOVER, at dedication of Herbert Hoover Junior High School, San Francisco, June 5, 1956.

There's no reason why the University should be stuck with me at 51 because I was a promising young man at 30.
> ROBERT M. HUTCHINS, announcing his resignation as chancellor of University of Chicago, *Time*, Jan. 8, 1951.

. . . Why is it that the boy or girl who on June 15 receives his degree, eager, enthusiastic, outspoken, idealistic, reflective, and independent, is on the following Sept. 15, or even June 16 . . . dull, uninspiring, shifty, pliable and attired in a double-breasted, blue serge suit? The answer must lie in the relative weakness of the higher education, compared with the forces that make everybody think and act like everybody else.
> ROBERT M. HUTCHINS, farewell address at University of Chicago, *Time*, Feb. 12, 1951.

166

Education is a kind of continuing dialogue, and a dialogue assumes, in the nature of the case, different points of view . . .

> ROBERT M. HUTCHINS, defining the nature of academic freedom, testimony to a House committee investigating grants to persons disloyal to U.S., *Time*, Dec. 8, 1952.

It is not so important to be serious as it is to be serious about the important things The monkey wears an expression of seriousness which would do credit to any college student, but the monkey is serious because he itches.

> ROBERT M. HUTCHINS, *Quote*, Aug. 3, 1958.

In the Middle West, the high school is the place where the band practices.

> ROBERT M. HUTCHINS, president, Fund for the Republic, in pamphlet quoted in *New York Herald Tribune*, April 22, 1963.

It has been said that we have not had the three R's in America, we had the six R's: remedial readin', remedial 'ritin', and remedial 'rithmetic.

> ROBERT M. HUTCHINS, *ibid.*

We have entered an age in which education is not just a luxury permitting some men an advantage over others. It has become a necessity without which a person is defenseless in this complex, industrialized society. . . . We have truly entered the century of the educated man.

> LYNDON B. JOHNSON, U.S. Vice President, Tufts University commencement address, June 9, 1963.

The scramble to get into college is going to be so terrible in the next few years that students are going to put up with almost anything, even an education.

> BARNABY C. KEENEY, president, Brown University, *Time*, Aug. 29, 1955.

Firm standards require that a distinction be made between success and failure, between excellence and mediocrity. . . . No man or woman is uniformly successful in mature life; we must all expect a rather high percentage of failure in the things we attempt.

> BARNABY KEENEY, *Atlantic*, November, 1960.

167

A kind of state-supported baby-sitting service.
> THE REVEREND GERALD KENNEDY, Methodist bishop, on American education, *Time*, April 11, 1960.

. . . The human mind is our fundamental resource.
> PRESIDENT KENNEDY, message to Congress on state of U.S. education, Feb. 20, 1961.

A child miseducated is a child lost.
> PRESIDENT KENNEDY, State of the Union address, Jan. 11, 1962.

I want to emphasize in the great concentration which we now place upon scientists and engineers how much we still need the men and women educated in the liberal tradition, willing to take the long look, undisturbed by prejudices and slogans of the moment, who attempt to make an honest judgment on difficult events.
> PRESIDENT KENNEDY, address at University of North Carolina, Oct. 12, 1962.

Modern cynics and skeptics. . . . see no harm in paying those to whom they entrust the minds of their children a smaller wage than is paid to those to whom they entrust the care of their plumbing.
> PRESIDENT KENNEDY, address on 90th anniversary of Vanderbilt University, May 19, 1963.

A university anywhere can aim no higher than to be as British as possible for the sake of the undergraduates, as German as possible for the sake of the public at large—and as confused as possible for the preservation of the whole uneasy balance.
> CLARK KERR, president, University of California, lecturing at Harvard on "The Uses of the University," *New York Times*, April 26, 1963.

The most important function of education at any level is to develop the personality of the individual and the significance of his life to himself and to others. This is the basic architecture of a life; the rest is ornamentation and decoration of the structure.
> GRAYSON KIRK, president, Columbia University, *Quote*, Jan. 27, 1963.

168

Remember that critics always want you to imitate the great artists of the present and the past, but that great artists never imitate their equals; they imitate (and plagiarize from) their inferiors. If you submit to the influence of the critics, they will hound you into the shadow of some imperious, if dead, perfection.

> JOHN KOUWENHOVEN, professor of English, Barnard College, "The Wellsprings of Design," *Architectural Record*, April, 1960.

Fulbright is responsible for the greatest movement of scholars across the face of the earth since the fall of Constantinople in 1453.

> R. B. McCALLUM, master of Pembroke College, Oxford, on Fulbright Fellowships, *Saturday Evening Post*, March 23, 1963.

There are few earthly things more beautiful than a university . . . a place where those who hate ignorance may strive to know, where those who perceive truth may strive to make others see.

> JOHN MASEFIELD, poet laureate, tribute to English universities quoted by President Kennedy in commencement address at American University, Washington, June 10, 1963.

The dearest hope of the parent for his child is that he become all that he is capable of being. This is precisely the goal of school and college and exactly what city, state and nation strive for.

> DR. MORRIS MEISTER, at installation as president of Bronx Community College, *New York Times*, May 12, 1959.

It is just as important, perhaps more important, for the teacher to have the benefit of personal counseling when he needs it as it is for the student.

> DR. WILLIAM MENNINGER, address to National Association of Secondary School Principals, news reports of Feb. 24, 1954.

I was well beaten myself, and I am the better for it.

> FIELD MARSHAL VISCOUNT MONTGOMERY, on corporal punishment in schools, news reports of Nov. 8, 1955.

Here the skeptic finds chaos and the believer further evidence that the hand that made us is divine.

> ROBERT MOSES, New York park commissioner, at reopening of Hayden Planetarium, *New York Herald Tribune*, Feb. 3, 1960.

There are two ways to teach mathematics. One is to take real pains toward creating understanding—visual aids, that sort of thing. The other is the old British system of teaching until you're blue in the face.

> JAMES R. NEWMAN, compiler of 2,535-page *The World of Mathematics,* quoted in *New York Times,* Sept. 30, 1956.

The true business of liberal education is greatness.

> NATHAN PUSEY, president, Harvard University, *Time,* March 1, 1954.

Our task is to keep American life reasonable. This is more than any two institutions alone—or sometimes, I think, all of us together, can do.

> NATHAN PUSEY, on being made an honorary Doctor of Laws by Yale, news reports of June 14, 1954.

The close observer soon discovers that the teacher's task is not to implant facts but to place the subject to be learned in front of the learner and, through sympathy, emotion, imagination, and patience, to awaken in the learner the restless drive for answers and insights which enlarge the personal life and give it meaning.

> NATHAN PUSEY, *New York Times,* March 22, 1959.

Each of us has a life to live and we shall want to spend it as well as may be . . . as alert, fair, concerned citizens of a complicated human world, aware in some fashion of God's high purpose for this earth of ours, eager to have a part in His plan for it, and to find joy in the process.

> NATHAN PUSEY, conclusion of baccalaureate address to Class of 1962 *

We live in a time of such rapid change and growth of knowledge that only he who is in a fundamental sense a scholar—that is, a person who continues to learn and inquire—can hope to keep pace, let alone play the role of guide. . . . We have created for ourselves a manner of living in America in which a little learning can no longer serve our needs.

> NATHAN PUSEY, *The Age of the Scholar: Observations on Education in a Troubled Decade,* Belknap Press of Harvard University Press, 1963.

---

* In his reply to Harvard students who protested abandonment of Latin in diplomas, Dr. Pusey quoted a poem written by Jane Hess, a junior at Bryn Mawr College:

What's pat in Latin,
And chic in Greek,
I always distinguish
More easily in English.

It is perhaps treason for me to say it but cast aside the richest book to listen to the right person.

> HERBERT PUTNAM, sometime librarian of Congress, news summaries of April 19, 1955.

Adjustment as an educational goal is a pricked balloon. To adjust to the twentieth century is to come to terms with madness. What is needed is the adjustment of our environment to ourselves, or rather to what we would like ourselves to be.

> MAX RAFFERTY, California state superintendent of public instruction, *Suffer Little Children*, Devin-Adair, 1962.

Russia's real threat to us will come through their educational and not through their military processes. Military systems and techniques are transitory—they now change every few years. An intelligent and well educated body of citizens is something you will have forever.

> VICE ADMIRAL HYMAN G. RICKOVER, *New York Herald Tribune*, Aug. 21, 1960.

When we exchanged the short undergraduate gown for the B.A.-M.A. gown and hood, we put on more than an emblem of brief scholastic achievement. We put on the mantle of humility before great learning; we put on the love of learning and belief in its significance; we put on the responsibility to use all that great teachers had given us, the duty not to let the torch go out unheeded.

> VIRGINIA RIDLEY, "American Girl at Oxford," *Christian Science Monitor*, Oct. 21, 1958.

Scholarship is polite argument.

> PHILIP RIEFF, associate professor, University of California, *New York Herald Tribune*, Jan. 1, 1961.

A degree is not an education, and the confusion on this point is perhaps the gravest weakness in American thinking about education.

> PROSPECT FOR AMERICA: *The Rockefeller Panel Reports*, Doubleday, 1961.

. . . A university where, at last, the Jews are hosts, and not guests as we have always been before.

> ABRAM SACHAR, president, Brandeis University, on his institution's tenth anniversary, Nov. 19, 1956.

171

Education is the established church of the United States. It is one of the religions that Americans believe in. It has its own orthodoxy, its pontiffs and its noble buildings.
> SIR MICHAEL SADLER, *New York Times*, Sept. 1, 1956.

Harvard [was a place of] generous intellectual sincerity . . . [but] such spiritual penury and moral confusion as to offer nothing but a lottery ticket or a chance at the grab-bag to the orphan mind.
> GEORGE SANTAYANA, on his 20 years as a philosophy professor at Harvard, *Santayana: The Later Years* by Daniel Cory, Braziller, 1963.

In education, the closeness of students to a good and great man or woman is the finest we can offer our children.
> SEYMOUR ST. JOHN, headmaster, Choate School, "Hard Education or Soft?" *Vogue*, Jan. 15, 1958.

I hitched my wagon to an electron rather than the proverbial star.
> DAVID SARNOFF, chairman of the board, Radio Corporation of America, on receiving an honorary high school diploma from New York high school he quit in 1906, *New York Times*, April 4, 1958.

You ought not to educate a woman as if she were a man, or to educate her as if she were not.
> GEORGE SCHUSTER, president emeritus, Hunter College, *The Ground I Walked On*, Farrar, Straus, 1961.

We have asked ourselves if beauty and brawn do not deserve a place on our campus as well as brains. The idea is not to lower our standards, but to attract a greater variety of Americans who are qualified to meet them. The ordinary American boy, who will only make a million in later life, the ordinary girl, who wants a husband as well as a diploma, are as welcome here as the Quiz Kid.
> ALAN SIMPSON, on becoming dean of reorganized undergraduate college, University of Chicago, in a move which erased last vestige of former President Robert Hutchins' controversial "A.B. in two years" program, *New York Times*, May 21, 1959.

172

I am not an educational theorist but I think I know what an educated man looks like. He is thoroughly inoculated against humbug, thinks for himself and tries to give his thoughts, in speech or on paper, some style.

> ALAN SIMPSON, on becoming president of Vassar College, *Newsweek*, July 1, 1963.

It is a rare thing for a student to be taught by only one tutor. If he should by rare chance have been indoctrinated by Mr. A., he will certainly be liberated by Mr. B.

> C. A. SIMPSON, dean, Christ Church, Oxford, answering a charge that American students might come to cherish British crown above Stars and Stripes, *Saturday Evening Post*, March 23, 1963.

Education is a weapon, whose effects depend on who holds it in his hands and at whom it is aimed.

> JOSEPH STALIN, interview with H. G. Wells, quoted in reports of Stalin's death, March 5, 1953.

. . . We must recover the element of quality in our traditional pursuit of equality. We must not, in opening our schools to everyone, confuse the idea that all should have equal chance with the notion that all have equal endowments.

> ADLAI E. STEVENSON, address to United Parents Association, *New York Times*, April 6, 1958.

Respect for intellectual excellence, the restoration of vigor and discipline to our ideas of study, curricula which aim at strengthening intellectual fiber and stretching the power of young minds, personal commitment and responsibility—these are the pre-conditions of educational recovery in America today; and, I believe, they have always been the pre-conditions of happiness and sanity for the human race.

> ADLAI E. STEVENSON, *ibid*.

A student is not a professional athlete. . . . He is not a little politician or junior senator looking for angles . . . an amateur promoter, a glad-hander, embryo Rotarian, café-society leader, quiz kid, or man about town. A student is a person who is learning to fulfill his powers and to find ways of using them in the service of mankind.

> HAROLD TAYLOR, author and educator, news summaries of Sept. 3, 1956.

There is only one way to read a book, to give yourself up to it, alone, without instruction as to what you should be finding in it, without the necessity of making it into a series of points, but enjoying it, coming to know in personal terms what is in the mind of the writer.
> HAROLD TAYLOR, "The Private World of the Man With A Book," *Saturday Review*, Jan. 7, 1961.

. . . Most of the most important experiences that truly educate cannot be arranged ahead of time with any precision. . . .
> HAROLD TAYLOR, *ibid*.

The ends are achieved by indirect means—something said in private conversation one day in the street, a remark by a teacher in the middle of a discussion, a book picked up in someone's room . . .
> HAROLD TAYLOR, *ibid*.

. . . Balliol College is a Victorian Gothic pile of no great distinction. . . . Yet it sits at the head of Oxford's intellectual table—a proud hatchery of Prime Ministers, archbishops, cardinals and viceroys.
> TIME, July 12, 1963, on 700th anniversary of one of Oxford's best known colleges.

Whether or not Balliol really was 700—an agreed age more than a historic fact—they cheerily drank the ancient toast, *Floreat domus de Balliol*, meaning, roughly, boola, boola Balliol.
> TIME, *ibid*.

Dignified, sequestered but not cut off, with a good table and a good cellar, with something but not too much to do, with ample scope for the acquired talent of bringing committees to the point, with real influence in a small and select community, the headship of an Oxford or Cambridge college seems just the job for an eminent public servant of scholarly tastes who may be contemplating a less strenuous occupation.
> THE TIMES, London, Feb. 13, 1962, editorial commending choice of prominent men for academic posts.

. . . Vice-chancellors belong to a new class of academic administrators, with a load of work which the permanent head of a government department would be in no hurry to exchange for his own. It might be different if they, too, were in the happy position of having at their disposal positions of dignity not devoid of influence and positions of ease not devoid of occupation.

> THE TIMES, London, on attracting prominent men for academic posts outside Cambridge and Oxford, *ibid.*

The function of genius is not to give new answers, but to pose new questions which time and mediocrity can resolve.

> H. R. TREVOR-ROPER, regius professor of modern history, Oxford University, *Men and Events*, Harper & Row, 1958.

For my confirmation, I didn't get a watch and my first pair of long pants, like most Lutheran boys. I got a telescope. My mother thought it would make the best gift.

> WERNHER VON BRAUN, rocket scientist, *Time*, Feb. 17, 1958.

. . . It is disturbing to have lost the feeling of belonging to one reassuring community, to New England, or to the United States, or to Western Civilization. . . . But it is exciting and inspiring to be among the first to hail and accept the only fraternal community that finally can be valid —that painfully emerging unity of those who live on the one inhabited star.

> THORNTON WILDER, playwright, commencement address at Harvard, *Time*, July 2, 1951.

The lexicographer is part Gallup, part IBM machine, part voting booth.

> GARRY WILLS, on *Webster's Third New International Dictionary*, in *National Review*, Feb. 13, 1962.

Schoolmasters and parents exist to be grown out of.

> SIR JOHN WOLFENDEN, *Sunday Times*, London, July 13, 1958.

We're trying to show that we're not a little bit of England in America, but a place for Americans to gain a better perspective on their own history. All the fundamental concepts which make up the kind of people we are today had their modern conception in the Tudor and Stuart periods. For us, that's the milk in the coconut.

> LOUIS BOOKER WRIGHT, director, Folger Shakespeare Library, Washington, news summaries of May 9, 1955.

Those who misrepresent the normal experiences of life, who decry being controversial, who shun risk, are enemies of the American way of life, whatever the piety of their vocal professions and the patriotic flavor of their platitudes.

HENRY WRISTON, president emeritus, Brown University, *Wall Street Journal*, June 1, 1960.

A guidance counselor who has made a fetish of security, or who has unwittingly surrendered his thinking to economic determinism, may steer a youth away from his dream of becoming a poet, an artist, a musician, or any other of thousands of things, because it offers no security, it does not pay well, there are no vacancies, it has no "future." Among all the tragic consequences of depression and war, this suppression of personal self-expression through one's life work is among the most poignant.

HENRY WRISTON, *ibid.*

Medicine

The dedicated physician is constantly striving for a balance between personal, human values [and] scientific realities and the inevitabilities of God's will.

> Dr. David Allman, president, AMA (American Medical Association), *The Brotherhood of Healing,* address to regional meeting, National Conference of Christians and Jews, Feb. 12, 1958.

Life is precious to the old person. He is not interested merely in thoughts of yesterday's good life and tomorrow's path to the grave. He does not want his later years to be a sentence of solitary confinement in society. Nor does he want them to be a death watch.

> Dr. David Allman, *The Right to Be Useful,* address to AMA Conference on Aging, Boston, Sept. 17, 1959.

There are no diseases of the aged, but simply diseases among the aged.

> American Medical Association, statement read by AMA president-elect Dr. Leonard Larson, to Senate Finance Committee, June 27, 1960.

When it comes to your health, I recommend frequent doses of that rare commodity among Americans—common sense. We are rapidly becoming a land of hypochondriacs, from the ulcer-and-martini executives in the big city to the patent medicine patrons in the sulphur-and-molasses belt.

> Dr. Vincent Askey, president, AMA, *The Land of Hypochondriacs,* address at Bakersfield, Calif., Oct. 20, 1960.

There are no such things as incurables, there are only things for which man has not found a cure.

> Bernard Baruch, address to President's Committee on Employment of the Physically Handicapped, news reports of May 1, 1954.

177

We sit at breakfast, we sit on the train on the way to work, we sit at work, we sit at lunch, we sit all afternoon . . . a hodgepodge of sagging livers, sinking gall bladders, drooping stomachs, compressed intestines, and squashed pelvic organs.

> Dr. John Button, Jr., address to American Osteopathic Association, *Newsweek*, Aug. 6, 1956.

Discoverer of the vaccine for the prevention of poliomyelitis, that scourge which has caused dread in the hearts of every family, not only in America, but throughout the world; his is a name that will go down in history and will be spoken amongst men in words of wonder and gratitude.

> Columbia University, conferring honorary Doctorate of Science on Jonas Edward Salk, June 1, 1955.

When has lasting greatness ever been achieved by one who sought greatness for itself rather than allowing it to move quietly upon him as he worked for others? It has never been done. It cannot be done. What Dooley, or what Rusk, or Kendall or Schweitzer set out to do anything but help his neighbor in the way he knew best?

> Dr. George Fister, president, AMA, address to Southwestern Surgical Conference, Mexico City, April 22, 1963.

A good gulp of hot whisky at bedtime—it's not very scientific, but it helps.

> Sir Alexander Fleming, discoverer of penicillin, on treatment of common cold, news summaries of March 22, 1954.

. . . The social climate must be changed so that smoking is looked upon as it used to be—a damned dirty habit and a vice.

> D. N. Goldstein, M.D., editorial, "Spare the Young," *Wisconsin Medical Journal*, September, 1963.

Striving to outdo one's companions on the golf course and tennis court or in the swimming pool constitutes several socially acceptable forms of suicide.

> Dr. George Griffith, professor of medicine, University of Southern California, on weekend athletics by men over forty, news summaries of Oct. 21, 1955.

When I began practice, if someone came to me with a pain in the lower right abdomen, I was relatively safe in assuming it was either appendicitis or green apples. Today, in addition to these two possibilities, it is also highly probable that the patient is suffering—really and acutely—from the fact that his wife of 40 years wants to leave him to join the Peace Corps or Richard Burton. Or the man might have Stockholder's Syndrome or Khrushchev Colic. It will be up to you to find out—you will get a very practical education in the symptoms of pressure.

> Dr. Gunnar Gundersen, past president, AMA, Commencement address, Strich School of Medicine, Loyola University, Chicago, June 7, 1962.

You will discover that while the patient wants the best and most modern treatment available, he is also badly in need of the old-fashioned friend that a doctor has always personified and which you must continue to be. In his mind's eye, the patient sees you as in the old paintings or in his real memories—rumpled and kindly, roused from your bed at 3 in the morning to come to his home and pull him through a crisis. But . . . you will treat him in the clinic or the hospital whenever possible because the care you can give is far better in those facilities. You will try to avoid night calls because you know you can diagnose better with your eyes *open.*

> Dr. Gunnar Gundersen, *ibid.*

If a man is good in his heart, then he is an ethical member of any group in society. If he is bad in his heart, he is an unethical member. To me, the ethics of medical practice is as simple as that.

> Dr. Elmer Hess, president, AMA, "Do Doctors Charge Too Much?" *American Weekly*, April 24, 1955.

There is no greater reward in our profession than the knowledge that God has entrusted us with the physical care of His people. The Almighty has reserved for Himself the power to create life but He has assigned to a few of us the responsibility of keeping in good repair the bodies in which this life is sustained.

> Dr. Elmer Hess, *ibid.*

Surgery is always second best. If you can do something else, it's better. Surgery is limited. It is operating on someone who has no place else to go.

> Dr. John Kirklin, heart surgeon, Mayo Clinic, *Time*, May 3, 1963.

The very success of medicine in a material way may now threaten the soul of medicine. Medicine is something more than the cold mechanical application of science to human disease. Medicine is a healing art. It must deal with individuals, their fears, their hopes and their sorrows. It must reach back further than a disease that the patient may have to those physical and emotional environmental factors which condition the individual for the reception of disease.

> Dr. WALTER MARTIN, "Medicine and the Public Welfare," inaugural address as president of AMA, news reports of June 23, 1954.

Medicine is for the patient. Medicine is for the people. It is not for the profits.

> GEORGE MERCK, leading pharmaceutical manufacturer, *Time*, Nov. 3, 1952.

. . . There is always serendipity. Remember the Three Princes of Serendip who went out looking for treasure? They didn't find what they were looking for, but they kept finding the things just as valuable. That's serendipity, and our business is full of it.

> GEORGE MERCK, *ibid.*

Interest in hair today has grown to the proportions of a fetish. Think of the many loving ways in which advertisements refer to scalp hair—satiny, glowing, shimmering, breathing, living. Living indeed! It is as dead as rope.

> Dr. WILLIAM MONTAGNA, dermatological researcher, Brown University, on decrease in hairiness in evolution of the human skin, *New York Herald Tribune*, Aug. 11, 1963.

Science will never be able to reduce the value of a sunset to arithmetic. Nor can it reduce friendship or statesmanship to a formula. Laughter and love, pain and loneliness, the challenge of accomplishment in living, and the depth of insight into beauty and truth: these will always surpass the scientific mastery of nature.

> Dr. LOUIS ORR, president, AMA, Commencement address, Emory University, June 6, 1960.

Middle-aged rabbits don't have a paunch, do have their own teeth and haven't lost their romantic appeal.

> Dr. AURELIA POTER, endocrinologist, on why "rabbit food" may be good for executives, *New York Times*, Sept. 22, 1956.

Why did Mozart compose music?

> DR. JONAS SALK, discoverer of antipolio vaccine, on why he has devoted his life to research, *Time*, March 29, 1954.

It is courage based on confidence, not daring, and it is confidence based on experience.

> DR. JONAS SALK, on how he experimented with his anti-polio vaccine by administering it to himself, his wife, and three sons, news summaries of May 9, 1955.

I feel that the greatest reward for doing is the opportunity to do more.

> DR. JONAS SALK, on receiving gold medal from President Eisenhower, news reports of Jan. 27, 1956.

I said the country will be very pleased—the country is so bowel-minded anyway . . . and it is important.

> DR. PAUL DUDLEY WHITE, heart specialist, on making public all details of President Eisenhower's condition following a heart attack, news summaries of Oct. 10, 1955.

To add life to years, not just years to life.

> UNOFFICIAL MOTTO of U.S. specialists in medicine for the aging and aged, "The Problem of Old Age," *Time*, July 23, 1956.

Psychology and Psychiatry

We now feel we can cure the patient without his fully understanding what made him sick. We are no longer so interested in peeling the onion as in changing it.

> DR. FRANZ ALEXANDER, address marking 50th anniversary of organized practice of psychoanalysis in U.S., *Time*, May 19, 1961.

The moment of health is the moment of unconscious creative synthesis, when, without thinking about it at all, we know that we make sense to ourselves and to others . . . I think that two new and important feelings come into the individual's experience: 1) the feeling that one is free and that life and its outcome are in one's own hands; 2) . . . a deeper sense

181

of relaxed participation in the present moment . . . Life ceases to be a course between birth and death, and becomes instead a fully realized experience of change . . .

> DR. FRANK BARRON, University of California, paper prepared for American Psychological Association, *Time*, Sept. 26, 1955.

The creative person is both more primitive and more cultivated, more destructive and more constructive, a lot madder and a lot saner, than the average person.

> DR. FRANK BARRON, *Think*, Nov.–Dec., 1962.

The main consequence of a "depressive" economic climate is an absence of positive satisfactions in life, rather than an increase in negative forces. It is the lack of joy in Mudville, rather than the presence of sorrow that makes the difference.

> DR. NORMAN BRADBURN, psychologist, University of Chicago, *In Pursuit of Happiness: A Pilot Study of Behavior Related to Mental Health*, National Opinion Research Center, 1963.

Happiness is a resultant of the relative strengths of positive and negative feelings rather than an absolute amount of one or the other.

> DR. NORMAN BRADBURN, *ibid.*

The truly independent person—in whom creative thinking is at its best— is someone who can accept society without denying himself.

> RICHARD CRUTCHFIELD, *Think*, Nov.–Dec., 1962.

√ Dreaming permits each and every one of us to be quietly and safely insane every night of our lives.

> DR. WILLIAM DEMENT, on research establishing that people dream in order to remain sane while awake, *Newsweek*, Nov. 30, 1959.

One cannot be deeply responsive to the world without being saddened very often.

> DR. ERIC FROMM, psychoanalyst, ABC-TV, May 25, 1958.

If it is true that one's ability to respect others is dependent upon the development of one's own self respect, then it follows that only a self-respecting pyschiatrist is capable of respecting his patients and of meeting them on the basis of mutual human equality.

> Dr. Frieda Fromm-Reichmann, *Principles of Intensive Psychotherapy*, University of Chicago Press, 1950.

Even those of us who never took a course in psychology and never saw a psychoanalyst in the flesh are probably a little happier—a little more understanding to our wives and children, a little kinder to our associates, a little less given to superstition and prejudice about human nature. All of us, even the myriads among us who have emotional problems ranging from the light to the serious, have far more hope for the future.

> Ernest Havemann, conclusion of a series of articles on growth, influence and outlook of modern psychology, *Life*, Feb. 4, 1957.

Being a good psychoanalyst, in short, has the same disadvantage as being a good parent: the children desert one as they grow up.

> Morton Hunt, "How the Analyst Stands the Pace," *New York Times*, Nov. 24, 1957.

A hundred doses of happiness are not enough: send to the drugstore for another bottle—and, when that is finished, for another . . . There can be no doubt that, if tranquilizers could be bought as easily and cheaply as aspirin, they would be consumed, not by the billions, as they are at present, but by the scores and hundreds of billions. And a good, cheap stimulant would be almost as popular.

> Aldous Huxley, *Brave New World Revisited*, Harper & Row, 1958.

The brain is viewed as an appendage of the genital glands.

> Dr. Carl Jung, Swiss psychoanalyst, on Freud's theory of sexuality, *Time*, Feb. 14, 1955.

Yes, how indeed? He copes, like everybody else, as well as he can, that's all. And it's usually deplorably enough.

> Dr. Carl Jung, on how a psychiatrist deals with personal problems, *Portraits of Greatness*, by Yousef Karsh, Thomas Nelson, 1960.

Death is psychologically just as important as birth. As the arrow flies to the target, so life ends in death . . . Shrinking away from it is something unhealthy and abnormal which robs the second half of life of its purpose.
> DR. CARL JUNG, quoted in report of his death at 85, *Time*, June 16, 1961.

With perception, you know something is there. Thinking tells you what it is. Feeling tells you what it is worth to you or to others. And intuition tells what the damn thing comes from or goes to.
> DR. CARL JUNG, on classifying basic personality types, *ibid*.

Man's task is to become conscious of the contents that press upward from the unconscious . . . As far as we can discern, the sole purpose of human existence is to kindle a light in the darkness of mere being. It may even be assumed that just as the unconscious affects us, increase in our consciousness likewise affects the unconscious.
> DR. CARL JUNG, *Memories, Dreams, Reflections*, Atlantic Monthly Press, 1962.

Anybody who is 25 or 30 years old has physical scars from all sorts of things, from tuberculosis to polio. It's the same with the mind.
> DR. M. RALPH KAUFMAN, director of psychiatry, Mt. Sinai Hospital, New York, *Newsweek*, May 29, 1961.

There were houses there and paths outside the houses but there were no paths leading from one house to another.
> DR. DORTHEA LEIGHTON, on high rate of mental illness in disorganized rural communities, *New York Herald Tribune*, May 9, 1962.

You must adjust. . . . This is the legend imprinted in every schoolbook, the invisible message on every blackboard. Our schools have become vast factories for the manufacture of robots.
> DR. ROBERT LINDNER, psychologist, *Must You Conform?* Holt, Rinehart and Winston, 1956.

Psychoanalysis has changed American psychiatry from a diagnostic to a therapeutic science, not because so many patients are cured by the psychoanalytic technique, but because of the new understanding of psychiatric patients it has given us and the new and different concept of illness and health.

DR. KARL MENNINGER, news reports of April 29, 1956.

It was his optimism that Freud bequeathed to America and it was the optimism of our youthfulness, our freedom from the sterner, sadder tradition of Europe which enabled us to seize his gift.

DR. KARL MENNINGER, *ibid.*

Unrest of spirit is a mark of life.

DR. KARL MENNINGER, *This Week,* Oct. 16, 1958.

Hope is a necessity for normal life, and the major weapon against the suicide impulse. Hope is not identical with optimism. Optimism is distant from reality; like pessimism, it emphasizes the importance of "I." Hope is modest, humble, selfless; it implies progress; it is an adventure, a going forward—a confident search for a rewarding life.

DR. KARL MENNINGER, on suicide, *Newsweek,* Nov. 2, 1959.

Money giving is a very good criterion, in a way, of a person's mental health. Generous people are rarely mentally ill people.

DR. KARL MENNINGER, *Quote,* June 19, 1960.

To "know thyself" must mean to know the malignancy of one's own instincts and to know as well one's power to deflect it.

DR. KARL MENNINGER, *Vogue,* June, 1961.

Mental health problems do not affect three or four out of every five persons but one out of one.

DR. WILLIAM MENNINGER, *New York Times,* Nov. 22, 1957.

It's among the intelligentsia, and especially among those who like to play with thoughts and concepts without really taking part in the cultural endeavors of their epoch, that we often find the glib compulsion to explain everything and to understand nothing.

DR. JOOST A. M. MEERLOO, *The Rape of the Mind,* World, 1956.

Among the millions of nerve cells that clothe parts of the brain there runs a thread. It is the thread of time, the thread that has run through each succeeding wakeful hour of the individual's past life.

> Dr. WILDER PENFIELD, Canadian neurosurgeon, *Reader's Digest*, July, 1958.

The repressed memory is like a noisy intruder being thrown out of the concert hall. You can throw him out, but he will hang on the door and continue to disturb the concert. The analyst opens the door and says, "If you promise to behave yourself, you can come back in."

> Dr. THEODOR REIK, *Saturday Review*, Jan. 11, 1958.

In our civilization, men are afraid that they will not be men enough and women are afraid that they might be considered only women.

> Dr. THEODOR REIK, quoted by Arthur Schlesinger, Jr., "The Crisis of American Masculinity," *Esquire*, Nov., 1958.

Work and love—these are the basics. Without them there is neurosis.

> Dr. THEODOR REIK, *Of Love and Lust*, Grove, 1959.

The essential nature of femininity is unknown except to women, who are neither interested in it nor willing to enlighten us men about it.

> Dr. THEODOR REIK, *The Need To Be Loved*, Farrar, Straus, 1963.

Frustrate a Frenchman, he will drink himself to death; an Irishman, he will die of angry hypertension; a Dane, he will shoot himself; an American, he will get drunk, shoot you, then establish a million dollar aid program for your relatives. Then he will die of an ulcer.

> Dr. STANLEY RUDIN, psychologist, Dalhousie University, Nova Scotia, correlation of national tendencies and individual psychological problems, address to International Congress of Psychology, *New York Times*, Aug. 22, 1963.

. . . There is no time at which a woman is more apt to go to pieces than when she is engaged in decorating her home. . . . It puts a woman under tremendous psychic pressure and, in doing so, brings to the surface her underlying weaknesses.

> Dr. MILTON R. SAPIRSTEIN, *Paradoxes in Everyday Life*, Random House, 1955.

The process of living is the process of reacting to stress.

> STANLEY J. SARNOFF, physiologist, National Institutes of Health, *Time*, Nov. 29, 1963.

Don't be afraid to enjoy the stress of a full life nor too naive to think you can do so without some intelligent thinking and planning. Man should not try to avoid stress any more than he would shun food, love, or exercise.

> DR. HANS SELYE, director, Institute of Experimental Medicine and Surgery, University of Montreal, *Newsweek*, March 31, 1958.

Anxiety seems to be the dominant fact—and is threatening to become the dominant cliché—of modern life. It shouts in the headlines, laughs nervously at cocktail parties, nags from advertisements, speaks suavely in the board room, whines from the stage, clatters from the Wall Street ticker, jokes with fake youthfulness on the golf course and whispers in privacy each day before the shaving mirror and the dressing table.

> TIME, March 31, 1961, on anxiety in modern life.

Science

There was once a twin brother named Bright
Who could travel much faster than light.
He departed one day, in a relative way,
And came home on the previous night.
> ANONYMOUS, poem on relativity, *Newsweek*, Feb. 3, 1958.

. . . The aims of pure basic science, unlike those of applied science, are neither fast-flowing nor pragmatic. The quick harvest of applied science is the useable process, the medicine, the machine. The shy fruit of pure science is Understanding.
> LINCOLN BARNETT, science writer, on Einstein's completion of mathematical formula for Unified Field Theory, *Life*, Jan. 9, 1950.

I think the school's involvement in the development of atomic energy and the bomb left a deep scar on the moral fiber of this place from which it has not really recovered. I do not believe they wish again to become involved in developments which are for the military.
> LUCIEN BIBERMAN, associate director, University of Chicago military research laboratory, announcement of closing of facilities because of the faculty's moral pangs over the University's pioneer development of the atomic bomb, *New York Times*, June 7, 1963.

Archeology sounds like dull sport in five syllables. It isn't. It's the Peeping Tom of the sciences. It is the sand-box of men who care not where they are going; they merely want to know where everybody else has been.
> JIM BISHOP, columnist, "Sifting the Sea for Time's Treasures," *New York Journal-American*, March 14, 1961.

A static hero is a public liability. Progress grows out of motion.
> ADMIRAL RICHARD E. BYRD, Arctic explorer, comment recalled in reports of his death, March 12, 1957.

Over increasingly large areas of the United States, spring now comes unheralded by the return of the birds, and the early mornings are strangely silent where once they were filled with the beauty of bird song.
> RACHEL CARSON, describing devastating effect of chemical insecticides indiscriminately sprayed on the land; her phrase furnished title for her much discussed book, *Silent Spring*, Houghton Mifflin, 1962.

As crude a weapon as the cave man's club, the chemical barrage has been hurled against the fabric of life. . . .
> RACHEL CARSON, *ibid.*

The grand aim of all science is to cover the greatest number of empirical facts by logical deduction from the smallest number of hypotheses or axioms.
> ALBERT EINSTEIN, *Life*, Jan. 9, 1950.

I assert that the cosmic religious experience is the strongest and the noblest driving force behind scientific research.
> ALBERT EINSTEIN, recalled in reports of his death, April 19, 1955.

The most incomprehensible thing about the world is that it is comprehensible.
> ALBERT EINSTEIN, *ibid.*

I think and think for months and years. Ninety-nine times, the conclusion is false. The hundredth time I am right.
> ALBERT EINSTEIN, *ibid.*

. . . A civilian-setting for the administration of space function will emphasize the concern of our nation that outer space be devoted to peaceful and scientific purposes.
> PRESIDENT EISENHOWER, message to Congress, recommending a civilian agency to direct U.S. aeronautical and space scientific activities other than primarily military projects, April 2, 1958.

189

Science is a little bit like the air you breathe—it is everywhere.
> PRESIDENT EISENHOWER, on the impracticality of establishing a Department of Science in federal government, June 18, 1958.

We stand now in the vestibule of a vast new technological age . . .
> PRESIDENT EISENHOWER, State of the Union message, Jan. 7, 1960.

I could have gone on flying through space forever.
> MAJOR YURI GAGARIN, describing in ecstatic terms his flight as the first man in space, *New York Times*, April 14, 1961.

A society committed to the search for truth must give protection to, and set a high value upon, the independent and original mind, however angular, however rasping, however socially unpleasant it may be; for it is upon such minds, in large measure, that the effective search for truth depends.
> CARYL HASKINS, president, Carnegie Institution of Washington, *New York Times*, Dec. 9, 1963.

I am hell-bent for the South Pole—God willing and crevasses permitting.
> SIR EDMUND HILLARY, eight days before reaching South Pole via overland route, news summaries of Jan. 5, 1958.

Steering by the sun from earlier fixes we came bang on base.
> SIR EDMUND HILLARY, *ibid*.

I think one of the things which warmed us most during this flight was the realization that however extraordinary computers may be, we are still ahead of them, and that man is still the most extraordinary computer of all.
> PRESIDENT KENNEDY, May 21, 1963, welcoming astronaut Gordon Cooper to Washington after the officer took over controls of his space capsule to achieve a safe "splash-down" in the Pacific.

Every time you scientists make a major invention, we politicians have to invent a new institution to cope with it—and almost invariably, these days, it must be an international institution.
> PRESIDENT KENNEDY, address to National Academy of Sciences, *Wall Street Journal*, Oct. 30, 1963.

The Wright Brothers flew right through the smoke screen of impossibility.

> CHARLES FRANKLIN KETTERING, *Professional Amateur*, by T. A. Boyd, Dutton, 1957.

Trying to answer students' questions, I soon learned there were great gaps in our scientific knowledge of sex—plenty of folktales, mythology and misunderstanding, of course, but little of the data we have on other phases of life. I resolved to try and fill the gaps.

> DR. ALFRED KINSEY, on the Kinsey Reports on sexual behavior, statement recalled in reports of his death, Aug. 26, 1956.

. . . We are recorders and reporters of the facts—not judges of the behavior we describe.

> DR. ALFRED KINSEY, in defense of the Kinsey Reports, *ibid.*

Not so long ago, when I was a student in college, just flying an airplane seemed a dream. But that dream turned into reality.

> CHARLES A. LINDBERGH, beginning his autobiography, *The Spirit of St. Louis*, Scribner's, 1953.

Science, freedom, beauty, adventure: What more could you ask of life? Aviation combined all the elements I loved. . . . I began to feel that I lived on a higher plane than the skeptics of the ground; one that was richer because of its very association with the element of danger they dreaded, because it was freer of the earth to which they were bound. In flying I tasted the wine of the gods of which they could know nothing . . .

> CHARLES A. LINDBERGH, *ibid.*

. . . At the end of the first half-century of engine-driven flight, we are confronted with the stark fact that the historical significance of aircraft has been primarily military and destructive.

> CHARLES A. LINDBERGH, on accepting medal of Institute of Aeronautical Sciences, news summaries of Feb. 1, 1954.

The laws of nature are written deep in the folds and faults of the earth. By encouraging men to learn those laws one can lead them further to a knowledge of the Author of all laws.

> JOHN JOSEPH LYNCH, S.J., noted seismologist-priest of Fordham University, on becoming president of the New York Academy of Sciences, *New York Times*, Dec. 5, 1963.

Which would you rather have, a bursting planet or an earthquake here and there?

> JOHN JOSEPH LYNCH, S.J., on his belief that earthquakes are usually maligned, *ibid.*

Comets are the nearest thing to nothing that anything can be and still be something.

> NATIONAL GEOGRAPHIC SOCIETY, announcing discovery of comet visible only by telescope, March 31, 1955.

I like people. I like animals, too—whales and quail, dinosaurs and dodos. But I like human beings especially, and I am unhappy that the pool of human germ plasm, which determines the nature of the human race, is deteriorating.

> DR. LINUS PAULING, scientist, California Institute of Technology, in a 1959 paper, *I Like People*, which dramatized his view of radioactive fallout's effect on human heredity; recalled when he was awarded Nobel Prize for Peace, *New York Times*, Oct. 13, 1963.

There is no magic formula for achieving creativity—it is simply a way of life in a laboratory dedicated to discovery and invention.

> DR. PAUL SALZBERG, director of research, E. I. du Pont de Nemours, *Think*, Nov.–Dec., 1962.

Atoms for peace. Man is still the greatest miracle and the greatest problem on this earth.

> BRIGADIER-GENERAL DAVID SARNOFF, first message ever sent with electricity produced by atomic energy, *New York Post*, Jan. 27, 1954.

. . . America, supremely the land of liberty, is also supremely the land of science. Freedom is the oxygen without which science cannot breathe.

> Brigadier-General David Sarnoff, "Electronics—Today and Tomorrow," *Profile of America,* compiled by Emily Davie, Crowell, 1954.

At their best, at their most creative, science and engineering are attributes of liberty—noble expressions of man's God-given right to investigate and explore the universe without fear of social or political or religious reprisals.

> Brigadier-General David Sarnoff, *ibid.*

The presence of humans, in a system containing high-speed electronic computers and high-speed, accurate communications, is quite inhibiting. Every means possible should be employed to eliminate humans in the data-processing chain.

> Stuart Luman Seaton, engineering consultant, address to American Institute of Electrical Engineers, *Time,* Feb. 17, 1958.

The human brain is a most unusual instrument of elegant and as yet unknown capacity.

> Stuart Luman Seaton, *ibid.*

The fairest thing we can experience is the mysterious. It is the fundamental emotion which stands at the cradle of true science. He who knows it not, and can no longer wonder, no longer feel amazement, is as good as dead. We all had this priceless talent when we were young. But as time goes by, many of us lose it. The true scientist never loses the faculty of amazement. It is the essence of his being.

> Dr. Hans Selye, *Newsweek,* March 31, 1958.

Science cannot stop while ethics catches up . . . and nobody should expect scientists to do all the thinking for the country.

> Elvin Stackman, University of Minnesota, speaking as president of American Association for Advancement of Science, *Life,* Jan. 9, 1950.

. . . There are some who have questioned the applicability of scientific methods to an investigation of human sexual behavior . . . It is as though the dietician and biochemist were denied the right to analyze foods and the processes of nutrition, because the cooking and proper serving of food may be rated a fine art, and because the eating of certain foods has been considered a matter for religious regulation.

> SEXUAL BEHAVIOR IN THE HUMAN FEMALE (Kinsey Report), "The Right to Investigate," Saunders, 1953.

The right of the scientist to investigate is akin to the academic freedom which our American standards demand for scholars in every field and not too remote from the freedom of speech which we have come to believe constitutes one of the foundation stones of our American way of living.

> SEXUAL BEHAVIOR IN THE HUMAN FEMALE, "The Individual's Right to Know," *ibid*.

A-OK full go.

> COMMANDER ALAN SHEPARD, JR., on blast-off of rocket carrying him aloft as America's first man in space, May 5, 1961. Defined as an engineering term for "double OK" or perfect, it became a U.S. idiom for "everything is going smoothly" and was later attributed by the Associated Press (*New York Times*, July 31, 1963) to Lieutenant-Colonel John Powers, public spokesman for astronauts.

The human body comes in only two shapes and three colors. I don't expect there will be any changes, so what we learn about it now will serve us for a long time to come.

> LIEUTENANT-COLONEL PAUL STAPP, on human endurance for space travel, *Time*, Sept. 12, 1955.

Spring One. Spring One. I am Eagle. I am Eagle. I can hear you very well. I feel excellent. My feeling is excellent.

> MAJOR GHERMAN TITOV, while circling globe every 88 minutes aboard Soviet spaceship Vostok II, *New York Times*, Aug. 7, 1961.

I knew that there was something in the nature of homesickness called nostalgia, but I found that there is also a homesickness for the earth. I don't know what it should be called but it does exist. There is nothing more splendid . . . than Mother Earth on which one can stand, work and breathe the wind of the steppes.

> MAJOR GHERMAN TITOV, on his 434,960-mile flight, *New York Herald Tribune*, Aug. 13, 1961.

It will free man from his remaining chains, the chains of gravity which still tie him to this planet. It will open to him the gates of heaven.

> WERNHER VON BRAUN, U.S. Army Ballistic Missile Agency, on meaning of space travel, *Time*, Feb. 10, 1958.

Travel

Christened with a name that has come to be the color of its reputation, clasped to the bosom of Long Island and yet, somehow, closer to the South Seas than the South Shore, surrounded completely by Friday and Monday and reached only by boat, seaplane, and, with less surety, telephone—this is Fire Island, a pile of sand beneath a pile of people.

> ALFRED ARONOWITZ, opening sentence in profile series on Fire Island, *New York Post*, July 27, 1959.

The Sussex lanes were very lovely in the autumn. I started going for long lone country walks among the spendthrift gold and glory of the year-end, giving myself up to the earth-scents and the skywinds and all the magic of the countryside which is ordained for the healing of the soul.

> MONICA BALDWIN, on the English countryside in *I Leap Over the Wall*, Rinehart, 1950.

Sheet upon sheet of blazing yellow, half-way between sulphur and celandine, with hot golden sunshine pouring down upon them out of a dazzling June sky. It thrilled me like music.

> MONICA BALDWIN, *ibid*.

On close inspection, this device turned out to be a funereal juke box—the result of mixing Lloyd's of London with the principle of the chewing gum dispenser.

> CECIL BEATON, on automatic insurance machines in U.S. airline terminals, *It Gives Me Great Pleasure*, John Day, 1955.

Americans . . . have an abiding belief in their ability to control reality by purely material means. Hence . . . airline insurance replaces the fear of death with the comforting prospect of cash.

> CECIL BEATON, *ibid*.

196

The eye remembers Lorca-like images: widows with beaten skin, an oyster eye and a black shawl over their heads; beggars having a good time exaggerating their poverty.

> CECIL BEATON, on Spain, *The Face of the World*, John Day, 1957.

. . . Scoops of mint ice cream with chips of chocolate cows.

> JIM BISHOP, columnist, on English countryside, *New York Journal-American*, Sept. 28, 1957.

Venice is like eating an entire box of chocolate liqueurs in one go.

> TRUMAN CAPOTE, news summaries of Nov. 26, 1961.

Yes, but I'd rather go by bus. There is nothing nicer in the world than a bus.

> CHARLES, PRINCE OF WALES, when asked if he was excited about sailing to Tobruk on royal yacht, news summaries of May 21, 1954.

We could never get our coffee hot when flying out of Cheyenne because of the altitude—and we were too dumb to know why.

> ELLEN CHURCH, history's first airline stewardess, recollection 30 years after her first commercial flight, *New York Times*, May 15, 1960.

A vice president of the company and a number of other people quit because they didn't want to have anything to do with an airline that would hire women . . . But it wasn't long before (pilots) discovered we were a help, not a hindrance. And besides they really didn't like serving coffee and cookies or holding somebody's head in their laps while he was sick.

> ELLEN CHURCH, *ibid.*

Vermont's a place where barns come painted
Red as a strong man's heart,
Where stout carts and stout boys in freckles
Are highest forms of art.

> ROBERT TRISTRAM COFFIN, "Vermont Looks Like A Man," last poem contributed to the *New York Herald Tribune* editorial page before his death, Jan. 20, 1955.

As a member of an escorted tour, you don't even have to know the Matterhorn isn't a tuba.

> TEMPLE FIELDING, *Fielding's Guide to Europe*, William Sloane Associates, 1963.

The most salient fact about Africa is that 190,800,000 people are suddenly making the transition with unbelievable velocity from wearing a string of beads to driving a Ford.

> JOHN GUNTHER, *New York Mirror*, Nov. 13, 1955.

[My hotels] are rather like the old Spanish mission stations, strung across the countryside just one day's journey apart.

> CONRAD HILTON, "In 19 Lands 'Instant America,'" by Dora Jane Hamblin, *Life*, Aug. 30, 1963.

It's wonderful to climb the liquid mountains of the sky. Behind me and before me is God and I have no fears.

> HELEN KELLER, at 74, on flight around the world, news reports of Feb. 5, 1955.

I'm leaving because the weather is too good. I hate London when it's not raining.

> GROUCHO MARX, news summaries of June 28, 1954.

In the space age, man will be able to go around the world in two hours—one hour for flying and the other to get to the airport.

> NEIL McELROY, U.S. Defense Secretary, *Look*, Feb. 18, 1958.

The East is a montage. The pictures that it calls to the mind are endless and bewildering—the stone fences of New England, New Haven's out-of-town theatre openings, day lilies in June, cities taller and more fabulous than Troy. It is whaling museums and subways and institutes of higher learning and some of the world's best restaurants. It is Maine's wildernesses and New York's Greenwich Village, clambakes and brownstone houses, dogwood and First Nights. It is old and it is young, very green in summer, very white in winter, gregarious, withdrawn, and at once both sophisticated and provincial.

> PHYLLIS McGINLEY, "The East Is Home," *Woman's Home Companion*, July, 1956.

Of all the women of Paris, the most impressive is what we call the concierge. In every building of Paris, there is a concierge, to serve as a human watchdog. Whoever you are, she knows about you. She knows how much money you make, and how foolishly you spend it, and where you are likely to end up. She knows all your friends. She does not like them. She talks about you secretly, and only to other concierges. They tell each other all they know. There is a good deal to tell. No matter how much Paris changes, nothing will dim her eye, which never sleeps. For she is a concierge. She knows. She knows, and she disapproves. There is a concierge in every building in Paris, like a tiger, guarding the old traditions of the city. Without her, Paris could no more be Paris than it could be Paris without its art . . . and artists.

> TED MILLS AND STEPHEN WHITE, *Maurice Chevalier's Paris*, NBC-TV, March 6, 1957.

The North Americans very naturally want to get away from North America. They are also after their own origins. Although they descend from people who could not succeed in Europe and furiously shook its dust from their feet, they have a sentimental feeling for ancestors.

> NANCY MITFORD, *The Water Beetle*, Harper & Row, 1963.

. . . There is a lull to the very air of the place, the creaking of the tall teak forests, the lapping of the canals, the gentle swaying of the little kingfishers who sit like neat blue idols on almost every telegraph wire.

> JAMES MORRIS, on Siam (Thailand), *The Road to Huddersfield: A Journey to Five Continents*, Pantheon, 1963.

God made the grass, the air and the rain; and the grass, the air and the rain made the Irish; and the Irish turned the grass, the air and the rain back into God.

> SEAN O'FAOLAIN, on Ireland, *Holiday*, June, 1958.

The Americans are always on a very right schedule, you know; they have to see Stratford and Hampton Court and Windsor all in one day. Once an American did come down here and he was just about to buy a pepper-mill when he suddenly looked at his watch and said he had to rush because he had only three and a half minutes left for Windsor.

> BEN OXLEY, proprietor of Mousehole Shop, Windsor, England, *Time & Tide*, Feb. 1, 1962.

. . . The life of the modern jet pilots tends to be most unexpectedly lonely. . . . Foreign countries are places to reach accurately and to leave on time. Distance is a raw material to work with. . . .

> JOHN PEARSON, "People of the 60's," *Sunday Times*, London, Feb. 4, 1962.

It is strange the way they come into the control room before a flight, the Trans-Atlantic jet pilots, with their brief cases and tidy moustaches, like bank managers prepared for a solid day's work. As they check through the pink wad of weather reports, there is little talk and everyone keeps his distance as if it were understood that piloting a £1,500,000 liner to New York in just under seven hours is something scrupulously to be played down.

JOHN PEARSON, *ibid.*

The old piston-engined aircraft that used to batter the 15-or-16 hour way to Gander or Idlewild demanded a different sort of personality from the pilot. . . . In those days, a man still flew an aircraft as he might sail a boat or drive a racing car. It was a thing to be done with a certain style, even a certain recklessness, and the most famous of these pilots came to be known as the North Atlantic Barons. It was a title of which they were proud. Some wore beards. Some wore monocles. They had a conscious personal myth inherited from wartime flying. But the big jets have changed all this . . . its pilots no longer need flair and doggedness so much as absolute precision. The pilot as man of action is being succeeded by the pilot as technocrat . . .

JOHN PEARSON, *ibid.*

Like a resplendent chandelier, Paris in winter is made up of many parts. It is a classic Degasesque ballet dancer rehearsing in the Opéra, the Champs-Élysées in the rain, the academic seriousness of study at the Beaux-Arts, the Bohemian bonhomie of all of St.-Germain-des-Prés, the light eating and deep conversation of Les Deux Magots, a formal concert by the visiting Viennese, the ever-changing patterns of the river Seine by night, the smile of service, the master music, youth and a dog, fresh flowers and wet pavements in the Étoile, the Gare des Invalides and its magnificent clock, the illuminated night tracery of leafless plane trees, the mysterious solace of the bridges, the glistening, triumphant majesty of the nighttime vistas . . . the heart-lifting silhouette of the Eiffel Tower, a businesslike bus and a proud set of arches. . . . It is Notre Dame . . . it is Paris . . . Fairest Lady of Europe.

W. A. POWERS, "Paris in Wintertime," *Town & Country*, Dec., 1956.

Serene and gracious, as though aware of its place in England's history, the Thames meanders through the green of Oxfordshire. It has time to dream here and be proud, time to laze and preen in the sun, time to remember and be quiet, before London's hubbub and the clamor of the docks surround it, at its journey's end, with a different kind of beauty.

V. S. Pritchett, "Thames River of History," *Holiday*, March, 1961.

Although Londoners are, more than any other city people, wary of foreigners, although London landladies are Britannias armed with helmet, shield, trident, and have faces with the word "No" stamped like a coat of arms on them, the place is sentimental and tolerant. The attitude to foreigners is like the attitude to dogs: Dogs are neither human nor British, but so long as you keep them under control, give them their exercise, feed them, pat them, you will find their wild emotions are amusing, and their characters interesting.

V. S. Pritchett, *London Perceived*, Harcourt, Brace & World, 1962.

The very name London has tonnage in it.

V. S. Pritchett, *ibid.*

. . . The helicopter has become the most universal vehicle ever created and used by man. It approaches closer than any other to fulfillment of mankind's ancient dreams of the flying horse and the magic carpet.

Igor Ivanovitch Sikorsky, Russian-born American inventor of helicopter, comment on 20th anniversary of its first flight, *New York Times*, Sept. 13, 1959.

When I was very young and the urge to be someplace else was on me, I was assured by mature people that maturity would cure this itch. When years described me as mature, the remedy prescribed was middle age. In middle age I was assured that greater age would calm my fever, and now that I am 58 perhaps senility will do the job.

John Steinbeck, *Travels With Charley*, Viking, 1962.

The city overwhelmed our expectations. The Kiplingesque grandeur of Waterloo Station, the Eliotic despondency of the brick row in Chelsea . . . the Dickensian nightmare of fog and sweating pavement and besmirched cornices. . . . We wheeled past mansions by Galsworthy and parks by A. A. Milne; we glimpsed a cobbled eighteenth-century alley, complete with hanging tavern boards, where Dr. Johnson might have reeled and gasped the night he laughed so hard . . .

John Updike, on London, in a short story, "A Madman," *New Yorker*, Dec. 22, 1962.

201

The West is color. . . . Its colors are animal rather than vegetable, the colors of earth and sunlight and ripeness. Tawny, buff, ocher, umber, tan, beige, sienna, sorel, bay, blood-bay, chestnut, roan, palomino: the colors of objects bleached, sun-drenched, dry, aromatic, warm; the color of stubble fields, of barley, of foothills, of sage, of ocean and desert sands; colors capable of reflecting light like a mirror. And this light itself is diamond hard and clear, and falls in Utah and New Mexico on fiercer hued colors, colors of blood and fire, of stump and sundown.

JESSAMYN WEST, "The West A Place to Hang Your Dreams," *Woman's Home Companion*, May, 1956.

Religion

Christians must realize that they have one Church, one Cross, one Gospel. Every church must put its treasures into a safe-deposit box and issue common money, a common money of love, which we need so much.
> ATHENAGORAS I, Ecumenical Patriarch of Constantinople, *Time*, July 5, 1963.

Conscience is the perfect interpreter of life.
> KARL BARTH, *The Word of God and the Word of Man*, Harper & Row, 1957.

Father, we thank you, especially for letting me fly this flight . . . for the privilege of being able to be in this position, to be in this wondrous place, seeing all these many startling, wonderful things that You have created.
> MAJOR GORDON COOPER, prayer while orbiting the earth in a space capsule; later used to conclude his address to Congress, *New York Times*, May 22, 1963.

I will try to make You as happy as the rambling piano keys on Easter Sunday morning, or a happy angel when she does a holy dance.
> "MISS BEAUTIFUL LOVE," in a letter to Father Divine, quoted in *Father Divine: Holy Husband* by Sara Harris with the assistance of Harriet Crittenden, Doubleday, 1953.

The soul of a civilization is its religion, and it dies with its faith.
> WILL AND ARIEL DURANT, *The Age of Reason Begins*, vol. VII of *The Story of Civilization*, Simon and Schuster, 1961.

I could not say I believe. I know! I have had the experience of being gripped by something that is stronger than myself, something that people call God.

> CARL JUNG, when asked if he believed in God, *Time*, Feb. 14, 1955.

Our heart glows, and secret unrest gnaws at the roots of our being. . . . Dealing with the unconscious has become a question of life for us. . . . I have treated many hundreds of patients. . . . Among [those] in the second half of life—that is to say, over thirty-five—there has not been one whose problem in the last resort was not that of finding a religious outlook on life. . . .

> CARL JUNG, *ibid.*

It gives me a deep comforting sense that "things seen are temporal and things unseen are eternal."

> HELEN KELLER, on reading Bible daily, news reports of June 26, 1955.

Infinite Spirit: Give us, we pray, the will and the capacity to grow, the sensitivity and receptivity to see in new ways, and the humility to understand how little we yet have grown and how little we yet have seen.

> DR. JAMES KILLIAN, prayer written as President Eisenhower's Special Assistant for Science and Technology, *Cosmopolitan*, April, 1958.

I propose that God should be openly and audibly invoked at the United Nations in accordance with any one of the religious faiths which are represented here. I do so in the conviction that we cannot make the United Nations into a successful instrument of God's peace without God's help—and that with His help we cannot fail.

> HENRY CABOT LODGE, JR., chief U.S. delegate to UN, letter to each member state, Dec. 30, 1955.

Religion which is interested only in itself, in its prestige and success, in its institutions and ecclesiastical niceties, is worse than vanity; it is essentially incestuous. Religion reveals itself in struggling to reveal the meaning of the world.

> S. H. MILLER, dean, Harvard Divinity School, *The Church of England* by Paul Ferris, Hodder and Stoughton, London, 1962.

Religion is a candle inside a multicolored lantern. Everyone looks through a particular color, but the candle is always there.

> MOHAMMED NAGUIB, former President of Egypt, news summaries of Dec. 31, 1953.

The final test of religious faith . . . is whether it will enable men to endure insecurity without complacency or despair, whether it can so interpret the ancient verities that they will not become mere escape hatches from responsibilities but instruments of insights into what civilization means.

> REINHOLD NIEBUHR, graduate professor of ethics and theology, Union Theological Seminary, "The Religious Traditions of Our Nations," *Saturday Evening Post*, July 23, 1960.

A vital religion proves itself both by moral responsibility in creating tolerable forms of community and justice, and by a humble awareness of human imperfectibility. Above all, it preserves a sense of ultimate majesty and meaning, transcending all our little majesties and partial meanings.

> REINHOLD NIEBUHR, *ibid.*

Nothing that is worth doing can be achieved in a lifetime; therefore we must be saved by hope. Nothing which is true or beautiful or good makes complete sense in any immediate context of history; therefore, we must be saved by faith. Nothing we do, however virtuous, can be accomplished alone; therefore we are saved by love.

> REINHOLD NIEBUHR, quoted by Eleanor Roosevelt in a book completed during final summer of her life, *Tomorrow Is Now*, Harper & Row, 1963.

All it required was a pen-knife, and guts, plus a humidifier.

> DR. J. A. SANDERS, American theologian, on his delicate task of unrolling Dead Sea scrolls * found in a cave in Jordan, *New York Times*, March 4, 1962.

---

* A translation of one of the Dead Sea scrolls, found in a cave in Judean desert, was released Nov. 8, 1956. It spoke of Abraham's sojourn in Egypt and of his wife, Sarah: "And how beautiful the look of her face. . . . And how fine is the hair of her head, how fair indeed are her eyes and how pleasing her nose and all the radiance of her face. . . . How beautiful her breast and how lovely all her whiteness. Her arms goodly to look upon, and her hands how perfect . . . all the appearance of her hands. How fair her palms and how long and fine all the fingers of her hands. Her legs how

Day by day we should weigh what we have granted to the spirit of the world against what we have denied to the spirit of Jesus, in thought and especially in deed.
> ALBERT SCHWEITZER, *Guideposts*, March, 1956.

Above all, I try to avoid the temptation to which anyone who speaks to heathens is subject, to "preach the law." It is difficult not to cite the Ten Commandments and thus prepare for the gospel people to whom lying, stealing and immorality are second nature. I strive to awaken in their hearts the longing for peace with God. When I speak of the difference between the restless and the peaceful heart, the wildest of my savages knows what is meant. And when I portray Jesus as He who brings peace with God to the hearts of men, they comprehend Him.
> ALBERT SCHWEITZER, "My Church in the Jungle," *American Weekly*, Oct. 5, 1958.

Do not our prayers for help mean: Help me to be better than I know myself to be . . . to do this thing that I am doing better than my own limited capacities would permit without help . . . to restrain my passions about to flare . . . to discipline my tired mind . . . to open my heart and imagination. Help me toward that wisdom which is more than knowledge. Help me to kindle and rekindle the divine spark of love . . . to find the fortitude by which I may endure this sorrow, frustration, injustice, or disappointment. God help me to know, love, and trust in God and to perform his particular will for me.
> DOROTHY THOMPSON, journalist, in anthology *How Prayer Helps Me*, Dial, 1955.

Religion is the substance of culture, and culture the form of religion.
> PAUL TILLICH, Protestant theologian, *Time*, Oct. 20, 1952.

The important thing is not that people go more to church, listen to evangelists and join churches. The important thing is that the younger generation asks the right questions . . . the meaning of our life, the

---

beautiful and without blemish her thighs. And all maidens and all brides that go beneath the wedding canopy are not more fair than she. And above all women she is lovely and higher is her beauty than that of them all, and with all her beauty there is much wisdom in her. And the tip of her hands is comely."

conflicts of our existence, the way to deal with anxiety in our life, the feeling of guilt, the feeling of emptiness.
> PAUL TILLICH, interviewed as he was finishing third volume of his magnum opus, *Systematic Theology, New York Times,* May 5, 1963.

Faith embraces itself and the doubt about itself.
> PAUL TILLICH, *ibid.*

The churches were urged by Paul in his letter to the Corinthians to give and take correction from each other. They are all responsible for each other. They must not be polite to each other but speak openly and frankly. There is no danger of self-righteousness from this, because correction is also a reminder to ourselves.
> WILLEM ADOLF VISSER'T HOOFT, General Secretary, World Council of Churches, in William Belden Noble Lecture at Memorial Church, Harvard University, *Christian Science Monitor,* Dec. 9, 1963.

Anglican

Mission is not the kindness of the lucky to the unlucky; it is mutual, united obedience to the one God Whose mission it is.
> ANGLICAN MANIFESTO entitled *Mutual Responsibility and Interdependence in the Body of Christ* presented by the Bishops of the Church at Anglican Congress, Toronto, Aug. 17, 1963; immediately regarded as a revolutionary declaration, it urged establishment of a central authority for the 18 national churches constituting the Anglican Communion.

Obedience, judgment, witness . . . these are the signposts to our salvation, in all the perplexities and busyness of our life.
> STEPHEN BAYNE, executive officer, Anglican Communion, conclusion of annual report to Archbishop of Canterbury, *Anglican World,* Easter, 1963.

Some Church members will have to cease thinking of the Church as a kind of memorial association for a deceased clergyman called Christ.
> STEPHEN BAYNE, on Anglican Manifesto presented at Anglican Congress, Toronto, *New York Herald Tribune,* Aug. 19, 1963.

Anyone closely connected with the affairs of the Church recognizes the thoughtful, creative, and conscientious contribution being made by the women. They are ready and able to share in the responsibility, the difficulties, and the satisfactions of toiling to "make straight in the desert a highway for our God."

> HORACE DONEGAN, Bishop of New York, plea that women be allowed to serve on parish vestries and as convention delegates, news reports of Sept. 8, 1955.

There are only two kinds of people in the modern world who know what they are after. One, quite frankly, is the Communist. The other, equally frankly, is the convinced Christian. . . . The rest of the world are amiable nonentities.

> GEOFFREY FISHER, Archbishop of Canterbury, news summaries of Aug. 26, 1954.

. . . If the typewriter was abolished tomorrow a mass of vapid thought that goes on between human beings would be vastly reduced and the danger of a war would be vastly decreased.

> GEOFFREY FISHER, at inauguration of new headquarters for British Council of Churches, London, March 15, 1955.

I say to you Baptists, "Go on being good Baptists, thinking that you are more right than anybody else." Unless you think it I have no use for you at all. The Church of England does precisely the same itself.

> GEOFFREY FISHER, to golden jubilee congress of Baptist World Alliance, news reports of July 17, 1955.

Until you know that life is interesting—and find it so—you haven't found your soul. . . . What matters is that we do our best for the Kingdom of God. If we say we're not doing too badly, we're sunk. But if we say, things are frightful and we'll do our best, we're okay.

> GEOFFREY FISHER, *Reader's Digest*, Oct., 1955.

It is true, as has been said, that in one sense what may pass between the Pope and myself may be trivialities. In another sense, the fact of talking trivialities is itself a portent of great significance. But the pleasantries which we exchange may, as one church leader said, be pleasantries about profundities.

> GEOFFREY FISHER, address to diocesan conference a month before first meeting in five centuries between a Pope and an Archbishop of Canterbury, *New York Times,* Nov. 6, 1960.

I hope that by going to visit the Pope I have enabled everybody to see that the words Catholic and Protestant, as ordinarily used, are completely out of date. They are almost always used now purely for propaganda purposes. That is why so much trouble is caused by them.

> GEOFFREY FISHER, on his belief that words "corporate" and "personal" almost exactly match words "Catholic" and "Protestant," *New York Times,* Jan. 11, 1961.

. . . My feelings are those of a schoolboy getting in sight of the holidays. Or more seriously, my feelings are perhaps those of a matador who has decided not to enter the bull ring.

> GEOFFREY FISHER, announcing plans to retire after a primacy of 16 years, *New York Times,* Jan. 18, 1961.

The anonymity of a gift is good for the recipient, and we want to think it is good also for the donor. As love is fulfilled in just the loving, so is giving fulfilled in just the giving; certainly there is something special about an anonymous gift. . . .

> H. L. FOLAND, *Anglican Digest,* Winter, A.D. 1962.

Out of our beliefs are born deeds. Out of our deeds we form habits; out of our habits grow our character; and on our character we build our destination.

> HENRY HANCOCK, dean, St. Mark's Cathedral, Minneapolis, *Alpha Xi Delta Magazine,* 1957.

If our Lord Jesus Christ had come back to earth in Scarsdale in time for the Holly Ball, he would not have been allowed to escort a young lady of this parish to that dance.

> GEORGE FRENCH KEMPSELL, rector, parish of St. James the Less, Scarsdale, N.Y., protesting barring of a Jewish youth from annual Christmas ball at Scarsdale Golf Club, page one article in New York newspapers, Jan. 13, 1961.

Fast from criticism, and feast on praise;
Fast from self-pity, and feast on joy;
Fast from ill-temper, and feast on peace;
Fast from resentment, and feast on contentment;
Fast from jealousy, and feast on love;
Fast from pride, and feast on humility;
Fast from selfishness, and feast on service;
Fast from fear, and feast on faith.

> ARTHUR LICHTENBERGER, Presiding Bishop, U.S. Episcopal Church, *Anglican Digest*, Spring, A.D. 1962.

The right to vote, to eat a hamburger where you want, to have a decent job, to live in a house fit for habitation: these are not rights to be litigated or negotiated. It is our shame that demonstrations must be carried out to win them. These constitutional rights *belong* to the Negro as to the white, because we are all men and we are all citizens.

> ARTHUR LICHTENBERGER, public statement, June 4, 1963.

We have relegated the Saints to a pink and blue and gold world of plaster statuary that belongs to the past; it is a hangover, a relic, of the Dark Ages when men were the children of fantasy's magic. We are content to place a statue of Francis of Assisi in the middle of a bird bath and let the whole business of the Saints go at that.

> C. KILMER MYERS, vicar, Chapel of the Intercession, New York, on lost role of Saints in Christian tradition, *New York Times*, March 19, 1962.

The 11 o'clock hour on Sunday is the most segregated hour in American life.

> JAMES A. PIKE, Bishop of California, *U.S. News & World Report*, May 16, 1960.

Heresy in embryo . . .

> JAMES A. PIKE, on glossolalia (speaking in tongues) and other over-emphasis on one form of worship, *Time*, May 17, 1963.

Help one another, serve one another, for the times are urgent and the days are evil. Help one another, serve one another, as from this hundredth ceremony at St. Augustine's throne there goes a band of those whose hearts God has touched.

> ARTHUR MICHAEL RAMSEY, Archbishop of Canterbury, conclusion of sermon upon his enthronement in Canterbury Cathedral, *The Hundredth Archbishop of Canterbury* by James B. Simpson, Harper & Row, 1962.

Learning to laugh at ourselves, we did not lack other things to laugh about. How should we, if the Christian life is indeed the knowledge of Him who is the author of laughter as well as tears?

> ARTHUR MICHAEL RAMSEY, on his days as a seminarian, *ibid.*

Take heed to thyself, that self which can deceive itself unless it is revealed in naked simplicity before its God. It is in this taking heed that a true devoutness, simple, generous, Godward, has its root and its renewing.

> ARTHUR MICHAEL RAMSEY, to men about to be ordained priests, *ibid.*

The supreme question is not what we make of the Eucharist but what the Eucharist is making of us. . . .

> ARTHUR MICHAEL RAMSEY, on the place of Holy Communion in the worship of God, *ibid.*

There is a simplicity born of shallowness, and falsely so called; and there is a simplicity which is the costly outcome of the discipline of mind and heart and will. Simplicity in preaching is properly the simplicity of the knowledge of God and of human beings. To say of someone "he preaches simply" is to say "he walks with God."

> ARTHUR MICHAEL RAMSEY, *ibid.*

Reason is an action of the mind; knowledge is a possession of the mind; but faith is an attitude of the person. It means you are prepared to stake yourself on something being so.

> ARTHUR MICHAEL RAMSEY, *ibid.*

I often think the doctrines of fasting in Lent and having meatless days are old-fashioned. . . . It might be better to give up television. That would be a more meaningful self-denial in this day and age.

> ARTHUR MICHAEL RAMSEY, *ibid.*

When an Anglican is asked, "Where was your Church before the Reformation?" his best answer is to put the counter-question, "Where was your face before you washed it?"

> ARTHUR MICHAEL RAMSEY, on continuity of the Church, *ibid.*

One is very fond of one's mother and listens to her advice, but does not consult her in everyday business.

> HENRY KNOX SHERRILL, Presiding Bishop, U.S. Episcopal Church, on affectionate but unbinding ties between American Church and primatial See of Canterbury, *Newsweek*, June 5, 1950.

Outward, for centuries, flowed the tide of British Empire; back, in hurried decades, it ebbed. On every foreign strand that it touched, the receding tide has left a church uniquely English, yet catholic enough to survive in any climate. It is grand and symbolic that as a typical consequence, there should be in the South Pacific a bishop who follows the ancient Church of England custom by styling himself Norman New Zealand. Empire is gone; the Church remains.

> TIME, Aug. 16, 1963, beginning of a major article on Anglican Communion.

Baptist

Every serious life has that experience where the profundities within ask for an answering profundity. No longer do the shallows suffice. Life within faces some profound abyss of experience, and the deep asks for an answering deep. So when deep calls unto deep and the deep replies, we face the essential experience of religion.

> HARRY EMERSON FOSDICK, pastor emeritus, Riverside Church, New York, "When Life Reaches Its Depths," *Riverside Sermons*, Harper & Row, 1958.

I would rather live in a world where my life is surrounded by mystery than live in a world so small that my mind could comprehend it.

> HARRY EMERSON FOSDICK, "The Mystery of Life," *ibid.*

Just because you were born in a garage, does that make you an automobile?

> BILLY GRAHAM, to listeners who said they were born in good Christian homes and therefore didn't need to be "converted," *Time*, Nov. 17, 1952.

May the Lord bless you real good.

> BILLY GRAHAM, favorite benediction, *Newsweek*, Feb. 1, 1954.

I just want to lobby for God.

> BILLY GRAHAM, on establishing a national headquarters in Washington, Dec. 12, 1955.

Segregation is the adultery of an illicit intercourse between injustice and immorality.

> MARTIN LUTHER KING, sermon in Brooklyn church, *New York Times*, July 1, 1963.

There is something distinctive that I always look for in men of serious purpose. Those who so live and work are, I find, believing men. Many are praying men. Again, many seem to do their praying not in words, but in the best work they can perform.

> J. C. PENNEY, noted merchandising executive, "Something to Lean On," *Rotarian*, Aug., 1956.

Jewish

A human life is like a single letter in the alphabet. It can be meaningless. Or it can be part of a great meaning.

> OPENING SENTENCES of an essay, "Who Takes Delight in Life?" printed on full pages purchased in *New York Times* and *New York Herald Tribune* by National Planning Committee, of Jewish Theological Seminary of America, on Rosh Hashana, Sept. 5, 1956.

A religious man is a person who holds God and man in one thought at one time, at all times, who suffers harm done to others, whose greatest passion is compassion, whose greatest strength is love and defiance of despair.

> ABRAHAM JOSHUA HESCHEL, Jewish Theological Seminary of America, *New York Journal-American*, April 5, 1963.

. . . Any man who is seeking public office and allows his ambition to affect his religious affiliation is not worthy of the confidence of his fellow citizens. . . .

> HERBERT LEHMAN, former Governor of New York, reply to a letter from a young Jewish boy asking if he would be handicapped in seeking public office; recalled on Mr. Lehman's death, *New York Herald Tribune*, Dec. 9, 1963.

America to us is a dream in the constant process of realization, a vision constantly being fulfilled. A dream and a vision, as old as the ancient Hebrew prophets, as new as the yearning in the hearts of men today.

> JUDAH NADICH, rabbi, invocation at Republican National Convention, news reports of Aug. 22, 1956.

I sing what is in my heart. My only thought now is to sing as I have never sung before.

> BETTY ROBBINS, Long Island housewife who became first woman cantor in Jewish history, news summaries of Aug. 15, 1955.

I felt there's a wealth in Jewish tradition, a great inheritance. I'd be a jerk not to take advantage of it.

> HERMAN WOUK, on his return to Orthodoxy, *Time*, Sept. 5, 1955.

Deep in the heart of both critical Christian and alienated Jew, there is . . . a feeling, not even a feeling, a shadow of a notion, nothing more substantial than the pointless but compelling impulse to knock on wood when one talks of the health of children—*something* that says there is more to Jews than meets the eye. There is a mystery about the Jews . . . and within this mystery lies the reason for the folk pride of the house of Abraham. This pride exists despite the disabilities that come from many centuries of ostracism.

> HERMAN WOUK, *This Is My God*, Doubleday, 1959.

214

Methodist

No one who has had a unique experience with prayer has a right to with-hold it from others.

> Madame Chiang Kai-shek, "The Power of Prayer," *Reader's Digest,* Aug., 1955.

. . . The Church recruited people who had been starched and ironed be-fore they were washed.

> John Wesley Lord, Methodist bishop, on post-war religious revival that swelled church memberships with people drawn by fear of war, hope of social prestige, or other non-religious reasons, *Time,* Feb. 1, 1963

Religion, in some quarters, is being identified with the cult of success, and prayer as but a means to promotion to the presidency of the company. This is not a worthy approach to the Eternal.

> G. Bromley Oxnam, Methodist bishop, news reports of Oct. 31, 1955.

I sit for six days a week like a weaver behind his loom busily fingering the threads of an intricate pattern. On the seventh day the church in its worship calls me around in front of the loom to look at the pattern on which I have been working. It bids me to compare the design of my days with the pattern shown me on Mount Sinai and the Mount of Olives. Some threads thereupon I have to cut, others I pull more tightly, and most of all I renew my picture of the whole plan.

> Ralph W. Sockman, Minister Emeritus, Christ Church, Methodist, New York; interview with James B. Simpson, 1961.

Our love for God is tested by the question of whether we seek Him or His gifts.

> Ralph W. Sockman, on loving God, *ibid.*

A service of worship is primarily a service to God. When we realize this and act upon it, we make it a service to men.

> Ralph W. Sockman, on going to church, *ibid.*

The hope of free man in a frightened world is the values which man puts ahead of inventions when his back is to the wall. These values are beauty, truth, goodness and having a faith, all of which are bomb-proof.

RALPH W. SOCKMAN, on values, *ibid.*

Religion is a vision of a world which, though invisible to the eye of flesh, is utterly real and endures forever, giving meaning to life, holding the higher goods of life and supplying power to achieve them. When men lose sight of this invisible, enduring world, they invariably play the present against the future, partly because they have no real faith that for them there is a future.

ERNEST FREMONT TITTLE, senior minister, First Methodist Church, Evanston, Ill., 1918–1949, sermon on "The Long View," included in his book *A Mighty Fortress*, Harper & Row, 1950.

Roman Catholic

. . . The true vocation [is] settled on the day the girl looks around her and sees a young woman her own age in pretty clothes wheeling a baby carriage by the convent. Then her heart takes an awful flop and she knows what it is God really is asking of her. If she stays—then she has a true calling and the making of a good religious.

MOTHER MARY AMBROSE of Marist Missionary Sisters, *Life*, March 15, 1963.

If [the birth control advocate] considers us souls to be rescued from stork worship and the hardship of large families, let us respect his motives, honor his altruism, accept as genuine his sense of civic responsibility. And wish he would do the same for us.

APRIL OURSLER ARMSTRONG, convert to Roman Catholicism and mother of seven youngsters, in her book, *Water In the Wine*, McGraw-Hill, 1963.

Living our faith in a world of men who consider sex apart from the Christian mystery, in a world convinced of the *virtue* of birth prevention, can be true heroic unsung martyrdom.

APRIL OURSLER ARMSTRONG, *ibid.*

216

Advocacy of conflicting opinions must always be the wellspring of the Church's intellectual life.

>   CATHOLIC COMMISSION ON INTELLECTUAL AND CULTURAL AFFAIRS, rebuke to administrator of Catholic University of America, Washington, for ban of four liberal theologians, *Harper's*, December, 1963.

. . . I call these children exceptional children because they give us an exceptional opportunity to manifest our love for God by loving the least of his children and these tots certainly are the least of the children of the Lord.

>   RICHARD CARDINAL CUSHING, Archbishop of Boston, on new home for children mentally handicapped, CBS-TV, April 16, 1954.

[I am] a fool for Christ.

>   DOROTHY DAY, quoted by critic Dwight Macdonald, *Esquire*, October, 1963, on her longtime editorship of *The Catholic Worker* and her work for various charities; a paraphrase of Paul (I Cor. 4:10): "We are fools for Christ's sake."

More than ever before the world has need of God-hunters, even though it may not understand this, and even though the apparent uselessness of your life scandalizes it. Hunting God is a great adventure.

>   MARIE DE FLORIS, Benedictine abbot of En-Calcat, France, to novices making their vows, quoted in *Benedictine and Moor* by Peter Beach and William Dunphy, Holt, Rinehart & Winston, 1960.

Lourdes is a land of miracles, but it is above all a place where an avalanche of grace takes place. It is a real hospital for souls.

>   PIERRE CARDINAL GERLIER, Archbishop of Lyons and Primate of France, on centennial of apparitions of Our Lady of Lourdes, *Time*, Feb. 24, 1958.

I am made to tremble and I fear!

>   JOHN XXIII (Angelo Giuseppe Cardinal Roncalli), on being told of his election to succeed the late Pius XII, news summaries of Oct. 30, 1958.

Dear sons and brothers, you could not come to see me so I have come to see you.

>   JOHN XXIII, on first papal visit to a prison since 1870, Dec. 26, 1958.

217

I have looked into your eyes with my eyes. I have put my heart near your heart.

> JOHN XXIII, to a prisoner who asked if Pope's message could be for him, *ibid.*

We ardently desire their return to the house of the common Father . . . they will not enter a strange house but their own.

> JOHN XXIII, surprise announcement calling Ecumenical Council to discuss unity of Christendom, news summaries of Feb. 9, 1959.

Love the soil. The work is hard and sometimes the return is little. . . . But you will find in the good earth and fields a sure refuge from dangerous materialism.

> JOHN XXIII, himself a tenant farmer's son, to an audience of 35,000 farmers, *New York Times*, April 23, 1959.

All are equally created to the glory of the Lord that sanctifies the peoples without discrimination of language, descent or color.

> JOHN XXIII, on first cardinals ever appointed for Japan, Tanganyika, and the Philippines, *New York Post*, March 28, 1960.

The Council now beginning rises in the Church like the daybreak, a forerunner of most splendid light.

> JOHN XXIII, opening Second Vatican Council in presence of 2,500 cardinals, patriarchs, and bishops and many non-Roman observers, *Newsweek*, Oct. 22, 1962.

Insofar as it concerns my humble person, I would not like to claim any special inspiration. I content myself with the sound doctrine which teaches that everything comes from God.

> JOHN XXIII, on papal power, *Time*, Oct. 26, 1962.

My eye ranged over the multitude of sons and brothers and suddenly as my glance rested upon your group, on each of you personally, I drew a special comfort from your presence. I will not say more about that at the moment but will content myself with recording the fact: *Benedictus Deus per singulos dies* [Blessed be God each day as it comes]. Yet, if you could read my heart, you would perhaps understand much more than words can say.

> JOHN XXIII, to non-Roman observers of opening Ecumenical Council, *ibid.*

It is now for the Catholic Church to bend herself to her work with calmness and generosity. It is for you to observe her with renewed and friendly attention.

> JOHN XXIII, to Ecumenical Council, *ibid.*

You have not come to see the son of a king, of an emperor, or one of the greats of this earth but only a priest, a son of poor people, who was called by the Lord and carries the burden of being the Supreme Pontiff.

> JOHN XXIII, on a visit to slums of Rome, *Newsweek*, Dec. 17, 1962.

Elizabeth Seton is the first officially recognized flower of sanctity which the United States of America offers to the world.

> JOHN XXIII, on beatification of Mother Seton, founder of parochial school system in the U.S., March 17, 1963.

. . . The conviction that all men are equal by reason of their natural dignity has been generally accepted. Hence racial discrimination can no longer be justified. . . . Consequently there are no political communities which are superior by nature and none which are inferior by nature.

> JOHN XXIII, in *Pacem in Terris*, last of eight encyclicals of his four-and-one-half-year reign and first in centuries of papal letters not addressed to Roman Catholics alone but to "all men of good will," April 10, 1963.

One must never confuse error and the person who errs . . .

> JOHN XXIII, *ibid.*

Universal peace is a good which interests everybody without distinction: To everybody, therefore, we have opened our soul.

> JOHN XXIII, speaking of *Pacem in Terris* on a radio and television broadcast following an unusual ceremony in which he publicly signed encyclical, *ibid.*

219

If God wants the sacrifice of the Pope's life, let it lead to copious favors for the Ecumenical Council, the Church, and humanity, which aspires to peace. If on the other hand God pleases to prolong this Pontifical service, let it serve for the sanctification of the Pope's soul.

> JOHN XXIII, comment on his final illness, *New York Herald Tribune*, May 27, 1963.

I have been able to follow my death step by step and now my life goes gently to its end.

> JOHN XXIII, in his last hours, *New York Daily News*, June 2, 1963.

The feelings of my smallness and my nothingness always kept me good company. . . .

> JOHN XXIII, in his will made public June 6, 1963.

Born poor, but of honored and humble people, I am particularly proud to die poor. . . .

> JOHN XXIII, *ibid.*

The most important thing about me is that I am a Catholic. It's a super-structure within which you can work, like the sonnet. I need that. A good director tells the actors where to move exactly; then they're free to *act.* I'm grateful for that discipline, and I've never had a crisis of conscience.

> JEAN KERR, *Time*, April 14, 1961.

Encased in ecclesiastical preferment, they [wield] from their invisible and inaccessible Roman offices a power which could make the parish priests of Pernambuco tremble and which could explode ecclesiastical bombs in San Francisco or Sydney.

> ROBERT KAISER, writing of the Roman Curia in his book, *Pope, Council and World*, Macmillan, 1963, a popular report that was banned during the second session of the Ecumenical Council.

[He symbolizes] the old order, its obstinacy, its refusal to change, its admitted strength, an antique cast in ancient bronze, silently unmalleable, quietly unreceptive.

> ROBERT KAISER, on Alfredo Cardinal Ottaviani, Secretary of the Sacred Congregation of the Holy Office (the Curia), *ibid.*

220

The United Nations Secretariat is more catholic than the Roman Curia of the Catholic Church.

> HANS KÜNG, dean, Catholic Theological Faculty, University of Tübingen, Germany, address during visit to New York, *Harper's*, December, 1963. During the Ecumenical Council, Father Küng came to be regarded as one of the most brilliant and articulate scholars on internal Church reform.

An unreformed Church cannot carry conviction. Apologetics without Church reform are worthless.

> HANS KÜNG, *ibid.*

Every manifestation in the Church of lack of freedom, however harmless, however much under cover, whatever religious trimmings it may have, contributes toward making the Church less believable in the eyes of the world and of men in general; and that is a miserable disaster.

> HANS KÜNG, *ibid.*

The prophet of despair gains a shouting audience. But one who speaks from hope will be heard long after the noise dies down.

> JOHN LAFARGE, S.J., "Hope in Your Heart," *This Week*, Oct. 9, 1960.

I am not so much trying to persuade people to walk on a certain road as I am to show them the road that I am convinced they are sooner or later going to walk on.

> JOHN LAFARGE, S.J., statement recalled on his death at 83, *New York Herald Tribune*, Nov. 25, 1963.

The religion of Christ is not aspirin to deaden the pain of living, it is not a discussion group, nor a miraculous medal nor a piety, nor bingo for God. Not anything less than a joyous adventure of being Christ in a world still skeptical of Him.

> JOHN MONAGHAN, Manhattan priest, "A Lenten Message," *New York Journal-American*, Feb. 16, 1961.

We open our arms to all those who glory in the name of Christ. We call them with the sweet name of brothers, and let them know they will find

221

in us constant comprehension and benevolence, that they will find in Rome the paternal house.

> PAUL VI (Giovanni Batista Cardinal Montini), in his first address as Pope, indicating he would continue his predecessor's quest for unity, June 22, 1963.

As our very first action, though it be in fear and trembling, we bow down in veneration before the hidden designs of God, who has willed to impose upon our slender powers an immense though most important burden— the Catholic Church, an institution than which there is most assuredly no greater or more holy upon the earth.

> PAUL VI, coronation address, June 30, 1963.

The fundamental attitude of Catholics who want to convert the world is loving it. We shall love our neighbors and those far afield. We shall love our country, we shall love other people's. We shall love Catholics, the schismatics, the Protestants, the Anglicans, the indifferent, the Moslems, the pagans and the atheists. We shall love those who merit and those who do not merit to be loved. We shall love our time, our civilization, our technical science, our art, our sport, our world. . . .

> PAUL VI, statement when in 1957, as Archbishop of Milan, he addressed World Congress for Lay Apostolate; recalled on his elevation to Papacy, *Life*, July 5, 1963.

We speak now to the representatives of the Christian denominations separated from the Catholic Church, who have nevertheless been invited to take part as observers in this solemn assembly. . . . If we are in any way to blame for that separation, we humbly beg God's forgiveness and ask pardon, too, of our brethren who feel themselves to have been injured by us.

> PAUL VI, in address opening second session of Ecumenical Council Vatican II, Sept. 29, 1963. His desire for "pardon" by non-Roman Catholics was considered one of the most remarkable aspects of his address.

. . . The Council will build a bridge toward the contemporary world.

> PAUL VI, *ibid.*

222

Let the world know this: the Church looks at the world with profound understanding, with sincere admiration and with the sincere intention not of conquering it but of serving it, not of despising it but of appreciating it, not of condemning it but of strengthening it.

> PAUL VI, *ibid.*

The episcopacy is not an institution independent of, or separated from, or still less, antagonistic to, the Supreme Pontificate of Peter, but with Peter and under him it strives for the common good and the supreme end of the Church.

> PAUL VI, on the relationship of bishops to the papacy; address at closing of second session of Ecumenical Council, Dec. 4, 1963.

We shall see that blessed land whence Peter set forth and where not one of his successors has returned.

> PAUL VI, disclosing his plans to visit the Holy Land, thus becoming the first Pope to leave Italy since 1809 and the only one since the apostle Peter to see the homeland of Christ.

Most humbly and briefly we shall return there as an expression of prayer, penance and renovation to offer to Christ His Church, to summon to this one holy Church our separated brethren, to implore divine mercy on behalf of peace among men . . . to beseech Christ our Lord for the salvation of the entire human race.

> PAUL VI, *ibid.*

If an atomic bomb falls on the world tomorrow, it is because I argued with my neighbor today.

> DOMINIQUE GEORGES HENRI PIRE, Dominican priest of Tihange le Huy, Belgium, who won 1958 Nobel Prize for Peace; comment during visit to U.S., *New York Journal-American*, Dec. 9, 1963.

. . . . The Year of the great return and pardon.

> PIUS XII (Eugenio Cardinal Pacelli), proclaiming Holy Year of 1950, *Life*, Jan. 9, 1950.

223

. . . The presence of Mary in soul and body in Heaven is a God-revealed truth. . . . Hence if anyone deliberately presumes to think otherwise, let him know that in his judgment he stands condemned, has suffered shipwreck in faith and has separated himself from the Church's unity.

> Pius XII, reading Papal Bull which proclaimed dogmatic belief in bodily assumption of the Virgin Mary into heaven, *Time*, Nov. 6, 1950.

It is true that Divine Providence has invested me, although unworthily, in this position as head of the Church, but as a man I am nothing . . . nothing . . . nothing.

> Pius XII, verbal reply to expression of loyalty given him by Fulton Sheen, Auxiliary Bishop of New York, *Look*, Aug. 22, 1955.

I shall be able to rest one minute after I die.

> Pius XII, to physicians who asked him to curtail his work, *ibid*.

Labor is not merely the fatigue of body without sense or value; nor is it merely a humiliating servitude. It is a service of God, a gift of God, the vigor and fullness of human life, the gage of eternal rest.

> Pius XII, message for Labor Day, *Guideposts*, Sept., 1955.

Bodily pain affects man as a whole down to the deepest layers of his moral being. It forces him to face again the fundamental questions of his fate, of his attitude toward God and fellow man, of his individual and collective responsibility and of the sense of his pilgrimage on earth.

> Pius XII, to international group of heart specialists received in audience, news summaries of Sept. 1, 1956.

God has no intention of setting a limit to the efforts of man to conquer space.

> Pius XII, on interplanetary explorations, news reports of Sept. 21, 1956.

I humbly ask pardon of all whom I may have offended, harmed or scandalized by word or by deed.

> Pius XII, in will, made public following his death, Oct. 8, 1958.

224

The concept of the woman of the shipyards, of the mines, of heavy labor as it is exalted and practiced by some countries that would want to inspire progress is anything but a modern concept. It is, on the contrary, a sad return toward epochs that Christian civilization buried long ago.

> Pius XII, address to several thousand members of an Italian feminist group, news reports of Oct. 15, 1956.

I have taken this step because I want the discipline, the fire and the authority of the Church. I am hopelessly unworthy of it, but I hope to become worthy.

> Dame Edith Sitwell, at 67, on being received into Roman Catholic Church, news summaries of Aug. 15, 1955.

My years in Carmel have taught me one thing: when God asks us to sacrifice the normal joys of living, it is only that He may give us a higher and holier joy. Living with God alone in the solitude of Carmel has proved sweeter far to me than all the pleasure and fickle applause of the world.

> Mother Catherine Thomas, *My Beloved: The Story of a Carmelite Nun*, McGraw-Hill, 1955.

We exchange the voice of a human suitor for the heavenly call of Christ, the Eternal Bridegroom; the earth, the here and the now, we exchange for the timelessness of the cloister; the tinsel treasures and the passing pleasures of the world we exchange for the priceless spiritual riches and the incomparable joy of living for others with Christ in poverty and penance. In exchange for running after shadows, we receive the privilege of touching reality. In exchange for the possibility of success in the world, we receive the certainty of the failure of Calvary; in exchange for social position and prestige, we accept the humility and hiddenness of Carmel. In exchange for the variable affections of the world, we receive the steadfast charity of Carmel; in exchange for radios and newspapers, we have the silence of Carmel; in exchange for mad jazz and concert music, we have the Gregorian chant whose only audience is God. . . .

> Mother Catherine Thomas, *ibid.*

Sometimes Christ is silent. Sometimes the Church is silent. Sometimes its priests must be silent. I have been silent for three years. But let us not

225

waste time with an assessment of the past. Forgiving everything, the Church has work to do.

> STEFAN CARDINAL WYSZYNSKI, on returning to Warsaw from Communist imprisonment, *Life*, Jan. 14, 1957.

I tell you, you will serve only your God, because man is too noble to serve anyone but God.

> STEFAN CARDINAL WYSZYNSKI, sermon against his Communist adversaries, *New York Times*, March 20, 1961.

Love

There is only one situation I can think of in which men and women make an effort to read better than they usually do. When they are in love and reading a love letter, they read for all they are worth. They read every word three ways; they read between the lines and in the margins . . . They may even take the punctuation into account. Then, if never before or after, they read.

MORTIMER J. ADLER, *Quote,* Dec. 26, 1961.

At the outset I was quite detached. I selected quite objectively from many girls the one who met all the requirements. That girl was Miss Shoda. It later turned to love. I am marrying her because I love her.

AKIHITO, Crown Prince of Japan, on becoming the first member of the Japanese royal family to wed a commoner, news summaries of April 12, 1959.

There is nothing enduring in life for a woman except what she builds in a man's heart.

JUDITH ANDERSON, *Coronet,* Sept., 1958.

If you haven't had at least a slight poetic crack in the heart, you have been cheated by nature. Because a broken heart is what makes life so wonderful five years later, when you see the guy in an elevator and he is fat and smoking a cigar and saying long-time-no-see. If he hadn't broken your heart, you couldn't have that glorious feeling of relief!

PHYLLIS BATTELLE, *New York Journal-American,* June 1, 1962.

On the whole, I haven't found men unduly loath to say, "I love you." The real trick is to get them to say, "Will you marry me?"

ILKA CHASE, *This Week,* Feb. 5, 1956.

227

He came into my life as the warm wind of spring had awakened flowers, as the April showers awaken the earth. My love for him was an unchanging love, high and deep, free and faithful, strong as death. Each year I learned to love him more and more . . .

> ANNA CHENNAULT, a daughter of Chinese aristocracy, on her romance and marriage to U.S. General Claire Chennault, *A Thousand Springs*, Taplinger, 1962.

Many a man has fallen in love with a girl in a light so dim he would not have chosen a suit by it.

> MAURICE CHEVALIER, news summaries, July 17, 1955.

An archeologist is the best husband any woman can have: the older she gets, the more interested he is in her.

> AGATHA CHRISTIE, news reports of March 9, 1954.

[My wife] told me one of the sweetest things one could hear—"I am not jealous. But I am truly sad for all the actresses who embrace you and kiss you while acting, for with them, you are only pretending."

> JOSEPH COTTEN, when asked if his wife had ever been jealous of his leading ladies; the interview's publication coincided with Mrs. Cotten's death at 55, *New York Herald Tribune*, Jan. 8, 1960.

I've sometimes thought of marrying—and then I've thought again.

> NOEL COWARD, *Theatre Arts*, Nov. 1956.

Most of them lead lives of unquiet desperation, continually seeking, in sex they wish was love and in the love they suspect is only sex, a center for their worlds to turn on.

> DAVID DEMPSEY, novelist, reviewing a story of Greenwich Village by Warren Miller, *New York Times*, April 27, 1958.

His people talk so tenderly and wittily of love, and yet love so badly. The men are confused in their masculinity, the women desperate in their womanness. Perhaps that's why the talk is so good. Otherwise there might have been less to say and more to do.

> DAVID DEMPSEY, *ibid.*

228

How do you know love is gone? If you said that you would be there at seven and you get there by nine, and he or she has not called the police yet—it's gone.

> MARLENE DIETRICH, *Marlene Dietrich's ABC's*, Doubleday, 1961.

Grumbling is the death of love.

> MARLENE DIETRICH, *ibid*.

To Mamie, For never-failing help since 1916—in calm and in stress, in dark days and in bright. Love—Ike, Christmas 1955.

> PRESIDENT EISENHOWER, message engraved on a gold medallion as Christmas gift to his wife, Dec. 25, 1955.

No, I haven't any formula. I can just say it's been a very happy experience . . . a successful marriage I think gets happier as the years go by, that's about all.

> PRESIDENT EISENHOWER, asked for a comment on his 43rd wedding anniversary; news conference of July 1, 1959.

Bitterness imprisons life; love releases it. Bitterness paralyzes life; love empowers it. Bitterness sours life; love sweetens it. Bitterness sickens life; love heals it. Bitterness blinds life; love anoints its eyes.

> HARRY EMERSON FOSDICK, *Riverside Sermons*, Harper & Row, 1958.

You can see them alongside the shuffleboard courts in Florida or on the porches of the old folks' homes up north: an old man with snow-white hair, a little hard of hearing, reading the newspaper through a magnifying glass; an old woman in a shapeless dress, her knuckles gnarled by arthritis, wearing sandals to ease her aching arches. They are holding hands, and in a little while they will totter off to take a nap, and then she will cook supper, not a very good supper, and they will watch television, each knowing exactly what the other is thinking, until it is time for bed. They may even have a good, soul-stirring argument, just to prove that they still really care. And through the night they will snore unabashedly, each resting content because the other is there. They are in love, they have always been in love, although sometimes they would have denied it. And because they have been in love they have survived everything that life could throw at them, even their own failures.

> ERNEST HAVEMANN, in concluding article in his series, "Love and Marriage," *Life*, Sept. 29, 1961.

229

. . . I was at a party feeling very shy because there were a lot of celebrities around, and I was sitting in a corner alone and a very beautiful young man came up to me and offered me some salted peanuts and he said, "I wish they were emeralds" as he handed me the peanuts and that was the end of my heart. I never got it back.

> HELEN HAYES, recollection of first meeting her husband, Charles MacArthur, CBS-TV, Jan. 14, 1955.

My Charlie would not have been spectacular enough to be a book. He was my gentle lover, my understanding husband, my gay companion, the sympathetic father of our children. How could you make a book out of that? But it made a lovely life.

> HELEN HAYES, writing of Charles MacArthur in an introduction to *Charlie* by Ben Hecht, Harper & Row, 1957.

The truth [is] that there is only one terminal dignity—love. And the story of a love is not important—what is important is that one is capable of love. It is perhaps the only glimpse we are permitted of eternity.

> HELEN HAYES, *Guideposts,* Jan. 1960.

. . . Love is a hole in the heart.

> BEN HECHT, in his play, *Winkelberg,* produced in New York in Jan., 1958.

A man nearly always loves for other reasons than he thinks. A lover is apt to be as full of secrets from himself as is the object of his love from him.

> BEN HECHT, *Think,* February, 1963.

Only the really plain people know about love—the very fascinating ones try so hard to create an impression that they soon exhaust their talents.

> KATHARINE HEPBURN, *Look,* Feb. 18, 1958.

As lovers, modern men and women may not be nearly as graceful as the Renaissance courtiers, as lusty as the rationalists, nor as sweetly eloquent as the Victorians; yet more than any of these they consider love the *sine qua non* of the happy life. Americans, who make more of marrying for love than any other people, also break up more of their marriages (close to 400,000 annually), but the figure reflects not so much the failure of love as the determination of people not to live without it.

> MORTON HUNT, *The Natural History of Love*, Knopf, 1959.

I have all my life, my brethren, hidden my worries, my problems and cares from you, wearing a smile on my face which never knew its way into my heart. I know loneliness eating my days and nights. I feel my spirit tearing and burning in a fire of gloomy loneliness and pitiful isolation. I needed affection.

> KING HUSSEIN, announcing his engagement to Toni Avril Gardiner, daughter of British army officer, *Time*, May 12, 1961.

How much do we know about love? The first thing we know about love is that, for most of us, it is the most absorbing and interesting subject in existence. There is an enormous range of meanings in this one little word "love." There are mother love and self-love, father love and children's love for their parents; there are brotherly love and love of one's home and one's country; love of money and love of power; making love and loving food; there are music lovers, sports lovers, bird lovers, sun lovers. Preachers insist that we should love God; Jesus adjures us to love our enemies. Love clearly includes all these usages: but the love in which one can be is the pre-eminent love for most of us.

> JULIAN HUXLEY, "All About Love," *Look*, July 12, 1955.

The Senior Prom is the point at which we learn how well we are doing thus far. A date means we are popular with at least one other person and, therefore, we are potentially lovable. Reassured, we press on.

> JULIAN HUXLEY, *ibid*.

When the wedding march sounds the resolute approach, the clock no longer ticks; it tolls the hour. . . . The figures in the aisle are no longer individuals; they symbolize the human race.

> ANNE MORROW LINDBERGH, *Dearly Beloved*, Harcourt, Brace & World, 1962.

So long as the emotional feelings between the couple are right, so long as there is mutual trust and love, their bodies will invariably make the appropriate responses.

> DR. DAVID R. MACE, *Time*, March 10, 1958.

231

Some women are wonderful and some of them are she-devils. Well, what are you going to do? You can't do with them, you can't do without them.

> BERNARR MACFADDEN, on being jailed at 86 for failure to pay alimony, news summaries of June 30, 1955.

. . . Man can live his truth, his deepest truth, but cannot speak it. It is for this reason that love becomes the ultimate human answer to the ultimate human question. Love, in reason's terms, answers nothing. We say that *Amor vincit omnia*, but, in truth, love conquers nothing—certainly not death—certainly not chance. What love does is to arm. It arms the worth of life in spite of life . . .

> ARCHIBALD MACLEISH, on his Broadway play, *J. B.*, *Time*, Dec. 22, 1958.

I would like it to be known that I have decided not to marry Group Captain Peter Townsend. I have been aware that subject to my renouncing my rights of succession it might have been possible for me to contract a civil marriage. But mindful of the Church's teaching that Christian marriage is indissoluble, and conscious of my duty to the Commonwealth, I have resolved to put these considerations before any others. I have reached this decision entirely alone and in doing so I have been strengthened by the unfailing support and devotion of Group Captain Townsend. I am deeply grateful for the concern of all those who have constantly prayed for my happiness.

> PRINCESS MARGARET of England, news reports of Nov. 1, 1955.

To be in love is merely to be in a state of perpetual anesthesia.

> H. L. MENCKEN, recalled in reports of his death, Jan. 29, 1956.

No normal man ever fell in love after thirty when the kidneys begin to disintegrate.

> H. L. MENCKEN, *ibid*.

I love, you love, we all love, why do we love, who do we love, how much do we love, where do we love, why did you stop loving me?

> MITCH MILLER, on the dominating themes of frustration, nostalgia, and love in popular songs, news summaries of May 24, 1954.

232

You study one another for three weeks, you love each other three months, you fight for three years, you tolerate the situation for 30.
> ANDRÉ DE MISSAN, French author, in a dictionary entitled *Pink and Black.*

A kiss can be a comma, a question mark or an exclamation point. That's basic spelling that every woman ought to know.
> MISTINGUETTE, French actress, *Theatre Arts*, Dec. 1955.

. . . To love means to communicate to the other that you are all for him, that you will never fail him or let him down when he needs you, but that you will always be standing by with all the necessary encouragements. It is something one can communicate to another only if one has it.
> ASHLEY MONTAGU, *The Cultured Man*, World, 1958.

Love is a dweller in strange places and has no proper address. It is no more remarkable to find it lighting the dim marble halls of a palace than blazing on the humble hearth, and the house that knows it not is dark and cold indeed. It is the penchant of poets to crown love with roses, discover it beside a limpid stream or in verdant meadows, but a lover knows this has no bearing on the matter, and given love, the desert springs with flowers.
> MARY PARRISH, "All the Love In the World," *McCall's*, June, 1961.

Love vanquishes time. To lovers, a moment can be eternity, eternity can be the tick of a clock. Across the barriers of time and the ultimate destiny, love persists, for the home of the beloved, absent or present, is always in the mind and heart. Absence does not diminish love.
> MARY PARRISH, *ibid.*

Great lovers will always be unhappy because, for them, love is of supreme importance.
> CESARE PAVESE, Italian author, *The Burning Brand*, Walker & Co., 1961.

This will change my life completely. Everything will become different for me. But what I have brought with me from the home of my childhood will always remain with me. I will remain the one I am.
> ANNE-MARIE RASMUSSEN, announcing at her home at Soegne, Norway, that she would marry Steven Rockefeller, son of New York Governor Nelson Rockefeller, news reports of Aug. 3, 1959. (On coming to the U.S. in 1956, she had been a maid in Rockefeller home.)

I say, when there are spats, kiss and make up before the day is done and live to fight another day.
> RANDOLPH RAY, rector, New York's "Little Church Around the Corner," favorite advice to brides and grooms, *New York World-Telegram & Sun*, June 30, 1956.

I would like to have engraved inside every wedding band, *Be kind to one another.* This is the Golden Rule of marriage, and the secret of making love last through the years.
> RANDOLPH RAY, *My Little Church Around the Corner*, Simon and Schuster, 1957.

It fulfills a most important function in propagation of the human species and is all the more interesting because it is involuntary and shows a readiness to be courted.
> DR. JOSEPH SANDLER, research psychologist, on blushing, news reports of Sept. 9, 1955.

If Marilyn is in love with my husband it proves she has good taste, for I am in love with him, too.
> SIMONE SIGNORET, on rumors linking her husband, Yves Montand, with actress Marilyn Monroe, *New York Journal-American*, Nov. 14, 1960.

. . . There is love, that is the same all over the world. That has always been there . . . the one thing we have really learned the importance of . . . and unless we have the element of love dominating this entire exhibition, we better take it down before we put it up.
> EDWARD STEICHEN, on photographic exhibition entitled, "The Family of Man," NBC-TV, 1955.

Man has survived everything, and we have only survived it on our optimism, and optimism means faith in ourselves, faith in the everydayness of our lives, faith in our universal qualities, and above all, faith in love.
> EDWARD STEICHEN, *ibid.*

A lady of 47 who has been married 27 years and has six children knows what love really is and once described it for me like this: "Love is what you've been through with somebody."
> JAMES THURBER, *Life*, March 14, 1960.

In my Sunday School class there was a beautiful little girl with golden curls. I was smitten at once and still am.

> HARRY TRUMAN, news summaries of Dec. 31, 1952.

We went to Sunday school, public school from the fifth grade through high school, graduated in the same class and marched down life's road together. For me she still has the blue eyes and golden hair of yesteryear.

> HARRY TRUMAN, *Years of Decision*, Doubleday, 1955.

Love is an act of endless forgiveness, a tender look which becomes a habit.

> PETER USTINOV, *Christian Science Monitor*, Dec. 9, 1958.

There is no more disturbing experience in the rich gamut of life than when a young man discovers, in the midst of an embrace, that he is taking the episode quite calmly, and is taking the kiss for what it is worth. His doubts and fears start from this point and there is no end to them. He doesn't know, now, whether it's love or passion. In fact, in the confusion of the moment he's not quite sure it isn't something else altogether, like forgery.

> E. B. WHITE, *New York Journal-American*, Feb. 12, 1961.

Love is an energy which exists of itself. It is its own value.

> THORNTON WILDER, on theme of *The Bridge of San Luis Rey; Time*, Feb. 3, 1958.

. . . Love, though it expends itself in generosity and thoughtfulness, though it gives birth to visions and to great poetry, remains among the sharpest expressions of self interest. Not until it has passed through a long servitude, through its own self-hatred, through mockery, through great doubts, can it take its place among the loyalties. Many who have spent a lifetime in it can tell us less of love than the child that lost a dog yesterday.

> THORNTON WILDER, quoted by Edmund Fuller in "The Notation of the of the Heart," from *The American Scholar Reader*, edited by Hiram Hayden and Betsy Saunders, Atheneum, 1960.

Ah! There will be a happy man, a grateful husband and father, in this old house next Friday if you all turn up safe and sound—a fellow with overflowing heart! Do you realize that I have been alone (what I consider alone) in this old mansion for just about half of the time I have been President? That's a h—— of a way to treat a President, isn't it?

> WOODROW WILSON, letter sent from White House in 1913 to his wife, Ellen Axson Wilson; one of a collection of 1,460 presented to Princeton University, *New York Mirror*, Oct. 26, 1962.

If 20 years were to be erased and I were to be presented with the same choice again under the same circumstances I would act precisely as I did then. . . . Perhaps I needed her even more in those searing lonely moments when I—I alone knew in my heart what my decision must be. I have needed her all these 20 years. I love her and need her now. I always will.

> DUKE OF WINDSOR, on 20th anniversary of his marriage to Wallis Warfield Simpson for whom he abdicated as Edward VIII of England, *New York Journal-American*, June 2, 1957.

Security is when I'm very much in love with somebody extraordinary who loves me back.

> SHELLEY WINTERS, news summaries, July 9, 1954.

The education of a woman's heart is a series of lessons with a series of men until she falls in love for the rest of her life.

> MAURICE ZOLOTOW, *Marilyn Monroe: A Biography*, Harcourt, Brace & World, 1960.

Family Life

Marriage is our last, best chance to grow up.

JOSEPH BARTH, minister, King's Chapel, Boston, *Ladies' Home Journal,*
April, 1961.

A boy is a magical creature—you can lock him out of your workshop,
but you can't lock him out of your heart. You can get him out of your
study, but you can't get him out of your mind. Might as well give up—
he is your captor, your jailer, your boss, and your master—a freckled-
faced, pint-sized, cat-chasing bundle of noise. But when you come home
at night with only the shattered pieces of your hopes and dreams he can
mend them like new with two magic words—"Hi, Dad!"

ALAN BECK, "What Is a Boy?" distributed by New England Mutual
Life Insurance Co., Boston, 1956.

Little girls are the nicest things that happen to people. They are born with
a little bit of angelshine about them and though it wears thin sometimes
there is always enough left to lasso your heart—even when they are sitting
in the mud, or crying temperamental tears, or parading up the street in
mother's best clothes.

ALAN BECK, "What Is a Girl?" *ibid.*

When a boy lays aside his tops, his marbles, and his bike in favor of a
girl, another girl, and still another girl, he becomes a youth. When the
youth discards his first girl and his second girl for *the* girl, he becomes a
bachelor. And when the bachelor can stand it no longer, he turns into a
husband.

ALAN BECK, "What Is A Husband?" *Good Housekeeping,* July, 1957.

A girl becomes a wife with her eyes wide open. She knows that those sweetest words, "I take thee to be my wedded Husband," really mean, "I promise thee to cook three meals a day for sixty years; thee will I clean up after; thee will I talk to even when thou art not listening; thee will I worry about, cry over, and take all manner of hurts from."

> ALAN BECK, "What Is A Wife?" *ibid.*

To succeed as both husband and subject, I believe you need a tightrope walker's sense of balance—and an understanding wife.

> BERNHARD, Prince Consort of the Netherlands, *Collier's*, June 6, 1954.

We just happen to like children.

> FRANCES BLESS on birth of her 18th child, news reports of June 15, 1959.

. . . If either side feels aggrieved, comfort rests in the knowledge that time will eventually even all scores. For yesterday's sittee is today's sitter. Today's employer of a sitter is tomorrow's parent of a sitter. And the sitter herself, incredibly soon, will have her own child to be sat for.

> JEAN LIBMAN BLOCK, conclusion of article on billion dollar business of 6,000,000 baby sitters, *New York Times*, May 22, 1960.

I'll tell you the real secret of how to stay married. Keep the cave clean. They want the cave clean and spotless. Air-conditioned, if possible. Sharpen his spear, and stick it in his hand when he goes out in the morning to spear that bear; and when the bear chases him, console him when he comes home at night, and tell him what a big man he is, and then hide the spear so he doesn't fall over it and stab himself . . .

> JEROME CHODOROV AND JOSEPH FIELDS, *Anniversary Waltz*, Random House, 1954.

A man should sleep sometime between lunch and dinner in order to be at his best in the evening when he joins his wife and friends at dinner. My wife and I tried two or three times in the last forty years to have breakfast together, but it was so disagreeable we had to stop.

> WINSTON CHURCHILL, letter to American friend, news summaries of Dec. 4, 1950.

238

My marriage was much the most fortunate and joyous event which happened to me in the whole of my life.

> WINSTON CHURCHILL, quoted in a biography of his wife, *My Darling Clementine*, by Jack Fishman, McKay, 1963.

My most brilliant achievement was my ability to be able to persuade my wife to marry me.

> WINSTON CHURCHILL, *ibid*.

I never thought that you should be rewarded for the greatest privilege of life.

> MAY ROPER COKER, Hartsville, S.C., on being named "Mother of the Year," *New York Daily News*, May 7, 1958.

The children despise their parents until the age of 40, when they suddenly become just like them—thus preserving the system.

> QUENTIN CREWE, in anthropological study of British upper class, *Saturday Evening Post*, Dec. 1, 1962.

I think housework is the reason most women go to the office.

> HELOISE CRUSE, author of widely syndicated column of housekeeping hints, *Editor & Publisher*, April 27, 1963.

Spoil your husband, but don't spoil your children—that's my philosophy.

> LOUISE SEVIER GIDDINGS CURREY, Lookout Mountain, Tenn., "Mother of the Year," *New York Post*, May 14, 1961.

From wherever men may look out from eternity to see the workings of our world, Jack Kennedy must beam with new pride in that valiant woman who shared his life, especially to the moment of its early and bitter end.

> RICHARD CARDINAL CUSHING, long-time friend of the Kennedy family, in eulogy for the dead President at a Mass in Boston, *New York Times*, Nov. 25, 1963.

239

Socks are a universally recognized symbol of the role relationship between a man and his wife. When a woman won't wash or darn her husband's socks, she is seen by both men and women as being lazy, dissatisfied with her husband, and in general a "no good wife." Or, if she is a good wife, something must be wrong with him.

> E. I. DU PONT DE NEMOURS, research report advising that advertising for men's socks should be directed primarily to women, *Advertising Age,* May 11, 1959.

My wife and I are just exactly like many thousands of other families in America tonight. We have home our son, and what is far more important . . . our grandchildren have home their Daddy.

> PRESIDENT EISENHOWER, on first Thanksgiving after Korean War, *Time,* Dec. 7, 1953.

. . . The external characteristics of home are not the same for each of us. On the coast of Maine, families labor to bring in their livelihood from the gray seas. In the vast reaches of the West many families live isolated from their neighbors. For each American, the meaning of home is unique and personal.

> PRESIDENT EISENHOWER, address to National Council of Catholic Women, Boston, Nov. 8, 1954.

The story of my boyhood and that of my brothers is important only because it could happen in any American family. It did, and will again.

> EARL EISENHOWER, brother of U.S. President, *American Weekly,* April 4, 1954.

Latch-key kids.

> ENGLAND's terminology for children whose parents are working away from home all day, quoted in London dispatch to *Christian Science Monitor,* Feb. 14, 1962.

My son is 7 years old. I am 54. It has taken me a great many years to reach that age. I am more respected in the community, I am stronger, I am more intelligent, and I think I am better than he is. I don't want to be a pal, I want to be a father.

> CLIFTON FADIMAN, on "togetherness" as promoted by American magazines, *Newsweek,* June 16, 1958.

240

The greatest thing in family life is to take a hint when a hint is intended
—and not to take a hint when a hint isn't intended.
>   ROBERT FROST, *Vogue*, March 15, 1963.

The father is always a Republican toward his son, and his mother's always
a Democrat.
>   ROBERT FROST, on parental attitudes, *Writers at Work*, Viking, 1963.

Love your children with all your hearts, love them enough to discipline
them before it is too late. . . . Praise them for important things, even if
you have to stretch them a bit. Praise them a lot. They live on it like bread
and butter and they need it more than bread and butter.
>   LAVINA CHRISTENSEN FUGAL, Pleasant Grove, Utah, "Mother of the
>   Year," news reports of May 3, 1955.

I've never met a mother, no matter how socially disorganized, who
wouldn't rather be socially disorganized in five rooms with a bath and a
kitchen, than in one room.
>   HORTENSE GABEL, Mayor's Assistant for Housing, *New York Times*,
>   May 1, 1961.

Only one woman in ten recognizes her husband as the same man he was
before she married him. Nine out of ten say he's changed. One in three
says he's changed for the worse.
>   GALLUP SURVEY, "The Woman's Mind," *Ladies' Home Journal*, Feb.,
>   1962.

Four is too big for his breeches,
Knows infinitely more than his mother,
Four is a matinee idol
To Two-and-a-Half, his brother.
Four is a lyric composer,
Ranconteur extraordinaire,
Four gets away with murder,
Out of line, and into hair.
Where Four is, there dirt is also,
And nails and lengths of twine,
Four is Mr. Fix-it
And all of his tools are mine.

241

Four barges into everything
(Hearts, too) without a knock.
Four will be five on the twelfth of July,
And I wish I could stop the clock.
> ELISE GIBBS, *Four,* copyright 1955, Curtis Publishing Company.

Just pray for a thick skin and a tender heart.
> RUTH GRAHAM (Mrs. Billy Graham), on being the wife of a famous preacher, news reports of April 22, 1954.

Back of every achievement is a proud wife and a surprised mother-in-law.
> BROOKS HAYS, on being sworn in as a presidential aide, *New York Herald Tribune,* Dec. 2, 1961.

A boy becomes an adult three years before his parents think he does, and about two years after he thinks he does.
> GENERAL LEWIS B. HERSHEY, director of Selective Service, news summaries of Dec. 31, 1951.

The most important thing a father can do for his children is to love their mother.
> THE REVEREND THEODORE HESBURGH, president, Notre Dame University, *Reader's Digest,* Jan. 1963.

Above all, I would teach him to tell the truth. . . . Truth telling, I have found, is the key to responsible citizenship. The thousands of criminals I have seen in 40 years of law enforcement have had one thing in common: every single one was a liar.
> J. EDGAR HOOVER, "What I Would Tell A Son," *Family Weekly,* July 14, 1963.

A woman is not a whole woman without the experience of marriage. In the case of a bad marriage, you win if you lose. Of the two alternatives —bad marriage or none—I believe bad marriage would be better. It is a bitter experience and a high price to pay for fulfillment, but it is the better alternative.
> FANNIE HURST, *Parade,* Sept. 18, 1960.

242

She invoked the understood silence of the long married. . . .
> McCREADY HUSTON, novelist, *The Platinum Yoke*, Lippincott, 1963.

The wife who always insists on the last word, often has it.
> DR. KENNETH HUTCHIN, on keeping husbands alive, *New York Times*, Feb. 26, 1960.

He may be wrong, he probably is, but why do you have to tell him? . . . The trouble is that men like to think they know best. Why not let him think it? It is not a very high price to pay for peace and security and good health.
> DR. KENNETH HUTCHIN, *ibid.*

I will try to be balm, sustainer and sometimes critic for my husband. I will try to help my children look at this job [of President] with all the reverence it is due, to get from it the knowledge their unique vantage point gives them and to retain the lightheartedness to which every teen-ager is entitled. As for my own self, my role must be merged in deeds, not words.
> LADY BIRD JOHNSON, on moving to the White House, *New York Herald Tribune*, Dec. 8, 1963.

Our child will not be raised in tissue paper! . . . We don't want her to even hear the word princess.
> JULIANA, Princess of the Netherlands, on engaging a nurse for her first child, *Ladies' Home Journal*, March, 1955.

Getting keys to their own front doors has done more to Westernize many Japanese than any other single factor. . . . The key will emancipate wives. Their husbands will now have no good excuse for leaving them at home and going off alone to the geisha houses.
> HISAAKIRA KANO, head of Japanese Housing Corporation, on placing locks on apartments, contrary to custom of open doors, *Time*, Nov. 10, 1958.

Jack doesn't belong any more to just a family. He belongs to the country. That's probably the saddest thing about all this. The family can be there.

But there is not much they can do sometimes for the President of the United States.

> JOSEPH P. KENNEDY, at 72, a few weeks before his son's inauguration, *John F. Kennedy, President*, by Hugh Sidey, Atheneum, 1963.

Today's family is built like a pyramid; with all the intrafamilial rivalries, tensions, jealousies, angers, hatreds, loves and needs focused on the untrained, vulnerable, insecure, young, inexperienced, and incompetent parental apex . . . about whose incompetence our vaunted educational system does nothing.

> LAWRENCE KUBIE, psychiatrist, *Newsweek*, March 7, 1960.

There's always room for improvement, you know—it's the biggest room in the house.

> LOUISE HEATH LEBER, New York State "Mother of the Year," *New York Post*, May 14, 1961.

Many a man wishes he were strong enough to tear a telephone book in half—especially if he has a teen-age daughter.

> GUY LOMBARDO, orchestra leader, news summaries of April 19, 1954.

Build me a son, O Lord, who will be strong enough to know when he is weak, and brave enough to face himself when he is afraid, one who will be proud and unbending in honest defeat, and humble and gentle in victory.

> GENERAL DOUGLAS MACARTHUR, "A Father's Prayer," *MacArthur: Rendezvous With History* by Major General Courtney Whitney, Knopf, 1955.

By profession I am a soldier and take pride in that fact. But I am prouder —infinitely prouder—to be a father. A soldier destroys in order to build; the father only builds, never destroys. The one has the potentiality of death; the other embodies creation and life. And while the hordes of death are mighty, the battalions of life are mightier still. It is my hope that my son, when I am gone, will remember me not from the battle but in the home repeating with him our simple daily prayer, "Our Father Who Art in Heaven."

> GENERAL DOUGLAS MACARTHUR, *ibid*.

. . . A great old-fashioned double brass bed, with big brass knobs at the four corners—the sort of bed that 50 years ago husband and wife slept in as a mark of respectability and a proof of the amenity of the married state.
> SOMERSET MAUGHAM, *New York Times*, April 1, 1962.

A successful marriage is an edifice that must be rebuilt every day.
> ANDRÉ MAUROIS, *Speaker's Encyclopedia*, compiled by Jacob M. Brande, Prentice-Hall, 1955.

I love the two of them so much because they are the *we* of me.
> CARSON McCULLERS, lines for role created by Julie Harris, speaking of her family in *The Member of the Wedding*, New Directions, 1951.

God knows that a mother needs fortitude and courage and tolerance and flexibility and patience and firmness and nearly every other brave aspect of the human soul. But because I happen to be a parent of almost fiercely maternal nature, I praise *casualness*. It seems to me the rarest of virtues. It is useful enough when children are small. It is important to the point of necessity when they are adolescents.
> PHYLLIS McGINLEY, *McCall's*, May, 1959.

. . . The most important phase of living with a person: the respect for that person as an individual.
> MILLICENT CAREY McINTOSH, "The Art of Living With Your Children," *Vogue*, Feb. 1, 1953.

The wife in curlpapers is replaced by the wife who puts on lipstick before she wakens her husband.
> MARGARET MEAD, anthropologist, on changes in American marriages, *Look*, Oct. 16, 1956.

One of my children wrote in a third grade piece on how her mother spent her time. She reported "one half time on home, one half time on outside things, one half time writing." An exact description of how it seemed to me, too.
> CHARLOTTE MONTGOMERY, columnist, *Good Housekeeping*, May, 1959.

Lee was such a fine, high-class boy. . . . He didn't waste time with comic books and trashy things. On Sundays I'd take him to church and then we'd have lunch somewhere and go to the zoo. If my son killed the President he would have said so. That's the way he was brought up.

> Marguerite Oswald, mother of alleged assassin of President Kennedy, Lee Harvey Oswald, who was himself slain by Dallas clubowner Jack Ruby, *Time*, Dec. 13, 1963.

Any woman who has a career and a family automatically develops something in the way of two personalities, like two sides of a dollar bill, each different in design. But one can complement the other to make a valuable whole. Her problem is to keep one from draining the life from the other. She can achieve happiness only as long as she keeps the two in balance.

> Ivy Baker Priest, U.S. Treasurer, *Green Grows Ivy*, McGraw-Hill, 1958.

Age seventeen is the point in the journey when the parents retire to the observation car; it is the time when you stop being critical of your eldest son and he starts being critical of you.

> Sally and James Reston, *Saturday Evening Post*, May 5, 1956.

Helping your eldest son pick a college is one of the great educational experiences of life—for the parents. Next to trying to pick his bride, it's the best way to learn that your authority, if not entirely gone, is slipping fast.

> Sally and James Reston, *ibid.*

Will it encourage you to know that I was once as ignorant, helpless and awkward a bride as was ever foisted on an impecunious young lawyer? Together we placed many a burnt offering on the altar of matrimony, and I have lived to serve a meal attractively and well and even to write a cookbook that has proved helpful to others.

> Irma Rombauer, in an introduction to *The Joy of Cooking*, extraordinarily popular cookbook; recalled in reports of her death at 83, *New York Herald Tribune*, Oct. 17, 1962.

The fundamental defect of fathers is that they want their children to be a credit to them.

> Bertrand Russell, *New York Times*, June 9, 1963.

246

You don't raise heroes, you raise sons. And if you treat them like sons, they'll turn out to be heroes, even if it's just in your own eyes.
>   WALTER SCHIRRA, SR., father of America's six-orbit astronaut, *This Week,* Feb. 3, 1963.

It sometimes happens, even in the best of families, that a baby is born. This is not necessarily cause for alarm. The important thing is to keep your wits about you and borrow some money.
>   ELINOR GOULDING SMITH, *The Complete Book of Absolutely Perfect Baby and Child Care,* Harcourt, Brace & World, 1957.

Any parent who has ever found a rusted toy automobile buried in the grass or a bent sand bucket on the beach knows that objects like these can be among the powerful things in the world. They can summon up in an instant, in colors stronger than life, the whole of childhood at its happiest —the disproportionate affection lavished on some strange possession, the concentrated self forgetfulness of play, the elusive expressions of surprise or elation that pass so transparently over youthful features . . .
>   SPORTS ILLUSTRATED, Dec. 26, 1960, introduction to portfolio of pictures, "The Timeless House of Children's Games."

The best games of children are timeless, and there seems to be nothing more natural than play.
>   SPORTS ILLUSTRATED, *ibid.*

. . . The more people have studied different methods of bringing up children the more they have come to the conclusion that what good mothers and fathers instinctively feel like doing for their babies is usually best after all.
>   DR. BENJAMIN SPOCK, quoted in "How to Survive Parenthood," *Life,* June 26, 1950.

First, there is the rocket-boosted mother-in-law. . . . She is queen of the melodrama when her acts of self-sacrifice and martyrdom go unnoticed and unrewarded. Her banner is the tear-stained hanky. She is as phony as a colic cure, transparent as a soap bubble. And as harmless as a barracuda. But she is really more wretched than wicked and needs more help than she can give.
>   ABIGAIL VAN BUREN, "After the Honeymoon," *McCall's,* September, 1962.

247

Then, there's the modern mother-in-law. In her mid-forties, she is the compact car of her breed: efficient, trim, attractive, and in harmony with her times. . . . She's pretty stiff competition for the plain young matron who's overweight and under-financed. If there is going to be friction in this relationship, it could start from envy and resentment in the younger woman. But Father Time is on her side, even if Mother Nature played her a dirty trick.

> ABIGAIL VAN BUREN, *ibid.*

Parents are wise to overlook seemingly disrespectful outbursts from time to time . . . The point must get across the idea that "I love you always, but sometimes I do not love your behavior."

> AMY VANDERBILT, on teen-agers, *Amy Vanderbilt's New Complete Book of Etiquette*, Doubleday, 1963.

My father asserted that there was no better place to bring up a family than in a rural environment. . . . There's something about getting up at 5 a.m., feeding the stock and chickens, and milking a couple of cows before breakfast that gives you a life-long respect for the price of butter and eggs.

> WILLIAM VAUGHN, president, Eastman Kodak Co., *Wall Street Journal*, June 12, 1963.

Perhaps host and guest is really the happiest relation for father and son.

> EVELYN WAUGH, novelist, "Father and Son," *Atlantic*, March, 1963.

She was like the embodiment of all women who have felt an astonished protest because their children have died before them.

> REBECCA WEST, writing of dowager Queen Mary at bier of her son, George VI, *Life*, Feb. 25, 1952.

The thing that impresses me most about America is the way parents obey their children.

> DUKE OF WINDSOR, *Look*, March 5, 1957.

Advice

If you practice an art, be proud of it and make it proud of you . . . It may break your heart, but it will fill your heart before it breaks it; it will make you a person in your own right.

> MAXWELL ANDERSON, author, *New York Herald Tribune*, March 7, 1959.

You must learn day by day, year by year, to broaden your horizon. The more things you love, the more you are interested in, the more you enjoy, the more you are indignant about—the more you have left when anything happens.

> ETHEL BARRYMORE, *New York Mirror*, May 6, 1955.

Let unswerving integrity ever be your watchword.

> BERNARD M. BARUCH, recalling his "most enduring lesson" from his father, news reports of Aug. 20, 1955.

Always do one thing less than you think you can do.

> BERNARD M. BARUCH, counseling businessmen on how to maintain good health, *Newsweek*, May 28, 1956.

If you are ready and able to give up everything else, and will study the market and every stock listed there as carefully as a medical student studies anatomy, and will glue your nose to the ticker tape at the opening of every day of the year and never take it off till night; if you can do all that, and in addition have the cool nerve of a gambler, the sixth sense of a clairvoyant and the courage of a lion—you have a Chinaman's chance.

> BERNARD M. BARUCH, on how to grow wealthy on stock speculations, *New York Mirror*, Jan. 3, 1957.

Never get up with the lark. Get up only for a lark.
> LORD BOYD-ORR, Nobel Prize winner, when asked about his spryness at the age of 75, *Boston Herald*, July 1, 1955.

The public is like a piano. You just have to know what keys to poke.
> AL CAPP, cartoonist, news summaries of March 1, 1954.

The first thing to do in life is to do with purpose what one proposes to do.
> PABLO CASALS, noted cellist, *New York Journal-American*, April 2, 1961.

Never answer a question, other than an offer of marriage, by saying Yes or No.
> SUSAN CHITTY, *The Intelligent Woman's Guide to Good Taste*, Mac-Gibbon & Kee, London, 1958.

If you have an important point to make, don't try to be subtle or clever. Use a pile driver. Hit the point once. Then come back and hit it again. Then hit it a third time—a tremendous whack.
> WINSTON CHURCHILL, advice to the young Prince of Wales on speech-making; quoted by Duke of Windsor in his autobiography, *A King's Story*, Putnam, 1951.

You will do foolish things, but do them with enthusiasm.
> COLETTE, French novelist, to her daughter, quoted by Hope Johnson, *New York World-Telegram & Sun*, April 28, 1961.

When you can, always advise people to do what you see they really want to do, so long as what they want to do isn't dangerously unlawful, stupidly unsocial or obviously impossible. Doing what they want to do, they may succeed; doing what they don't want to do, they won't.
> JAMES GOULD COZZENS, *By Love Possessed*, Harcourt, Brace, 1957.

If a man is vain, flatter. If timid, flatter. If boastful, flatter. In all history, too much flattery never lost a gentleman.
> KATHRYN CRAVENS, *Pursuit of Gentlemen*, Coward-McCann, 1952.

250

The graveyards are full of women whose houses were so spotless you could eat off the floor. Remember the second wife always has a maid.

> HELOISE CRUSE, in her widely published column of advice on housekeeping, *Saturday Evening Post*, March 2, 1963.

You never get promoted when no one else knows your current job. The best basis for being advanced is to organize yourself out of every job you're put into. Most people are advanced because they're pushed up by the people underneath them rather than pulled by the top.

> DONALD DAVID, former dean, Harvard Business School, in *Men At The Top*, by Osborn Elliott, Harper & Row, 1959.

The first and great commandment is, Don't let them scare you.

> ELMER DAVIS, news commentator, *But We Were Born Free*, Bobbs-Merrill, 1954.

To speak ill of others is a dishonest way of praising ourselves; let us be above such transparent egotism. . . . If you can't say good and encouraging things, say nothing. Nothing is often a good thing to say, and always a clever thing to say.

> WILL DURANT, philosopher and author, *New York World-Telegram & Sun*, June 6, 1958.

Don't let life discourage you; everyone who got where he is had to begin where he was.

> RICHARD L. EVANS, veteran radio spokesman for Mormonism, *Time*, July 26, 1963.

You've got to love what's lovable, and hate what's hateable. It takes brains to see the difference.

> ROBERT FROST, interviewed at 84, *New York Post*, May 18, 1958.

Always fall in with what you're asked to accept. Take what is given, and make it over your way. My aim in life has always been to hold my own with whatever's going. Not against: with.

> ROBERT FROST, *Vogue*, March 14, 1963.

251

You have to do a little bragging on yourself even to your relatives—man doesn't get anywhere without advertising.
> JOHN NANCE GARNER, news summaries of Feb. 15, 1954.

I am not a career woman; I am a *woman*. It is because I am a woman that I *have* the career. You are hired *because* you are a woman. If they wanted a man in the job, they would hire one. . . . Don't slip out of your high heels and clobber around in a pair of brogues too big and too tough to fill. Stay in your I. Miller's, kids. Be sure they're pretty, and be sure you fill them well, and you'll do better than you ever dreamed.
> SALLY GIBSON, advertising executive, "It's a Man's World—Enjoy It," address to University of Minnesota co-eds, *Printers' Ink*, Nov. 20, 1959.

On the first sign of a cold, go to bed with a bottle of whisky and a hat. Place hat on left-hand bedpost. Take a drink of whisky and move hat to right-hand post. Take another drink and shift it back again. Continue until you drink the whisky but fail to move the hat. By then the cold is probably cured.
> DR. RICHARD GORDON, "The Common Cold," *Atlantic*, Jan., 1955.

The person who gets the benefit of your décolleté is the minister—and he doesn't want it. Bear in mind that it is a wedding you are arranging, not a chorus line-up.
> CHARLES GRICE, English parson, advising prospective brides, *Newsweek*, Feb. 11, 1963.

The best way I know of to win an argument is to start by being in the right.
> LORD HAILSHAM (Quintin Hogg), *New York Times*, Oct. 16, 1960.

Fill your mouth with marbles and make a speech. Every day, reduce the number of marbles in your mouth and make a speech. You will become an accredited public speaker—as soon as you have lost all your marbles.
> BROOKS HAYS, former Arkansas Congressman, on his secret for swaying an audience, *New York Herald Tribune*, June 15, 1960.

[Senator McCarthy said] that he followed a maxim taught to him by an Indian named "Charlie" . . . the rule of conduct that if one was ever approached by another person in a not completely friendly fashion, one should start kicking at the other person as fast as possible below the belt until the other person was rendered helpless.

> H. STRUVE HENSEL, Assistant Secretary of Defense, in an affidavit made public June 20, 1954. At outset of Army-McCarthy hearings, Senator Joseph McCarthy had accused Hensel of joining attacks on him because the McCarthy subcommittee was investigating Hensel's record.

Speak up like you do to your wives.

> JAMES HOFFA, on administering membership oath to recruits of International Brotherhood of Teamsters, *Life*, May 18, 1959.

If you haven't struck oil in five minutes, stop boring.

> GEORGE JESSEL, on after-dinner speakers, *Look*, Jan. 10, 1955.

An after-dinner speech is like a love letter. Ideally, you should begin by not knowing what you are going to say, and end by not knowing what you've said.

> LORD JOWITT, *Look*, Dec. 14, 1954.

Never bend your head. Always hold it high. Look the world straight in the face.

> HELEN KELLER, to a five-year-old blind child, news reports of May 31, 1955.

If you cannot catch a bird of paradise, better take a wet hen.

> NIKITA KHRUSHCHEV, to Russian peasants, *Time*, Jan. 6, 1958.

Find out where you can render a service, and then render it. The rest is up to the Lord.

> S. S. KRESGE, dime store tycoon, on 90th birthday, *International News Service* reports, July 31, 1957.

Find a nice man, marry him, have babies and shut up.

> WAUHILLAU LA HAY, advertising executive, advice to career girls, *Advertising Age,* Oct. 26, 1959.

. . . It is always well to accept your own shortcomings with candor but to regard those of your friends with polite incredulity.

> RUSSELL LYNES, "The Art of Accepting," *Vogue,* Sept. 1, 1952.

The art of acceptance is the art of making someone who has just done you a small favor wish that he might have done you a greater one.

> RUSSELL LYNES, *Reader's Digest,* Dec., 1954.

The only gracious way to accept an insult is to ignore it; if you can't ignore it, top it; if you can't top it, laugh at it; if you can't laugh at it, it's probably deserved.

> RUSSELL LYNES, *Reader's Digest,* British Edition, Dec., 1961.

I tell her that when she goes to bed, she should just say her prayers, tell everybody to go to hell and then go to sleep.

> DOUGLAS McKAY, Secretary of Interior, advice to his wife on how to live with criticism, *Reader's Digest,* May, 1955.

In many businesses, today will end at five o'clock. Those bent on success, however, make today last from yesterday right through tomorrow.

> LAWRENCE H. MARTIN, Boston banker, *Wall Street Journal,* March 9, 1962.

Laugh at yourself first, before anybody else can.

> ELSA MAXWELL, quoting death-bed advice of her father, NBC-TV interview, Sept. 28, 1958.

Your mental health will be better if you have lots of fun outside of that office.

> DR. WILLIAM MENNINGER, "The Care and Preservation of the American Executive," *New York Herald Tribune,* April 21, 1959.

Sit by the homely girls so you'll look better by comparison. Practice smiling. Smile at lamp posts and mail boxes. Don't be modest—this isn't the time. Always eat a snack before going to a luncheon meeting so you can spend your time charming, not chewing.

> JACQUE MERCER, former Miss America, on how to win a beauty contest, *New York Post*, Sept. 9, 1960.

I always play a party by ear.

> PERLE MESTA, on starting some new action at a party when she senses that guests are losing interest, news summaries of Jan. 16, 1954.

Limit your predinner cocktail period to 30 minutes and don't fret if you left someone off your guest list—just start planning another party. . . .

> PERLE MESTA, *Celebrity Register*, Harper & Row, 1963.

If you achieve success, you will get applause, and if you get applause, you will hear it. My advice to you concerning applause is this: Enjoy it but never quite believe it.

> ROBERT MONTGOMERY, comment to his daughter as she began an acting career, *Woman's Home Companion*, Dec., 1955.

Never grow a wishbone, daughter, where your backbone ought to be.

> CLEMENTINE PADDLEFORD, food editor, quoting advice from her mother, *This Week*, May 11, 1958.

After you've done a thing the same way for two years, look it over carefully. After five years, look at it with suspicion. And after ten years, throw it away and start all over.

> ALFRED EDWARD PERLMAN, president, New York Central Railroad, *New York Times*, July 3, 1958.

When you read, *read!* Too many students just half read. I never read without summarizing—and so understanding what I read. The art of memory is the art of understanding.

> ROSCOE POUND, dean emeritus, Harvard Law School, *Reader's Digest*, Feb., 1961.

No girl in her right mind should deliberately set out to become a model.
JOHN ROBERT POWERS, *This Week*, Nov. 20, 1955.

Any woman who wants to make her mark in business must make men forget she's a woman between nine and five, and must make them remember she's a woman for the balance of her waking hours.
MARY G. ROEBLING, president, Trenton Trust Co., *Saturday Evening Post*, May 11, 1960.

No one can make you feel inferior without your consent.
ELEANOR ROOSEVELT, quoted in *Catholic Digest*, Aug., 1960.

Never invest your money in anything that eats or needs repainting.
BILLY ROSE, *New York Post*, Oct. 26, 1957.

What good are vitamins? Eat four lobsters, eat a pound of caviar—live! If you are in love with a beautiful blonde with an empty face and no brain at all, don't be afraid, marry her—live!
ARTUR RUBINSTEIN, concert pianist, on the good, healthy life, *New York Times*, June 13, 1958.

One of the best ways to persuade others is with your ears—by listening to them.
DEAN RUSK, *Reader's Digest*, July, 1961.

Give the best that you have to the highest you know—and do it now.
RALPH W. SOCKMAN, on achieving goals, 1952.

Be careful that victories do not carry the seeds of future defeats.
RALPH W. SOCKMAN, in sermon of March 26, 1961.

Never answer a telephone that rings before breakfast. It is sure to be one of three types of persons that is calling: a strange man in Minneapolis who has been up all night and is phoning collect; a salesman who wants to come over and demonstrate a new, patented combination Dictaphone and music box that also cleans rugs; or a woman out of one's past.

> JAMES THURBER, *Lanterns and Lances*, Harper & Row, 1961.

Devote six years to your work but in the seventh go into solitude or among strangers so that your friends, by remembering what you were, do not prevent you from being what you have become.

> LEO SZILARD, atomic scientist, *Harper's*, July, 1960.

I have found the best way to give advice to your children is to find out what they want and then advise them to do it.

> HARRY TRUMAN, CBS-TV, May 27, 1955.

Never lick your chopsticks to get at last grains of rice sticking to them.

> TOKYO POLICE, in official etiquette pamphlet distributed to 23,000 policemen in the Japanese capital city, *Time*, April 27, 1959.

I keep myself in puffect shape. I get lots of exercise—in my own way—and I walk every day. . . . Knolls, you know, small knolls, they're very good for walking. Build up your muscles, going up and down the knolls.

> MAE WEST, at 61, pronouncing herself in "puffect" health, news summaries of Nov. 1, 1954.

Save a boyfriend for a rainy day—and another, in case it doesn't rain.

> MAE WEST, *New York Mirror*, April 6, 1958.

Have the mental equipment to do your job, then take the job seriously, yourself not too seriously.

> FRANCES WILLIS, U.S. ambassador to Switzerland, comment on a successful career, *Look*, Nov. 17, 1953.

Perhaps one of the only positive pieces of advice that I was ever given was that supplied by an old courtier who observed: Only two rules really count. Never miss an opportunity to relieve yourself; never miss a chance to sit down and rest your feet.

> DUKE OF WINDSOR, in his autobiography, *A King's Story*, Putnam, 1951.

Be temperate in your work, but don't carry the practice over into your leisure hours; never diet; never buy a suit for $100 if you can find one that costs more; avoid like the plague being out of debt; shun all avoidable exercise; learn to be a catnapper so you can stay out all night.

> MONTY WOOLLEY, advice to young actors, *New York Herald Tribune*, May 7, 1963.

A man is a fool if he drinks before he reaches the age of 50, and a fool if he doesn't afterward.

> FRANK LLOYD WRIGHT, on his before-dinner custom of a single Irish whisky with water chaser, *New York Times*, June 22, 1958.

My final warning to you is always pay for your own drinks. . . . All the scandals in the world of politics today have their cause in the despicable habit of swallowing free drinks.

> Y. YAKIGAWA, president, Kyoto (Japan) University, to graduating class, news summaries of June 13, 1954.

Humor and Wit

Women like silent men. They think they're listening.
> Marcel Achard, French playwright, *Quote*, Nov. 4, 1956.

Never play cards with a man called Doc. Never eat at a place called Mom's. Never sleep with a woman whose troubles are worse than your own.
> Nelson Algren, quoting a convict's advice which he also recommended to young writers, *Newsweek*, July 2, 1956.

The American arrives in Paris with a few French phrases he has culled from a conversational guide or picked up from a friend who owns a beret. He speaks the sort of French that is really understood by another American who also has just arrived in Paris.
> Fred Allen, introduction to *Paris After Dark*, by Art Buchwald, Little, Brown, 1954.

A vice-president in an advertising agency is a "molehill man." A molehill man is a pseudo-busy executive who comes to work at 9 A.M. and finds a molehill on his desk. He has until 5 P.M. to make this molehill into a mountain. An accomplished molehill man will often have his mountain finished even before lunch.
> Fred Allen, *Treadmill to Oblivion*, Little, Brown, 1954.

A celebrity is a person who works hard all his life to become well known, then wears dark glasses to avoid being recognized.
> Fred Allen, *ibid.*

Asthma doesn't seem to bother me any more unless I'm around cigars or dogs. The thing that would bother me most would be a dog smoking a cigar.
> STEVE ALLEN, television comedian, news summaries of July 15, 1955.

The hair is real—it's the head that's a fake.
> STEVE ALLEN, on being asked if he wore a toupee, NBC-TV, Dec. 15, 1957.

A "good" family, it seems, is one that used to be better.
> CLEVELAND AMORY, *Who Killed Society?*, Harper & Row, 1960.

Coats of arms are family badges indicating descent from a common ancestor—a phrase that many of those who want "coats" don't like to begin with.
> CLEVELAND AMORY, *ibid.*

He's certain to get the divorce vote and remember that's one in four these days.
> CLEVELAND AMORY, on Governor Rockefeller's political future following his divorce, *London Daily Telegraph*, Feb. 8, 1962.

The opera is like a husband with a foreign title: expensive to support, hard to understand, and therefore a supreme social challenge.
> CLEVELAND AMORY, NBC-TV, April 6, 1962.

The longest running road show in history.
> CLEVELAND AMORY, on the trans-Atlantic comings-and-goings of the Duke and Duchess of Windsor, *New York World-Telegram and Sun*, April 6, 1962.

My vigor, vitality, and cheek repel me. I am the kind of woman I would run from.
> NANCY, LADY ASTOR, comment during a visit to Washington, news reports of March 29, 1955.

260

I am interested in physical medicine because my father was. I am interested in medical research because I believe in it. I am interested in arthritis because I have it.

> BERNARD BARUCH, *New York Post*, May 1, 1959.

A jay is a bird of the crow family, which can be found in fields and meadows. A jaywalker, on the other hand, is a bird of the Schmoe family who can be found in traffic jams and morgues.

> PHYLLIS BATTELLE, *New York Journal-American*, Nov. 28, 1955.

I am rather like a mosquito in a nudist camp; I know what I ought to do, but I don't know where to begin.

> STEPHEN BAYNE, on assuming newly created post of executive officer of Anglican Communion, *Time*, Jan. 25, 1960.

What is elegance? Soap and water!

> CECIL BEATON, *New York Times*, Jan. 30, 1959.

The English may not like music, but they absolutely love the noise it makes.

> SIR THOMAS BEECHAM, conductor, Royal Philharmonic Orchestra, *New York Herald Tribune*, March 9, 1961.

A private railroad car is not an acquired taste. One takes to it immediately.

> MRS. AUGUST BELMONT, *Fabric of Memory*, Farrar, Straus, 1957.

He never spares himself in conversation. He gives himself so generously that hardly anybody else is permitted to give anything in his presence.

> ANEURIN BEVAN, Socialist leader, on Sir Winston Churchill, news summaries of April 26, 1954.

I always remember the first script that I wrote [on *The Goldbergs*]. Jake came home for supper with a little ambitious bug in his brain. He wanted to go into business and he told this to Molly and Molly had some money she had put away anticipating just such a time and she gave it to him, and as they sat down to the dinner table he said to her, "Molly, darling, some

261

day we will be eating out of golden plates," and Molly turned to him and said, "Jake, darling, will it taste any better?" I always remember that.
GERTRUDE BERG, CBS-TV, June 4, 1954.

A committee is a group that keeps minutes and loses hours.
MILTON BERLE, news summaries of July 1, 1954.

Humor is falling downstairs if you do it while in the act of warning your wife not to.
KENNETH BIRD, editor of *Punch*, news summaries of May 3, 1954.

It isn't as if the Pittsburgh Pirates won a ball game.
ROGER BLOUGH, refusing to celebrate his appointment as board chairman of U.S. Steel, news summaries of May 5, 1955.

A Frenchwoman, when double-crossed, will kill her rival; the Italian woman would rather kill her deceitful lover; the Englishwoman simply breaks off relations—but they all will console themselves with another man.
CHARLES BOYER, news summaries of July 20, 1954.

Nine out of ten people don't know who threw the overalls in Mrs. Murphy's chowder. Mrs. Murphy did, the old fun-lover!
HAL BOYLE, AP columnist, *New York Post*, Sept. 4, 1957.

After all, what is a pedestrian? He is a man who has two cars—one being driven by his wife, the other by one of his children.
ROBERT BRADBURY, Liverpool city official, *New York Times*, Sept. 5, 1962.

. . . Rhetoric that rolls like a freight train over a bridge.
DAVID BRINKLEY, NBC commentator, on speechmaking of union czar John L. Lewis, *Newsweek*, March 13, 1961.

Earnest people are often people who habitually look on the serious side of things that have no serious side.
VAN WYCK BROOKS, *From a Writer's Notebook*, Dutton, 1958.

Mannerism is the sign of a second-rate mind; pride in mannerism is the sign of a third-rate mind.

VAN WYCK BROOKS, *ibid.*

I look at you and I see rebellion. I see the scars of liquor and dope. I see pain and reckless abandon. Oh, Ronald, it's such a *good* face!

WILLIAM F. BROWN, in *Beat, Beat, Beat,* essay spoofing America's "beat generation," *The Christian Science Monitor,* May 12, 1959.

He says he was born too late for the Lost Generation and too soon for the Beat Generation, so he decided to give in to his natural optimism.

WILLIAM F. BROWN, *ibid.*

A bad liver is to a Frenchman what a nervous breakdown is to an American. Everyone has had one and everyone wants to talk about it.

ART BUCHWALD, *New York Herald Tribune,* Jan. 16, 1958.

No woman has ever stepped on Little America—and we have found it to be the most silent and peaceful place in the world.

ADMIRAL RICHARD BYRD, on eve of his fifth expedition to the Antarctic, news reports of Nov. 27, 1955.

Well, I'm about as tall as a shotgun, and just as noisy.

TRUMAN CAPOTE, when asked to describe himself, *Time,* March 3, 1952.

. . . that hour-glass of Big Ben figures.

TRUMAN CAPOTE, on Mae West, *Observations,* Simon and Schuster, 1959.

Li'l Abner never knows what to do about a succession of eager, luscious girls who throw their juicy selves at him. That makes every male who reads Li'l Abner feel fine. No matter how fumbling or stupid he has been, compared with Li'l Abner he is Don Juan.

AL CAPP, on his cartoon character, *Life,* Jan. 14, 1957.

Like all New York hotel lady cashiers she had red hair and had been disappointed in her first husband.

> AL CAPP, on cashing a check in Manhattan, *New York Herald Tribune*, Jan. 29, 1961.

Having served on various committees, I have drawn up a list of rules: Never arrive on time; this stamps you as a beginner. Don't say anything until the meeting is half over, this stamps you as being wise. Be as vague as possible; this avoids irritating the others. When in doubt, suggest that a sub-committee be appointed. Be the first to move for adjournment; this will make you popular; it's what everyone is waiting for.

> HARRY CHAPMAN, *Greater Kansas City Medical Bulletin*, 1963 issue.

A fanatic is one who can't change his mind and won't change the subject.

> SIR WINSTON CHURCHILL, news summaries of July 5, 1954.

An appeaser is one who feeds a crocodile—hoping it will eat him last.

> SIR WINSTON CHURCHILL, *Reader's Digest*, December, 1954.

The trouble about the Academie is that by the time they get around to electing us to a seat, we really need a bed.

> JEAN COCTEAU, on his election to the Academie Française, comment recalled at his death, *New York Post*, Oct. 13, 1963.

Out of the 93 persons who have sat on the Supreme Court, not one yet has been a woman. Too bad, for they always have the last word, except here, where the last word really counts.

> TOM CLARK, Associate Justice, U.S. Supreme Court, *McCall's*, September, 1963.

I have enough money to get by. I'm not independently wealthy, just independently lazy, I suppose.

> MONTGOMERY CLIFT, actor, *New York Post*, April 13, 1958.

My ignorance of science is such that if anyone mentioned copper nitrate I should think he was talking about policemen's overtime.

> DONALD COGGAN, Archbishop of York, *New York Journal-American*, Sept. 20, 1961.

264

Sex is the great amateur art. The professional, male or female, is frowned on; he or she misses the whole point and spoils the show.

> DAVID CORT, *Social Astonishments*, Macmillan, 1963.

If enough people told enough people to put their heads under trucks, I'm sure they would do so. I wonder why no one has thought of doing that.

> NOEL COWARD, on lukewarm reception given by Broadway critics to his stage adaptation of *Look After Lulu*, *New York Journal-American*, April 29, 1959.

And he murmured soft endearments,
And she talked of Dostoevsky. . . .
As they landed at the airport
Braves in blue restrained the tribesfolk
Held at bay the howling pressmen. . . .
Some there were who liked her front view;
Some more partial to the back view.
Others strove to take her sideways
Thus to get the best of both worlds. . . .
And the grateful British public
Rose rejoicing from its breakfast.

> PERCY CUDLIPP, *London News Chronicle*, poem inspired by arrival in England of film star Marilyn Monroe and her new husband, playwright Arthur Miller, news summaries of July 30, 1956.

He has shaken up a diocese founded by Episcopalians of innate conservatism. They accept as a truism that whereas Presbyterians, Methodists, Roman Catholics, Mormons and atheists came with the Gold Rush, they themselves waited for the Pullmans.

> LAWRENCE DAVIES, on Bishop James Pike and Episcopal Diocese of California, *New York Times*, April 3, 1960.

Hearing Mass is the ceremony I most favor during my travels. Church is the only place where someone speaks to me . . . and I do not have to answer back.

> CHARLES DE GAULLE, *Newsweek*, Oct. 1, 1962.

I always thought I was Jeanne d'Arc and Bonaparte. How little one knows oneself.

> CHARLES DE GAULLE, reply to speaker who compared him to Robespierre, *Time*, June 16, 1958.

These people really aim very badly.
> CHARLES DE GAULLE, on emerging unharmed after 120 bullets were fired at his car in an assassination attempt, *Wall Street Journal*, Aug. 24, 1962.

How can you be expected to govern a country that has 246 kinds of cheese?
> CHARLES DE GAULLE, quoted by a former Cabinet aide, Constantin Melnick, *Newsweek*, Oct. 1, 1962.

Gladys, at thirteen, was a wanton little nymphomaniac. Edmund, at fifteen, was a complete thug with halitosis and an advanced case of satyriasis. . . . Eleven-year-old Enid was a kleptomaniac, and whenever anything was missing one only had to look in Enid's room to find it. Giner was an illegitimate child who exploded the old theory that love children are always the loveliest. . . . Albert, at ten, was just despicable, and his little sister, Margaret Rose, although the best of the lot, was a chronic bed wetter and no bargain.
> PATRICK DENNIS (Edward Everett Tanner), on adoption of six English war refugees, *Auntie Mame*, Vanguard Press, 1955.

Dear Sir: Thank you very much for your crank letter.
> PATRICK DENNIS (Edward Everett Tanner), reply to critical letters, *Newsweek*, Oct. 5, 1959.

Ultimately we want to teach men how to be free—free to love. We hardly dare use the word in school—we are so afraid it will be taken to mean "get into bed with each other."
> THE REVEREND HUGH DICKINSON, chaplain, Trinity College, Cambridge, *Sunday Telegram*, London, Feb. 11, 1962.

Latins are tenderly enthusiastic. In Brazil they throw flowers at you. In Argentina they throw themselves.
> MARLENE DIETRICH, on being mauled by a crowd in Buenos Aires, *Newsweek*, Aug. 24, 1959.

A man who buys two of the same morning paper from the doorman of his favorite night club when he leaves with his girl.
> MARLENE DIETRICH, defining a gentleman, *Marlene Dietrich's ABC's*, Doubleday, 1961.

266

. . . Will somebody please explain to me why public relations people are almost invariably "associates"? Whom do they associate with, and who can stand it?

> GEORGE DIXON, King Features Syndicate, *PR: The Quarterly Review of Public Relations*, Oct. 1957.

New York has many wonderful restaurants . . . but I personally prefer a nice frozen TV dinner at home, mainly because it's so little trouble. All you have to do is have another drink, while you're throwing it in the garbage.

> JACK DOUGLAS, *Never Trust a Naked Bus Driver*, E. P. Dutton, 1960.

Don't put no constrictions on da people. Leave 'em ta hell alone.

> JIMMY DURANTE, *Great Quotations*, compiled by George Seldes; Lyle Stuart, 1960.

When a man sits with a pretty girl for an hour, it seems like a minute. But let him sit on a hot stove for a minute—and it's longer than any hour. That's relativity.

> ALBERT EINSTEIN, quotation recalled in obituaries, *New York Times*, April 19, 1955.

When I see you on the street will you please say "hello"—because some people who don't belong to the university occasionally pass me on 116th Street and they think I'm crazy when I say hello.

> DWIGHT EISENHOWER, address to students shortly after becoming President of Columbia University, *Time*, July 24, 1950.

An atheist is a guy who watches a Notre Dame–SMU football game and doesn't care who wins.

> PRESIDENT EISENHOWER, news summaries of Nov. 6, 1954.

Oh yes, I studied dramatics under him for 12 years.

> DWIGHT EISENHOWER, when asked if he knew General Douglas Mac-Arthur, quoted in the autobiographical *By Quentin Reynolds*, McGraw-Hill, 1963.

267

The adjective is the banana peel of the parts of speech.
> CLIFTON FADIMAN, *Reader's Digest*, Sept., 1956.

A woman can look both moral and exciting—if she also looks as if it was quite a struggle.
> EDNA FERBER, *Reader's Digest*, Dec., 1954.

She was a free-lance castrater.
> JULES FEIFFER, humorist, describing a character in his book, *Harry, The Rat With Women*, McGraw-Hill, 1963.

Dare I say that when he is at home I wish he was overseas, and still more profoundly when he is overseas I wish he was at home?
> GEOFFREY FISHER, ninety-ninth Archbishop of Canterbury, on "Red Dean" of Canterbury, Hewlett Johnson, *Time*, July 3, 1950.

The long and distressing controversy over capital punishment is very unfair to anyone meditating murder.
> GEOFFREY FISHER, *Sunday Times*, London, Feb. 24, 1957.

I have asked myself once or twice lately what was my natural bent. I have no doubt at all: it is to look at each day for the evil of that day and have a go at it, and that is why I have never failed to have an acute interest in each morning's letters.
> GEOFFREY FISHER, in reply to farewells of his colleagues upon his retirement, news reports of Jan. 18, 1961.

What does it take to be an Archbishop of Canterbury? The strength of a horse—and the ability to be a cart horse one day and a race horse the next.
> GEOFFREY FISHER, quoted in biography of his successor, *The Hundredth Archbishop of Canterbury*, by James B. Simpson, Harper & Row, 1962.

A bore is a fellow who opens his mouth and puts his feats in it.
> HENRY FORD, humorous jottings made public on 50th anniversary of founding of Ford Motor Company, printed privately by the Company, 1953.

268

Never thank anybody for anything, except a drink of water in the desert
—and then make it brief.
> GENE FOWLER, author, *New York Mirror*, April 9, 1954.

I had delusions of humility.
> GENE FOWLER, on giving away to needy friends $1,500,000 earned as
> a Hollywood writer, *Holiday*, May, 1959.

I didn't know the full facts of life until I was 17. My father never talked
about his work.
> MARTIN FREUD, son of late Sigmund Freud, news summaries of Nov.
> 15, 1957.

I'd hate this to get out but I really like opera.
> FORD FRICK, baseball commissioner, news summaries of Feb. 8, 1954.

A true sonnet goes eight lines and then takes a turn for better or worse
and goes six or eight lines more.
> ROBERT FROST, news summaries of March 29, 1954.

Now see here! I cut my own hair. I got sick of barbers because they talk
too much. And too much of their talk was about my hair coming out.
> ROBERT FROST, *Quote*, March 11, 1962.

Try thinking up a gift; intimate enough to be person-to-person, significant enough to be president-to-president, creative and lasting enough
eventually to become a museum piece.
> BESS FURMAN, Washington writer for *New York Times*, Feb. 22, 1960,
> on protocol of gift-giving on Presidential trips.

I support myself in a way I am accustomed to live and I tell you, dolling,
I can barely afford myself. But I want you to know there's not one rich
man in this country I could not have married later or sooner.
> ZSA ZSA GABOR, *New York Herald Tribune*, April 9, 1958.

Every woman should have three husbands.
> ZSA ZSA GABOR, *New York Mirror*, May 18, 1958.

He gave me the car and every time I drove with the top down, I got chilly. So naturally he did what any gentleman would do and offered me a coat.

>ZSA ZSA GABOR, after receiving a mink coat from Lieut.-Gen. Raphael Trujillo of Dominican Republic, *New York Journal-American*, May 25, 1958.*

A man in love is incomplete until he has married. Then he's finished.

>ZSA ZSA GABOR, *Newsweek*, March 28, 1960.

Husbands are like fires. They go out when unattended.

>ZSA ZSA GABOR, *ibid.*

If brides, they should be very cautious about asking their husbands to dry the dinner dishes. The right start is important to a marriage. Make them wash 'em right from the beginning.

>GEORGIE STARBUCK GALBRAITH, "Horoscope for Housewives," *McCall's*, January, 1963.

People come by here to see me. . . . They expect to see some big, imposing man. And it's me. I'm just a little old Democrat.

>JOHN NANCE GARNER, former U.S. Vice President, news summaries of Jan. 30, 1954.

Old burglars never die, they just steal away.

>GLEN GILBREATH, 72, on facing 13th robbery charge, *Chicago Sun-Times*, April 26, 1958.

All we Jews have to do is take a one-shot ad in all the big papers saying that we hereby serve notice that the next time we hear of any anti-Semitism we will all become Christians the next day. Jews, who are mostly middle class, would join what church? Why, the Episcopal Church, of course! The prospect of having 5,000,000 Jews joining their church would send Episcopalians into a frenzy. They would organize anti-defamation

---

* Commented *New York Post* columnist Earl Wilson: "Zsa Zsa does social work among the very wealthy."

270

leagues, and police anti-Semitism for us! Just think of it! We would have all those Episcopalians working for us Jews!

> HARRY GOLDEN, author and columnist, lecture at St. Paul's Episcopal Church, Jackson, Michigan, *Time*, Feb. 22, 1960.

Marilyn has married a Protestant, a Catholic and a Jew, in that order, and divorced all of them, impartially, with the proper amount of tears. That's what I call brotherhood.

> HARRY GOLDEN, nominating actress Marilyn Monroe for his Interfaith Brotherhood Week Award, *Time*, March 17, 1961.

I wish she was smart enough to teach second grade, too, next year.

> WILLIAM GOUMAS, first-grade pupil, "favorite teacher" essay, *Christian Science Monitor*, March 17, 1958.

Moscow is the city where, if Marilyn Monroe should walk down the street with nothing on but shoes, people would stare at her feet first.

> JOHN GUNTHER, *Inside Russia Today*, Harper & Row, 1958.

There are only about twenty murders a year in London and not all are serious—some are just husbands killing their wives.

> COMMANDER G. H. HATHERILL, Scotland Yard, news reports of July 1, 1954.

I don't care what is written about me so long as it isn't true.

> KATHARINE HEPBURN, on gossip and publicity, news summaries of May 24, 1954.

The thing I enjoyed most were visits from children. They did not want public office.

> HERBERT HOOVER, on his years in the White House, *On Growing Up*, Morrow, 1962.

Middle age is when your age starts to show around your middle.

> BOB HOPE, news summaries of Feb. 15, 1954.

. . . With the exception of unreformed scrooges, most humans fall into five gift-list categories: children who want everything, people who collect everything or try anything, people who don't do anything, people who need everything, people who have everything.
HOUSE & GARDEN, Nov., 1962.

More free time means more time to waste. The worker who used to have only a little time in which to get drunk and beat his wife now has time to get drunk, beat his wife—and watch TV.
ROBERT HUTCHINS, news summaries of Jan. 2, 1954.

Here I am at the end of the road and at the top of the heap.
JOHN XXIII, shortly after succeeding the late Pius XII, *Time*, Nov. 24, 1958.

It often happens that I wake at night and begin to think about a serious problem and decide I must tell the Pope about it. Then I wake up completely and remember that I am the Pope.
JOHN XXIII, *Time*, Feb. 1, 1960.

Italians come to ruin most generally in three ways—women, gambling, and farming. My family chose the slowest one.
JOHN XXIII, *Newsweek*, Dec. 17, 1962.

When I eat alone I feel like a seminarian being punished. . . . I tried it for one week and I was not comfortable. Then I searched through Sacred Scripture for something saying I had to eat alone. I found nothing, so I gave it up and it's much better now.
JOHN XXIII, on breaking papal precedent of dining alone, recalled in reports of his death, June 3, 1963.

Please don't make my lion look so cross.
JOHN XXIII, when shown design for his papal coat-of-arms, *ibid*.

The trouble with photographing beautiful women is that you never get into the dark room until after they've gone!
YUSSEF KARSH, *New York Mirror*, May 2, 1963.

The Massachusetts ticket is all Irish; its members have the cold eyes and slack faces of IRA members who have gone into another line of work.

> Murray Kempton, journalist, *America Comes Of Middle Age*, Little, Brown, 1963.

I do not think it altogether inappropriate to introduce myself to this audience. I am the man who accompanied Jacqueline Kennedy to Paris, and I have enjoyed it.

> President Kennedy, opening a news conference, June 3, 1961, after French acclaim for First Lady.

I think this is the most extraordinary collection of talent, of human knowledge, that has ever been gathered together at the White House—with the possible exception of when Thomas Jefferson dined alone.

> President Kennedy, at dinner for 49 Americans who hold the Nobel Prize, April 29, 1962.

It might be said now that I have the best of both worlds. A Harvard education and a Yale degree.

> President Kennedy, on receiving honorary degree from Yale University, *New York Times*, June 12, 1962.

I find that the three major administrative problems on a campus are sex for the students, athletics for the alumni and parking for the faculty.

> Clark Kerr, President, University of California, *Time*, Nov. 17, 1958.

I was square and looked like a refrigerator approaching.

> Jean Kerr, on being pregnant with twins, *Vogue*, May, 1958.

A lawyer is never entirely comfortable with a friendly divorce, any more than a good mortician wants to finish his job and then have the patient sit up on the table.

> Jean Kerr, *Time*, April 14, 1961.

There's an old cliché, "Sick as a dog." After you have seen as many sick dogs as I have, you realize it's more truth than cliché. A dog who hurts can't reason that he has felt bad before and recovered to chase cats. He

273

can't comfort himself that this too will pass. He doesn't even care whether the doctor, the nurse or the other patients in the waiting room think he's a coward. He's sick as a dog.

> JAMES R. KINNEY, on veterinary medicine, "Most of My Patients Are Dogs," written with Isabella Taves, *McCall's*, Dec., 1957.

A gossip is one who talks to you about others; a bore is one who talks to you about himself; and a brilliant conversationalist is one who talks to you about yourself.

> LISA KIRK, singer, *New York Journal-American*, March 9, 1954.

It is now proved beyond doubt that smoking is one of the leading causes of statistics.

> FLETCHER KNEBEL, *Reader's Digest*, British Edition, Dec., 1961.

No well-bred European girl would chat with a stranger on a bus or if she did, she wouldn't date him the same day; or if she did, she wouldn't bring him home; or if she did, her parents would have a fit.

> HANS KONINGSBERGER, novelist, "The Female of Our Species," *Holiday*, July, 1963.

It helps to have a rather odd face like mine. People always recognize you.

> ELSA LANCHESTER, English actress, *New York Journal-American*, Feb. 19, 1961.

Research is something that tells you that a jackass has two ears.

> ALBERT D. LASKER, founder of modern advertising, *Taken at the Flood: The Story of Albert D. Lasker*, by John Gunther, Harper & Row, 1960.

This is nice and I appreciate it very much. But who ever heard of Paul Revere's horse?

> CHARLES LAWRENCE, at dinner honoring him for development of engine for Charles Lindbergh's non-stop flight to Paris, *New York Journal-American*, March 14, 1957.

A "woman driver" is one who drives like a man and gets blamed for it.

> PATRICIA LEDGER, winner in National Junior Chamber of Commerce driver-ability tests, in testimony to Congressional committee, *New York Herald Tribune*, April 15, 1958.

274

All they wanted of me were head shots. That certainly seemed strange. Nobody's ever paid attention to my face before.

> GYPSY ROSE LEE, on her television debut as an actress, *New York Herald Tribune,* Sept. 24, 1956.

Every time I tell them my name down here, they knock me down. They think I'm being sacrilegious or something.

> ROBERT E. LEE, an Ohio-born man who complained to Tampa, Florida, police of being forced into street fights with strangers, *Time,* June 25, 1956.

Any time someone gathers a group of girls together for employment purposes in France, the police are bound to think you're up to no good.

> DORIAN LEIGH, head of London model agency supplying mannequins for Paris designers, *Time,* Jan. 27, 1961.

I don't drink. I don't like it. It makes me feel good.

> OSCAR LEVANT, *Time,* May 5, 1958.

This is Oscar Levant speaking. It's an identification that I have to make because I suffer from amnesia.

> OSCAR LEVANT, opening statement at musical program, *ibid.*

I'm a study of a man in chaos in search of frenzy.

> OSCAR LEVANT, *ibid.*

Epigram: a wisecrack that played Carnegie Hall.

> OSCAR LEVANT, *Coronet,* Sept., 1958.

Call me Mister, call me friend,
A loving ear to all I lend,
But do not my soul with anguish rend,
Please stop calling me Reverend.

> HENRY LEWIS, Episcopal chaplain, University of Michigan Medical Center, on forms of address for clergy, *Time,* Nov. 30, 1962.

The tanned appearance of many Londoners is not sunburn—it is rust.

> LONDON EVENING STANDARD, on Britain's wettest winter on record, *Time,* Jan. 2, 1961.

275

She teaches girls to be women and inspires our sons to deserve such ladies . . .

> HENRY LUCE, introducing Mary Bunting, president of Radcliffe, *Time*, May 17, 1963.

. . . A lady is nothing very specific. One man's lady is another man's woman; sometimes, one man's lady is another man's wife. Definitions overlap but they almost never coincide.

> RUSSELL LYNES, "Is There a Lady in the House?" *Look*, July 22, 1958.

It's nature's way of telling you to slow down.

> MADISON AVENUE definition of death, *Newsweek*, April 25, 1960.

An unnerving squeal went up, like forty thousand Persian cats having their tails trodden on simultaneously.

> MANCHESTER GUARDIAN, on Liberace's appearance in Royal Festival Hall, London, before a capacity audience which was 90% female. news summaries of Oct. 3, 1956.

(Newspapers) can be used by men as barriers against their wives. It is still the only effective screen against the morning features of the loved one, and as such performs a unique human service. The second advantage is that you can't line a garbage pail with a television set—it's usually the other way around.

> MARYA MANNES, author and critic, *New York Times*, April 22, 1960.

I propose to anybody. I say it to a hat-check girl. I say it to anybody— a sort of form of introduction.

> TOMMY MANVILLE, much married millionaire, news summaries of July 14, 1955.

It was the usual "zoo tea." You know, we eat—the others watch.

> PRINCESS MARGARET of England, on public receptions attended by royalty, news summaries of July 19, 1954.

There's one way to find out if a man is honest—ask him. If he says "yes," you know he is crooked.

> GROUCHO MARX, news summaries of July 28, 1954.

Money is like a sixth sense—and you can't make use of the other five without it.
SOMERSET MAUGHAM, *New York Times,* Oct. 18, 1958.

I have always been convinced that if a woman once made up her mind to marry a man, nothing but instant flight could save him.
SOMERSET MAUGHAM, *New York Times,* Nov. 25, 1962.

There are certain compensations for overweight women. Men do not suspect them and other women do not fear them as competition.
ELSA MAXWELL in her autobiography, *RSVP,* Little, Brown, 1954.

I'm going to introduce a resolution to have the Postmaster General stop reading dirty books and deliver the mail.
SENATOR GALE McGEE, on efficiency before censorship, *Quote,* Sept. 13, 1959.

A bad little boy is a canoe—behaves better if paddled from the rear.
DON McNEILL, on his radio program, "The Breakfast Club," in 1954.

If, after I depart this vale, you ever remember me and have thought to please my ghost, forgive some sinner and wink your eye at some homely girl.
H. L. MENCKEN, epitaph for himself, recalled in obituaries reporting his death, Jan. 29, 1956.

I set up my pitch in life on a busy and interesting street. I did a good business and I have no regrets.
H. L. MENCKEN, *ibid.*

I am by nature a vulgar fellow. . . . I delight in beef stews, limericks, burlesque shows, New York City, and the music of Haydn, that beery, delightful old rascal! I swear in the presence of old ladies and archdeacons. When the mercury is above ninety-five, I dine in my shirt sleeves and write poetry naked.
H. L. MENCKEN, self-description, *ibid.*

277

I've made it a rule never to drink by daylight and never to refuse a drink after dark.

> H. L. Mencken, *ibid.*

Fog rolled in late last night. It came not on the little cat feet of Carl Sandburg's phrase, but with the authority of an elephant and with just about the same coloring.

> Drew Middleton, reporting from London on one of England's worst fogs in many years, *New York Times*, Jan. 30, 1959.

They treat us like an orphan asylum. . . . A man is forbidden as if he were an apple.

> Edna St. Vincent Millay, on being an undergraduate at Vassar, *Letters of Edna St. Vincent Millay*, edited by Allen Ross Macdougall, Harper & Row, 1952.

It is not true that life is one damn thing after another—it's one damn thing over and over . . .

> Edna St. Vincent Millay, *ibid.*

In determining whether a person is a child, the prime consideration is his age.

> Ministry of Pensions and National Insurance, instructions quoted in *Sunday Times*, London, Dec. 22, 1957.

I've been on a calendar, but never on time.

> Marilyn Monroe, *Look*, Jan. 16, 1962.

I asked a Burmese why women, after centuries of following their men, now walk ahead. He said there were many unexploded land mines since the war.

> Robert Mueller, American pianist, *Look*, March 5, 1957.

I drink to make other people interesting.

> George Jean Nathan, critic and author, news reports of April 8, 1958.

Marriage is based on the theory that when a man discovers a particular brand of beer exactly to his taste he should at once throw up his job and go to work in the brewery.

> GEORGE JEAN NATHAN, *ibid.*

To enjoy women at all one must manufacture an illusion and envelop them with it; otherwise they would not be endurable.

> GEORGE JEAN NATHAN, *ibid.*

A ship is always referred to as a "she" because it costs so much to keep her in paint.

> ADMIRAL CHESTER NIMITZ, *New York Times*, May 24, 1959.

. . . His thinning red hair gave me the impression of violence reduced to witty resignation.

> LOUIS NIZER, attorney, describing Brendan Bracken, secretary to Winston Churchill, *My Life in Court*, Doubleday, 1961.

It would have been 12 cows if I had been kind, or 24 if I had been harsh. No woman is worth more than 24 cattle.

> WALTER ODEDE, African nationalist, on establishing a dowry for his daughter's marriage, *Time*, Jan. 12, 1962.

Flirting is to a woman what experimentation is to electricity.

> JOSÉ ORTEGA Y GASSET, philosopher, "The Duality of Feminine Nature," *Harper's Bazaar*, Jan., 1957.

Some American cemeteries have adopted the slogan, "Foreverness." In California one advertised "Next Attraction Starring—You!" Another cemetery manager piped organ music to the graves but he quit when a complaint came in.

> JACK PAAR, NBC-TV, March 22, 1962.

He and I had an office so tiny that an inch smaller and it would have been adultery.

> DOROTHY PARKER, on sharing space at *Vanity Fair* with Robert Benchley, *Writers at Work*, Viking, 1958.

279

I do everything for a reason. . . . Most of the time the reason is money.
SUZY PARKER, actress and fashion model, *Newsweek*, Feb. 18, 1963.

There is no stronger craving in the world than that of the rich for titles, except that of the titled for riches.
HESKETH PEARSON, English author and biographer, *The Marrying Americans*, Coward-McCann, 1961.

If weight of "brass" alone could insure the success of an exhibition, this one is already comfortable, home and dry.
PHILIP, DUKE OF EDINBURGH, welcoming dignitaries as he opened British Exposition in Manhattan's Coliseum, *New York Journal-American*, June 10, 1960.

Dentopedalogy is the science of opening your mouth and putting your foot in it. I've been practicing it for years.
PHILIP, DUKE OF EDINBURGH, in an address to Britain's General Dental Council, *Time*, Nov. 21, 1960.

If my husband would ever meet a woman on the street who looked like the women in his paintings, he would fall over in a dead faint.
MRS. PABLO PICASSO, *Quote*, July 3, 1955.

A speech is like an airplane engine. It may sound like hell but you've got to go on.
WILLIAM THOMAS PIPER, president, Piper Aircraft Corporation, *Time*, Jan. 13, 1961.

We women don't care too much about getting our pictures on money as long as we can get our hands on it.
IVY BAKER PRIEST, U.S. Treasurer, *Look*, Aug. 10, 1954.

. . . the general look of an elderly fallen angel traveling incognito.
PETER QUENELL, on André Gide, *The Sign of the Fish*, Viking Press, 1960.

Perhaps they wanted a woman in the street—no, that sounds a bit shocking. Let's say a woman in the pew.
> MILDRED RAWLINSON, widow of Bishop of Derby, on being appointed only woman member of Archbishops' Commission on Crown Appointments, *The Sunday Times*, London, Feb. 11, 1962.

If you see a snake coming toward you in a jungle, you have a right to be anxious. If you see it coming down Park Avenue, you're in trouble.
> DR. THEODOR REIK, psychoanalyst, *Saturday Review*, Jan. 11, 1958.

. . . Women would often be terrified if men could intuitively grasp their motives, and some women would not be caught dead with their intimate feelings exposed.
> DR. THEODOR REIK, psychoanalyst, *The Need To Be Loved*, Farrar, Straus, 1963.

Even the wisest men make fools of themselves about women, and even the most foolish women are wise about men.
> DR. THEODOR REIK, *ibid*.

Ever since Eve gave Adam the apple, there has been a misunderstanding between the sexes about gifts.
> NAN ROBERTSON, on Christmas shopping, *New York Times*, Nov. 28, 1957.

Thanks a thousand.
> NELSON ROCKEFELLER, a favorite "conservative" expression as opposed to the familiar "thanks a million," news summaries of Jan. 2, 1956.

The reason there are so few women comics is that so few women can bear being laughed at.
> ANNA RUSSELL, *Sunday Times*, London, Aug. 25, 1957.

Men have more problems than women. In the first place, they have to put up with women.
> FRANÇOISE SAGAN, *New York Times*, Oct. 27, 1957.

I said "yes." Isn't that enough?

> FRANÇOISE SAGAN, asked for comment on her wedding, *New York Mirror*, March 16, 1958.

When I was a young man I vowed never to marry until I found the ideal woman. Well, I found her—but, alas, she was waiting for the ideal man.

> ROBERT SCHUMAN, French Foreign Minister, news summaries of Dec. 31, 1952.

Rising, dressing, feeding, with its inevitable sequels, working, snoozing, undressing and going to bed. Provided, of course, I do not spend an earlier date . . . being cremated.

> GEORGE BERNARD SHAW, on plans for his 94th birthday, *Time*, Aug. 7, 1950.

Baloney is the unvarnished lie laid on so thick you hate it. Blarney is flattery laid on so thin you love it.

> FULTON SHEEN, Auxiliary Bishop of New York, news reports of March 22, 1954.

I feel it is time that I also pay tribute to my four writers, Matthew, Mark, Luke, and John.

> FULTON SHEEN, on receiving award for his television addresses, *New York World-Telegram and Sun*, Dec. 24, 1954.

An atheist is a man who has no invisible means of support.

> FULTON SHEEN, *Look*, Dec. 14, 1955.

The all-round player has the conceit of a peacock, night habits of an owl, rapacity of a crocodile and the sly inscrutability of a snake. Along with these he needs the memory of an elephant, the boldness of a lion, endurance of a bulldog and killer instinct of a wolf. In such company, the average bridge player is nothing but a kibitzing monkey.

> MARSHALL SMITH, "Savage World of Big Bridge," *Life*, March 18, 1957.

Next to reading somebody else's love letters, there's nothing quite so delightful as being privy to the facts of his financial life, especially if they tend toward the disastrous.

> A. C. SPECTORSKY, *The Exurbanites*, Lippincott, 1955.

A diplomat is a person who can tell you to go to hell in such a way that you actually look forward to the trip.

> CASKIE STINNETT, *Out of the Red*, Random House, 1960.

. . . Tattoo artists, a durable breed of craftsmen whose interests in mankind may be only skin deep, but whose impressions usually last a lifetime.

> GAY TALESE, *New York: A Serendipiter's Journey*, Harper & Row, 1961.

Most men are afraid of opera singers. They think of them as people in another world. So I say I'm in the lingerie line. That puts them at their ease.

> BLANCHE THEBOM, Metropolitan Opera star, on how she meets men when traveling, *Newsweek*, Dec. 8, 1958.

When my mother gets angry, boy does she yell. Then my father comes along and tries to calm her but then he takes over. And when they both yell at the same time, boy they could win first prize in a yelling contest.

> THIRD-GRADER in Brooklyn Avenue School, Valley Stream, N.Y., writing on what he thought of parents and himself, quotations from "their Big Ben tablets, that last refuge of frank commentary," *New York Herald Tribune*, June 15, 1961.

I can't make people like me but if I wasn't me I would like me.

> THIRD-GRADER, *ibid.*

I was a code clerk in Washington at the time, when we received an urgent message that twelve code clerks were needed by President Wilson at the Versailles Peace Conference. What they really wanted were twelve code books, but somebody got the message mixed up.

> JAMES THURBER, on his first trip to Paris, *New York Herald Tribune*, May 15, 1955.

Seeing is deceiving. It's eating that's believing.

> JAMES THURBER, *Further Fables for Our Time*, Simon and Schuster, 1956.

Man wants a great deal here below, and Woman even more.
JAMES THURBER, *ibid.*

I'm 65 and I guess that puts me in with the geriatrics. But if there were 15 months in every year, I'd only be 48. That's the trouble with us. We number everything. Take women, for example. I think they deserve to have more than twelve years between the ages of 28 and 40.
JAMES THURBER, *Time,* Aug. 15, 1960

Waggish non-Yale men never seem to weary of calling "For God, for Country and for Yale," the outstanding single anti-climax in the English language.
TIME, June 11, 1951.

Stretch pants—the garment that made skiing a spectator sport. . . .
TIME, on feminine ski attire, Feb. 23, 1962.

I've never been poor, only broke. Being poor is a frame of mind. Being broke is only a temporary situation.
MIKE TODD, theatrical entrepreneur, *Newsweek*, March 31, 1958.

America is a large, friendly dog in a very small room. Every time it wags its tail, it knocks over a chair.
ARNOLD TOYNBEE, news summaries, July 14, 1954.

The only interesting thing that can happen in a Swiss bedroom is suffocation by a feather mattress.
DALTON TRUMBO, screenwriter, advising a teen-age daughter about to tour Europe, *Time*, Jan. 2, 1961.

Never steal more than you actually need, for the possession of surplus money leads to extravagance, foppish attire, frivolous thought.
DALTON TRUMBO, on stealing, *ibid.*

Let the lie be delivered full-face, eye to eye, and without scratching of the scalp, but let it, for all its simplicity, contain one fantastical element of creative ingenuity.

> DALTON TRUMBO, on lying, *ibid.*

We never discuss the heir's hair.

> TRUMPER'S, a London barbershop, when a national controversy raged on why Prince Charles's hair was allowed to cover his forehead, Oct. 11, 1956.

People who are uncommonly sensitive about disclosing their private affairs may as well make plans to spend the night of Mar. 31, 1960, at home. That's the night the census taker will ask you what bed you are sleeping in, if not your own.

> UNITED PRESS INTERNATIONAL, on advance planning of 1960 decennial census and its confidential nature, *New York Journal-American*, April 9, 1959.

Unlike his unmarried sister, a bachelor need give no thought at all to his appearance. . . . Everyone knows that a man can always marry even if he reaches 102, is penniless, and has all faculties gone. There is always some woman willing to take a chance on him.

> AMY VANDERBILT, on the unmarried man, *Complete Book of Etiquette*, Doubleday, 1952.

The refreshing definition of a camel: a horse planned by a committee.

> VOGUE, July, 1958.

We can lick gravity, but sometimes the paperwork is overwhelming.

> WERNHER VON BRAUN, scientist, on outer-space and governmental "red tape," *Chicago Sun-Times*, July 10, 1958.

. . . She looked as composed as a sea anemone digestively sealed on its prey.

> SYLVIA TOWNSEND WARNER, short-story writer, describing a possessive mother, *New Yorker*, May 11, 1963.

It's great. It's wonderful *per se.*
> EARL WARREN, Chief Justice, U.S. Supreme Court, legalistic comment on learning of birth of a grandson, *Newsweek,* March 19, 1956.

I let Earl go with me to a delicatessen just once. We never could afford it again.
> MRS. EARL WARREN, explaining that she does her marketing by telephone, news summaries of Dec. 14, 1954.

Poets, we know, are terribly sensitive people, and in my observation, one of the things they are most sensitive about is cash.
> ROBERT PENN WARREN, on receiving a $1,000 check with National Book Award, *Publishers' Weekly,* March 24, 1958.

A neurotic is the man who builds a castle in the air. A psychotic is the man who lives in it. And a psychiatrist is the man who collects the rent.
> LORD WEBB-JOHNSON, British surgeon, *Look,* Oct. 4, 1955.

A fox is a wolf who sends flowers.
> RUTH WESTON, actress, *New York Post,* Nov. 8, 1955.

Free speech is like garlic. If you are perfectly sure of yourself, you enjoy it and your friends tolerate it.
> LYNN WHITE, JR., president, Mills College, *Look,* April 17, 1956.

Whatever women do they must do twice as well as men to be thought half as good. Luckily, this is not difficult.
> CHARLOTTE WHITTON, Mayor of Ottawa, *Canada Month,* June, 1963.

Back in Detroit we had a saying that an expert is a mechanic away from home.
> CHARLES E. WILSON, Secretary of Defense, news summaries of Jan. 11, 1954.

Platonic love is love from the neck up.
> THYRA SAMTER WINSLOW, novelist, interview with James Simpson, Aug. 10, 1952.

It was so cold I almost got married.
>SHELLEY WINTERS, *New York Times*, April 29, 1956.

To hell with you. Offensive letter follows.
>IRATE CITIZEN's telegram quoted by Lord Home, Britain's Foreign Secretary, *Wall Street Journal*, July 11, 1962.

He was white and shaken, like a dry martini.
>P. G. WODEHOUSE, describing a startled Englishman, *Cocktail Time*, Simon & Schuster, 1958.

An alcoholic is someone who drinks too much—and you don't like anyway.
>VARIOUSLY ATTRIBUTED, a popular saying of 1956.

Wisdom, Philosophy, and
Other Musings

. . . No matter how big a nation is, it is no stronger than its weakest people, and as long as you keep a person down, some part of you has to be down there to hold him down,* so it means you cannot soar as you might otherwise.

> MARIAN ANDERSON, when asked by a woman commentator in India about U.S. Negroes, CBS-TV, Dec. 30, 1957.

Sometimes, it's like a hair across your cheek. You can't see it, you can't find it with your fingers, but you keep brushing at it because the feel of it is irritating.

> MARIAN ANDERSON, on racial prejudice, quoted by Emily Kimbrough, "My Life in a White World," *Ladies' Home Journal*, Sept., 1960.

Manliness is not all swagger and swearing and mountain climbing. Manliness is also tenderness, gentleness, consideration. You men think you can decide on who is a man, when only a woman can really know.

> ROBERT ANDERSON, *Tea and Sympathy*, Random House, 1953.

Did it ever occur to you that you persecute in Tom, that boy up there, you persecute in him the thing you fear in yourself?

> ROBERT ANDERSON, *ibid.*

Any man should be happy who is allowed the patience of his wife, the tolerance of his children and the affection of waiters.

> MICHAEL ARLEN, author, news reports of June 24, 1956.

---

* Paraphrase of statement by Booker T. Washington.

288

Reality is always more conservative than ideology.
> RAYMOND ARON, French philosopher, *The Opium of the Intellectuals,*
> Doubleday, 1957.

What passes for optimism is most often the effect of an intellectual error.
> RAYMOND ARON, *ibid.*

Youth is a fast gallop over a smooth track to the bright horizon . . . The
time of great expectations for yourself and expectations of others for you
—to be fulfilled at an unspecified time called "Someday."
> HAROLD AZINE, author of *The House in Webster Groves,* NBC-TV,
> Feb. 16, 1958.

Time is a dressmaker specializing in alterations.
> FAITH BALDWIN, *Face Toward the Spring,* Rinehart, 1956.

We, too, the children of earth, have our moon phases all through any
year; the darkness, the delivery from darkness, the waxing and waning.
None lives, except the mindless, who does not in some degree experience
this; hours of despair followed by hope or, perhaps, slow adjustment;
times of fear, even panic, and then the light, however small. For in the
normal human being it is impossible to live every day under emotional
stress; there have to be, on this seesaw, periods of even balance.
> FAITH BALDWIN, "The Open Door," *Woman's Day,* Feb., 1961.

The wonder is not that so many Negro boys and girls are ruined but that
so many survive.
> JAMES BALDWIN, Negro essayist and novelist, *Notes of a Native Son,*
> Beacon, 1955.

Negro servants have been smuggling odds and ends out of white homes for
generations, and white people have been delighted to have them do it, because it has assuaged a dim guilt and testified to the intrinsic superiority
of white people. . . .
> JAMES BALDWIN, *Time,* May 17, 1963.

The fear I heard in my father's voice . . . when he realized that I really
believed I could do anything a white boy could do, and had every inten-

289

tion of proving it, was not at all like the fear I heard when one of us was ill or had fallen down the stairs or strayed too far from the house. It was another fear, a fear that the child, in challenging the white world's assumptions, was putting himself in the path of destruction.

JAMES BALDWIN, *The Fire Next Time*, Dial, 1963.

I have always felt that the moment when first you wake up in the morning is the most wonderful of the 24 hours. No matter how weary or dreary you may feel, you possess the certainty that, during the day that lies before you, absolutely anything may happen. And the fact that it practically always *doesn't*, matters not one jot. The possibility is always there.

MONICA BALDWIN, *I Leap Over the Wall*, Holt, Rinehart and Winston, 1950.

Regrets are as personal as fingerprints. . . . Discarding what is vain or false, facing the facts that should truly disturb your conscience, is worth whatever time it takes or pain it may cause. It can pay to the future what you owe to the past.

MARGARET CULKIN BANNING, "Living With Your Regrets," *Reader's Digest*, Oct., 1958.

The idea of strictly minding our own business is moldy rubbish. Who could be so selfish?

MYRTIE BARKER, Indianapolis newspaper columnist, *I Am Only One*, Bobbs-Merrill, 1963.

Conceit is God's gift to little men.

BRUCE BARTON, *Coronet*, Sept., 1958.

To me, old age is always fifteen years older than I am.

BERNARD BARUCH, on 85th birthday, news reports of Aug. 20, 1955.

Age is only a number, a cipher for the records. A man can't retire his experience. He must use it. Experience achieves more with less energy and time.

BERNARD BARUCH, *ibid*.

290

Great cultural changes begin in affectation and end in routine.
>   JACQUES BARZUN, *The House of Intellect*, Harper & Row, 1959.

Intellect has nothing to do with equality except to respect it as a sublime convention.
>   JACQUES BARZUN, *ibid.*

Along about dusk today, the frantic search for joy begins—the annual struggle toward midnight, and an obligatory oblivion to society. . . . Tonight turns out to be the wildest, mildest, happiest, saddest, friendliest, loneliest night of the year—depending on the emotional condition of the man in the celebrant's seat.
>   PHYLLIS BATTELLE, on New Year's Eve, *New York Journal-American*, Dec. 31, 1957.

A complete life may be one ending in so full an identification with the not-self that there is no self left to die.
>   BERNARD BERENSON, comment recalled in report of the connoisseur-critic's death at 94, *Time*, Oct. 19, 1959.

A friend is someone who stimulates me and to whom I am stimulated to talk. . . . When the stimulation no longer occurs, it is a spent and exhausted friendship, and continues as a burden and a bore. . . . Unfortunately in a long life one gets barnacled over with the mere shells of friendship and it is difficult without hurting one's self to scrape them off.
>   BERNARD BERENSON, quoted in biography by Iris Origo, *Sunset and Twilight: From the Diaries of 1947–1958*, Harcourt, Brace & World, 1963.

The toughest thing about success is that you've got to keep on being a success. Talent is only a starting point in this business. You've got to keep on working that talent. Someday I'll reach for it and it won't be there.
>   IRVING BERLIN, *Theatre Arts*, Feb., 1958.

Everybody ought to have a lower East Side in their life.
>   IRVING BERLIN, *Vogue*, Nov. 1, 1962.

The bird of paradise alights only upon the hand that does not grasp.
> JOHN BERRY, novelist, on happiness, *Flight of White Crows*, Macmillan, 1961.

. . . What is known as success assumes nearly as many aliases as there are those who seek it. Like love, it can come to commoners as well as courtiers. Like virtue, it is its own reward. Like the Holy Grail, it seldom appears to those who don't pursue it.
> STEPHEN BIRMINGHAM, "Young Men of Manhattan," *Holiday*, March, 1961.

Courage is a good word. It has a ring. It is a substance that other people, who have none, urge you to have when all is lost. To have courage, one must first be afraid. The deeper the fear, the more difficult the climb toward courage.
> JIM BISHOP, columnist, *New York Journal-American*, March 14, 1959.

The future is an opaque mirror. Anyone who tries to look into it sees nothing but the dim outlines of an old and worried face.
> JIM BISHOP, *New York Journal-American*, Oct. 15, 1959.

It is difficult to live in the present, ridiculous to live in the future, and impossible to live in the past. Nothing is as far away as one minute ago.
> JIM BISHOP, *New York Journal-American*, May 7, 1961.

At 19, everything is possible and tomorrow looks friendly . . .
> JIM BISHOP, *New York Journal-American*, May 9, 1961.

Wit is a treacherous dart. It is perhaps the only weapon with which it is possible to stab oneself in one's own back.
> GEOFFREY BOCCA, *The Woman Who Would Be Queen: A Biography of the Duchess of Windsor*, Holt, Rinehart and Winston, 1954.

Probably no one alive hasn't at one time or another brooded over the possibility of going back to an earlier, ideal age in his existence and living a different kind of life. It is perhaps mankind's favorite daydream.
> HAL BOYLE, Associated Press columnist, *Quote*, May 28, 1961.

If a little nobody like me and a little nobody son of mine can arouse people as you have been aroused, then it is God's work and he hasn't died in vain.

> Mrs. Mamie Bradley, address to 8,000 Harlem residents assembled to protest Mississippi murder of her Negro son, Emmett Louis Till, news reports of Sept. 26, 1955.

The greatest danger to human beings is their consciousness of the trivialities of their aims.

> Gerald Brennan, novelist, *A Holiday by the Sea*, Farrar, Straus, 1962.

Madness comes from the refusal to develop, to adjust, to dilute one's true self in the sordid mush of the world. If we want to find the true self of each of us, we must go to the county lunatic asylum.

> Gerald Brennan, *ibid.*

Nothing is so soothing to our self-esteem as to find our bad traits in our forbears. It seems to absolve us.

> Van Wyck Brooks, *From a Writer's Notebook*, Dutton, 1958.

So often we rob tomorrow's memories by today's economies.

> John Mason Brown, essay in *The Arts of Living*, Simon & Schuster, 1954.

Charm is a glow within a woman that casts a most becoming light on others.

> John Mason Brown, *Vogue*, Nov. 15, 1956.

A good conversationalist is not one who remembers what was said, but says what someone wants to remember.

> John Mason Brown, *Esquire*, April, 1960.

Summer is a sailor in a rowboat and ice-cream on your dress when you're four years old. Summer is a man with his coat off, wet sand between your toes, the smell of a garden an hour before moonrise. Oh, summer is silk itself, a giant geranium and music from a flute far away!

> Michael Brown, excerpt from script for 1956 March of Dimes Fashion Show.

293

As I watched her at play . . . it came to me that this child would pass through life as the angels live in Heaven. The difficulties of existence would never be hers . . .

> PEARL BUCK, on her mentally retarded daughter, *The Child Who Never Grew*, John Day, 1950.

[Psychologists] have been able to discover, exactly as though in a slow-motion picture, the way the human creature acquires new knowledge and new habits. Our educational techniques for normal children have been vastly improved by what the retarded children have taught us. . . . Be proud of your child, accept him as he is and do not heed the words and stares of those who know no better. This child has a meaning for you and for all children. . . . Lift up your head and go your appointed way.

> PEARL BUCK, *ibid.*

It is my belief that a child is a child, regardless of religion or race, and that they all need homes and loving care. I believe that is the modern attitude. At least, it is the attitude of most intelligent people, and they will lead the way for others to follow.

> PEARL BUCK, on adopting an eight-year-old Negro-Japanese girl, *New York Herald Tribune*, March 25, 1958.

They resemble us in more ways than they differ from us.

> PEARL BUCK, on retarded children and her work for them, *Parade*, Nov. 13, 1960.

You cannot live on other people's promises, but if you promise others enough, you can live on your own.

> MARK CAINE, *The S-Man: A Grammar of Success*, Houghton, Mifflin, 1961.

In the midst of winter, I finally learned that there was in me an invincible summer.

> ALBERT CAMUS, author, *Christian Science Monitor*, Jan. 6, 1960.

On that road of the informer, it is always night. I who have traveled it from end to end, and know its windings, switchbacks and sheer drops—I

294

cannot say at what point, where or when, the ex-Communist must make his decision to take it. That depends on the individual man. . . . I cannot ever inform against anyone without feeling something die within me. I inform without pleasure, because it is necessary.

> WHITTAKER CHAMBERS, former Red spy whose disclosures were a sensation of the early 1950's, writing in his autobiographical *Witness*, Random House, 1952.

. . . When you understand what you see, you will no longer be children. You will know that life is pain, that each of us hangs always upon the Cross of himself. And when you know that this is true of every man, woman and child on earth, you will be wise.

> WHITTAKER CHAMBERS, letter to his children, concluding his autobiography, *ibid*.

Nature gives you the face you have at twenty; it is up to you to merit the face you have at fifty.

> GABRIELLE "COCO" CHANEL, designer, *Ladies' Home Journal*, Sept., 1956.

How many cares one loses when one decides not to be something, but to be someone.

> GABRIELLE "COCO" CHANEL, *This Week*, Aug. 20, 1961.

Those who create are rare: those who cannot are numerous. Therefore, the latter are stronger.

> GABRIELLE "COCO" CHANEL, *ibid*.

Old age isn't so bad when you consider the alternative. ———

> MAURICE CHEVALIER, at 72, *New York Times*, Oct. 9, 1960.

One does not leave a convivial party before closing time.

> WINSTON CHURCHILL, parrying persistent queries as to when he would retire as Prime Minister, news summaries of March 22, 1954.

It will be the same, I trust, as it has been since the days of Adam and Eve.

> WINSTON CHURCHILL, when asked by an ardent American feminist about future role of women, news summaries of May 31, 1954.

295

. . . I don't know whether you have them here but football pools, and all that, constitutes the sustaining background of the life of a man upon whose faithful daily toil and exertion all the progress of society depends.

> WINSTON CHURCHILL, at New York news conference, evaluating the football pool, a game of chance highly popular in Britain, news reports of June 29, 1954.

I am an optimist. It does not seem too much use being anything else.

> WINSTON CHURCHILL, news reports of Nov. 10, 1954.

It is easy enough to praise men for the courage of their convictions. I wish I could teach the sad young of this mealy generation the courage of their confusions.

> JOHN CIARDI, *Saturday Review*, June 2, 1962.

I wanted to go higher than Rockefeller Center, which was being erected across the street from Saks Fifth Avenue and was going to cut off my view of the sky. . . . Flying got into my soul instantly but the answer as to why must be found somewhere back in the mystic maze of my birth and childhood and the circumstances of my earlier life. Whatever I am is elemental and the beginnings of it all have their roots in Sawdust Road. I might have been born in a hovel, but I determined to travel with the wind and stars.

> JACQUELINE COCHRAN, on how she became internationally famous aviatrix, *The Stars at Noon*, Little, Brown, 1954.

The best compliment to a child or a friend is the feeling you give him that he has been set free to make his own inquiries, to come to conclusions that are right for him, whether or not they coincide with your own.

> ALISTAIR COOKE, "The Art of Curiosity," *Vogue*, Jan., 1953.

. . . Curiosity is free-wheeling intelligence. . . . It endows the people who have it with a generosity in argument and a serenity in their own mode of life which spring from the cheerful willingness to let life take the forms it will.

> ALISTAIR COOKE, *ibid.*

296

Suspicion is a thing very few people can entertain without letting the hypothesis turn, in their minds, into fact. . . .

DAVID CORT, *Social Astonishments*, Macmillan, 1963.

We do not agree, really, on very much, because we do not propose to confess very much about what is going on in our heads.

DAVID CORT, *ibid*.

My importance to the world is relatively small. On the other hand, my importance to myself is tremendous. I am all I have to work with, to play with, to suffer and to enjoy. It is not the eyes of others that I am wary of, but my own. I do not intend to let myself down more than I can possibly help, and I find that the fewer illusions I have about myself or the world around me, the better company I am for myself.

NOEL COWARD, *Cosmopolitan*, March, 1958.

Life's a pretty precious and wonderful thing. You can't sit down and let it lap around you . . . you have to plunge into it; you have to dive through it! And you can't save it, you can't store it up; you can't horde it in a vault. You've got to taste it; you've got to use it. The more you use, the more you have . . . that's the miracle of it!

KYLE CRICHTON, *The Happiest Millionaire*, hit Broadway comedy of 1956–57, speech by the title-role character, Anthony J. Drexel Biddle.

To be nobody-but-myself—in a world which is doing its best, night and day, to make you everybody else—means to fight the hardest battle which any human being can fight, and never stop fighting.

E. E. CUMMINGS, poet, quoted in *The Magic-Maker*, by Charles Norman, Macmillan, 1958.

. . . There is a case for keeping wrinkles. They are the long-service stripes earned in the hard campaign of life. . . . A wrinkled face is a firm face, a steady face, a safe face. Wrinkles are the dried-up riverbeds of a lifetime's tears. Wrinkles are the nostalgic remnants of a million smiles.

297

Wrinkles are the crannies and footholds on the smooth visage of life on which man can cling and gain some comfort and security.

DAILY MAIL, London, Jan. 20, 1961, editorial "In Praise of Wrinkles."

As a general thing, people marry most happily with their own kind. The trouble lies in the fact that people usually marry at an age where they do not really know what their own kind is.

ROBERTSON DAVIES, Canadian author and educator, *A Voice From the Attic*, Knopf, 1960.

. . . The world is full of people whose notion of a satisfactory future is, in fact, a return to the idealized past.

ROBERTSON DAVIES, *ibid.*

Glory gives herself only to those who have always dreamed of her.

CHARLES DE GAULLE, *New York Times*, June 1, 1958.

Women never use their intelligence—except when they need to prop up their intuition.

JACQUES DEVAL, French playwright, news summaries of May 10, 1954.

The charms that work on others count for nothing in that devastatingly well-lit back alley where one keeps assignations with one's self: no winning smiles will do here, no prettily drawn lists of good intentions.

JOAN DIDION, "Self-Respect, Its Sources and Power," *Vogue*, Aug. 1, 1961.

The average man is more interested in a woman who is interested in him than he is in a woman—any woman—with beautiful legs.

MARLENE DIETRICH, news summaries of Dec. 13, 1954.

I love them, because it is a joy to find thoughts one might have, beautifully expressed with much authority by someone recognizedly wiser than oneself.

MARLENE DIETRICH, on quotations, *Marlene Dietrich's ABC's*, Doubleday, 1961.

Zest is the secret of all beauty. There is no beauty that is attractive without zest.

> CHRISTIAN DIOR, *Ladies' Home Journal*, April, 1956.

The strongest are those who renounce their own times and become a living part of those yet to come. The strongest, and the rarest.

> MILOVAN DJILAS, former Vice President of Yugoslavia, in autobiography written prior to imprisonment by Communists, *Land Without Justice*, Harcourt, Brace and World, 1958.

Life is like a B-picture script. It is that corny. If I had my life story offered to me to film, I'd turn it down.

> KIRK DOUGLAS, actor, *Look*, Oct. 4, 1955.

This is the great folly of grownups—wanting what lasts, wanting to last. Only two things last: shoes too small and foolishness.

> MINOU DROUET, eight-year-old Parisian girl who in late 1955 caused lively controversy among French critics over whether she was literary genius or fraud, news summaries of Nov. 19, 1955.

Humanity, let us say, is like people packed in an automobile which is traveling down hill without lights on a dark night at terrific speed and driven by a four-year-old child. The signposts along the way are all marked "Progress."

> LORD DUNSANY, Irish poet, news summaries of Jan. 11, 1954.

. . . Everyone's future is, in reality, an urn full of unknown treasures from which all may draw unguessed prizes.

> LORD DUNSANY, "Nothing Is Final," *This Week*, Dec. 1, 1957.

Civilization is a stream with banks. The stream is sometimes filled with blood from people killing, stealing, shouting and doing the things historians usually record, while on the banks, unnoticed, people build homes, make love, raise children, sing songs, write poetry and even whittle statues. The story of civilization is the story of what happened on the banks. Historians are pessimists because they ignore the banks for the river.

> WILL DURANT, co-author of the monumental *The Story of Civilization*, when challenged to sum up civilization in half an hour, *Life*, Oct. 18, 1963.

If a man has good manners and is not afraid of other people, he will get by —even if he is stupid.

> SIR DAVID ECCLES, Britain's Minister of Education, *Look*, Jan. 10, 1955.

If A equals success, then the formula is A equals X plus Y plus Z. X is work. Y is play. Z is keep your mouth shut.

> ALBERT EINSTEIN, defining success, news summaries of April 19, 1955.

The true value of a human being is determined primarily by the measure and the sense in which he has attained liberation from the self.

> ALBERT EINSTEIN, *ibid.*

The bitter and the sweet come from the outside, the hard from within, from one's own efforts. For the most part I do the thing which my own nature drives me to do.

> ALBERT EINSTEIN, *ibid.*

I suppose I am concerned more with man's inhumanity to himself than with man's inhumanity to man. Life as it presents itself in New York, say, does not ask to be embraced. Everywhere you turn in New York you see people who are sacrifices. They are, in the main, self-sacrifices to their own insurance policies, or their own life programs; they are caught in the closets of their own perceptions.

> ALEXANDER ELIOT, author and critic, *New York Post*, Nov. 28, 1962.

Life is a fatal adventure. It can only have one end. So why not make it as far ranging and free as possible?

> ALEXANDER ELIOT, *ibid.*

Most of the trouble in the world is caused by people wanting to be important.

> T. S. ELIOT, *The Cocktail Party*, hit play of 1950. According to the producer, Henry Sherek, it was this line in the script which first interested him in the play.

The years between fifty and seventy are the hardest. You are always being asked to do things, and yet you are not decrepit enough to turn them down.

> T. S. ELIOT, *Time*, Oct. 23, 1950.

300

I don't believe one grows older. I think that what happens early on in life is that at a certain age one stands still and stagnates.

> T. S. ELIOT, on 70th birthday, *New York Times*, Sept. 21, 1958.

Wisdom is knowing when you can't be wise.

> PAUL ENGLE, *Poems In Praise*, Random House, 1959.

There is no necessary connection between the desire to lead and the ability to lead, and even less the ability to lead somewhere that will be to the advantage of the led. . . .

> BERGEN EVANS, writer and educator, *The Spoor of Spooks and Other Nonsense*, Knopf, 1954.

Legislators who are of even average intelligence stand out among their colleagues. Many Governors and Senators have to be seen to be believed. A cultured college president has become as much a rarity as a literate newspaper publisher. A financier interested in economics is as exceptional as a labor leader interested in the labor movement. For the most part our leaders are merely following out in front; they do but marshal us the way that we are going.

> BERGEN EVANS, *ibid.*

Youth is so sure the rules have changed. Age is sure they haven't. Youth feels it knows how far it can go. Age is deeply aware of the danger. Youth feels it can always apply the brakes in time to save itself. Age knows it isn't always so.

> RICHARD L. EVANS, radio broadcast from Salt Lake City Tabernacle, March 4, 1956.

To divide one's life by years is of course to tumble into a trap set by our own arithmetic. The calendar consents to carry on its dull wall-existence by the arbitrary timetables we have drawn up in consultation with those permanent commuters, Earth and Sun. But we, unlike trees, need grow no annual rings.

> CLIFTON FADIMAN, "On Being Fifty," *Holiday*, Feb., 1955.

For most men life is a search for the proper manila envelope in which to get themselves filed.

> CLIFTON FADIMAN, quoted in *International Celebrity Register*, Celebrity Service, Inc., 1960.

I love Virginians because Virginians are all snobs and I like snobs. A snob has to spend so much time being a snob that he has little time left to meddle with you.

> WILLIAM FAULKNER, *Memphis Commercial Appeal*, July 7, 1962.

A gentleman can live through anything. He faces anything. A gentleman accepts the responsibilities of his actions and bears the burden of their consequences, even when he did not himself instigate them but only acquiesced to them, didn't say No though he knew he should.

> WILLIAM FAULKNER, *The Reivers*, Random House, 1962.

I decline to accept the end of man. It is easy enough to say that man is immortal simply because he will endure: that when the last ding-dong of doom has clanged and faded from the last worthless rock hanging tideless in the last red and dying evening, that even then there will still be one more sound: that of his puny inexhaustible voice, still talking. I refuse to accept this. I believe that man will not merely endure: he will prevail. He is immortal, not because he alone among creatures has an inexhaustible voice, but because he has a soul, a spirit capable of compassion and sacrifice and endurance.

> WILLIAM FAULKNER, Nobel Prize acceptance speech recalled in reports of his death, July 6, 1962.

. . . I have found that the greatest help in meeting any problem with decency and self-respect and whatever courage is demanded, is to know where you yourself stand. That is, to have in words what you believe and are acting from.

> WILLIAM FAULKNER, letter to a University of Alabama student during riots over enrollment of a Negro girl; letter was not published until seven years later, *National Observer*, June 17, 1963.

In cities, no one is quiet but many are lonely; in the country, people are quiet but few are lonely.

> GEOFFREY FISHER, Archbishop of Canterbury, news summaries of Feb. 22, 1954.

The world is covered with places I'm going to retire to—New Zealand, America, and every county of England.

> GEOFFREY FISHER, news summaries of Aug. 27, 1954.

302

Who knows whether in retirement I shall be tempted to the last infirmity of mundane minds, which is to write a book.

> GEOFFREY FISHER, in final address as Archbishop of Canterbury, *Time*, May 12, 1961.

One has two duties—to be worried and not to be worried.

> E. M. FORSTER, *The Observer*, London, Dec. 20, 1959.

Men are not against you; they are merely for themselves.

> GENE FOWLER, *Skyline*, Viking, 1961.

Love and memory last and will so endure till the game is called because of darkness.

> GENE FOWLER, *ibid*.

Happiness makes up in height for what it lacks in length.

> ROBERT FROST, *Reader's Digest*, March, 1959.

There is the fear that we shan't prove worthy in the eyes of someone who knows us at least as well as we know ourselves. That is the fear of God. And there is the fear of Man—fear that men won't understand us and we shall be cut off from them.

> ROBERT FROST, on the two fears that follow man through life, *Newsweek*, Feb. 11, 1963.

The reason why worry kills more people than work is that more people worry than work.

> ROBERT FROST, *Vogue*, Mar. 15, 1963.

. . . The first of our senses which we should take care never to let rust through disuse is that sixth sense, the imagination . . . I mean the wide-open eye which leads us always to see truth more vividly, to apprehend more broadly, to concern ourselves more deeply, to be, all our life long, sensitive and awake to the powers and responsibilities given to us as human beings.

> CHRISTOPHER FRY, playwright, "On Keeping the Sense of Wonder," *Vogue*, Jan., 1956.

303

I have been boycotted, followed to my house by a mob of mothers who used obscene language with threats of beating if I did not take my child out of school. Let it be said that I feel nothing but compassion toward these women who in fear and hatred forget so easily what America stands for: freedom of thought, freedom of speech, freedom of action. It is these qualities, divine in essence, that are the core of civilization. Tyranny and suppression can only thwart their own purposes in the end. For the sake of our beloved children, may every American mother remember in time.

> MRS. DAISY GABRIELLA, on enrolling her young daughter in integrated New Orleans school, "The Mother Who Stood Alone," by Isabella Taves, *Redbook*, April, 1961.

The rich man who deludes himself into behaving like a mendicant may conserve his fortune although he will not be very happy. The affluent country which conducts its affairs in accordance with rules of another and poorer age also forgoes opportunities. And in misunderstanding itself it will, in any time of difficulty, implacably prescribe for itself the wrong remedies.

> JOHN KENNETH GALBRAITH, Professor of Economics, Harvard University, *The Affluent Society*, Houghton Mifflin, 1958. The title of his book has sometimes been used as a synonym for the 50's and 60's in America.

No one can be as calculatedly rude as the British, which amazes Americans, who do not understand studied insult and can only offer abuse as a substitute.

> PAUL GALLICO, *New York Times*, Jan. 14, 1962.

For every talent that poverty has stimulated it has blighted a hundred.

> JOHN W. GARDNER, president, Carnegie Foundation, in his book, *Excellence*, Harper & Row, 1961.

The society which scorns excellence in plumbing because plumbing is a humble activity, and tolerates shoddiness in philosophy because philosophy is an exalted activity, will have neither good plumbing nor good philosophy. Neither its pipes nor its theories will hold water.

> JOHN W. GARDNER, *Saturday Evening Post*, Dec. 1, 1962.

Humor is an affirmation of dignity, a declaration of man's superiority to all that befalls him.

ROMAIN GARY, *Promise At Dawn*, Harper & Row, 1961.

I sincerely regret all my divorces, because I don't like anything to be unsuccessful.

JOHN PAUL GETTY, international industrialist, *Time*, Feb. 24, 1958.

I always wanted to be somebody. If I made it, it's half because I was game enough to take a lot of punishment along the way and half because there were a lot of people who cared enough to help me.

ALTHEA GIBSON, *Think*, February, 1963.

Are there still virgins? One is tempted to answer no. There are only girls who have not yet crossed the line, because they want to preserve their market value, having been told that desirable customers buy only unused merchandise; and girls who are afraid of men, of *Man*, the enemy who must be avoided because he wounds, or must be captured in order to make him a husband. Call them virgins if you wish, these travelers in transit.

FRANÇOISE GIROUD, French novelist, *Coronet*, Nov., 1960.

The angel sent down to expel Adam and Eve was the first Reno judge, but we are conservative; despite all thunder, trouble, and waste of spirit, we failed to recognize him. Now the day of natural virtue, when divorce was almost inconceivable, is over.

HERBERT GOLD, "Divorce As A Moral Act," *Atlantic*, Nov., 1957.

If the new love is happy, the old marriage is vindicated: *Through me you have learned to love.* Or if not so much, at least this: I left you with the strength to be happy, an ambition to know love, the suspicion that it is possible. Perhaps I have even left you with a belief and a brilliant need. Together we have put an end to the monstrous expectations of first marriage, and without cynicism we may now go on to what is possible.

HERBERT GOLD, *ibid*.

Back of tranquility lies always conquered unhappiness.

DAVID GRAYSON, American author, quoted in *The Autobiography of Eleanor Roosevelt*, Harper & Row, 1961.

305

Most people say that as you get old, you have to give up things. I think you get old because you give up things.

> SENATOR THEODORE FRANCIS GREEN of Rhode Island, at 87, news summaries of June 28, 1954.

Have you ever seen a room from which faith has gone? . . . Like a marriage from which love has gone. All that's left are habits and pet names and sentimental objects picked up on beaches and in foreign towns that don't mean anything any more. And patience, patience everywhere like a fog.

> GRAHAM GREENE, *The Potting Shed*, reprinted in *Theatre Arts*, March, 1958.

Society itself suffers when people are allowed to sacrifice identity in the damp laundry of mediocrity.

> CRAWFORD GREENEWALT, president, E. I. du Pont de Nemours & Company, *Business Week*, May 10, 1958.

The human race has had long experience and a fine tradition in surviving adversity. But we now face a task for which we have little experience, the task of surviving prosperity.

> ALAN GREGG, Rockefeller Foundation, *New York Times*, Nov. 4, 1956.

Self-respect cannot be hunted. It cannot be purchased. It is never for sale. It cannot be fabricated out of public relations. It comes to us when we are alone, in quiet moments, in quiet places, when we suddenly realize that, knowing the good, we have done it; knowing the beautiful, we have served it; knowing the truth, we have spoken it.

> WHITNEY GRISWOLD, president, Yale University, baccalaureate address, news summaries of June 24, 1957.

All happiness depends on a leisurely breakfast.

> JOHN GUNTHER, *Newsweek*, April 14, 1958.

[It] is a sort of "white book" concerning my negotiations with myself—and God.

> DAG HAMMARSKJÖLD, former Secretary-General of the United Nations, note explaining diary he kept from 1925 to his death in 1961, published in 1963 as a book, *Road Signs*.

Silence is the space surrounding every action and every communion of people. Friendship needs no words—it is a loneliness relieved of the anguish of loneliness.

> DAG HAMMARSKJÖLD, *ibid.*

To let oneself be bound by a duty from the moment you see it approaching is a part of the integrity that alone justifies responsibility.

> DAG HAMMARSKJÖLD, in 1955, more than two years after he became UN Secretary-General, *ibid.*

The truth is so simple that it is regarded as pretentious banality.

> DAG HAMMARSKJÖLD, *ibid.*

We shall succeed only so far as we continue that most distasteful of all activity, the intolerable labor of thought.

> JUDGE LEARNED HAND, at 25th anniversary dinner of Research Institute of America, April 27, 1960.

Life is something like this trumpet. If you don't put anything in it you don't get anything out. And that's the truth.

> W. C. HANDY, jazz musician and composer, news summaries of Feb. 15, 1954.

Perseverance is the most overrated of traits, if it is unaccompanied by talent; beating your head against a wall is more likely to produce a concussion in the head than a hole in the wall.

> SYDNEY J. HARRIS, columnist, *Chicago Daily News*, Jan. 9, 1958.

More trouble is caused in the world by indiscreet answers than by indiscreet questions.

> SYDNEY J. HARRIS, *Chicago Daily News*, March 27, 1958.

. . . What the small town may have contributed in the past is one side of the coin; the other side is urbanism and the greatest opportunity in the history of man for him to reach his full potential. Where the small town kept him prisoner, urbanism gives him freedom of choice—choice of education, choice of profession, choice of marriage. If the small town is passing, we can't bemoan it.

PHILIP HAUSER, sociologist, *Newsweek*, July 8, 1963.

Each of us has his own little private conviction of rightness and almost by definition, the Utopian condition of which we all dream is that in which all people finally see the error of their ways and agree with us. And underlying practically all our attempts to bring agreement is the assumption that agreement is brought about by changing people's minds—other people's.

S. I. HAYAKAWA, quoted by Martin Mayer, *Where, When and Why: Social Studies in American Schools*, Harper & Row, 1963.

It is the individual who knows how little he knows about himself who stands a reasonable chance of finding out something about himself before he dies.

S. I. HAYAKAWA, *Symbol, Status, and Personality*, Harcourt, Brace & World, 1963.

. . . Time is a circus always packing up and moving away.

BEN HECHT, *Charlie*, Harper & Row, 1957.

One's lifework, I have learned, grows with the working and the living. Do it as if your life depended on it, and first thing you know, you'll have made a life out of it. A good life, too.

THERESA HELBURN, *A Wayward Quest*, Little, Brown, 1960.

I am not willing, now or in the future, to bring bad trouble to people who, in my past association with them, were completely innocent of any talk or any action that was disloyal or subversive. . . . I cannot and will not cut my conscience to fit this year's fashions, even though I long ago came to the conclusion that I was not a political person and could have no comfortable place in any political group.

LILLIAN HELLMAN, letter to Committee on Un-American Activities, *Nation*, May 31, 1952.

308

Worry a little bit every day and in a lifetime you will lose a couple of years. If something is wrong, fix it if you can. But train yourself not to worry. Worry never fixes anything.

> Mrs. Ernest Hemingway, "Words to Live By," *This Week*, Nov. 7, 1954.

After the first million, it doesn't matter. You can only eat three meals a day—I tried eating four and I got sick. You can't sleep in more than one bed a night. Maybe I have twenty suits, but I can only wear one at a time, and I can't use more than two shirts a day.

> Joseph Hirshhorn, American multimillionaire, *Time*, July 25, 1955.

Man is the only animal that contemplates death, and also the only animal that shows any sign of doubt of its finality.

> William Ernest Hocking, professor of philosophy, Harvard University, *The Meaning of Immortality in Human Experience*, Harper & Row, 1957.

When people are free to do as they please, they usually imitate each other.

> Eric Hoffer, *The Passionate State of Mind*, Harper & Row, 1955.

Intolerance is the "Do Not Touch" sign on something that cannot bear touching. We do not mind having our hair ruffled, but we will not tolerate any familiarity with the toupee which covers our baldness.

> Eric Hoffer, *ibid.*

Our credulity is greatest concerning the things we know least about. And since we know least about ourselves, we are ready to believe all that is said about us. Hence the mysterious power of both flattery and calumny.

> Eric Hoffer, *ibid.*

Every new adjustment is a crisis in self-esteem. . . .

> Eric Hoffer, *The Ordeal of Change*, Harper & Row, 1963.

The longer I live, the more convinced I am that material progress is not only valueless without spiritual progress; it is, in the long term, impossible.

> Eugene Holman, president, Standard Oil of New Jersey, 1944–54, quoted in *Profile of America*, Crowell, 1954.

Experience is awareness of the encompassing totality of things.

> SIDNEY HOOK, professor of philosophy, New York University, *New York Times*, Feb. 16, 1958.

A boy has two jobs. One is just being a boy. The other is growing up to be a man.

> HERBERT HOOVER, address to fiftieth anniversary celebration of the Boys' Clubs of America, May 21, 1956.

In my opinion, we are in danger of developing a cult of the Common Man, which means a cult of mediocrity.

> HERBERT HOOVER, *This Week*, Aug. 5, 1956.

Wisdom consists not so much in knowing what to do in the ultimate as in knowing what to do next.

> HERBERT HOOVER, *Reader's Digest*, July, 1958.

Money alone can't bring you happiness, but money alone has not brought me unhappiness. . . . I won't say my previous husbands thought only of my money, but it had a certain fascination for them.

> BARBARA HUTTON, news summaries of June 4, 1956.

Experience is not what happens to you; it is what you do with what happens to you.

> ALDOUS HUXLEY, *Reader's Digest*, Mar., 1956.

Intellectuals . . . regard over-simplification as the original sin of the mind and have no use for the slogans, the unqualified assertions and sweeping generalizations which are the propagandist's stock in trade.

> ALDOUS HUXLEY, *Brave New World Revisited*, Harper & Row, 1958.

An impersonal generation will take the place of Nature's hideous system. In vast state incubators, rows upon rows of gravid bottles will supply the world with the population it requires. The family system will disappear; society, sapped at its very base, will have to find new foundations; and

Eros, beautifully and irresponsibly free, will flit like a gay butterfly from flower to flower.

ALDOUS HUXLEY in his first published novel, *Crome Yellow*, which foreshadowed his *Brave New World;* taken together, they were considered a picture of a scientific Utopia that might become a reality; quoted on his death, Nov. 23, 1963.

Reading is one of our bad habits . . . We read, most of the time, not because we wish to instruct ourselves, not because we long to have our feelings touched and our imagination fired, but . . . because we have time to spare.

ALDOUS HUXLEY, among comments quoted in his obituaries, *ibid.*

The surest way to work up a crusade in favor of some good cause is to promise people that they will have a chance of maltreating someone. . . . To be able to destroy with good conscience, to be able to behave badly and call your bad behavior "righteous indignation"—this is the height of psychological luxury, the most delicious of moral treats.

ALDOUS HUXLEY, *ibid.*

I think that one possible definition of our modern culture is that it is one in which nine-tenths of our intellectuals can't read any poetry.

RANDALL JARRELL, on receiving National Book Award for Poetry, *New York Herald Tribune*, March 19, 1961.

One of the wisest things my daddy ever told me was that "so-and-so is a damned smart man, but the fool's got no sense."

SENATOR LYNDON JOHNSON, *Time*, March 17, 1958.

I doubt if there is one married person on earth who can be objective about divorce. It is always a threat, admittedly or not, and such a dire threat that it is almost a dirty word.

NORA JOHNSON, "A Marriage on the Rocks," *Atlantic*, July, 1962.

Some of the best of men make their lives tolerable by the fantasy that the spiritual torments they have lived through, the cruelty of friends, of parents, or of children, the sickening loss of love, had really been quite

311

funny at the time. Be fond of the man who jests at his scars, if you like; but never believe he is being on the level with you.

> PAMELA HANSFORD JOHNSON, *An Error of Judgement*, Harcourt, Brace & World, 1962.

There are as many nights as days, and the one is just as long as the other in the year's course. Even a happy life cannot be without a measure of darkness, and the word "happy" would lose its meaning if it were not balanced by sadness. It is far better to take things as they come along with patience and equanimity.

> DR. CARL JUNG, on happiness, *Newsweek*, Aug. 1, 1960.

You do what you have to do in life, when you form a philosophy that you can't talk yourself out of. . . . People who decide they came to earth to work, who make work their personal philosophy, are kept very busy.

> CONSTANTINE KARAMANLIS, Prime Minister of Greece, news reports of Nov. 14, 1956.

If there is a single quality that is shared by all great men, it is vanity. But I mean by "vanity" only that they appreciate their own worth. Without this kind of vanity they would not be great. And with vanity alone, of course, a man is nothing.

> YUSSEF KARSH, internationally known photographer, *Cosmopolitan*, Dec., 1955.

I can see, and that is why I can be so happy, in what you call the dark, but which to me is golden. I can see a God-made world, not a man-made world.

> HELEN KELLER, reply to question, "Can you see a world?" in *The Unconquered*, filmed documentary of her life, 1955.

Self-pity is our worst enemy and if we yield to it, we can never do anything wise in the world.

> HELEN KELLER, news reports of June 26, 1955.

Life is an exciting business and most exciting when it is lived for others.

> HELEN KELLER, *ibid*.

312

It has been a happy life. My limitations never make me sad. Perhaps there is just a touch of yearning at times. But it is vague, like a breeze among flowers. Then, the wind passes, and the flowers are content.

> HELEN KELLER, *ibid.*

The courage of life is often a less dramatic spectacle than the courage of a final moment; but it is no less than a magnificent mixture of triumph and tragedy. A man does what he must—in spite of personal consequences, in spite of obstacles and dangers and pressures—and that is the basis of all human morality.

> JOHN F. KENNEDY, *Profiles In Courage*, Harper & Row, 1955, a book for which the future President was awarded a Pulitzer Prize.

The ones who are mad to live, mad to talk, mad to be saved, desirous of everything at the same time, the ones who never yawn or say a commonplace thing, but burn, burn, burn.

> JACK KEROUAC, on the "beat generation" of the 1950's, *On the Road*, Viking, 1957.

Where there is an open mind, there will always be a frontier.

> CHARLES KETTERING, retired research chief for General Motors, quoted in *Profile of America*, Crowell, 1954.

My definition of an educated man is the fellow who knows the right thing to do at the time it has to be done. . . . You can be sincere and still be stupid.

> CHARLES KETTERING, quoted in *Professional Amateur* by T. A. Boyd, Dutton, 1957.

It is man's destiny to ponder on the riddle of existence and, as a by-product of his wonderment, to create a new life on this earth.

> CHARLES KETTERING, *Time*, Dec. 8, 1958.

Every day has been so short, every hour so fleeting, every minute so filled with the life I love that time for me has fled on too swift a wing.

> AGA KHAN, biographical statement recalled in reports of his death at 79, July 11, 1957.

I want to be the white man's brother, not his brother-in-law.
> MARTIN LUTHER KING, civil rights leader, *New York Journal-American*, Sept. 10, 1962.

The Negro lives on a lonely island of poverty in the midst of a vast ocean of material prosperity and finds himself an exile in his own land.
> MARTIN LUTHER KING, address at Lincoln Memorial to 200,000 participants in "march on Washington," Aug. 28, 1963.

The sweltering summer of the Negro's legitimate discontent will not pass until there is an invigorating autumn of freedom and equality.
> MARTIN LUTHER KING, *ibid.*

I have a dream that one day on the red hills of Georgia, the sons of former slaves and the sons of former slave-owners will be able to sit together at the table of brotherhood. . . . That one day even the State of Mississippi, a state sweltering with the heat of injustice, sweltering with the heat of oppression, will be transformed into an oasis of freedom and justice. . . . That my four little children will one day live in a nation where they will not be judged by the color of their skin but by the content of their character.
> MARTIN LUTHER KING, *ibid.*

Before you tell someone how good you are, you must tell him how bad you used to be.
> SEMON EMIL KNUDSEN, president, Pontiac Division, General Motors, *Time*, May 25, 1959.

The trouble with our age is all signposts and no destination.
> LOUIS KRONENBERGER, *Look*, May 17, 1954.

Experience is a hard teacher because she gives the test first, the lesson afterwards.
> VERNON LAW, pitcher, Pittsburgh Pirates, "How To Be A Winner," *This Week*, Aug. 14, 1960.

314

When you're through learning, you're through.
VERNON LAW, *ibid.*

Egotism is the anesthetic that dulls the pain of stupidity.
FRANK LEAHY, former Notre Dame football coach, *Look*, Jan. 10, 1955.

A man takes a drink, the drink takes another, and the drink takes the man.
SINCLAIR LEWIS, to his future wife Dorothy Thompson, *Dorothy and Red*, by Vincent Sheean, Houghton Mifflin, 1963.

The most exhausting thing in life, I have discovered, is being insincere. That is why so much social life is exhausting; one is wearing a mask.
ANNE MORROW LINDBERGH, *Gift From the Sea*, Pantheon, 1955.

I believe that what woman resents is not so much giving herself in pieces as giving herself purposelessly.
ANNE MORROW LINDBERGH, *ibid.*

If one sets aside time for a business appointment, a trip to the hairdresser, a social engagement, or a shopping expedition, that time is accepted as inviolable. But if one says: I cannot come because that is my hour to be alone, one is considered rude, egotistical or strange. What a commentary on our civilization, when being alone is considered suspect; when one has to apologize for it, make excuses, hide the fact that one practices it—like a secret vice!
ANNE MORROW LINDBERGH, *ibid.*

I have a hankering to go back to the Orient and discard my necktie. Neckties strangle clear thinking.
LIN YUTANG, Chinese-American philosopher and writer, news summaries of Feb. 22, 1954.

Where all think alike, no one thinks very much.
WALTER LIPPMANN, columnist, *Speaker's Encyclopedia*, compiled by Jacob M. Braude, Prentice-Hall, 1955.

315

The opiate of the intellectuals . . . but no cure, except as a guillotine might be called a cure for a case of dandruff.

> CLARE BOOTHE LUCE, on Communism, *Newsweek*, Jan. 24, 1955.

The baleful beep of the Sputnik, which is heard in every land, every hour, on the hour, is an intercontinental outer-space raspberry to a decade of American pretensions that the American way of life was a gilt-edged guarantee of our material superiority.

> CLARE BOOTHE LUCE, on Russia's artificial satellite in outer space, *New York Herald Tribune*, Oct. 18, 1957.

Charm is that extra quality that defies description.

> ALFRED LUNT, *Ladies' Home Journal*, April, 1956.

Cynicism is the intellectual cripple's substitute for intelligence. It is the dishonest businessman's substitute for conscience. It is the communicator's substitute, whether he is advertising man or editor or writer, for self-respect.

> RUSSELL LYNES, managing editor, *Harper's*, address to American Association of Advertising Agencies, *How High Is the American Brow?*, April 25, 1963.

There is no security on this earth; there is only opportunity.

> GENERAL DOUGLAS MACARTHUR, *MacArthur: His Rendezvous With History* by Major General Courtney Whitney, Knopf, 1955.

The curtain is lifting. We can have triumph, or tragedy, for we are the playwrights, the actors and the audience. Let us book our seats for triumph. The world is sickened of tragedy.

> JOHN MACAULEY, Chairman, League of Red Cross Societies, address accepting Nobel Peace Prize for the organization, *New York Times*, Dec. 12, 1963.

The dissenter is every human being at those moments of his life when he resigns momentarily from the herd and thinks for himself.

> ARCHIBALD MACLEISH, "In Praise of Dissent," *New York Times*, Dec. 16, 1956.

316

J. B., like Job, covers his mouth with his hand; acquiesces in the vast indifference of the universe as all men must who truly face it; takes back his life again. In love. To live.

> ARCHIBALD MACLEISH, on *J. B.*, his 1959 Pulitzer Prize play, *Life*, May 18, 1959.

There are those, I know, who will reply that the liberation of humanity, the freedom of man and mind, is nothing but a dream. They are right. It is. It is the American dream.

> ARCHIBALD MACLEISH, in debate on "The National Purpose," *New York Times*, May 30, 1960.

All neurotics are pretty bourgeois. Madness is too revolutionary for them. . . . We madmen are the aristocrats of mental illness.

> MARY MCCARTHY, dialogue for an amiably unstable father in her novel, *The Group*, Harcourt, Brace & World, 1963.

Practical people would be a lot more practical if they were just a little more dreamy.

> J. P. MCEVOY, author, *Reader's Digest*, June, 1954.

One of the shameful chapters of this country was how so many of the comfortable—especially those who profited from the misery of others—abused her . . . But she got even in a way that was almost cruel. She forgave them.

> RALPH MCGILL, Atlanta newspaper editor, quoted by Helen Gahagan Douglas in *The Eleanor Roosevelt We Remember*, Hill and Wang, 1963.

Gossip isn't scandal and it's not merely malicious. It's chatter about the human race by lovers of the same. Gossip is the tool of the poet, the shoptalk of the scientist, and the consolation of the housewife, wit, tycoon and intellectual. It begins in the nursery and ends when speech is past.

> PHYLLIS MCGINLEY, "A New Year and No Resolutions," *Woman's Home Companion*, Jan., 1957.

It is, of course, a trite observation to say that we live "in a period of transition." Many people have said this at many times. Adam may well have made the remark to Eve on leaving the Garden of Eden.

> HAROLD MACMILLAN, British Prime Minister, *New York Times*, June 9, 1958.

Of all the traps and pitfalls in life, self-disesteem is the deadliest, and the hardest to overcome; for it is a pit designed and dug by our own hands, summed up in the phrase, "It's no use—I can't do it." . . . It is that good hard second look—taken not just for one's own sake but for everyone else's too—that very often reveals that the "impossible" task is quite possible after all.

> DR. MAXWELL MALTZ, "You Can Do the Impossible," *This Week*, July 24, 1955.

The last half century has been a retrogression of humanity, a frightening atrophy of culture of the most sinister kind, a loss in education, in decorum, in feeling for law, in truth and faith, in the most simple dependability.

> THOMAS MANN, part of an identical lecture delivered in West Germany and in East Germany a few weeks before his 80th birthday, news reports of Jan. 28, 1955.

Do not the most moving moments of our lives find us all without words?

> MARCEL MARCEAU, French pantomimist, *Reader's Digest*, June, 1958.

There is an old saying here that a man must do three things during life: plant trees, write books and have sons. I wish they would plant more trees and write more books.

> LUIS MUÑOZ MARÍN, Governor of Puerto Rico, *Time*, June 23, 1958.

Healthy people do not neglect the unknown, or deny it, or run away from it, or try to make believe it really is known. [Some people] have a wonderful capacity to appreciate again and again, freshly and naively, the basic goods of life, with awe, pleasure, wonder, and even ecstasy.

> A. H. MASLOW, professor, Brandeis University, quoted by S. I. Hayakawa, *Symbol, Status, and Personality*, Harcourt, Brace & World, 1963.

If you are small, death may quite likely overlook you.

> SOMERSET MAUGHAM, at 84, *Time*, Feb. 3, 1958.

Invention is a curious faculty. It is an attribute of youth and with age it is lost.

> SOMERSET MAUGHAM, *Points of View*, Heinemann, London, 1958.

318

As far as I can judge, with women it is all take and no give. There must be some women who are not liars. I do know a few women I am extremely fond of, but at my age one's attitude is rather different from a young man's.

SOMERSET MAUGHAM, at 86, *Time*, Oct. 17, 1960.

Where does discipline end? Where does cruelty begin? Somewhere between these, thousands of children inhabit a voiceless hell.

FRANÇOIS MAURIAC, *Second Thoughts*, World, 1961.

Growing old is no more than a bad habit which a busy man has no time to form.

ANDRÉ MAUROIS, in *The Aging American* by Milton Barron, Crowell, 1961.

Position is only what you are yourself and what you give to those around you.

ELSA MAXWELL, on social standing, *New York Journal-American*, Aug. 4, 1956.

. . . Party-giving is loving. It is giving. It is sharing. It is everybody's chance to light a little candle in the sometimes gloomy corners of the world. Someone has said that life itself is a party; you join after it's started and you leave before it's finished.

ELSA MAXWELL, *How To Do It*, Little, Brown, 1957.

I've done my small part to stamp out boredom in certain quarters of this world where it threatened to become rampant. If I accomplish little else, I shall consider my life justified by that one fact. Down with boredom. It has to go.

ELSA MAXWELL, on her role as a leading hostess of international café society, recalled in report of her death at 80, *Time*, Nov. 8, 1963.

Women want mediocre men, and men are working hard to be as mediocre as possible.

MARGARET MEAD, anthropologist, *Quote*, May 15, 1958.

319

There is no leisure time today except for the totally shiftless living in a shack with a hound dog.
> MARGARET MEAD, *New York Mirror*, May 18, 1958.

Everybody is overworked. Now the main occupation of the educated man is not his job, but helping his wife at home.
> MARGARET MEAD, *ibid*.

In almost any society, I think, the quality of the non-conformists is likely to be just as good as and no better than that of the conformists.
> MARGARET MEAD, *Redbook*, Jan., 1961.

Some people mistake weakness for tact. If they are silent when they ought to speak and so feign an agreement they do not feel, they call it being tactful. Cowardice would be a much better name. Tact is an active quality that is not exercised by merely making a dash for cover. Be sure, when you think you are being extremely tactful, that you are not in reality running away from something you ought to face.
> SIR FRANK MEDLICOTT, *Reader's Digest*, July, 1958.

Metaphysics is almost always an attempt to prove the incredible by an appeal to the unintelligible.
> H. L. MENCKEN, *Minority Report: H. L. Mencken's Notebooks*, Alfred A. Knopf, Inc., 1956.

There are some people who read too much: the bibliobibuli. I know some who are constantly drunk on books, as other men are drunk on whiskey or religion. They wander through this most diverting and stimulating of worlds in a haze, seeing nothing and hearing nothing.
> H. L. MENCKEN, *ibid*.

I now live in my work and in a few relationships with the few people I can really count on. Fame will go by and, so long, I've had you, fame. If it goes by, I've always known it was fickle. So at least it's something I experienced, but that's not where I live.
> MARILYN MONROE, concluding long tape-recorded conversation published in *Life*, Aug. 3, 1962; its publication ironically coincided with her death at 36 from an overdose of sleeping-pills.

If misery loves company, then triumph demands an audience.
> BRIAN MOORE, *A Message From Limbo*, Atlantic–Little, Brown, 1962.

I look back on my life like a good day's work, it was done and I am satisfied with it. I was happy and contented, I knew nothing better and made the best out of what life offered. And life is what we make it, always has been, always will be.
> ANNA MARY MOSES, American artist known as Grandma Moses, in her autobiography, *My Life's History*, Harper & Row, 1951.*

Everyone is a prisoner of his own experiences. No one can eliminate predjudices—just recognize them.
> EDWARD R. MURROW, news commentator, Dec. 31, 1955.

There are gatherers and scatterers of work. You, Edna, are a gatherer.
> CONDÉ NAST, former publisher of *Vogue*, quoted by veteran *Vogue* editor Edna Woolman Chase in autobiography, *Always In Vogue*, Doubleday, 1954.

Most advocates of realism in this world are hopelessly unrealistic.
> JAWAHARLAL NEHRU, Prime Minister of India, address to World Council of Churches, New Delhi, Dec. 4, 1961.

Nobody can live in the past or the future without being something of a nut. I live for the Everlasting Now.
> EVELYN NESBIT, figure in famed Thaw-White murder case, on life story as a motion picture, news summaries of Sept. 26, 1955.

When a man points a finger at someone else, he should remember that four of his fingers are pointing at himself.
> LOUIS NIZER, on accusations, *My Life In Court*, Doubleday, 1962.

---

* ". . . She had become by her hundredth year one of those old people who, as old buildings civilize a city or spindly church spires bind up a landscape, make the world seem safer. Shaw and Brancusi were examples; Churchill and Schweitzer still are. They pay the world the great compliment of being reluctant to leave it, and their reluctance becomes a benediction." *New Yorker*, Dec. 23, 1961, on death of Grandma Moses.

The visionless demigod of our new materialistic myth—a Success!
> EUGENE O'NEILL, characterization of the outwardly happy American businessman as presented in his 1926 play *The Great God Brown;* recalled in report of his death at 65, *Time,* Dec. 7, 1953.

This is Daddy's bedtime secret for today: Man is born broken. He lives by mending. The grace of God is glue.
> EUGENE O'NEILL, *ibid.*

. . . No one of us can help the things life has done to us. They're done before you realize it, and once they're done, they make you do other things until at last everything comes between you and what you'd like to be, and you've lost your true self forever.
> EUGENE O'NEILL, *Long Day's Journey Into Night,* Yale University Press, 1955.

The past is the present, isn't it? It's the future, too. We all tried to lie out of that but life won't let us.
> EUGENE O'NEILL, *ibid.*

The profound oblivion . . . descended on my name (is) the rational necessity of a historical situation imposed by destiny.
> VITTORIO EMANUELE ORLANDO, last surviving member of First World War "Big Four," *Time,* Dec. 8, 1952.

Oratory is just like prostitution: you must have little tricks. One of my favorite tricks is to start a sentence and leave it unfinished. Everyone racks his brains and wonders what I was going to say. . . .
> VITTORIO EMANUELE ORLANDO, *ibid.*

I am I plus my circumstances.
> JOSÉ ORTEGA Y GASSET, *Time,* Oct. 31, 1955.

The most difficult secret for a man to keep is his own opinion of himself.
> MARCEL PAGNOL, French playwright, news summaries of March 15, 1954.

322

Work expands so as to fill the time available for its completion. . . . The thing to be done swells in importance and complexity in a direct ratio with the time to be spent.

> C. NORTHCOTE PARKINSON, *Parkinson's Law and Other Studies in Administration*, Houghton Mifflin, 1957.

Expenditure rises to meet income. . . . Individual expenditure not only rises to meet income but tends to surpass it . . . [and] what is true of individuals is also true of governments . . .

> C. NORTHCOTE PARKINSON, *The Law and the Profits*, Houghton Mifflin, 1960.

In life it is more necessary to lose than to gain. A seed will only germinate if it dies. One has to live without getting tired, one must look forward and feed on one's living reserves, which oblivion no less than memory produces.

> BORIS PASTERNAK, *I Remember*, Pantheon, 1959.

"Segregation" is such an active word that it suggests someone is trying to segregate somebody else. So the word "apartheid" was introduced. Now it has such a stench in the nostrils of the world, they are referring to "autogenous development."

> ALAN PATON, South African author, *New York Times*, Oct. 24, 1960.

Pain makes man think. Thought makes man wise. Wisdom makes life endurable.

> JOHN PATRICK, in his 1954 play, *Teahouse of the August Moon*.

All sins have their origin in a sense of inferiority, otherwise called ambition.

> CESARE PAVESE, Italian author, *The Burning Brand*, Walker & Co., 1961.

We do not remember days, we remember moments.

> CESARE PAVESE, *ibid.*

The art of living is the art of knowing how to believe lies.

> CESARE PAVESE, *ibid.*

323

A note of triumph flowers inevitably in the voice that pronounces someone else insane, since to this verdict the answer is never definitive.

> VIRGILIA PETERSON, author and critic, in her autobiography, *A Matter of Life and Death*, Atheneum, 1961.

Happiness doesn't come from doing what we like to do but from liking what we have to do.

> WILFRED PETERSON, "The Art of Happiness," *This Week*, Feb. 5, 1961.

The art of being yourself at your best is the art of unfolding your personality into the man you want to be. . . . Be gentle with yourself, learn to love yourself, to forgive yourself, for only as we have the right attitude toward ourselves can we have the right attitude toward others.

> WILFRED PETERSON, *This Week*, Oct. 1, 1961.

If you are honest, it is the best thing in the world. It goes above intelligence.

> PANAYOTIS PIPINELIS, Premier of Greece, *New York Times*, July 12, 1963.

. . . Adventure is something you seek for pleasure, or even for profit, like a gold rush or invading a country; for the illusion of being more alive than ordinarily, the thing you *will* to occur; but experience is what really happens to you in the long run; the truth that finally overtakes you.

> KATHERINE ANNE PORTER, "Adventure in Living," *Mademoiselle*, Aug., 1955.

Life is full of internal dramas, instantaneous and sensational, played to an audience of one.

> ANTHONY POWELL, English novelist, *New York Times*, July 22, 1958.

The world is round and the place which may seem like the end may also be only the beginning.

> IVY BAKER PRIEST, Treasurer of the United States, *Parade*, Feb. 16, 1958.

We cannot get grace from gadgets. In the bakelite house of the future, the dishes may not break, but the heart can. Even a man with ten shower baths may find life flat, stale and unprofitable.

> J. B. PRIESTLEY, British novelist, news summaries of April 1, 1956.

324

Between midnight and dawn, when sleep will not come and all the old wounds begin to ache, I often have a nightmare vision of a future world in which there are billions of people, all numbered and registered, with not a gleam of genius anywhere, not an original mind, a rich personality, on the whole packed globe. The twin ideals of our time, organization and quantity, will have won forever.

>   J. B. Priestley, *Thoughts in the Wilderness*, Harper & Row, 1958.

Children are entitled to their otherness, as anyone is; and when we reach them, as we sometimes do, it is generally on a point of sheer delight, to us so astonishing, but to them so natural.

>   Alastair Reid, *Places, Poems, Preoccupations*, Atlantic–Little, Brown, 1963.

. . . In about the same degree as you are helpful, you will be happy.

>   Karl Reiland, former rector of St. George's Church, New York, *New York Herald Tribune*, Nov. 6, 1961.

My mother was given to a typical question: "We have always done this. Why should we do anything else?" But my wife's typical question was "We have always done this. Why not do it another way or, better still, why not do something else?"

>   John D. Rockefeller, Jr., *Fortune*, Feb., 1955.

How shall I tell you what the years have taught—that courage does not always march to airs blown by a bugle: is not always wrought out of the fabric ostentation wears.

>   Frances Rodman, "For A Six-Year-Old," poem in *New York Times*, May 13, 1961.

Courage is sometimes frail as hope is frail: A fragile shoot between two stones, that grows brave toward the sun though warmth and brightness fail, striving and faith the only strength it knows.

>   Frances Rodman, *ibid.*

"Queuemania" is an ailment that afflicts people with a compulsive urge to line up behind someone or something, even a lamp-post. . . . Usually it is used to describe disparagingly the alleged British inclination to line up in sheeplike fashion for any reason or no reason at all.

THOMAS P. RONAN, London correspondent, *New York Times*, Aug. 23, 1955.

I have never given very deep thought to a philosophy of life, though I have a few ideas that I think are useful to me. One is that you do whatever comes your way to do as well as you can, and another is that you think as little as possible about yourself and as much as possible about other people and about things that are interesting. The third is that you get more joy out of giving joy to others and should put a good deal of thought into the happiness that you are able to give.

ELEANOR ROOSEVELT, when asked about her philosophy of life, *McCall's*, Sept., 1957.

You gain strength, courage and confidence by every experience in which you really stop to look fear in the face. You are able to say to yourself, "I lived through this horror. I can take the next thing that comes along." . . . *You must do the thing you think you cannot do.*

ELEANOR ROOSEVELT, *You Learn by Living*, Harper & Row, 1960.

Perhaps the most important thing that has come out of my life is the discovery that if you prepare yourself at every point as well as you can, with whatever means you may have, however meager they may seem, you will be able to grasp opportunity for broader experience when it appears. Without preparation you cannot do it.

ELEANOR ROOSEVELT, *The Autobiography of Eleanor Roosevelt*, Harper & Row, 1961.

Life was meant to be lived, and curiosity must be kept alive. One must never, for whatever reason, turn his back on life.

ELEANOR ROOSEVELT,* *ibid.*

---

* In life and death, Eleanor Roosevelt received many tributes. Said *Time*, April 7, 1952: ". . . Kind, literal, awesomely helpful and endlessly patient, she has trotted up and down the stairways of the world, year after year—straightening its curtains, eyeing its plumbing, and occasionally admonishing landlords of those political slums behind the Iron Curtain, in sharp but hopeful tones." The Rev. Gordon Kidd, Rector, St. James Church, Hyde Park, said in a graveside eulogy Nov. 10, 1962: "The entire world becomes one family orphaned by her passing."

I accept life unconditionally. . . . Most people ask for happiness on condition. Happiness can only be felt if you don't set any condition.

ARTUR RUBINSTEIN, concert pianist, news reports of Feb. 5, 1956.

I have always thought respectable people scoundrels and I look anxiously at my face every morning for signs of my becoming a scoundrel.

BERTRAND RUSSELL, in *Bertrand Russell: The Passionate Skeptic* by Alan Wood, Simon & Schuster, 1958.

. . . It is possible, and authentic wise men have proved that it is possible, to live in so large a world that the vexations of daily life come to feel trivial and that the purposes which stir our deeper emotions take on something of the immensity of our cosmic contemplations. Some can achieve this in a greater degree, some only in a lesser, but all who care to do so can achieve this in some degree and, in so far as they succeed in this, they will win a kind of peace which will leave activity unimpeded but not turbulent. The state of mind which I have been trying to describe is what I mean by wisdom, and it is undoubtedly more precious than rubies.

BERTRAND RUSSELL, "The Expanding Mental Universe," *Saturday Evening Post*, July 18, 1959.

If there were in the world today any large number of people who desired their own happiness more than they desired the unhappiness of others, we could have a paradise in a few years.

BERTRAND RUSSELL, interviewed by Seth King, *New York Times*, May 18, 1961.

The answer to our prayer may be the echo of our resolve.

LORD SAMUEL (Herbert Louis Samuel, 1st Viscount), *Reader's Digest*, May, 1963.

Memory is when you look back and the answers float in to who, what, when, and where . . .

CARL SANDBURG, news summaries of June 30, 1954.

Not often in the story of mankind does a man arrive on earth who is both steel and velvet, who is as hard as rock and soft as drifting fog, who holds

327

in his heart and mind the paradox of terrible storm and peace unspeakable and perfect.

> CARL SANDBURG, address to joint session of Congress on 150th anniversary of Abraham Lincoln's birth, news reports of Feb. 13, 1959.

Always the path of American destiny has been into the unknown. Always there arose enough of reserves of strength, balances of sanity, portions of wisdom to carry the nation through to a fresh start with ever-renewing vitality.

> CARL SANDBURG, on 96th anniversary of Lincoln's Gettysburg address, *New York Times*, Nov. 20, 1959.

In these times you have to be an optimist to open your eyes when you awake in the morning.

> CARL SANDBURG, *New York Post*, Sept. 9, 1960.

To me, the distinction between happiness and unhappiness in childhood was one of small families and of large families, rather than of wealth and poverty.

> MARGARET SANGER, originator of the term "birth control," on receiving citation from World Population Emergency Conference, *New York Times*, May 12, 1961.

No woman can call herself free who does not own and control her body. No woman can call herself free until she can choose consciously whether she will or will not be a mother.

> MARGARET SANGER, frequently quoted statement which, when first voiced in 1913, caused her to be indicted by U.S. government on nine counts of law violation; it was recalled in interview following her 85th birthday, *Parade*, Dec. 1, 1963.

I can still see them, those poor, weak, wasted, frail women, pregnant year after year like so many automatic breeding machines. . . . Realizing that there was no one, no man on the scene, no doctor, no nurse, no social worker who would help them, I resolved that women should have some knowledge of their own bodies, some knowledge of contraception, that they should be rescued from their sex servitude. You ask me how I could face all the persecution, the martyrdom, the opposition. I'll tell you how. I knew I was right. It was as simple as that. *I knew I was right.*

> MARGARET SANGER, *ibid.*

328

Those who do not remember the past are condemned to relive it.

> GEORGE SANTAYANA, philosopher, quoted near frontispiece of William Shirer's history, *The Rise and Fall of the Third Reich*, Simon & Schuster, 1960.

The greatest happiness you can have is knowing that you do not necessarily require happiness.

> WILLIAM SAROYAN, news summaries of Dec. 16, 1957.

Good people are good because they've come to wisdom through failure. We get very little wisdom from success, you know. Success makes a fool of you, but failure can come only from great effort. One who doesn't try cannot fail and become wise.

> WILLIAM SAROYAN, *New York Journal-American*, Aug. 23, 1961.

Happiness is not having what you want, but wanting what you have.

> HYMAN JUDAH SCHACHTEL, rabbi, *The Real Enjoyment of Living*, Dutton, 1954.

Peace is art. Peace is when time doesn't matter as it passes by.

> MARIA SCHELL, actress, *Time*, March 3, 1958.

An optimist is a person who sees a green light everywhere, while the pessimist sees only the red stop light. . . . But the truly wise person is colorblind.

> DR. ALBERT SCHWEITZER, news summaries of Jan. 14, 1955.

That's my private ant. You're liable to break its legs.

> DR. ALBERT SCHWEITZER, asking a 10-year-old American boy not to brush an insect from his sleeve; the remark was considered a prime example of Dr. Schweitzer's famous "reverence for life," *Time*, April 19, 1963.

Tenterhooks are the upholstery of the anxious seat.

> ROBERT SHERWOOD, playwright, news reports of Nov. 15, 1955.

If you choose to work, you will succeed; if you don't, you will fail.

If you neglect your work, you will dislike it; if you do it well, you will enjoy it.

If you join little cliques, you will be self-satisfied; if you make friends widely, you will be interesting.

If you gossip, you will be slandered; if you mind your own business, you will be liked.

If you act like a boor, you will be despised; if you act like a human being, you will be respected.

If you spurn wisdom, wise people will spurn you; if you seek wisdom, they will seek you.

If you adopt a pose of boredom, you will be a bore; if you show vitality, you will be alive.

If you spend your free time playing bridge, you will be a good bridge-player; if you spend it in reading, discussing and thinking of things that matter, you will be an educated person.

> SIDNEY SMITH, president, University of Toronto, address to students, *Queen's Journal*, Kingston, Ontario, Oct. 2, 1956.

No one is fit to be trusted with power. . . . No one. . . . Any man who has lived at all knows the follies and wickedness he's capable of. If he does not know it, he is not fit to govern others. And if he does know it, he knows also that neither he nor any man ought to be allowed to decide a single human fate.

> C. P. SNOW, dialogue in *The Light and the Dark*, Scribner's, 1961.

What do I mean by magnanimity? Nothing very difficult. . . . The virtue consists, first, of seeing oneself and another person, any other person, as both really are: for there is no virtue without clear sight. And then, exerting oneself to see the best in the other person, and trying to get that best out of him. Which means, of course, that in the process one is trying to get the best out of oneself.

> C. P. SNOW, on becoming Rector of St. Andrew's University *Harper's*, July, 1962.

Gentleness is a divine trait: nothing is so strong as gentleness, and nothing is so gentle as real strength.

> RALPH W. SOCKMAN, Methodist minister, *New York Mirror*, June 8, 1952.

330

The roots of responsibility run out to the ends of the earth and we can no more isolate our consciences from world issues than we can fence off our oyster beds from the tides of the ocean.

RALPH W. SOCKMAN, in a sermon in 1953.

It is one thing to be moved by events; it is another to be mastered by them.

RALPH W. SOCKMAN, bulletin of Fourth Presbyterian Church, Chicago, Nov. 17, 1957.

. . . Perhaps a child who is fussed over gets a feeling of destiny, he thinks he is in the world for something important and it gives him drive and confidence.

DR. BENJAMIN SPOCK, *New York Sunday News*, May 11, 1958.

Photography records the gamut of feelings written on the human face, the beauty of the earth and skies that man has inherited, and the wealth and confusion man has created. It is a major force in explaining man to man.

EDWARD STEICHEN, *Time*, April 7, 1961.

We all cry and laugh but never at the same time or for the same reason. It is up to the photographer to catch the instant that is the reality of the person or of the moment.

EDWARD STEICHEN, *ibid.*

While I am not in favor of maladjustment, I view this cultivation of neutrality, this breeding of mental neuters, this hostility to eccentricity and controversy with grave misgiving. One looks back with dismay at the possibility of a Shakespeare perfectly adjusted to bourgeois life in Stratford, a Wesley contentedly administering a country parish, George Washington going to London to receive a barony from George III, or Abraham Lincoln prospering in Springfield with nary a concern for the preservation of the crumbling Union.

ADLAI E. STEVENSON, commencement address at Smith College, news reports of June 7, 1955.

There is nothing so fine as to be twenty-one and an American. One is for a fleeting instant—and the other is forever. So live—decently, fearlessly,

331

joyously—and don't forget that in the long run it is not the years in your life but the life in your years that counts!

> ADLAI E. STEVENSON, "If I Were Twenty-One," *Coronet*, Dec. 1955.

You will find that the truth is often unpopular and the contest between agreeable fancy and disagreeable fact is unequal. For, in the vernacular, we Americans are suckers for good news.

> ADLAI E. STEVENSON, commencement address at Michigan State University, *New York Times*, June 9, 1958.

With the supermarket as our temple and the singing commercial as our litany, are we likely to fire the world with an irresistible vision of America's exalted purposes and inspiring way of life?

> ADLAI E. STEVENSON, *Wall Street Journal*, June 1, 1960.

The face which we present to the world . . . is the face of the individual or the family as a high consumption unit with minimal social links or responsibilities—father happily drinking his beer, mother dreamily fondling soft garments newly rinsed in a wonderful new detergent, the children gaily calling from the new barbecue pit for a famous sauce for their steak.

> ADLAI E. STEVENSON, *ibid.*

Freedom is not an ideal, it is not even a protection, if it means nothing more than the freedom to stagnate.

> ADLAI E. STEVENSON, *Putting First Things First: A Democratic View*, Random House, 1960.

We have confused the free with the free and easy.

> ADLAI E. STEVENSON, *ibid.*

The secret of a good life is to have the right loyalties and to hold them in the right scale of values.

> NORMAN THOMAS, *Great Dissenters*, Norton, 1962.

Last night I dreamed of a small consolation enjoyed only by the blind: Nobody knows the trouble I've *not* seen! Visual images stimulate creativity, but may depress the spirit.

> JAMES THURBER, on his failing eyesight, *Newsweek*, June 16, 1958.

Humor is emotional chaos remembered in tranquillity.
JAMES THURBER, *New York Post*, Feb. 29, 1960.

Let the meek inherit the earth—they have it coming to them.
JAMES THURBER, *Life*, March 14, 1960.

I used to wake up at 4 a.m. and start sneezing, sometimes for five hours. I tried to find out what sort of allergy I had but finally came to the conclusion that it must be an allergy to consciousness.
JAMES THURBER, *ibid*.

A pinch of probably is worth a pound of perhaps.
JAMES THURBER, *Lanterns and Lances*, Harper & Row, 1961.

. . . The character of human life, like the character of the human condition, like the character of all life, is "ambiguity": the inseparable mixture of good and evil, the true and false, the creative and destructive forces —both individual and social.
PAUL TILLICH, theologian, address to 40th anniversary dinner of *Time* (reported in their May 17, 1963, issue).

The awareness of the ambiguity of one's highest achievements (as well as one's deepest failures) is a definite symptom of maturity.
PAUL TILLICH, *ibid*.

. . . The repository for washed-away cares? It must lie somewhere in the ocean, for nothing can vanish as completely as cares seem to vanish, just beyond the breakers. There is a twisting, slithering mass of them somewhere, perhaps in a deep cavern, many fathoms down. The spot should be discovered and then charted, so that no chance voyager might accidentally stumble upon it. All the cares of the world is better as a figure of speech than it would be as a reality. . . . On vacation, and out beyond the breakers, all men are millionaires, at least for the time. It is good to turn over out there, and float, and to think about those vanished cares, wherever they may be.
"TOPICS OF THE TIMES," *New York Times*, Aug. 1, 1955.

333

History not used is nothing, for all intellectual life is action, like practical life, and if you don't use the stuff—well, it might as well be dead.
ARNOLD TOYNBEE, historian, NBC-TV, April 17, 1955.

Civilization is a movement and not a condition, a voyage and not a harbor.
ARNOLD TOYNBEE, *Reader's Digest*, Oct., 1958.

. . . we human beings do have some genuine freedom of choice and therefore some effective control over our own destinies. I am not a determinist. But I also believe that the decisive choice is seldom the latest choice in the series. More often than not, it will turn out to be some choice made relatively far back in the past.
ARNOLD TOYNBEE, "Some Great 'If's' Of History," *New York Times*, Mar. 5, 1961.

We have been God-like in our planned breeding of our domesticated plants and animals, but we have been rabbit-like in our unplanned breeding of ourselves.
ARNOLD TOYNBEE, on growths in population, to World Food Congress at Washington, *National Observer*, June 10, 1963.

What a holler would ensue, if people had to pay the minister as much to marry them as they have to pay a lawyer to get them a divorce.
CLAIRE TREVOR, *New York Journal-American*, Oct. 12, 1960.

Character is something each one of us must build for himself, out of the laws of God and nature, the examples of others, and—most of all—out of the trials and errors of daily life. Character is the total of thousands of small daily strivings to live up to the best that is in us. Character is the final decision to reject whatever is demeaning to oneself or to others and with confidence and honesty to choose the right.
GENERAL ARTHUR G. TRUDEAU, chief, Research and Development, U.S. Army, *This Week*, March 27, 1960.

. . . the Bible tells us so often to give thanks, to praise God, and to acknowledge all His benefits. Surely it's not that God, like us, needs appreciation for His own well-being. It must be because He knows that when

334

we learn to give thanks, we are learning to concentrate not on the bad things, but on the good things in our lives.

> Amy Vanderbilt, "Your Amazing Power to Appreciate," *Guideposts*, Sept., 1957.

The modern rule is that every woman must be her own chaperone.

> Amy Vanderbilt, WNTA-TV, May 17, 1960.

. . . the world is hard to love, though we must love it because we have no other, and to fail to love it is not to exist at all.

> Mark Van Doren, *Autobiography of Mark Van Doren*, Harcourt, Brace and World, 1958.

Memory is the mother of imagination, reason and skill. . . . We like signs of richness in an individual, and most of all we like a great memory. Memory performs the impossible for man; holds together past and present, gives continuity and dignity to human life. This is the companion, this is the tutor, the poet, the library, with which you travel.

> Mark Van Doren, *Liberal Education*, Holt, Rinehart & Winston, 1960.

Any piece of knowledge I acquire today has a value at this moment exactly proportioned to my skill to deal with it. Tomorrow, when I know more, I recall that piece of knowledge and use it better.

> Mark Van Doren, *ibid.*

There is beauty in space, and it is orderly. There is no weather, and there is regularity. It is predictable. . . . Everything in space obeys the laws of physics. If you know these laws, and obey them, space will treat you kindly. And don't tell me man doesn't belong out there. Man belongs wherever he wants to go—and he'll do plenty well when he gets there.

> Wernher Von Braun, *Time*, Feb. 17, 1958.

Individual life does not rebel; there is too little of it for rebellion. One soul mingles with another like smoke.

> Heimito von Doderer, on life in Eastern world, *The Demons*, Knopf, 1961.

335

. . . every life has its own special, if invisible garden plot. . . . A man stands alone between the tended flower beds and the little porticoes of a house from which no one, by law and equity, is entitled to expel him. He stands alone by himself; the soft blue air is around him; he is unencumbered on all sides, like a statue. This is the only way he knows how to be; only in this way can he be big or little, crooked or straight, good or bad.

HEIMITO VON DODERER, on life in Western world, *ibid*.

Who gives a good book gives more than cloth, paper, and ink . . . more than leather, parchment and words. He reveals a foreword of his thoughts, a dedication of his friendship, a page of his presence, a chapter of himself, and an index of his love.

WILLIAM A. WARD, Texas Wesleyan College, *Quote*, Dec. 2, 1962.

Zen does not confuse spirituality with thinking about God while one is peeling potatoes. Zen spirituality is just to peel the potatoes. . . . Zen is a way of liberation, concerned not with discovering what is good or bad or advantageous, but what is.

ALAN WATTS, former priest who became an exponent of Zen, *Life*, April 21, 1961.

Trying to define yourself is like trying to bite your own teeth.

ALAN WATTS, *ibid*.

To live with fear and not be afraid is the final test of maturity.

EDWARD WEEKS, author and editor, "A Quarter Century: Its Retreats," *Look*, July 18, 1961.

If you must publish this book, please, make molehills out of mountains.

CHAIM WEIZMANN, first President of Israel, quoted in *Chaim Weizmann: A Biography by Several Hands*, Atheneum, 1963; on learning of the book's preparation.

When you are down and out, something always turns up—and it is usually the noses of your friends.

ORSON WELLES, *New York Times*, April 1, 1962.

336

Success is a fickle jade. The clothes on her back may be put there by hard work, but her jewels are the gifts of chance.

> SIR CHARLES WHEELER, president, Royal Academy of Art, *Sunday Times*, London, April 27, 1958.

The world is a funny paper read backwards. And that way it isn't so funny.

> TENNESSEE WILLIAMS, self-interview, *The Observer*, London, April 7, 1957.

Life is an unanswered question, but let's still believe in the dignity and importance of the question.

> TENNESSEE WILLIAMS, quoting a line from his *Camino Real, ibid.*

It haunts me, the passage of time. I think time is a merciless thing. I think life is a process of burning oneself out and time is the fire that burns you. But I think the spirit of man is a good adversary.

> TENNESSEE WILLIAMS, *New York Post*, April 30, 1958.

If the American dream is for Americans only, it will remain our dream and never be our destiny.

> RENE DE VISME WILLIAMSON, Dept. of Government, Louisiana State University, *Christianity Today*, June 19, 1961.

It's futile to talk too much about the past—something like trying to make birth control retroactive.

> CHARLES E. WILSON, Secretary of Defense, news summaries of May 22, 1955.

If it keeps up, man will atrophy all his limbs but the push-button finger.

> FRANK LLOYD WRIGHT, on automation, *New York Times*, Nov. 27, 1955.

Taste . . . is a matter of ignorance. You taste, and you like the taste, and you taste again because it pleases you, but you taste because you don't know. If you knew you wouldn't have to taste. . . .

FRANK LLOYD WRIGHT, "The Architect Preaches a Sermon," Church of the Divine Paternity, New York, June 3, 1956.

Authors

You can't make the Duchess of Windsor into Rebecca of Sunnybrook Farm. The facts of life are very stubborn things.
> CLEVELAND AMORY, on the Duchess of Windsor's memoirs, news reports of Oct. 6, 1955.

It often happens that only from the words of a good story-teller do we realize what we have done and what we have missed, and what we should have done and what we shouldn't have. It is perhaps in these stories, oral and written, that the true history of mankind can be found and that through them one can perhaps sense if not fully know the meaning of that history.
> Ivo ANDRIC of Yugoslavia, accepting Nobel Prize, *New York Times*, May 13, 1962.

Talent is like a faucet; while it is open, one must write. Inspiration is a farce that poets have invented to give themselves importance.
> JEAN ANOUILH, author of *Becket* and other plays, *New York Times*, Oct. 2, 1960.

It has always been much like writing a check. . . . It is easy to write a check if you have enough money in the bank, and writing comes more easily if you have something to say.
> SHOLEM ASCH, *New York Herald Tribune*, Nov. 6, 1955.

. . . Fiction is not a dream. Nor is it guesswork. It is imagining based on facts, and the facts must be accurate or the work of imagining will not stand up.
> MARGARET CULKIN BANNING, *The Writer*, March, 1960.

My gifts are small. I've used them very well and discreetly, never straining them, and the result is that I have made a charming little reputation.
> Sir Max Beerbohm, news reports of May 20, 1956.

I don't keep any copy of my books around. . . . They would embarrass me. When I finish writing my books, I kick them in the belly, and have done with them.
> Ludwig Bemelmans, *New York Herald Tribune*, Dec. 15, 1957.

To me it seems the sign of a second-rate imagination to assume that the impact of an obscene word can only be conveyed by showing it in cold print.
> Nicholas Bentley, English author and illustrator, *A Choice of Ornaments*, Taplinger, 1962.

There are a great many things I know nothing about but concerning which I know very well what I like.
> Nicholas Bentley, *ibid.*

What makes a good writer of history is a guy who is suspicious. Suspicion marks the real difference between the man who wants to write honest history and the one who'd rather write a good story.
> Jim Bishop, *New York Times*, Feb. 5, 1955.

A good writer is not, *per se*, a good book critic. No more so than a good drunk is automatically a good bartender.
> Jim Bishop, *New York Journal-American*, Nov. 26, 1957.

Writing, I think, is not apart from living. Writing is a kind of double living. The writer experiences everything twice. Once in reality and once in that mirror which waits always before or behind him. . . . A double life is a double burden. But it has also a double reward.
> Catherine Drinker Bowen, *Atlantic*, Dec., 1957.

Writers seldom choose as friends those self-contained characters who are never in trouble, never unhappy or ill, never make mistakes, and always count their change when it is handed to them.
> Catherine Drinker Bowen, *ibid.*

Of one of my earlier books, someone said I wrote like a disgruntled schoolteacher. I felt that was unjust. I wasn't a schoolteacher.

> CATHERINE DRINKER BOWEN, *New York Herald Tribune,* March 16, 1958.

In writing biography, fact and fiction shouldn't be mixed. And if they are, the fiction parts should be printed in red ink, the fact parts in black ink.

> CATHERINE DRINKER BOWEN, *Publishers' Weekly,* March 24, 1958.

Being a writer in a library is rather like being a eunuch in a harem.

> JOHN BRAINE, author of *Room At the Top, New York Times,* Oct. 7, 1962.

There is small chance in our fickle air for the hope of a durable fame that has always been thought a legitimate spur of writers, for we throw away our [literary] riches like a drunken sailor.

> VAN WYCK BROOKS, *Saturday Review,* Aug. 18, 1956.

I'm very healthy. And I have an eternal curiosity. Then, I think I'm not dependent on any person. I love people, I love my family, my children. . . . But inside myself is a place where I live all alone and that's where you renew your springs that never dry up.

> PEARL BUCK, *New York Post,* April 26, 1959.

I think you must remember that a writer is a simple-minded person to begin with and go on that basis. He's not a great mind, he's not a great thinker, he's not a great philosopher, he's a story-teller.

> ERSKINE CALDWELL, *Atlantic,* July, 1958.

I have never been able to forget the sunlight, the daylight in life, the freedom in which I grew up. But although that nostalgia explains many of my mistakes and shortcomings, it doubtless helped me to understand my calling, and it still helps me to stand implicitly beside all those silent men who, throughout the world, endure the life that has been made for them only because they remember or fleetingly re-experience free moments of happiness.

> ALBERT CAMUS, accepting Nobel Prize, Dec. 10, 1957.

341

I know with certainty that a man's work is nothing but the long journey to recover, through the detours of art, the two or three simple and great images which first gained access to his heart.
ALBERT CAMUS, *New York Times*, Jan. 24, 1960.

In the dream of life is man who finds his truths and loses them, on death's earth, in order to return . . . toward the peaceful land where death itself is a happy silence.
ALBERT CAMUS, *ibid*.

Of course no writers ever forget their first acceptance. . . . One fine day when I was seventeen I had my first, my second and third, all in the same morning's mail. Oh, I'm here to tell you, dizzy with excitement is no mere phrase!
TRUMAN CAPOTE, *Paris Review*, Spring-Summer, 1957.

We romantic authors are there to make people feel and not think. A historical romance is the only kind of book where chastity really counts.
BARBARA CARTLAND, address to Romantic Novelists' Association of England, *Queen*, Jan. 30, 1962.

When a book, any sort of book, reaches a certain intensity of artistic performance it becomes literature. That intensity may be a matter of style, situation, character, emotional tone, or idea, or half a dozen other things. It may also be a perfection of control over the movement of a story similar to the control a great pitcher has over the ball.
RAYMOND CHANDLER, *Raymond Chandler Speaking*, edited by Dorothy Gardiner and Kathrine S. Walker, Houghton Mifflin, 1962.

The novel remains for me one of the few forms—where we can record man's complexity and the strength and decency of his longings; where we can describe, step by step, minute by minute, our not altogether unpleasant struggle to put ourselves into a viable and devout relationship to our beloved and mistaken world.
JOHN CHEEVER, accepting National Book Award for Fiction, *The Writer*, Sept., 1958.

The novelist in America today benefits, I think, from the versatility and power of his language, from the breadth of his landscapes, from the company of many brilliant, gifted and adventurous colleagues and from a group of readers who, beset with an unprecedented variety of diversions, continue to read with great taste and intelligence.

JOHN CHEEVER, *ibid.*

I've always believed in writing without a collaborator, because where two people are writing the same book, each believes he gets all the worries and only half the royalties.

AGATHA CHRISTIE, news summaries of March 15, 1955.

The best time for planning a book is while you're doing the dishes.

AGATHA CHRISTIE, *ibid.*

I specialize in murders of quiet, domestic interest. Give me a nice deadly phial to play with and I am happy.

AGATHA CHRISTIE, *Life,* May 14, 1956.

It is ridiculous to set a detective story in New York City. New York City is itself a detective story.

AGATHA CHRISTIE, *ibid.*

I am proud but also, I must admit, awe-struck at your decision to include me. I do hope you are right. I feel we are both running a considerable risk and that I do not deserve it. But I shall have no misgivings if you have none.

SIR WINSTON CHURCHILL, accepting Nobel Prize for Literature, recalled in news reports on his eightieth birthday, Nov. 30, 1954.

Writing a book is an adventure; to begin with it is a toy and an amusement, then it becomes a master, and then it becomes a tyrant; and the last phase is just as you are about to be reconciled to your servitude—you kill the monster and fling him . . . to the public.

SIR WINSTON CHURCHILL, *Saturday Review,* July 13, 1963.

The Library's a lovely place. It should have many, many books dedicated to it. It's large, easygoing, generous—like New York itself.

MARCHETTE CHUTE, on dedicating a book to New York Public Library, *New York Times,* Oct. 18, 1953.

I've never signed a contract, so never have a deadline. A deadline's an unnerving thing. I just finish a book, and if the publisher doesn't like it that's his privilege. There've been many, many rejections. If you want to write in your own way, that's the chance you take.

> MARCHETTE CHUTE, *ibid*.

Listen carefully to first criticisms made of your work. Note just what it is about your work that the critics don't like—then cultivate it. That's the only part of your work that's individual and worth keeping.

> JEAN COCTEAU, advice to group of young artists, *New York Post*, June 27, 1956.

What is history after all? History is facts which become lies in the end; legends are lies which become history in the end. We writers are legends and legends become stronger than ourselves. We really are fabulous creatures.

> JEAN COCTEAU, *The Observer*, London, Sept. 22, 1957.

But children, you know, do really talk rather formally if you listen to them. Colloquialism comes later. It is what people pick up.

> IVY COMPTON-BURNETT, quoted by Frank Kermode, *The House of Fiction*, Heinemann, London, 1963.

I am convinced that all writers are optimists whether they concede the point or not. . . . How otherwise could any human being sit down to a pile of blank sheets and decide to write, say two hundred thousand words on a given theme?

> THOMAS COSTAIN, *Guideposts*, Oct., 1955.

In America only the successful writer is important, in France all writers are important, in England no writer is important, and in Australia you have to explain what a writer is.

> GEOFFREY COTTRELL, *New York Journal-American*, Sept. 22, 1961.

I write at high speed because boredom is bad for my health. It upsets my stomach more than anything else. I also avoid green vegetables. They're grossly overrated.

> NOEL COWARD, *Tempo*, Jan. 15, 1956.

344

. . . I meditate and put on a rubber tire with three bottles of beer. Most of the time I just sit picking my nose and thinking.

> JAMES GOULD COZZENS, on what he does in his study, *Time*, Sept. 2, 1957.

The thing you have to know is yourself; you are people. . . . I have no thesis except that people get a very raw deal from life. To me, life is what life is.

> JAMES GOULD COZZENS, *ibid.*

I always start writing with a clean piece of paper and a dirty mind.

> PATRICK DENNIS (Edward Everett Tanner), *Vogue*, Feb. 15, 1956.

It's so depressing. On every dollar the government gives me exactly nine cents to play around with.

> PATRICK DENNIS (Edward Everett Tanner), on tax tribulations of a best-selling author, *Newsweek*, Aug. 25, 1958.

It circulated for five years, through the halls of 15 publishers, and finally ended up with Vanguard Press, which as you can see, is rather deep into the alphabet.

> PATRICK DENNIS (Edward Everett Tanner), on his novel, *Auntie Mame, Saturday Review*, Feb. 25, 1961.

Writing isn't hard; no harder than ditch-digging.

> PATRICK DENNIS (Edward Everett Tanner), *Life*, Dec. 7, 1962.

People don't choose their careers: they are engulfed by them.

> JOHN DOS PASSOS, *New York Times*, Oct. 25, 1959.

If there is a special Hell for writers it would be in the forced contemplation of their own works, with all the misconceptions, the omissions, the failures that any finished work of art implies. . . . Naturally you do find passages that seem to come through. Invention isn't all failure: I suppose in Hell the successful passages would fade away just as you were starting to read them.

> JOHN DOS PASSOS, *ibid.*

Most of us, I believe, would like to so write about America that our contemporaries can say, "Yes, we see ourselves." And in a later day if men happen to come across the record we left, they may say to one another, "This is how it was—in that country—in that time."

> ALLEN DRURY, on *Advise and Consent*, his best-selling novel on Washington, *New York Times*, Sept. 6, 1959.

Every book is like a purge; at the end of it one is empty . . . like a dry shell on the beach, waiting for the tide to come in again.

> DAPHNE DU MAURIER, *Ladies' Home Journal*, Nov., 1956.

People in doubt, people mystified, people groping their way from one situation to another, from childhood to middle age, from joy to sorrow —these are the figures in the true suspense novel. They are traveling along a road of uncertainty toward an unseen goal. The suspense novel succeeds if the reader says to himself at the final page, "Yes—it couldn't happen any other way."

> DAPHNE DU MAURIER, *New York Times*, Dec. 22, 1957.

All novels are about certain minorities: the individual is a minority.

> RALPH ELLISON, *Writers At Work*, Viking, 1963.

When you reread a classic you do not see more in the book than you did before; you see more in *you* than there was before.

> CLIFTON FADIMAN, *Any Number Can Play*, World, 1957.

Great editors do not discover nor produce great authors; great authors create and produce great publishers.

> JOHN FARRAR, American publisher, *What Happens in Book Publishing*, Columbia University Press, 1957.

The only environment the artist needs is whatever peace, whatever solitude, and whatever pleasure he can get at not too high a cost.

> WILLIAM FAULKNER, *Life*, June 11, 1956.

No man can write who is not first a humanitarian.

> WILLIAM FAULKNER, *Time*, Feb. 25, 1957.

346

Everything goes by the board: honor, pride, decency . . . to get the book written. If a writer has to rob his mother, he will not hesitate; the *Ode to a Grecian Urn* is worth any number of old ladies.
WILLIAM FAULKNER, *Writers At Work*, Viking, 1958.

Why, that's a hundred miles away. That's a long way to go just to eat.
WILLIAM FAULKNER, on declining invitation to White House dinner honoring America's Nobel Prize winners, *Life*, Jan. 20, 1962.

. . . The young man or woman writing today has forgotten the problems of the human heart in conflict with itself which alone can make good writing because only that is worth writing about, worth the agony and the sweat. He must learn them again . . . leaving no room in his workshop for anything but pity and pride and compassion and sacrifice.
WILLIAM FAULKNER, *ibid*.

A writer is congenitally unable to tell the truth and that is why we call what he writes fiction.
WILLIAM FAULKNER, recalled on his death, July 6, 1962.*

I sat staring up at a shelf in my workroom from which 31 books identically dressed in neat dark green leather stared back at me with a sort of cold hostility, like children who resent their parents. Don't stare at us like that! they said. Don't blame us if we didn't turn out to be the perfection you expected. We didn't ask to be brought into the world.
EDNA FERBER, *A Kind of Magic*, autobiography, Doubleday, 1963.

---

* President Kennedy's statement issued from the White House: "A Mississippian by birth, an American by virtue of those forces and loyalties which guided his work, a guiding citizen of our civilization by virtue of his art, William Faulkner now rests, the search done, his place secure among the great creators of this age." A year later, *Saturday Evening Post*, July 13, 1963, reporting for the first time that Faulkner died in an alcoholic clinic, quoted a statement made by the author's brother, Murry Faulkner, to reporters gathered at the Ole Miss Hotel, Oxford, Miss.: "Ordinarily, in a matter of this kind, we would not tolerate the publicity and notoriety which will attend my brother's funeral. However, we are well aware of his fame and of his accomplishments, and we understand that you gentlemen are here from a sense of duty to your employers, rather than morbid curiosity. We wish to help you all we can. But decorum and dignity must be preserved. I know you all appreciate that."

347

I think that in order to write really well and convincingly, one must be somewhat poisoned by emotion. Dislike, displeasure, resentment, fault-finding, imagination, passionate remonstrance, a sense of injustice—they all make fine fuel.

> EDNA FERBER, *ibid.*

Mostly, we authors must repeat ourselves—that's the truth. We have two or three great moving experiences in our lives—experiences so great and moving that it doesn't seem at the time that anyone else has been caught up and pounded and dazzled and astonished and beaten and broken and rescued and illuminated and rewarded and humbled in just that way ever before.

> F. SCOTT FITZGERALD, *Afternoon Of An Author, A Selection Of Uncollected Stories and Essays,* Scribner's, 1958.

Art for art's sake? I should think so, and more so than ever at the present time. It is the one orderly product which our middling race has produced. It is the cry of a thousand sentinels, the echo from a thousand labyrinths, it is the lighthouse which cannot be hidden . . . it is the best evidence we can give of our dignity.

> E. M. FORSTER, address to P.E.N. Club Congress, quoted by Huw Wheldon in his compilation of BBC-TV programs, *Monitor,* Macdonald & Co., 1962.

I have only got down on to paper, really, three types of people: the person I think I am, the people who irritate me, and the people I'd like to be. When you come to the really great writers like Tolstoy you find they can get hold of all types.

> E. M. FORSTER, *ibid.*

Sometimes I think it sounds like I walked out of the room and left the typewriter running.

> GENE FOWLER, on his own work, *Newsweek,* Nov. 1, 1954.

Reality is not an inspiration for literature. At its best, literature is an inspiration for reality.

> ROMAIN GARY, *New York Herald Tribune,* Jan. 13, 1960.

348

A kid is a guy I never write down to. He's interested in what I say if I make it interesting. He is also the last container of a sense of humor, which disappears as he gets older, and he laughs only according to the way the boss, society, politics, or race, want him to. Then he becomes an adult. And an adult is an obsolete child.

> THEODORE GEISEL (Dr. Seuss), *New York Mirror*, May 18, 1958.

As far back as I remember, long before I could write, I had played at making stories. . . . But not until I was seven or more, did I begin to pray every night, "O God, let me write books! Please, God, let me write books!"

> ELLEN GLASGOW, in her autobiography, *The Woman Within*, Harcourt, Brace and World, 1954.

. . . It was enough, and it is now over. Not for everything that the world could give would I consent to live over my life unchanged, or to bring back, unchanged, my youth. . . . Only on the surface of things have I ever trod the beaten path. So long as I could keep from hurting anyone else, I have lived, as completely as it was possible, the life of my choice. I have been free. Yet I have not stolen either the ponderable or the imponderable material of happiness. I have done the work I wished to do for the sake of that work alone. And I have come, at last, from the fleeting rebellion of youth into the steadfast—or is it merely the seasonable—accord without surrender of the unreconciled heart.

> ELLEN GLASGOW, *ibid.*

. . . For a dyed-in-the-wool author nothing is as dead as a book once it is written. . . . She is rather like a cat whose kittens have grown up. While they were a-growing she was passionately interested in them but now they seem hardly to belong to her—and probably she is involved with another batch of kittens as I am involved with other writing.

> RUMER GODDEN, *New York Times*, Dec. 1, 1963.

I was last in Rome in 540 A.D., when it was full of Goths and their heavy horses. It has changed a great deal since then.

> ROBERT GRAVES, on his first visit to Rome, scene of many of his historical works, *Time*, Jan. 6, 1958.

349

Intuition, the supra-logic that cuts out all routine processes of thought and leaps straight from problem to answer.

ROBERT GRAVES, *Five Pens in Hand*, Doubleday, 1958.

Unless a writer has a strong sense of pity he is bound to be in some sense a maimed writer.

GRAHAM GREENE, *The Observer*, London, Sept. 15, 1957.

What it all adds up to is that I write novels about what interests me and I can't write about anything else. And one of the things which interests me most is discovering the humanity in the apparently inhuman character.

GRAHAM GREENE, *ibid.*

They're fancy talkers about themselves, writers. If I had to give young writers advice, I would say don't listen to writers talking about writing or themselves.

LILLIAN HELLMAN, *New York Times*, Feb. 21, 1960.

. . . A writer of fiction has to invent out of what he knows in order to make something not photographic, or naturalistic, or realistic, which will be something entirely new and invented out of his own knowledge. What a writer should try to do is to make something which will be so written that it will become a part of the experience of those who read him.

ERNEST HEMINGWAY, on learning that he had been chosen to receive Nobel Prize, news reports of Nov. 7, 1954.

Writing, at its best, is a lonely life. Organizations for writers palliate the writer's loneliness, but I doubt if they improve his writing. He grows in public stature as he sheds his loneliness and after his work deteriorates. For he does his work alone and if he is a good enough writer he must face eternity, or the lack of it, each day.

ERNEST HEMINGWAY, accepting Nobel Prize, news reports of Dec. 11, 1954.

No classic resembles any previous classic, so do not be discouraged.

ERNEST HEMINGWAY, advice to young people who would be writers, *McCall's*, May, 1956.

350

I am very happy for any writer who deserves it to get the prize. I am sorry about any writer who deserves it and doesn't get it. This makes me very humble in accepting it.

ERNEST HEMINGWAY, on Nobel Prize, *ibid.*

When I am working on a book or a story I write every morning as soon after first light as possible. There is no one to disturb you and it is cool or cold and you come to your work and warm as you write . . . When you stop you are as empty, and at the same time never empty but filling, as when you have made love to someone you love. Nothing can hurt you, nothing can happen, nothing means anything until the next day when you do it again. It is the wait until the next day that is hard to get through.

ERNEST HEMINGWAY, *Paris Review*, Spring, 1958.

The most essential gift for a good writer is a built-in, shock-proof shit detector. This is the writer's radar and all great writers have had it.

ERNEST HEMINGWAY, *ibid.*

In stating as fully as I could how things really were, it was often very difficult and I wrote awkwardly and the awkwardness is what they called my style. All mistakes and awkwardnesses are easy to see, and they called it style.

ERNEST HEMINGWAY, *This Week*, Oct. 18, 1959.

A big lie is more plausible than truth. People who write fiction, if they had not taken it up, might have become very successful liars.

ERNEST HEMINGWAY, *ibid.*

We are all apprentices in a craft where no one ever becomes a master.

ERNEST HEMINGWAY, *New York Journal-American*, July 11, 1961.

. . . Journalism allows its readers to witness history; fiction gives its readers an opportunity to live it.

JOHN HERSEY, *Time*, March 13, 1950.

Any writer worth the name is always getting into one thing or getting out of another thing.

FANNIE HURST, *New York Mirror*, Aug. 28, 1956.

351

. . . Writing is the lonelist job in the world. There's always that frustrating chasm to bridge between the concept and the writing of it. We're a harassed tribe, we writers.

> FANNIE HURST, *ibid.*

I have knocked at the door of the experience of others. Almost universally, even for the humble among us, the survey adds up to blood and tears. Sweat and ink are part of the terrible dilemma of authorohip.

> FANNIE HURST, in her autobiography, *The Anatomy of Me*, Doubleday, 1958.

A bad book is as much of a labor to write as a good one, it comes as sincerely from the author's soul.

> ALDOUS HUXLEY, *Newsweek*, Jan. 2, 1956.

The chief defeat of the novel of ideas is that you must write about people who have ideas to express which excludes all but about .01 per cent of the human race.

> ALDOUS HUXLEY, *New York Herald Tribune*, Nov. 24, 1963.

I think . . . that American writers, once they become writers, and become reasonably successful, they stop being people and they become writers. They sort of cut off their own material . . . they're forced continually to turn to their youthful experiences before they became "writers" in order to find material.

> JAMES JONES on *The Writer Speaks*, radio series quoted in *Christian Science Monitor*, June 6, 1963.

In a very real sense, the writer writes in order to teach himself, to understand himself, to satisfy himself; the publishing of his ideas, though it brings gratifications, is a curious anticlimax.

> ALFRED KAZIN, *Think*, February, 1963.

Confronted by an absolutely infuriating review it is sometimes helpful for the victim to do a little personal research on the critic. Is there any truth to the rumor that he had no formal education beyond the age of eleven? In any event, is he able to construct a simple English sentence? Are his modifiers misplaced? Do his participles dangle? When moved to lyricism does he write "I had a fun time"? Was he ever arrested for burglary? I don't know that you will prove anything this way, but it is perfectly harmless and quite soothing.

JEAN KERR, *The Snake Has All the Lines,* Doubleday, 1960.

. . . Some day some author might ask some critic whether he had really read the book or seen the play or heard the music or whatever. If the critic shoots right back: "Do you cheat at cards?" just say: "I don't play cards." That should stun him. If his high calling has not put him in the sorry state of being above stunning. A cad of that stripe has no place in this beguiling world of shared masterpieces.

JEAN KERR, *ibid.*

Literature plays an important role in our country, helping the Party to educate the people correctly, to instill in them advanced, progressive ideas by which our Party is guided. And it is not without reason that writers in our country are called engineers of the human soul.

NIKITA KHRUSHCHEV, Soviet premier, interview with Henry Shapiro of United Press, Nov. 14, 1957.

Right now, anyone who finds a way to make a lamp out of a Coca-Cola bottle gets more protection than a man who creates a work of art.

CHRISTOPHER LAFARGE, plea for a universal copyright law, news summaries of April 9, 1954.

In Monroeville [Alabama], well, they're Southern people, and if they know you are working at home they think nothing of walking right in for coffee. But they wouldn't dream of interrupting you on the golf course.

HARPER LEE, on why she does most of her creative thinking while golfing, *Time,* May 12, 1961.

. . . The middle class, that prisoner of the barbarian 20th century.

SINCLAIR LEWIS, speaking of the theme of the novel that still lay unfinished at his death, Jan. 10, 1951.

Nothing feeds the center (of being) so much as creative work. . . . The curtain of mechanization has come down between the mind and the hand.

ANNE MORROW LINDBERGH, *Gift From the Sea,* Pantheon, 1955.

353

. . . I have a stern, perhaps Puritan, feeling that—wonderful as it is to receive awards for one's work—somehow one ought not to be dwelling on one's past efforts, or patting oneself on the back for them, or allowing others to do so; but that one should rather resolutely leave them behind and go ahead, devoting one's present thoughts and energies to new work . . .
> ANNE MORROW LINDBERGH, letter declining an invitation to receive literary award, *McCall's,* Oct., 1956.

Writers, if they are worthy of that jealous designation, do not write for other writers. They write to give reality to experience.
> ARCHIBALD MACLEISH, *Saturday Review,* Nov. 26, 1960.

The critics will be waiting for you with meat cleavers the next time around.
> JOHN P. MARQUAND, warning to Herman Wouk, after success of Wouk's *The Caine Mutiny,* news reports of Nov. 18, 1955.

I wrote the scenes . . . by using the same apprehensive imagination that occurs in the morning before an afternoon's appointment with my dentist.
> JOHN P. MARQUAND, *Atlantic,* Sept., 1956.

You don't get better by worrying. You get better by writing and you have to do it every day—for hours.
> JOHN P. MARQUAND, *Variety,* April 3, 1957.

Mr. Moto was my literary disgrace. I wrote about him to get shoes for the baby.
> JOHN P. MARQUAND, *New York Times,* Aug. 3, 1958.

If you have one strong idea, you can't help repeating it and embroidering it. Sometimes I think that authors should write one novel and then be put in a gas chamber.
> JOHN P. MARQUAND, *New York Herald Tribune,* Oct. 5, 1958.

Some books are written in anguish, others just write themselves and these are jolly to write. . . . But d'you know even when a thing is difficult, if you are a writer you are never so happy as when you are writing.
> SOMERSET MAUGHAM, interview in *New York Times,* Nov. 19, 1950.

The real reason for the universal applause that comforts the declining years of the author who exceeds the common span of man is that intelligent people, after the age of thirty, read nothing at all. As they grow older, the books they read in their youth are lit with its glamour, and with every year that passes they ascribe greater merit to the author that wrote them.
>   SOMERSET MAUGHAM, comment recalled in reports of his 80th birthday, Jan. 25, 1954.

I am a relic of the Edwardian era. It may seem rather old fashioned to you, but I believe in *story-telling*. . . . I don't think that either politics or philosophy are suitable material for genuine story-telling. They clog the narrative and action which distinguishes fiction from other forms of writing.
>   SOMERSET MAUGHAM, *The Observer*, London, Nov. 10, 1957.

What I really believe in is the personal drama of the human relations. . . . The genesis of a story in my mind was always the particular situation between individuals, never the silent wish to illustrate a general truth.
>   SOMERSET MAUGHAM, *ibid.*

I have written because I had a fertile invention and the ideas for plays and stories that thronged my brain would not let me rest till I had got rid of them by writing them.
>   SOMERSET MAUGHAM, preface to *The Gentleman From Cap Ferrat* by Klaus Jonas, published by The Center of Maugham Studies, New Haven, 1957.

What has influenced my life more than any other single thing has been my stammer. Had I not stammered I would probably . . . have gone to Cambridge as my brothers did, perhaps have become a don and every now and then published a dreary book about French literature.
>   SOMERSET MAUGHAM, *Newsweek*, May 23, 1960.

The need to express one's self in writing springs from a maladjustment to life, or from an inner conflict which the adolescent (or the grown man) cannot resolve in action. Those to whom action comes easily as breathing rarely feel the need to break loose from the real, to rise above, and describe it. . . . I do not mean that it is enough to be maladjusted to become a

355

great writer, but writing is, for some, a method of resolving a conflict, provided they have the necessary talent.

André Maurois, *The Art of Writing*, Dutton, 1960.

Style is the hallmark of a temperament stamped upon the material at hand.

André Maurois, *ibid.*

Almost all the great novels have as their *motif*, more or less disguised, the "passage from childhood to maturity," the clash between the thrill of expectation, and the disillusioning knowledge of the truth. *Lost Illusion* is the undisclosed title of every novel.

André Maurois, *ibid.*

Writing is a difficult trade which must be learned slowly by reading great authors; by trying at the outset to imitate them; by daring then to be original; by destroying one's first productions; by comparing subsequent works to recognized materpieces and, once more, by destroying them; by crossing out whole passages; by weeping from despair; by being more severe with oneself than even the critics will be. After ten years of such arduous activity, if one has talent, one may begin to write in an acceptable manner.

André Maurois, *New York Journal-American*, July 31, 1963.

. . . A thermos of tea, a quiet room in the early morning hours.

Carson McCullers, on the ideal atmosphere for writing, *Playbill*, Oct. 28, 1957.

A writer soon discovers he has no single identity but lives the lives of all the people he creates and his weathers are independent of the actual day around him. I live with the people I create and it has always made my essential loneliness less keen.

Carson McCullers, preface to *The Square Root of Wonderful*, Houghton Mifflin, 1958.

The dimensions of a work of art are seldom realized by the author until the work is accomplished. It is like a flowering dream. Ideas grow, budding silently, and there are a thousand illuminations coming day by day as the work progresses. A seed grows in writing as in nature. The seed of the idea is developed by both labor and the unconscious, and the struggle that goes on between them.

CARSON McCULLERS, *Esquire*, Dec., 1959.

The writer by nature of his profession is a dreamer and a conscious dreamer. How, without love and the intuition that comes from love, can a human being place himself in the situation of another human being? He must imagine, and imagination takes humility, love, and great courage. How can you create a character without love and the struggle that goes with love?

CARSON McCULLERS, *ibid.*

I know that my works are a credit to this nation, and I dare say they will endure longer than the McCarran Act. . . . I have made more friends for American culture than the State Department. Certainly I have made fewer enemies, but that isn't very difficult.

ARTHUR MILLER, on being refused a passport, *New York Herald Tribune*, March 31, 1954.

When you're a writer, you no longer see things with the freshness of the normal person. There are always two figures that work inside you, and if you are at all intelligent you realize that you have lost something. But I think there has always been this dichotomy in a real writer. He wants to be terribly human, and he responds emotionally, and at the same time there's this cold observer who cannot cry.

BRIAN MOORE, *Saturday Review*, Oct. 13, 1962.

Slang is a token of man's lively spirit ever at work in unexpected places. . . . For slang, after all, is a kind of metaphor and metaphor, we have agreed, is a kind of poetry; you might say indeed that slang is a poor-man's poetry.

JOHN MOORE, English novelist, *You English Words*, Lippincott, 1961.

Scientists will have rifled the secrets of the moon and of Mars long before they will know the secret and subtle workings of the myriad-minded force which shapes the course of the language.

JOHN MOORE, *ibid.*

357

Literature is not a commodity that can be valued at an appraising warehouse. It seems grotesque to have to insist on it again and again, but literature is the sudden expression of the fierce, hilarious lives of human beings.

> CHRISTOPHER MORLEY, *Saturday Review*, April 13, 1957.

Most writers have an island, a center of refuge, within themselves. It is the mind's anchorage, and the soul's Great Good Place. . . . These are holy provinces, and within them lies what we come to recognize as the author's field of vision.

> WRIGHT MORRIS, accepting National Book Award for fiction, *New York Herald Tribune*, March 24, 1957.

All my major works have been written in prison. . . . I would recommend prison not only to aspiring writers but to aspiring politicians, too.

> JAWAHARLAL NEHRU, Prime Minister of India, on his years as a political prisoner, *Look*, April 5, 1955.

I write what I would like to read—what I think other women would like to read. If what I write makes a woman in the Canadian mountains cry and she writes and tells me about it, especially if she says, "I read it to Tom when he came in from work and he cried, too," I feel I have succeeded.

> KATHLEEN NORRIS, on the publication of her seventy-eighth book, *New York Times*, Feb. 5, 1955.

The hallway of everyman's life is paced with pictures; pictures gay and pictures gloomy, all useful for, if we be wise, we can learn from them a richer and braver way to live.

> SEAN O'CASEY, on his autobiographical play, *Pictures in the Hallway*, *New York Times*, Sept. 16, 1956.

Between the writing of plays, in the vast middle of the night, when our children and their mother slept, I sat alone, and my thoughts drifted back in time, murmuring the remembrance of things past into the listening ear of silence; fashioning thoughts to unspoken words, and setting them down upon the sensitive tablets of the mind.

> SEAN O'CASEY, *ibid*.

I have learned in my thirty-odd years of serious writing only one sure lesson: stories, like whiskey, must be allowed to mature in the cask.
    SEAN O'FAOLAIN, *Atlantic*, Dec., 1956.

A legend has a life of its own. . . . People stick a label on you and, thirty years later, it's still there because they haven't the patience to look and see that it no longer fits.
    JOHN O'HARA, *Cosmopolitan*, Sept., 1960.

They started dropping honorary degrees all around me, but never hit me.
    JOHN O'HARA, novelist, on why he quit giving his manuscripts to Yale, *Newsweek*, June 3, 1963.

Wit has truth in it; wisecracking is simply calisthenics with words.
    DOROTHY PARKER, *Paris Review*, Summer, 1956.

As artists they're rot, but as providers they're oil wells—they gush.
    DOROTHY PARKER, on lady novelists, *The Years With Ross*, by James Thurber, *Atlantic*, 1958.

Immensely grateful, touched, proud, astonished, abashed.
    BORIS PASTERNAK, telegram to Swedish Academy, accepting Nobel Prize, *New York Mirror*, Oct. 26, 1958.

In view of the meaning given to this honor in the community to which I belong, I should abstain from the undeserved prize that has been awarded to me. Do not meet my voluntary refusal with ill-will.
    BORIS PASTERNAK, cable reversing acceptance of Nobel Prize after outburst of criticism by the government of the Soviet Union, *New York Times*, Oct. 30, 1958.

The writer is the Faust of modern society, the only surviving individualist in a mass age. To his orthodox contemporaries he seems a semi-madman.
    BORIS PASTERNAK, *The Observer*, London, Dec. 20, 1959.

One must live and write restlessly, with the help of the new reserves that life offers. I am weary of this notion of faithfulness to a point of view at all costs.

> Boris Pasternak, *Writers At Work*, Viking, 1963.

An essayist is a lucky person who has found a way to discourse without being interrupted

> Charles Poore, *New York Times*, May 31, 1962.

It began as a diary . . . little by little it began to turn itself into a story, by that mysterious process which I cannot explain, but which I recognize when it begins, and I go along with it out of a kind of curiosity, as if my mind which knows the facts is watching to see what my story-telling mind will finally make of them.

> Katherine Anne Porter, on the writing of a novel, *Atlantic*, March, 1956.

I am nowhere and everywhere. I am the captain and the seasick bulldog and the man in the cherry-colored shirt who sings and the devilish children and all of the women and lots of the men. . . . You know, I got attached to my gang on the boat. I hated to give them up.

> Katherine Anne Porter, on *Ship of Fools*, her best-selling novel, *Saturday Review*, March 31, 1962.

Most people won't realize that writing is a craft. You have to take your apprenticeship in it like anything else.

> Katherine Anne Porter, *ibid.*

Of course I wasn't working on it all that time, it was working on me.

> Katherine Anne Porter, on the 30-year period in which she wrote *Ship of Fools*, *McCall's*, April, 1963.

If I didn't know the ending of a story, I wouldn't begin. I always write my last line, my last paragraphs, my last page first.

> Katherine Anne Porter, *Writers At Work*, Viking, 1963.

. . . Really, in the end, the only thing that can make you a writer is the person that you are, the intensity of your feeling, the honesty of your vision, the unsentimental acknowledgment of the endless interest of the life around you and within you. Virtually nobody can help you deliberately—many people will help you unintentionally.

SANTHA RAMA RAU, *Harper's Bazaar*, Aug., 1956.

When anyone tells me he wants to write, I say to him—first pick your ancestors carefully. The farther from an author, the better. Miners are fine. Stonecutters are better. So are farmers and stockmen. Their innocence of literary creation leaves plenty of good oxygen in the blood stream. Even ancestors who indulged in a little reading are suspect.

CONRAD RICHTER, on receiving National Book Award for fiction, *Saturday Review*, April 1, 1961.

I'm having a wonderful time. I can't figure out who did the killing.

MARY ROBERTS RINEHART, comment at 81 on re-reading one of her earliest murder mysteries, *Quote*, Aug. 25, 1957.

I shall live bad if I do not write and I shall write bad if I do not live.

FRANÇOISE SAGAN, French novelist, *New York Times*, Nov. 11, 1956.

There are no new plots, there are only new people, new treatment, new reactions, new locations, new times. . . . A professional writer will starve if he waits for inspiration; he must learn to combine spontaneity of emotion with sound technique to make the result read like inspiration.

ADELA ROGERS ST. JOHNS, *How to Write a Story and Sell It*, Doubleday, 1956.

Some of my best friends are children. In fact, all of my best friends are children.

J. D. SALINGER, *Time*, July 16, 1951.

To be out of jail. To eat and sleep regular. To get what I write printed in a free country for free people. To have a little love in the home and esteem outside the home.

CARL SANDBURG, "personal happiness prescription," *Newsweek*, Jan. 16, 1956.

Slang is a language that rolls up its sleeves, spits on its hands and goes to work.
> CARL SANDBURG, *New York Times*, Feb. 13, 1959.

A writer lives, at best, in a state of astonishment. Beneath any feeling he has of the good or evil of the world lies a deeper one of wonder at it all. To transmit that feeling, he writes.
> WILLIAM SANSOM, *Blue Skies, Brown Studies*, Atlantic–Little, Brown, 1961.

The writer is a spiritual anarchist, as in the depth of his soul every man is. . . . He neither walks with the multitude nor cheers with them. The writer who is a writer is a rebel who never stops.
> WILLIAM SAROYAN, preface to *The Whole Voyald*, Little, Brown, 1956.

When the going is good a writer knows very little, if any, loneliness. When it is bad he believes he knows nothing else. The flaw is the same in either event: when the writer thought the going was good and therefore felt no loneliness, the writing was not necessarily good, and when he believed the going was bad and therefore felt ineffective, the writing may actually have been good. He just happened to feel loneliness at the time. If it wasn't something he ate, it was surely something that was eating him.
> WILLIAM SAROYAN, *Saturday Review*, Feb. 25, 1961.

The writer goes into another world when he goes to work—into another womb, if you prefer. . . . He goes there because it's a good place for him to be, since he discovered it, explored it, mapped it, populated it, and gave it its rules, regulations, laws, crimes, and punishments.
> WILLIAM SAROYAN, *ibid.*

It's not entirely useless to remember how things were in the middle of the world's greatest city (New York) when I was a kid, before TV dinners, and homemade bomb shelters, when there was still glory in war and it wasn't un-American to call your team the Cincinnati Reds . . .
> RALPH SCHOENSTEIN, writing his autobiography at 27, *The Block* (Random House), *New York Journal-American*, Oct. 30, 1960.

Every writer is a frustrated actor who recites his lines in the hidden auditorium of his skull.

> Rod Serling, *Vogue*, April 1, 1957.

Literature is like any other trade; you will never sell anything unless you go to the right shop.

> George Bernard Shaw, message on a postcard sent to a young author and later exhibited in a New York department store, *New York Herald Tribune*, May 4, 1955.

The duty of dramatists is to express their times and guide the public through the perplexities of those times.

> Robert Sherwood, news reports of Nov. 15, 1955.

I write fast, because I have not the brains to write slow.

> Georges Simenon, author of an average of six novels per year, written at a pace of thirty-three hours per novel, *Look*, Dec. 15, 1953.

The lust of the era I manage beautifully.

> Edith Sitwell, on writing about the 16th century, *Time*, Dec. 1, 1952.

It is music to my ears. I have always said that if I were a rich man, I would employ a professional praiser.

> Osbert Sitwell, on hearing his books read aloud, NBC-TV, Jan. 2, 1955.

I wanted to write a special kind of book—a book wherein people loved the things that other people in higher economic and cultural brackets thought were terrible. I wrote about people who *liked* fake fireplaces in their parlor, who thought a brass horse with a clock embedded in its flank was *wonderful*.

> Betty Smith, on her novels of Brooklyn, *Parade*, June 29, 1958.

Those big-shot writers . . . could never dig the fact that there are more salted peanuts consumed than caviar.

> Mickey Spillane, on popularity of mystery books, *New York Herald Tribune*, Aug. 18, 1961.

Hard-covered books break up friendships. You loan a hard-covered book to a friend and when he doesn't return it you get mad at him. It makes you mean and petty. But twenty-five cent books are different.
> JOHN STEINBECK, news summaries of April 25, 1954.

One man was so mad at me that he ended his letter: "Beware. You will never get out of this world alive."
> JOHN STEINBECK, "The Mail I've Seen," *Saturday Review*, Aug. 3, 1956.

I feel wrapped and shellacked.
> JOHN STEINBECK, on learning from a television newscast that he had been awarded Nobel Prize, *New York Times*, Oct. 26, 1962.

I am impelled, not to squeak like a grateful and apologetic mouse, but to roar like a lion out of pride in my profession.
> JOHN STEINBECK, accepting Nobel Prize, *Newsweek*, Dec. 24, 1962.

The writer is delegated to declare and to celebrate man's proven capacity for greatness of heart and spirit, for gallantry in defeat, for courage, compassion, and love. In the endless war against weakness and despair, these are the bright rally-flags of hope and emulation.
> JOHN STEINBECK, *ibid.*

I hold that a writer who does not passionately believe in the perfectibility of man has no dedication nor any membership in literature.
> JOHN STEINBECK, *ibid.*

The profession of book-writing makes horse racing seem like a solid, stable business.
> JOHN STEINBECK, *ibid.*

With sixty staring me in the face, I have developed inflammation of the sentence structure and a definite hardening of the paragraphs.
> JAMES THURBER, at age 59, *New York Post*, June 30, 1955.

Humor is the other side of tragedy. Humor is a serious thing. I like to think of it as one of our greatest and earliest national resources which must be preserved at all costs. It came over on the *Mayflower* and we should have it, all of it.

> JAMES THURBER, CBS-TV, March 4, 1956.

The devoted writer of humor must continue to try to come as close to the truth as he can, even if he gets burned in the process, but I don't think he will get too badly burned. His faith in the good will, the soundness, and the sense of humor of his countrymen will always serve as his asbestos curtain.

> JAMES THURBER, *Newsweek*, Feb. 4, 1957.

I am told that I talk in shorthand and then smudge it.

> J. R. R. TOLKIEN, British author, on reports his writing was difficult to understand, *New York Times*, March 3, 1957.

When I had got my notes all written out, I thought that I'd polish it off in two summers, and it took me twenty-seven years.

> ARNOLD TOYNBEE, on completing ten volumes of *A Study of History*, NBC-TV, April 17, 1955.

I don't believe a commitee can write a book. There are all kinds of things a committee can do. It can, oh, govern a country, perhaps, but I don't believe it can write a book. I think a book has to be written by some single mind. But, of course, that's a very large and formidable undertaking, and I think if a writer is wise, he gets all the help he can from other people. The responsibility is on him, it must pass through his mind, but he takes help where he can get it.

> ARNOLD TOYNBEE, when asked if *A Study of History* could have been written by a group of people working together, *ibid*.

Immature artists imitate. Mature artists steal.

> LIONEL TRILLING, *Esquire*, Sept., 1962.

The machine has several virtues. . . . One may lean back in his chair and work it. It piles an awful stack of words on one page. It don't muss things or scatter ink blots around.

> MARK TWAIN's first typewritten letter, addressed to his brother, quoted by Bruce Bliven, *The Wonderful Writing Machine*, Random House, 1954.

365

A talent for drama is not a talent for writing, but is an ability to articulate human relationships.

GORE VIDAL, *New York Times*, June 17, 1956.

Once you start illustrating virtue as such you had better stop writing fiction. Do something else, like Y-work. Or join a committee. Your business as a writer is not to illustrate virtue but to show how a fellow may move toward it or away from it.

ROBERT PENN WARREN, *Paris Review*, Spring-Summer, 1957.

Words should be an intense pleasure just as leather should be to a shoemaker. If there isn't that pleasure for a writer maybe he ought to be a philosopher.

EVELYN WAUGH, *New York Times*, Nov. 19, 1950.

It is harder to write good fiction today . . . that little "so what?" begins to ask itself at the end of each paragraph—they are horrible words but they are those of an age of self-doubt.

EDWARD WEEKS, *Christian Science Monitor*, Oct. 31, 1957.

My relationships with every writer who was dear to us had constantly to be redefined. What is true of friendship is true of editing; the understanding must be continually refreshed. . . . I have tried to remember that it was my job to help when the author needed it, to reassure him, to call out of him his best, but always to bear in mind that the final decision was his.

EDWARD WEEKS, *In Friendly Candor*, Atlantic–Little, Brown, 1959.

Editing is the most companionable form of education.

EDWARD WEEKS, *ibid*.

A writer should describe reality with a touch of unreality, an element of distortion. That's the magic of creativeness. A literal transcription—a photograph—isn't enough. Maybe this is why it's better to write about places and people you don't know too well. The writer must leave something to his imagination.

JESSAMYN WEST, *New York Times*, Jan. 3, 1954.

There is no royal path to good writing; and such paths as exist do not lead through neat critical gardens, various as they are, but through the jungles of self, the world, and of craft.

JESSAMYN WEST, *Saturday Review*, Sept. 21, 1957.

It is a great pity that every human being does not, at an early stage of his life, have to write a historical work. He would then realize that the human race is in quite a jam about truth.

REBECCA WEST, "The Art of Skepticism," *Vogue*, Nov. 1, 1952.

Just how difficult it is to write biography can be reckoned by anybody who sits down and considers just how many people know the real truth about his or her love affairs.

REBECCA WEST, *ibid.*

. . . My skepticism long ago led me to the belief that writers write for themselves and not for their readers, and that art has nothing to do with communication between person and person, only with communication between different parts of a person's mind.

REBECCA WEST, *ibid.*

Literature is the orchestration of platitudes.

THORNTON WILDER, *Time*, Jan. 12, 1953.

I think I write in order to discover on my shelf a new book which I would enjoy reading, or to see a new play that would engross me.

THORNTON WILDER, *Writers at Work*, Viking, 1958.

I am writing seven one-act plays on the seven deadly sins. You can find many of the sins right here in St. Moritz.

THORNTON WILDER, on a winter of work in Switzerland, *New York Herald Tribune*, Feb. 24, 1959.

If I am no longer disturbed myself, I will deal less with disturbed people. I don't regret having concerned myself with such people, because I think

367

that most of us are disturbed. . . . It would be good if I could write with serenity.

> TENNESSEE WILLIAMS, disclosing that he was undergoing psycho-analysis, *New York Herald Tribune,* Jan. 5, 1958.

When I stop (working) the rest of the day is posthumous. I'm only really alive when I'm writing.

> TENNESSEE WILLIAMS, *Pittsburgh Press,* May 30, 1960.

. . . I was certainly surprised. I was so surprised that I woke one morning and started to get up and fainted dead away on the floor, tried to get up again, fainted again, and fainted five times in two hours.

> KATHLEEN WINSOR, reaction to success of *Forever Amber,* CBS-TV, Feb. 4, 1955.

I just sit at a typewriter and curse a bit.

> P. G. WODEHOUSE, on his technique as a writer, *Collier's,* Aug. 31, 1956.

The Edwardian butler has joined the Great Auk, Mah Jong, and the snows of yesterday in limbo. The change in conditions in English life has made it rather difficult for my kind of writing. Comedy does so depend on prosperity. But I suppose a couple of wars have made the English more earnest. Yet there are still, I think, people who behave oddly . . .

> P. G. WODEHOUSE, creator of the famous butler Jeeves, *Time,* Aug. 4, 1958.

I can always find plenty of women to sleep with but the kind of woman that is really hard for me to find is a typist who can read my writing.

> THOMAS WOLFE, quoted in Elizabeth Nowell's biography, *Thomas Wolfe,* Doubleday, 1960.

Poets

Before people complain of the obscurity of modern poetry, they should first examine their consciences and ask themselves with how many people and on how many occasions they have genuinely and profoundly shared some experience with another. . . .

> W. H. AUDEN, *Newsweek,* March 17, 1958.

A poet is, before anything else, a person who is passionately in love with language.
> W. H. AUDEN, *New York Times*, Oct. 9, 1960.

Poetry is the impish attempt to paint the color of the wind.
> MAXWELL BODENHEIM, poet, quoted in Ben Hecht's play, *Winkelberg*, produced in New York, Jan., 1958.

. . . It's silly to suggest the writing of poetry as something ethereal, a sort of soul-crashing emotional experience that wrings you. I have no fancy ideas about poetry. It doesn't come to you on the wings of a dove. It's something you work hard at.
> LOUISE BOGAN, on winning $5,000 "distinguished poetic achievement" award of Academy of American Poets, *New York World-Telegram and Sun*, Jan. 28, 1959.

. . . You don't have to suffer to be a poet. Adolescence is enough suffering for anyone.
> JOHN CIARDI, *Simmons Review*, Fall, 1962.

We poets have a mania for truth, we attempt to report in detail what strikes us . . . The poet never asks for admiration; he wants to be believed.
> JEAN COCTEAU, *Newsweek*, April 7, 1958.

We German poets have lost our readers—the Jews.
> GREGORY CORSO, *Evergreen Review No. 16*, 1961.

Modern poets are bells of lead. They should tinkle melodiously but usually they just klunk.
> LORD DUNSANY, Irish poet, news summaries, Jan. 11, 1954.

. . . The intolerable wrestle with words and meanings.
> T. S. ELIOT, on the writing of poetry, *Time*, March 6, 1950.

The method is to take a well-known poem . . . analyze it stanza by stanza and line by line, and extract, squeeze, tease, press every drop of meaning out of it. It might be called the lemon-squeezer school of criticism.

> T. S. ELIOT, on contemporary literary criticism, *On Poetry and Poets*, Farrar, Straus, 1957.

I was too slow a mover. It was much easier to be a poet.

> T. S. ELIOT, on giving up boxing in college, *New York Herald Tribune*, May 11, 1958.

All poetry is an ordered voice, one which tries to tell you about a vision in the unvisionary language of farm, city and love. Writing is like this—you dredge for the poem's meaning the way police dredge for a body. They think it is down there under the black water, they work the grappling hooks back and forth. But maybe it's up in the hills under the leaves or in a ditch somewhere. Maybe it's never found. But what you find, whatever you find, is always only part of the missing, and writing is the way the poet finds out what it is he found.

> PAUL ENGLE, *Life*, May 28, 1956.

. . . Poetry is ordinary language raised to the nth power. Poetry is boned with ideas, nerved and blooded with emotions, all held together by the delicate, tough skin of words.

> PAUL ENGLE, *New York Times*, Feb. 17, 1957.

There's absolutely no reason for being rushed along with the rush. Everybody should be free to go very slow. . . . What you want, what you're hanging around in the world waiting for, is for something to occur to you.

> ROBERT FROST, news reports of Mar. 21, 1954.

I don't call myself a poet yet. It's for the world to say whether you're a poet or not. I'm one-half teacher, one-half poet and one-half farmer; that's three halves.

> ROBERT FROST, comment on 80th birthday, news summaries of March 29, 1954.

I guess one way of putting it would be that you have freedom when you're easy in your harness.

> ROBERT FROST, news summaries of May 10, 1954.

370

That's the way I write a poem—getting a small piece of it in my hands and pulling it out and not knowing whether it is a man or a woman. I have never started a poem yet whose end I knew. Writing a poem is discovering.
> ROBERT FROST, *New York Times*, Nov. 7, 1955.

I'd just as soon play tennis with the net down.
> ROBERT FROST, on writing "free verse," *Newsweek*, Jan. 30, 1956.

Modern poets talk against business, poor things, but all of us write for money. Beginners are subjected to trial by market, poor things.
> ROBERT FROST, *New York Post*, May 18, 1958.

Poets are like baseball pitchers. Both have their moments. The intervals are the tough things.
> ROBERT FROST, *ibid.*

If you can bear at your age the honor of being made President of the United States, I ought to be able at my age to bear the honor of taking some part in your inauguration. I may not be equal to it but I can accept it for my cause—the arts, poetry—now for the first time taken into the affairs of statesmen. I am glad the invitation pleases your family. It will please my family to the fourth generation and my family of friends and, were they living, it would have pleased inordinately the kind of Grover Cleveland Democrats I had for parents.
> ROBERT FROST, at 86, replying by telegram to President-elect Kennedy, *New York Times*, Jan. 15, 1961.

Discipline. Tightness. Firmness. Crispness. Sternness. And sternness in our lives. Life is tons of discipline. Your first discipline is your vocabulary; then your grammar and your punctuation, you see. Then, in your exuberance and bounding energy you say you're going to add to that. Then you add rhyme and meter. And your delight is in *that* power.
> ROBERT FROST, *Life*, Dec. 1, 1961.

You can be a little ungrammatical if you come from the right part of the country.
> ROBERT FROST, *Atlantic*, Jan., 1962.

There is no challenge except the challenge of life to pull off something that *is* something. What is the idea? If you remember only one thing I've said, remember that *an idea is a feat of association,* and the height of it is a good metaphor. If you have never made a good metaphor, then you don't know what it's all about.

> ROBERT FROST, *ibid.*

I would have written of me on my stone: I had a lover's quarrel with the world.

> ROBERT FROST, epitaph recalled in reports of his death, Jan. 29, 1963.

Talking is a hydrant in the yard and writing is a faucet upstairs in the house. Opening the first takes the pressure off the second.

> ROBERT FROST, *Vogue,* March 15, 1963.

Poetry is a way of taking life by the throat.

> ROBERT FROST, *ibid.*

A poem . . . begins as a lump in the throat, a sense of wrong, a homesickness, a lovesickness.

> ROBERT FROST, *The Letters of Robert Frost to Louis Untermeyer,* Holt, Rinehart & Winston, 1963.

[Style is] that which indicates how the writer takes himself and what he is saying. . . . It is the mind skating circles around itself as it moves forward.

> ROBERT FROST, *ibid.*

Poetry is the language in which man explores his own amazement . . . says heaven and earth in one word . . . speaks of himself and his predicament as though for the first time. It has the virtue of being able to say twice as much as prose in half the time, and the drawback, if you do not give it your full attention, of seeming to say half as much in twice the time.

> CHRISTOPHER FRY, *Time,* April 3, 1950.

Prose books are the show dogs I breed and sell to support my cat.

> ROBERT GRAVES, on writing novels to support his love of writing poetry, *New York Times,* July 13, 1958.

Poetry is no more a narcotic than a stimulant; it is a universal bittersweet mixture for all possible household emergencies and its action varies accordingly as it is taken in a wine-glass or a tablespoon, inhaled, gargled or rubbed on the chest by hard fingers covered with rings.

> ROBERT GRAVES, *New York Times*, Oct. 9, 1960.

I believe that every English poet should read the English classics, master the rules of grammar before he attempts to bend or break them, travel abroad, experience the horror of sordid passion, and—if he is lucky enough —know the love of an honest woman.

> ROBERT GRAVES, first lecture as Professor of Poetry at Oxford, *Time*, Dec. 15, 1961.

There's no money in poetry, but then there's no poetry in money either.

> ROBERT GRAVES, quoted by Huw Wheldon in his compilation of BBC-TV programs, *Monitor*, Macdonald, 1962.

I don't really feel my poems are mine at all. I didn't create them out of nothing; I owe them to my relations with other people.

> ROBERT GRAVES, *New York Mirror*, April 1, 1963.

The business of a poet is not to clarify, but to suggest; to imply, to employ words with auras of association, with a reaching out toward a vision, a probing down into an emotion, beyond the compass of explicit definition.

> HAROLD HOBSON, critic, *New York Journal-American*, Jan. 31, 1958.

When power leads man toward arrogance, poetry reminds him of his limitations. When power narrows the area of man's concern, poetry reminds him of the richness and diversity of his existence. When power corrupts, poetry cleanses.

> PRESIDENT KENNEDY, at dedication of Robert Frost Library, Amherst College, Oct. 26, 1963.

In these days of nuclear energy, can the earthenware lamp of the poet still suffice? Yes, if its clay reminds us of our own. And it is sufficient mission for the poet to be the guilt conscience of his time.

> ALEXIS LEGER (Saint-John Perse), on receiving Nobel Prize, *New York Times*, Dec. 11, 1960.

In the power and splendor of the universe, inspiration waits for the millions to come. Man has only to strive for it. Poems greater than the *Iliad*, plays greater than *Macbeth*, stories more engaging than *Don Quixote* await their seeker and finder.

> JOHN MASEFIELD, poet laureate of England, *New York Times*, June 1, 1958.

Journalism is concerned with events, poetry with feelings. Journalism is concerned with the look of the world; poetry with the feel of the world. Journalism wishes to tell what it is that has happened everywhere as though the same things had happened for every man. Poetry wishes to say what it is like for any man to be himself in the presence of a particular occurrence as though only he were alone there. . . . To separate journalism and poetry, therefore—history and poetry—to set them up at opposite ends of the world of discourse, is to separate seeing from the feel of seeing, emotion from the acting of emotion, knowledge from the realization of knowledge.

> ARCHIBALD MACLEISH, "The Poet and the Press," *Atlantic*, March, 1959.

The crown of literature is poetry. It is its end and aim. It is the sublimest activity of the human mind. It is the achievement of beauty and delicacy. The writer of prose can only step aside when the poet passes.

> SOMERSET MAUGHAM, *Saturday Review*, July 20, 1957.

Poetry is a peerless proficiency of the imagination. I prize it, but am myself an observer. I see no reason for calling my work poetry except that there is no other category in which to put it.

> MARIANNE MOORE, on accepting National Book Award for poetry, *New York Mirror*, May 31, 1959.

A connoisseur of tame excitement . . .

> MARIANNE MOORE, self-description, *Vogue*, Aug. 1, 1960.

Any writer overwhelmingly honest about pleasing himself is almost sure to please others.

> MARIANNE MOORE, *Vogue*, Aug. 15, 1963.

374

My verses. I cannot say poems. . . . I was following in the exquisite footsteps of Miss Millay, unhappily in my own horrible sneakers.
> DOROTHY PARKER, *Writers At Work*, Viking, 1958.

I can't write five words but that I change seven.
> DOROTHY PARKER, *ibid*.

Poetry is a rich, full-bodied whistle, cracked ice crunching in pails, the
night that numbs the leaf, the duel of two nightingales, the sweet pea that
has run wild, Creation's tears in shoulder-blades.
> BORIS PASTERNAK, *Life*, June 13, 1960.

Poetry is the revelation of a feeling that the poet believes to be interior and
personal (but) which the reader recognizes as his own.
> SALVATORE QUASIMODO, winner of 1959 Nobel Prize, *New York Times*,
> May 14, 1960.

I'll die propped up in bed trying to do a poem about America.
> CARL SANDBURG, on eve of 79th birthday, Jan. 6, 1957.

. . . A sliver of the moon lost in the belly of a golden frog.
> CARL SANDBURG, describing poetry, *New York Times*, Feb. 13, 1959.

To trembling harmonies of field and cloud,
Of flesh and spirit was my worship vowed.
Let form, let music, let all-quickening air
Fulfill in beauty my imperfect prayer.
> GEORGE SANTAYANA, last stanza of five verses of *The Poet's Testament*
> found among his papers on his death at 88 and read at his funeral in
> Rome, *Time*, Oct. 27, 1952.

Poetry ennobles the heart and the eyes, and unveils the meaning of all
things upon which the heart and the eyes dwell. It discovers the secret rays
of the universe, and restores to us forgotten paradises.
> EDITH SITWELL, "Of What Use Is Poetry?" *Reader's Digest*, Aug., 1955.

375

Poetry is the light of the Great Morning wherein the beings whom we see passing in the street are transformed for us into the epitome of all beauty, or of all joy, or of all sorrow.

> EDITH SITWELL, *ibid.*

I am not an eccentric. It's just that I am more alive than most people. I am an unpopular electric eel in a pool of catfish.

> EDITH SITWELL, *Life,* Jan. 4, 1963.

Poetry is the deification of reality . . .

> EDITH SITWELL, *ibid.*

Great poetry is always written by somebody straining to go beyond what he can do.

> STEPHEN SPENDER, *New York Times,* March 26, 1961.

Accuracy of observation is the equivalent of accuracy of thinking.

> WALLACE STEVENS, *Opus Posthumous: Poems, Plays, Prose,* Knopf, 1958.

It's what I meant it to be. It's a tender Valentine that's going out into the world.

> GLORIA VANDERBILT, on her first book, *Love Poems,* news reports of Aug. 14, 1955.

The poem . . . is a little myth of man's capacity for making life meaningful. And in the end, the poem is not a thing we see—it is, rather, a light by which we may see—and what we see is life.

> ROBERT PENN WARREN, *Saturday Review,* March 22, 1958.

You will find that at the times when life becomes most real, in the great times of life, almost every man or woman becomes a poet at heart, as when in love or in the moments of great loss or bereavement. . . .

> JOHN HALL WHEELOCK, news summaries of Sept. 13, 1955.

It is true that the poet does not directly address his neighbors; but he does address a great congress of persons who dwell at the back of his mind, a

congress of all those who have taught him and whom he has admired; they constitute his ideal audience and his better self. To this congress the poet speaks not of peculiar and personal things, but of what in himself is most common, most anonymous, most fundamental, most true of all men . . .
> RICHARD WILBUR, accepting National Book Award for poetry for *Things of This World, New York Herald Tribune,* March 24, 1957.

I would love to be the poet laureate of Coney Island. I would feel enormous satisfaction in being regarded as the voice of the average American.
> THORNTON WILDER, *New York Journal-American,* Nov. 11, 1955.

I think all writing is a disease. You can't stop it.
> WILLIAM CARLOS WILLIAMS, *Newsweek,* Jan. 7, 1957.

A poet's autobiography is his poetry. Anything else can be only a footnote.
> YEVGENY YEVTUSHENKO, quoted by Professor William T. Moynihan in an article on Dylan Thomas, *New York Times,* Nov. 3, 1963.

The world no heart may find untaught,
No mortal eyes unpurged may view
It is with beauty so enwrought:
The world the old magicians sought,
And long ago the wise men knew.
> ELLA YOUNG, poetic summary of mysticism which characterized her work, quoted in reports of her death, July 24, 1956.

377

Books

Supper was at six and was over by half past. There was still daylight, shining softly and with a tarnish, like the lining of a shell; and the carbon lamps lifted at the corners were on in the light, and the locusts were started, and the fire-flies were out, and a few frogs were flopping in the dewy grass.

> James Agee, *A Death In the Family*, describing a summer's night a half century ago in Knoxville, Tenn.; McDowell, Obolensky, Inc., 1957.

The children ran out first, hell bent and yelling those names by which they were known; then the fathers sank out leisurely in crossed suspenders, their collars removed and their necks looking tall and shy. The mothers stayed back in the kitchen washing and drying, putting things away, recrossing their traceless footsteps like the life-time journeys of bees, measuring out the dry cocoa for breakfast. When they came out they had taken off their aprons and their skirts were dampened and they sat in rockers on their porches quietly.

> James Agee, *ibid.*

A giraffe is so much a lady that one refrains from thinking of her legs, but remembers her as floating over the plain in long garbs, draperies of morning mist or mirage.

> Isak Dinesen, *Shadows In the Grass*, Random House, 1961.

[It was] the Age of the Shrug . . . too large and too insistent and too frightening to be grasped, and so everybody would rather sigh and shrug and concentrate instead on bigger and bigger cars and shinier and shinier appliances and longer and longer vacations . . .

> Allen Drury, *Advise and Consent*, Doubleday, 1959.

378

This volume is neither an apology nor a recrimination . . . [it] will expose wounds; by doing so it could help to heal them.
> ANTHONY EDEN, Lord Avon, in his autobiography, *Full Circle*, Houghton Mifflin, 1960.

. . . A screaming, sooty, scythe-winged, short-tailed sprite that makes a swallow seem slow.
> JAMES FISHER, description of a swift, *Bird Recognition* 3, Pelican Books, 1957.

They share the insult of each other's presence.
> CHRISTOPHER ISHERWOOD, on characters in his novel, *Down There On A Visit*, Simon & Schuster, 1962.

To the alley and the canal and the little houses and the pachinko parlor and to the flutes at night—sayonara. And you, Japan, you crowded islands, you tragic land—sayonara, you enemy, you friend.
> JAMES MICHENER, *Sayonara* ("sad goodbye"), Random House, 1954.

I don't say he's a great man. Willy Loman never made a lot of money. His name was never in the paper. He's not the finest character that ever lived. But he's a human being and a terrible thing is happening to him. So attention must be paid. He's not to be allowed to fall into his grave like an old dog. Attention, attention must be finally paid to such a person.
> ARTHUR MILLER, *Death of a Salesman*, speech for wife of Willy Loman, *Theatre Arts*, March, 1951.

Willy was a salesman. And for a salesman, there is no rock bottom to the life. He don't put a bolt to a nut, he don't tell you the law or give you medicine. He's a man 'way out there in the blue, riding on a smile and a shoeshine. And when they start not smiling back—that's an earthquake. And then you get yourself a couple of spots on your hat and you're finished . . .
> ARTHUR MILLER, *ibid.*

. . . Wherever they go, and whatever happens to them on the way, in that enchanted place on the top of the Forest, a little boy and his Bear will always be playing.
> A. A. MILNE, closing line in the last of his famed series on Winnie-the-Pooh; recalled in reports of his death, Jan. 31, 1956.

He was a wanderer who had sought the bluebird. . . . He looked up at the sky. Gray clouds ballooned down like the dirty underside of a great circus tent. Yet, oh! Never since he had lain in a field as a small boy had the heavens seemed so soaring, so illimitable. And in that moment his heart filled with an unpredictable joy. He was free. . . . No longer was he a man running uphill against hope, his shins kicked, his luck running out. He was no one: he was eyes staring at the sky. He was the sky. A passer-by bumped against him. . . . The moment detached itself, leaving him weak and wondering. That was happiness. Would it ever come again? Wishing would not bring it back, nor ambitions, nor sacrifice, nor love. Why was it that true joy, this momentary release, could come even in his hour of loss and failure? It could not be wished for: it came unawares. It came more often in childhood but it might come again and again, even at the end of a life.

> BRIAN MOORE, *The Luck of Ginger Coffey*, Atlantic–Little, Brown, 1960.

Here, with whitened hair, desires failing, strength ebbing out of him, with the sun gone down and with only the serenity and the calm warning of the evening star left to him, he drank to Life, to all it had been, to what it was, to what it would be. Hurrah!

> SEAN O'CASEY, final paragraph of his autobiography, *Sunset and Evening Star*, Macmillan, 1954.

. . . You can learn just as much here about people and things as you can learn any place else. . . . Some of the people are good and some of them are bad—just like the fruit on a tree. . . . No matter if you go or stay, think of it like that till the day you die—let it be your learnin' tree.

> GORDON PARKS, quoting his mother in fictionalized autobiography of a Negro boy growing up in Kansas, *The Learning Tree*, Harper & Row, 1963.

Now what is history? It is the centuries of systematic explorations of the riddle of death, with a view to overcoming death. That's why people discover mathematical infinity and electromagnetic waves, that's why they write symphonies. . . .

> BORIS PASTERNAK, *Doctor Zhivago*, Pantheon, 1958.

Believe me . . . the first 24 hours of the invasion will be decisive . . . for
the Allies, as well as Germany, it will be the longest day.
>   GENERAL ERWIN ROMMEL, on World War II invasion of Europe;
>   his phrase "the longest day" became the title of a popular book in
>   1959 and a motion picture in 1963.

I keep picturing all these little kids in this big field of rye. . . . If they're
running and they don't look where they're going I have to come out from
somewhere and catch them. That's all I'd do all day. I'd just be the catcher
in the rye and all. I know it's crazy . . .
>   J. D. SALINGER, dialogue for Holden Caulfield which gave title to best-
>   selling *The Catcher in the Rye*, Little, Brown, 1951.

Thus Anne Frank's voice was preserved out of the millions that were
silenced. No louder than a child's whisper, it speaks for those millions and
has outlasted the raucous shouts of the murderers, soaring above the
clamorous voices of passing time.
>   ERNST SCHNABEL, on famed World War II diary of a Jewish girl,
>   *Anne Frank: A Portrait in Courage*, Harcourt, Brace, & World, 1958.

. . . she died peacefully, in the certitude that death was not a calamity.
>   SURVIVOR OF BELSEN, describing death of Anne Frank, *ibid.*

. . . Too many freeways, too much sun, too much abnormality taken
normally, too many pink stucco houses and pink stucco consciences.
>   CLANCY SIGAL, on Hollywood, in his novel, *Going Away*, Houghton
>   Mifflin, 1962.

Our eyes met. I was certain, as one can be certain in a duel across the
table . . .
>   C. P. SNOW, *The Light and the Dark*, Scribner's, 1961.

The muffled tongue of Big Ben tolled nine by the clock as the cortege left
the palace, but on history's clock it was sunset, and the sun of the old world
was setting in a dying blaze of splendor never to be seen again.
>   BARBARA TUCHMAN, on funeral of Edward VII, May, 1910, *The Guns
>   of August*, Macmillan, 1962.

A barn, in day, is a small night.
> JOHN UPDIKE, *Pigeon Feathers and Other Stories*, Knopf, 1962.

Shaped like a sickle, her life whipped through grasses of confusion and lethargy that in a summer month grew up again as tall as before.
> JOHN UPDIKE, describing an old lady, *ibid.*

. . . Beauty was a world of its own whose anarchy had a sort of godly license.
> TENNESSEE WILLIAMS, *The Roman Spring of Mrs. Stone*, New Directions, 1950.

The sensuality of that hour was exquisite as the jam of the gods.
> TENNESSEE WILLIAMS, on a gigolo's visit to a barbershop, *ibid.*

Literary Criticism

If the Man in the Grey Flannel Suit married Marjorie Morningstar on my front porch at high noon, I wouldn't bother to go to the wedding.
> NELSON ALGREN, on novelists Sloan Wilson and Herman Wouk, quoted by Myrick Land, *The Fine Art of Literary Mayhem*, Holt, Rinehart and Winston, 1963.

Autobiography is now as common as adultery, and hardly less reprehensible.
> LORD ALTRINCHAM, *Sunday Times*, London, Feb. 28, 1962.

In disguises thinner than a Chicago strip-teaser's work clothes. . . .
> RUSSELL BAKER, on flimsy characterizations in flood of novels on Washington, D.C., *New York Times*, April 28, 1962.

The chatter is endless, the mood determinedly gay, the egotism effortlessly immense.
> JOHN BARKHAM, *New York World-Telegram and Sun*, May 10, 1963, on Elsa Maxwell's *The Celebrity Circus*.

The clear, icy poet in her, hated the spaghetti of contemporary prose.

> CLAIRE BURCH on her former teacher, Professor Eda Lou Walton of New York University, *Saturday Review*, June 29, 1963.

Adorned with cape, with tricorn, saintly soul singing in librarian tones an enameled song that coolly celebrates her chewing-gum enthusiasms: the subway, baseball, the horses at Hialeah; her starry universe of zoological passions—what swims, what slithers, peers from forest-night or across the noon-desert crawls: all are caught on the coral-reef of her sensibility, corraled and made captive inside the bowl of a poem, the cages of art.

> TRUMAN CAPOTE, on poetess Marianne Moore, *Observations*, Simon & Schuster, 1959.

That's not writing, that's typing.

> TRUMAN CAPOTE, on the work of Jack Kerouac, quoted by Myrick Land, *The Fine Art of Literary Mayhem*, Holt, Rinehart and Winston, 1963.

There have been too many [books] in which some young man is looking forward, backward or sideways in anger. Or in which some Southern youth is being chased through the magnolia bushes by his aunt. She catches him on page 28 with horrid results.

> BENNETT CERF, news summaries of June 9, 1958.

. . . We have to accept the verbal portraits, as indeed we have to accept paintings and sculptures, as well as photographs, of the immortals whose influence on our lives is often greater than that of our own family members.

> RICHARD CHURCH, English author, in praise of biography, *Christian Science Monitor*, April 30, 1963.

. . . Pencil, pad and purpose.

> EDNA FERBER, on the work of writer Edmund Wilson, *Time*, March 31, 1958.

He carried his childhood like a hurt warm bird held to his middle-aged breast. . . .

> HERBERT GOLD, vignette of Sherwood Anderson, *The Age of Happy Problems*, Dial, 1962.

The public examination of homosexuality in our contemporary life is still so coated with distasteful moral connotations that even a reviewer is bound to wonder uneasily why *he* was selected to evaluate a book on the subject, and to assert defensively at the outset that he is happily married, the father of four children, and the one-time adornment of his college boxing, track, and tennis teams.

> SYDNEY J. HARRIS, columnist, beginning a review of *The Sixth Man* (Doubleday, 1961), in *Saturday Review*, April 22, 1961.

A writer and nothing else: a man alone in a room with the English language, trying to get human feelings right.

> JOHN K. HUTCHENS' study of Stephen Crane, *New York Herald Tribune*, Sept. 10, 1961.

Irony . . . is the thing by which we save our own lives. And the writer who sets out to tell the whole truth about himself needs a bit of it, unless he is to disarm criticism in a fashion that is not critically defensible.

> PAMELA HANSFORD JOHNSON, on reviewing an autobiography, *New York Times*, Sept. 17, 1961.

He doesn't know what he means, and doesn't know he doesn't know.

> F. R. LEAVIS, *Two Cultures? The Significance of C. P. Snow*, Pantheon, 1963.

It is one test of a fully developed writer that he reminds us of no one but himself.

> MELVIN MADDOCKS, on novelist Anthony Powell, *Christian Science Monitor*, May 2, 1963.

From the moment I picked your book up until I laid it down I was convulsed with laughter. Some day I intend reading it.

> GROUCHO MARX, on *Dawn Ginsbergh's Revenge*, S. J. Perelman's first book, *Life*, Feb. 9, 1962.

In literature as in love, we are astonished at what is chosen by others.

> ANDRÉ MAUROIS, *New York Times*, April 14, 1963.

384

A person who publishes a book willfully appears before the populace with his pants down. . . . If it is a good book nothing can hurt him. If it is a bad book, nothing can help him.

> EDNA ST. VINCENT MILLAY, *Letters of Edna St. Vincent Millay*, edited by Allen Ross Macdougall, Harper & Row, 1952.

Radford Center . . . turns out indeed to possess a homey familiarity for anybody who has ever lingered in King's Row or Peyton Place. The hotel-keeper's daughter is a nymphomaniac, the cabdriver's wife is a prostitute, the druggist and the newspaper editor are rivals in lechery, and the corresponding secretary of the WCTU is a dope addict. Just folks, one and all.

> NEWSWEEK, Feb. 29, 1960, review of *Chautauqua*, novel by Day Keene and Dwight Vincent.

The fine art of fiction regards each individual as unique, elaborate, perhaps greatly puzzling, worthy of sensitive study.

> NEWSWEEK, Jan. 23, 1961, on book review pages.

Dipping into Marianne Moore is like trying potluck at Cartier's.

> NEWSWEEK, Nov. 27, 1961, on *A Marianne Moore Reader*.

. . . Her book is a marvelous and implausible edifice built of glittering scraps in a make-believe land by a magpie.

> NEWSWEEK, Nov. 27, 1961, on *Tell It to Louella* by Hollywood columnist Louella Parsons, Putnam, 1961.

There is an ancient tradition, likely sponsored by the dour and envious, that novelists never do any real work. Sloppily dressed, they sit around, passing the time of day well into the late night, getting nothing worth doing done. At a casual glance, the pictures of eleven of them here do seem to bear this out. Sweaters, shirtsleeves, food, animals are with them—no typewriter in view. Yet they have worked, and hard, these eleven, and now, awaiting the summer or fall publication of their latest books, are entitled to the open spaces. And to a stillness from the dour and envious.

> NEW YORK TIMES, June 8, 1958, article picturing eleven writers in various states of mood and mind.

385

Here lived, here died Colette, whose work is a window wide open on life.
> CITY OF PARIS, inscription on plaque placed at home of novelist, Colette,
> quoted by Maurice Goudeket, *Close to Colette*, Farrar, Straus, 1957.

We were all imitative. We all wandered in after Miss Edna St. Vincent
Millay. We were all being dashing and gallant, declaring we weren't
virgins, whether we were or not.
> DOROTHY PARKER, on poetry of the 1920's, *New York Herald Tribune*,
> Oct. 13, 1963.

Satire is the most aggressive form of flattery. In it imitation is fired by
indignation. The satirist elevates the importance of what he is tearing
down. He cannot ignore what he sets out to deplore.
> CHARLES POORE, on *The Anatomy of Satire* by Gilbert Highet, *New
> York Times*, Sept. 29, 1962.

Scores of books a day, thousands in a year, many of them good and all of
them dressed up in brightly colored jackets. And all of them free. Could a
booklover imagine a better version of the earthly paradise?
> ORVILLE PRESCOTT, on being a book reviewer, *New York Times*, Dec.
> 2, 1956.

What was once Sinclair Lewis is buried in no ground. Even in life he was
fully alive only in his writing. He lives in public libraries from Maine to
California, in worn copies in the bookshelves of women from small towns
who, in their girlhood, imagined themselves as Carol Kennicotts, and of
medical men who, as youths, were inspired by Martin Arrowsmith. . . .
He survives in every college and university library. He does not live as do
those few stupendous novelists revealing the human condition for all places
and all times. . . . But he is an ineradicable part of American cultural history in the Twenties and Thirties, and no one seeking to recapture and
record the habits, frames of mind, social movements, speech, aspirations,
admirations, radicalisms, reactions, crusades, and Gargantuan absurdities of
the American *demos* during those twenty years will be able to do without
him.
> DOROTHY THOMPSON, after visiting the grave of her former husband,
> the first American to win Nobel Prize for Literature; "The Boy From
> Sauk Center," *Atlantic*, November, 1960.

. . . All her usual period impediments: details of dress, description and houses and plantations.

> TIME, Nov. 10, 1952, on novels of Francis Parkinson Keyes.

When disaster causes the familiar ground to shudder beneath the feet of a child, a neurotic is sometimes born, or a writer, and often both.

> TIME, May 20, 1957.

Two of the most difficult tasks a writer can undertake, to write the truth about himself and about his mother . . .

> TIME, March 31, 1961, on Frank O'Connor's *An Only Child*, Knopf, 1961.

Research is the opium of the biographers; when the fit is on them, any fact, no matter how small, must be included just because it is available.

> TIME, Oct. 13, 1961, on *Sinclair Lewis* by Mark Schorer, McGraw-Hill, 1961.

. . . She . . . compels the reader finally to accept as looming mountains the emotional molehills that are the topography of starved lives.

> TIME, Oct. 26, 1962, on Jane Frame's *The Edge of the Alphabet*, Braziller, 1962.

Sex is too often not only Topic A, but also Topics B and C as well.

> TIME, June 7, 1963, on novels of John O'Hara.

. . . That rare literary phenomenon, a Southern novel with no mildew on its magnolia leaves.

> VOGUE, Jan. 15, 1961, review of *To Kill a Mockingbird*.

. . . Thurber did not write the way a surgeon operates, he wrote the way a child skips rope, the way a mouse waltzes.

> E. B. WHITE, tribute to James Thurber, *New Yorker*, Nov. 11, 1961.

Press

We are going to have to decide what kind of people we are—whether we obey the law only when we approve of it, or whether we obey it no matter how distasteful we may find it.

> HARRY ASHMORE, executive editor, *The Arkansas Gazette*, Sept. 4, 1957, editorial on integration of Little Rock High School. (Eight months later *The Gazette* and Ashmore received Pulitzer Prizes for this editorial stand, the first newspaper to win both the public service prize and editorial prize for its work on same news story.)

I have some fears that in this profession of ours the loss of our own loco-motion threatens us—that the handout and the "spokesman" threaten our diligence, our ingenuity, our skepticism, our zeal. For zealots we must be. Not for a cause. For facts and for truth—and all of the truth.

> FRANK BARTHOLOMEW, president, United Press, address at University of Washington, Feb. 21, 1958.

Like the newspapers dependent upon us for news, ours will be a business organization, collecting and distributing one of the world's most perishable products, *news*. We believe private enterprise with a profit incentive is the best guarantee of objective coverage of world news, exactly as it is for the subsequent publishing of that news in the great independent news-papers of the world.

> FRANK BARTHOLOMEW, announcing merger of United Press and International News Service, *New York Times*, May 25, 1958.

Rumor, that most efficient of press-agents. . . .

> BRUCE BARTON, JR., art editor of *Time*, Nov. 24, 1961, on behind-the-scenes talk in galleries of New York.

388

A reporter discovers, in the course of many years of interviewing celebrities, that most actors are more attractive behind a spotlight than over a spot of tea. . . . They are more comfortable in the role of someone else than they are as themselves.

> Phyllis Battelle, *New York Journal-American*, April 30, 1961.

I suppose I will go on selling newspapers until at last will come the late night final.

> Lord Beaverbrook, publisher, on 75th birthday, news summaries of June 7, 1954.

Perhaps the quickest and best phrasemaker who ever inhabited the White House, F.D.R. was a President after a newsman's heart. He talked in headline phrases. He acted, he emoted; he was angry, he was smiling. He was persuasive, he was demanding; he was philosophical, he was elemental. He was sensible, he was unreasonable; he was benevolent, he was malicious. He was satirical, he was soothing; he was funny, he was gloomy. He was exciting. He was human. He was copy.

> Jack Bell, Washington correspondent, *The Splendid Misery*, Doubleday, 1960.

. . . New York, the Jerusalem of journalism.

> Jim Bishop, columnist, *New York Journal-American*, April 30, 1961.

All I have to do to get a story on the front page of every one of the AP's 2,000 clients is to mention in the lead a treatment for piles, ulcers, or sexual impotence—three conditions that every telegraph editor has, or is worried about.

> Alton Blakeslee, science editor, The Associated Press, *Newsweek*, Oct. 21, 1957.

Habits form our pattern of living, and when we have become accustomed, through the years, to traverse the whole world every morning through the imposing size of your newspapers and the abundance of your news reports, it is going to be hard to give up this intellectual morning feast. It is to me the little glass of white wine that the workman in my country still prefers to milk before setting out on his hard day's work.

> Henri Bonnet, French ambassador to U.S., farewell address to National Press Club, news reports of Dec. 16, 1954.

389

. . . The day of the printed word is far from ended. Swift as is the delivery of the radio bulletin, graphic as is television's eyewitness picture, the task of adding meaning and clarity remains urgent. People cannot and need not absorb meanings at the speed of light.

> ERWIN CANHAM, editor, *Christian Science Monitor*, on future role of newspapers, *New York Times*, Jan. 5, 1958.

The composing room has an unlimited supply of periods available to terminate short, simple sentences.

> TURNER CATLEDGE, managing editor, *New York Times*, memo to staff, *Time*, Dec. 20, 1954.

Hell, that's what the news is—an emergency. Why, we look at this as pretty much routine.

> TURNER CATLEDGE, on coverage of sinking of *Andrea Doria* in *New York Times'* final edition issued seven hours after learning of accident; *Time*, Aug. 6, 1956.

I saw their flat sallow faces, their Sunday-best clothes, their curious capacity for enjoying themselves without displaying any sign of emotion. I saw them all as a challenge. It was my job to interest them in everything that was happening, to make the arrival of the *Daily Express* each morning an event, to show them the world outside Bolton and Bacup, to give them courage and confidence to overcome the drabness of their lives.

> ARTHUR CHRISTIANSEN, London editor, in his autobiography, *Headlines All My Life*.

News, news, news—that is what we want. You cannot beat news in a newspaper.

> ARTHUR CHRISTIANSEN, quoted in report of his death, *New York Herald Tribune*, Sept. 28, 1963.

I am always in favor of the free press but sometimes they say quite nasty things.

> WINSTON CHURCHILL, news reports of July 1, 1954.

The reader deserves an honest opinion. If he doesn't deserve it, give it to him anyhow.

> JOHN CIARDI, "The Reviewer's Duty to Damn," *Saturday Review*, Feb. 16, 1957.

A man knows less about his reading habits than he does his sex habits.
> NORMAN COUSINS, editor, *Saturday Review, New York Herald Tribune*, Feb. 27, 1961.

. . . When these [press conferences] started, they were on the basis of questions submitted by you people . . . they were selected then by the press officers, and maybe even answers, drafts of answers given, and the President approved them and that was a press conference. Now, to my mind, that is just not good enough in modern America. I believe they want to see the President capable of going through the whole range of subjects that can be fired at him and giving to the average citizen some concept of what he is thinking about the whole works. . . . The press conference is a very fine latter-day American institution.
> PRESIDENT DWIGHT D. EISENHOWER, April 30, 1958.

I don't attempt to be a poker player before this crowd. I try to tell you exactly what I am thinking at the moment when the question is posed.
> PRESIDENT DWIGHT D. EISENHOWER, *ibid.*

News is history shot on the wing. The huntsmen from the Fourth Estate seek to bag only the peacock or the eagle of the swifting day.
> GENE FOWLER, newspaperman and author, in his autobiography, *Skyline*, Viking, 1961.

Freedom of the press is not an end in itself but a means to the end of a free society.
> JUSTICE FELIX FRANKFURTER, *New York Times*, Nov. 28, 1954.

The first thing I am going to do is to rejoin the American people and find out what Americans are thinking about.
> JOHN GATES, on resigning after ten years as editor of the *Daily Worker* and 27 years as a member of the Communist Party, *Editor & Publisher*, Jan. 18, 1958.

I usually start with a repulsive character and go on from there.
> CHESTER GOULD, creator of *Dick Tracy* comic strip, *New York Daily News*, Dec. 18, 1955.

I am insatiably curious about the state of our world. I revel in the recitation of the daily and weekly grist of journalism. . . . So let us drudge on about our inescapably impossible task of providing every week a first rough draft of a history that will never be completed about a world we can never understand.

> PHILIP GRAHAM, publisher, *Newsweek*, addressing his editors and correspondents; statement recalled in issue of Aug. 12, 1963, reporting his death.

It takes a long time to educate a community and it can't be done by spellbinders, moneybags, hypnotizers or magicians . . . or Aladdin's lamp. Character is what matters on a paper.

> HARRY GRANT, of the *Milwaukee Journal*, *Time*, Feb. 1, 1954.

We're not a loved paper. But we're a respected one.

> HARRY GRANT, *ibid*.

It's the equivalent of putting on the brakes suddenly while driving uphill.

> JOHN GUNTHER, on writing magazine articles to pay for travel necessary for his books, *Saturday Review*, Dec. 13, 1962.

We looked on the hopheads, crooks and gunsels and on their bawdy ladies as members of a family among whom we were privileged to move. . . . There was no caste system, moral or social, in our manners. We trotted, coach-dog fashion, at the heels of the human race, our tails a-wag.

> BEN HECHT, on crime reporting in Chicago, *Charlie*, Harper & Row, 1957.

I have enjoyed writing this book more than most I have written. Its hero, myself, appealed to me as one of the finest of humans. He knew almost nothing. His achievements were nil. He was as void of ambition as an eel of feathers. He misunderstood himself and the world around him. He thought journalism was some kind of stoop-tag. He was a pauper without troubles or problems. And he was as in love with life as an ant on a summer blade of grass.

> BEN HECHT, *Gaily, Gaily: Memoirs Of a Cub Reporter in Chicago*, Doubleday, 1963.

It must be wonderful sport to contradict each other. You are interested in the kitchen of the world—you want to find out what is cooking . . . who has a finger in the pie and who will burn his finger.

> QUEEN JULIANA of the Netherlands, to a Washington correspondent, on a visit to the U.S., *Time*, April 14, 1952.

Let there be a fresh breeze of new honesty, new idealism, new integrity. And there, gentlemen, is where you come in. You have typewriters, presses and a huge audience. How about raising hell?

> JENKIN LLOYD JONES, editor, *Tulsa Tribune*, address to Inland Daily Press Association, *U.S. News & World Report*, May 28, 1962.

In college circles, journalism is thought of a possible stepping stone to literature or political life and not as a career that presents good opportunities in and for itself. If these colleges will encourage young men to look toward journalism, there will be more well-equipped recruits whom we can trust with the task of guiding the king of America—public opinion.

> H. V. KALTENBORN, commentator, news summaries of Feb. 5, 1955.

In my job, [there are] moments when tragedy and comedy are all mixed up, and God and the devil contend like scorpions in a bottle inside the soul of a man before us.

> MURRAY KEMPTON, Washington columnist, *America Comes Of Middle Age*, Little, Brown, 1963.

The newspaper critic's obligation is not to the man who has invested a thousand dollars in a project he hopes to make a profit on; it is to the reader who has invested five cents in his newspaper and is on the verge of investing an additional $7.50 in a theatre seat.

> WALTER KERR, drama critic, *New York Mirror*, Sept. 14, 1958.

The press is our chief ideological weapon. Its duty is to strike down the enemies of the working class, the foes of the working people.

> NIKITA KHRUSHCHEV, Soviet Premier, *New York Times*, Sept. 29, 1957.

Every President after Jefferson has professed agreement with Jefferson's concept that the freedom of the American press to print its versions of the

393

facts, background, and likely consequences of human events was a constitutional principle permanently reserved from any form of interference by government. Consequently Jefferson denounced . . . either direct or indirect attempts by government to do what in current parlance has become known as "management of the news."

> ARTHUR KROCK, veteran Washington reporter for *New York Times* in an article, "Mr. Kennedy's Management of the News," *Fortune*, March, 1963, that set off conjecture on Administration's juggling of news events.

There is nothing so valueless as the curbstone utterances of people passing through.

> JOHN L. LEWIS, on being interviewed on a visit to Savannah, *Time*, Apr. 21, 1952.

. . . To bring to light the hidden facts, to set them into relation with each other, and make a picture of reality on which men can act.

> WALTER LIPPMANN, on a newspaper's responsibility, *Saturday Review*, Nov. 9, 1963.

Here lies a nuisance dedicated to sanity.

> DAVID LOW, New Zealander who became Britain's best known newspaper cartoonist, epitaph for himself quoted in reports of his death at 72, *New York Times*, Sept. 29, 1963.

The American public highly overrates its sense of humor. We're great belly laughers and prat fallers, but we never really did have a real sense of humor. Not satire anyway. We're a fat-headed, cotton-picking society. When we realize finally that we aren't God's given children, we'll understand satire. Humor is really laughing off a hurt, grinning at misery.

> BILL MAULDIN, cartoonist, *Time*, July 21, 1961.

. . . You don't have a democracy. It's a photocracy.

> ROBERT MENZIES, Prime Minister of Australia, on being followed by news photographers during a visit to Washington, D.C., news reports of Nov. 6, 1954.

A good newspaper, I suppose, is a nation talking to itself.

> ARTHUR MILLER, *The Observer*, London, Nov. 26, 1961.

Good taste and humor are a contradiction in terms, like a chaste whore.
>   MALCOLM MUGGERIDGE, explaining his editorship of *Punch; Time*, Sept.
>   14, 1953.

It is well to remember that freedom through the press is the thing that comes first. Most of us probably feel we couldn't be free without newspapers, and that is the real reason we want the newspapers to be free.
>   EDWARD R. MURROW, commentator, *New York Herald Tribune*,
>   March 12, 1958.

It reflects the Danish mind. It smiles when it speaks.
>   VINCENT NEAL, on *Berlingske Tidende*, Denmark's largest daily news-
>   paper, of which he is principal stockholder, *Time*, Jan. 4, 1963.

Somebody was using the pencil.
>   DOROTHY PARKER, to Harold Ross, on missing a *New Yorker* deadline,
>   quoted by James Thurber, *The Years With Ross*, Atlantic Monthly
>   Press, 1959.

The trouble with me is that I am a vindictive old shanty-Irish bitch.
>   CISSY PATTERSON, American heiress and publisher, *Time*, Sept. 13,
>   1954.

My hates have always occupied my mind much more actively and have given greater spiritual satisfactions than my friendships . . . The wish to favor a friend is not as active as one's instinct to annoy some person or institution I detest.
>   WESTBROOK PEGLER, columnist, *Pegler: Angry Man of the Press*, by
>   Oliver Pilat, Beacon, 1963.

Somehow—I don't know why—peace seems to have a better chance in the *Times*. Everybody else seems to be shouting at us and giving the human race six weeks to get out. But the *Times* is always saying that there was trouble in the Sixteenth Century too. It never seems to think anything is quite as good or as bad as others make it out to be.
>   JAMES RESTON, *New York Times* Washington correspondent, *New
>   Leader*, Jan. 7, 1963.

395

People are always dying in the *Times* who don't seem to die in other papers, and they die at greater length and maybe even with a little more grace.

JAMES RESTON, *ibid.*

. . . How do I know what to think if I can't read what I write?

JAMES RESTON, comment during New York newspaper strike, *ibid.**

Like officials in Washington, we suffer from Afghanistanism. If it's far away, it's news, but if it's close at home, it's sociology.

JAMES RESTON, in an address at a Columbia University academic convocation, *Wall Street Journal*, May 27, 1963.

The trouble with daily journalism is that you get so involved with "Who hit John?" that you never really know why John had his chin out in the first place.

CHALMERS ROBERTS, Washington reporter, *Newsweek*, Jan. 6, 1958.

Editing is the same as quarreling with writers—same thing exactly.

HAROLD ROSS, founder and editor of *The New Yorker*, on the magazine's 25th anniversary, *Time*, March 6, 1950.

. . . There aren't any embarrassing questions—just embarrassing answers.

CARL ROWAN, U.S. Ambassador to Finland, on news conferences, *New Yorker*, Dec. 7, 1963.

. . . My advice to any diplomat who wants to have a good press is to have two or three kids and a dog.

CARL ROWAN, *ibid.*

Communications today put a special emphasis on what happens next, for an able and sophisticated and competitive press today knows that what

---

* When newspapers resumed publication April 1, 1963, after a strike of almost four months, a *New York Times* report quoted a ranking official of the Publishers' Association of New York as saying: "Our professionals miscalculated on every major point. . . . Always their approach was 'Give 'em nothing—and do it retroactively.' "

happens today is no longer news—it is what is going to happen tomorrow that is the object of interest and concern. . . . Unless we can find some way to keep our sights on tomorrow, we cannot expect to be in touch with today.

> DEAN RUSK, Secretary of State, addressing 40th Anniversary Dinner of *Time*, quoted in issue, May 17, 1963.

In America journalism is apt to be regarded as an extension of history: in Britain, as an extension of conversation.

> ANTHONY SAMPSON, *Anatomy of Britain*, Harper & Row, 1962.

Valor is a gift. Those having it never know for sure whether they have it till the test comes. And those having it in one test never know for sure if they will have it when the next test comes. No one knows better than the tested overseas correspondent how a brave man can be rash, can take such risks that he goes down and never lives to file what might have been his greatest story.

> CARL SANDBURG, at dedication of Overseas Press Club, news reports of Dec. 14, 1954.

The lovely and luminous moon has become a public issue. For quite a few thousand years it was a private issue; it figured in purely bilateral negotiations between lovers; poets from attic windows issued the statements about the moon, and they made better reading than the handouts now being issued by Assistant Secretaries of Defense.

> ERIC SEVAREID, in a CBS newscast, "Be Careful With the Moon!" *Reader's Digest*, July, 1958.

The relationship between a reporter and a President is exactly the same as that between a pitcher and a batter . . . they both are trying to keep each other away.

> MERRIMAN SMITH, White House correspondent, United Press International, NBC-TV, Aug. 2, 1961.

I like to get where the cabbage is cooking and catch the scents.

> RED SMITH, sports columnist, on departure to cover California-based games of Giants and Dodgers, *Newsweek*, April 21, 1958.

We tell the public which way the cat is jumping. The public will take care of the cat.

> ARTHUR HAYS SULZBERGER, publisher, *New York Times*, on impartial news reporting, *Time*, May 8, 1950.

The First Duty of a newspaper is to be Accurate. If it be Accurate, it follows that it is Fair.

> HERBERT BAYARD SWOPE, letter to *New York Herald Tribune*, March 16, 1958.

Pick out the best story of the day and then hammer the living hell out of it. . . . Don't forget that the only two things people read in a story are the first and last sentences. Give them blood in the eye on the first one.

> HERBERT BAYARD SWOPE, editor of old *New York World*, statement recalled on his death, June 30, 1958.

Surely no other editor has ever been lost and saved so often in the course of a working week. When his heart leaped up, it leaped up a long way, because it started from so far down, and its commutings over the years from the depths to the heights made Ross a specialist in appreciation.

> JAMES THURBER, on late *New Yorker* editor Harold Ross, *The Years With Ross*, Atlantic Monthly Press, 1959.

(I am) a journalist in the field of etiquette. I try to find out what the most genteel people regularly do, what traditions they have discarded, what compromises they have made.

> AMY VANDERBILT, author and columnist, *Newsweek*, Aug. 11, 1958.

Who needs a book of etiquette? Everyone does . . . for we must all learn the socially acceptable ways of living. . . . Even in primitive societies there are rules, some . . . as complex and inexplicable as many of our own. Their original *raison d'être* or purpose is lost, but their acceptance is still unquestioned.

> AMY VANDERBILT, *ibid.*

398

The modern world is not given to uncritical admiration. It expects its idols to have feet of clay, and can be reasonably sure that press and camera will report their exact dimensions.

>BARBARA WARD, British writer, reviewing an autobiography, *Saturday Review*, Sept. 30, 1961.

The younger people, who grew up during the paper shortage, aren't used to filling the space. But that is journalism—an ability to meet the challenge of filling the space.

>REBECCA WEST, *New York Herald Tribune*, April 22, 1956.

Radio and Television

There is no doubt at all that between 9 and 10 a.m. the American radio is concerned almost exclusively with love. . . . It seems a little like ending breakfast with a stiff bourbon.
>DEAN ACHESON, former U.S. Secretary of State, on "soap operas" that flourished until the 1960's, *The Reporter*, Sept. 19, 1957.

When a radio comedian's program is finally finished it slinks down Memory Lane into the limbo of yesteryear's happy hours. All that the comedian has to show for his years of work and aggravation is the echo of forgotten laughter.
>FRED ALLEN, *Treadmill to Oblivion*, Little, Brown, 1954.

Ed Sullivan will be around as long as someone else has talent.
>FRED ALLEN, on tenth anniversary of Ed Sullivan variety show, *TV Guide*, June 21, 1958.

That Was the Week That Was
>BRITISH BROADCASTING CORPORATION, title of weekly satirical show on current events, premiered Nov. 24, 1962.

Some television programs are so much chewing gum for the eyes.
>JOHN MASON BROWN, interview with James B. Simpson, July 28, 1955.

Get a genie in a bottle. Make the genie head writer. Keep reminding him you've got to be funnier this week than last. That you've got to get a big

400

rating. That you've got to please the agency, the network and the public. A genie could do it for you. An ordinary mortal, no.

> RED BUTTONS, on pressure for a fresh, witty show each week, *New York World-Telegram & Sun*, April 25, 1958.

They are simple and true and they compose one.

> PABLO CASALS, on watching Westerns on television, *Cellist In Exile*, by Bernard Taper, McGraw-Hill, 1962.

A very bad thing happened to the advertising business 30 years ago, and that was the invention of radio—I say bad because the advertising people, both in companies and in agencies, then got into show business. They loved it. This was just what they had been waiting for. . . . Then along came television and this made it worse.

> FAIRFAX CONE, advertising executive, *Christian Science Monitor*, March 20, 1963.

He is forced to be literate about the illiterate, witty about the witless and coherent about the incoherent.

> JOHN CROSBY, on role of a television critic, news summaries of March 20, 1955.

You have debased [my] child . . . You have made him a laughingstock of intelligence . . . a stench in the nostrils of the gods of the ionosphere.

> DR. LEE DE FOREST, inventor of audion tube, to National Association of Broadcasters, recalled in obituary in *Time*, July 7, 1961.

I might have had trouble saving France in 1946—I didn't have television then.

> CHARLES DE GAULLE, President of France, *Newsweek*, Aug. 19, 1963.

. . . The bright grey blackboard.

> HENRI DIEUZEIDE, director, French educational television, *Réalités*, July, 1963.

401

It is a medium of entertainment which permits millions of people to listen to the same joke at the same time, and yet remain lonesome.

> T. S. ELIOT, on his dislike for television, *New York Post*, Sept. 22, 1963.

It's inevitable that I should seem a rather remote figure to many of you— a successor to the Kings and Queens of history; someone whose face may be familiar in newspapers and films but who never touches your personal lives. But now, at least for a few minutes, I welcome you to the peace of my own home.

> ELIZABETH II, opening first telecast of her annual Christmas address to British Commonwealth, Dec. 25, 1957.

Students learn as well or better by instruction over TV as they do in traditional classroom work. This is a case of Mark Hopkins on one end of the log and a half-million students on the other.

> ALVIN EURICH of the Fund for the Advancement of Education, *Fortune*, April, 1961.

Conversation in this country has fallen upon evil days. . . . It is drowned out in singing commercials by the world's most productive economy that has so little to say for itself it has to hum it. It is hushed and shushed in dimly lighted parlors by television audiences who used to read, argue, and even play bridge, an old-fashioned card game requiring speech.

> WHITNEY GRISWOLD, President, Yale University, *New York Herald Tribune*, April 20, 1963.

We are drowning our youngsters in violence, cynicism and sadism piped into the living room and even the nursery. The grandchildren of the kids who used to weep because the Little Match Girl froze to death now feel cheated if she isn't slugged, raped and thrown into a Bessemer converter.

> JENKIN LLOYD JONES, editor, *Tulsa Tribune*, address to Inland Daily Press Association, *U.S. News & World Report*, May 28, 1962.

. . . It merely expresses one of the elements of our times, the indifference to personal privacy, the assumption that a free press means a licensed press and the fact that today there is too much privilege on the part of the reporter to invade the privacy, the decency, the self-respect of the individual who is being interviewed.

> H. V. KALTENBORN, on the popularity of "penetrating" interviews, *New York Herald Tribune*, April 20, 1958.

I read in the newspapers they are going to have 30 minutes of intellectual stuff on television every Monday from 7:30 to 8. They're going to educate America. They couldn't educate America if they started at 6:30.

> GROUCHO MARX, *Boston Evening Globe*, Jan. 22, 1960.

. . . You will observe a vast wasteland.

> NEWTON MINOW, chairman, Federal Communications Commission, on television programing, address to National Association of Broadcasters, *New York Times*, May 10, 1961.

Children will watch anything, and when a broadcaster uses crime and violence and other shoddy devices to monopolize a child's attention, it's worse than taking candy from a baby. It is taking precious time from the process of growing up.

> NEWTON MINOW, testimony to Senate Subcommittee on Juvenile Delinquency, *New York Post*, June 19, 1961.

We never said we were putting on a show "for housewives"—as though housewives were equated with cretins. They're the same women who watch at night. They don't suddenly become brains at sunset.

> GARRY MOORE, television emcee, urging quality in daytime programs, *Newsweek*, May 26, 1958.

A bar or tavern is a place where you can buy a glass of draught beer for fifteen cents. Unfortunately, these are the very places that are most corrupted by TV. No more real talking! No more real drinking! The end of an era!

> MIKE MORIARTY, proprietor, Moriarty's Bar & Grill, *New Yorker*, July 16, 1960.

Bars used to be the bulwark of social life in the city, but what's the use of coming into a bar nowadays to meet your friends? All you'll get is that damnable blat, blat, blat from the box!

> MIKE MORIARTY, *ibid.*

A reporter is always concerned with tomorrow. There's nothing tangible of yesterday. All I can say I've done is agitate the air ten or fifteen minutes and then boom—it's gone.

> EDWARD R. MURROW, news commentator, news summaries of Dec. 31, 1955.

Almost from the moment the horror occurred, television changed, It was no longer a small box containing entertainment, news, and sports; suddenly, it was a window opening onto violently unpredictable life in Washington and in Dallas, where a President had been assassinated.

> NEWSWEEK, Dec. 9, 1963, on coverage of events surrounding death of President Kennedy.

The greatest escapist medium ever devised made escape impossible, and at one time or other the screen drew an estimated total of 175-million Americans. . . . It would be impossible to think of the instrument in the old, easy way again.

> NEWSWEEK, *ibid.*

More than a hundred million Americans watched the late President's funeral, but the funeral did not take place in Arlington Cemetery alone. It took place in a living room in Los Angeles, in Grand Central Terminal in New York, in kitchens and offices across the U.S. John F. Kennedy's casket did not ride down Pennsylvania Avenue only. It rode down Main Street.

> NEWSWEEK, *ibid.*

The theory has always been to present only guests who are acceptable in livingrooms. But we're on pretty late at night. Statistics show that many people watch our show from the bedroom. . . . And people you ask into your bedroom have to be more interesting than those you ask into your livingroom. I kid you not!

> JACK PAAR, emcee of NBC-TV's "Tonight Show," *New York Herald Tribune*, April 22, 1958.

After all, what was *Medea?* Just another child custody case.

> FRANK PIERSON, producer, on sameness of television story plots, *New York Times*, March 23, 1962.

404

The impact of television on our culture is just indescribable. There's a certain sense in which it is nearly as important as the invention of printing.
>   CARL SANDBURG, news summaries of Dec. 30, 1955.

You should realize that the community with which you deal is not the one of Forty-Second and Broadway, or Hollywood and Vine. These are the crusts on the great American sandwich. The meat is in between.
>   FULTON SHEEN, Auxiliary Bishop of New York, to broadcasting executives, news summaries of Nov. 9, 1955.

It was through TV that the Kennedy profile, the sincere Kennedy tones, the Kennedy thoughts could get to the people. He did not have to run the risk of having his ideas and his words shortened and adulterated by a correspondent. This was the TV era, not only in campaigning, but in holding the presidency.
>   HUGH SIDEY, *Time* correspondent, on the 1960 campaign, *John F. Kennedy, President*, Atheneum, 1963.

. . . There are days when any electrical appliance in the house, including the vacuum cleaner, seems to offer more entertainment possibilities than the TV set.
>   HARRIET VAN HORNE, columnist, *New York World-Telegram and Sun*, June 7, 1957.

One who roams the channels after dark, searching for buried treasure . . .
>   HARRIET VAN HORNE, on her role as television critic, *New York World-Telegram and Sun*, Feb. 27, 1958.

Now is the time of year when the viewer is tempted to throw an old Spanish shawl over his TV set and leave it there until Halloween. For the happy home-entertainment season now is ended. The time of the rack and the screws is come. Summer television has set in with its usual severity. And the small screen, where late the sweet birds sang, is now awash with repeats, reruns, rejects, replacements and reversions to the primitive.
>   HARRIET VAN HORNE, "Time to Buy A Polo Mallet," *New York World-Telegram and Sun*, June 2, 1958.

405

There come evenings—and one of them crept in last night—when I think fondly of that ancient king who offered a casket of jewels to any subject who could invent a new pleasure for him. Did any sly, sandaled genius, any jackanapes or gypsy, ever claim the reward? If so, he should be living at this hour. And under contract to a TV network.

> HARRIET VAN HORNE, *New York World-Telegram and Sun*, Jan. 12, 1961.

Television is now so desperately hungry for material that they're scraping the top of the barrel.

> GORE VIDAL, novelist and television writer, July 20, 1955.

. . . I hate television. I hate it as much as peanuts. But I can't stop eating peanuts.

> ORSON WELLES, on watching television, *New York Herald Tribune*, Oct. 12, 1956.

Scaring an audience to death is the first objective of all melodrama, the first duty of its author—book, story, play, movie or network thriller. . . . Having the imagination briefly seized and shaken by fear—fear that is naked and primitive and right-in-the-room—is not only the goal of all storytellers in this field but one of the few exhilarating pleasures of living.

> MAX WYLIE, author and critic, on violence in American life, *Clear Channels*, Funk & Wagnalls, 1955.

Films

I went out there for a thousand a week, and I worked Monday, and I got fired Wednesday. The guy that hired me was out of town Tuesday.

> NELSON ALGREN, on being a Hollywood writer, *Writers At Work*, Viking, 1958.

The reason good women like me and flock to my pictures is that there is a little bit of vampire instinct in every woman.

> THEDA BARA, on her many roles as a "vamp," quoted in reports of her death, April 8, 1955.

To understand those days, you must consider that people believed what they saw on the screen. Nobody had destroyed the grand illusion. They thought the stars of the screen were the way they saw them. Now they know it's all just make-believe.

> THEDA BARA, *ibid.*

. . . Fundamentally I feel that there is as much difference between the stage and the films as between a piano and a violin. Normally you can't become a virtuoso in both.

> ETHEL BARRYMORE, *New York Post*, June 7, 1956.

Where great-grandmothers dread to grow old. . . .

> PHYLLIS BATTELLE, on Hollywood, *New York Journal-American*, March 15, 1958.

She has a face that belongs to the sea and the wind, with large rocking horse nostrils and teeth that you know just bite an apple every day.

> CECIL BEATON, on photographing Katharine Hepburn, news summaries of March 29, 1954.

407

In *The Entertainer* the smell of decay hangs over everything, decay and shabby misery. It has set itself to scratching the dandruff out of the mane of life.
> PAUL V. BECKLEY, critic, *New York Herald Tribune*, Oct. 4, 1960.

I came out here with one suit and everybody said I looked like a bum. Twenty years later Marlon Brando came out with only a sweatshirt and the town drooled over him. That shows how much Hollywood has progressed.
> HUMPHREY BOGART, quotation recalled in reports of his death, Jan. 15, 1957.

The whole world is about three drinks behind.
> HUMPHREY BOGART, *ibid*.

Sometimes you just get the feeling that here it is 11 o'clock in the morning and you're not in school.
> MARLON BRANDO, on Western films, *New York Post*, May 11, 1959.

. . . People in Hollywood can't face the truth in themselves or in others. This town is filled with people who make adventure pictures and who have never left this place. They make religious pictures and they haven't been in a church or a synagogue in years. They make pictures about love and they haven't been in love—ever.
> RICHARD BROOKS, film director, *New York Post*, Dec. 7, 1960.

You may be as vicious about me as you please. You will only do me justice.
> RICHARD BURTON, on being interviewed for cover-story in *Time*, April 26, 1963.

A film is a petrified fountain of thought.
> JEAN COCTEAU in his film, "Le Testament d'Orphee," quoted in *Esquire*, Feb., 1961.

Honestly, I think I've stretched a talent which is so thin that it's almost opaque over a quite unbelievable term of years.
> BING CROSBY, *Time*, Oct. 15, 1956.

Believe it or not, it is a picture about two young people romantically in love—in love with each other, that is, not with a tractor, or the Soviet state . . . the Russians have finally found romance.

> Bosley Crowther, film critic, reviewing USSR's "The Cranes Are Flying," *New York Times*, March 27, 1960.

There is another word for being a good trouper, a word that show business would think too grand to use. That word is dedication. And that word, I think, is Mary Pickford's secret, as it is the secret of anyone who succeeds at anything.

> Cecil B. de Mille, introduction to *Sunshine and Shadow*, autobiography of Mary Pickford, Doubleday, 1955.

Most of us serve our ideals by fits and starts. The person who makes a success of living is the one who sees his goal steadily and aims for it unswervingly. That is dedication.

> Cecil B. de Mille, *ibid*.

Creation is a drug I can't do without.

> Cecil B. de Mille, *New York Times*, Aug. 12, 1956.

There's nothing funnier than the human animal.

> Walt Disney, on changing from films about animals to shows about people, news reports of Dec. 5, 1954.

American motion pictures are written by the half-educated for the half-witted.

> St. John Ervine, *New York Mirror*, June 6, 1963.

After my screen test, the director clapped his hands gleefully and yelled: "She can't talk! She can't act! She's sensational!"

> Ava Gardner, on "crashing" Hollywood, news summaries of Dec. 11, 1954.

God makes the star. God gives them the talent. It is up to the producers to recognize that talent and develop it.

> Samuel Goldwyn, CBS-TV, Feb. 19, 1954.

A wide screen just makes a bad film twice as bad.
> SAMUEL GOLDWYN, *Quote*, Sept. 9, 1956.

Film directors say, "Stop acting!" If you stop acting, what is the point? You are then just talking and behaving.
> SIR CEDRIC HARDWICKE, *Theatre Arts*, Feb., 1958.

I believe that God felt sorry for actors so He created Hollywood to give them a place in the sun and a swimming pool. The price they had to pay was to surrender their talent.
> SIR CEDRIC HARDWICKE, *A Victorian In Orbit*, his memoirs as told to James Brough, Doubleday, 1961.

There never was an actress with whom it was easy to work. I have yet to see one completely unspoiled star, except for the animals—like Lassie. Each thinks she knows more than I do about her bust and hips.
> EDITH HEAD, seven-time Oscar winner for her costumes designed for Hollywood pictures, *Saturday Evening Post*, Nov. 30, 1963.

The movie-makers are able to put more reality into a picture about the terrors of life at the ocean bottom than into a tale of two Milwaukeeans in love.
> BEN HECHT, news reports of June 13, 1954.

The honors Hollywood has for the writer are as dubious as tissue-paper cuff links.
> BEN HECHT, *Charlie*, Harper & Row, 1957.

People's sex habits are as known in Hollywood as their political opinions, and much less criticized.
> BEN HECHT, *New York Mirror*, April 24, 1959.

The average Hollywood film star's ambition is to be admired by an American, courted by an Italian, married to an Englishman and have a French boy friend.
> KATHARINE HEPBURN, *New York Journal-American*, Feb. 22, 1954.

I am a typed director. If I made *Cinderella,* the audience would immediately be looking for a body in the coach.

>ALFRED HITCHCOCK, *Newsweek,* June 11, 1956.

It is self-evident that the poloist, the steeplechaser, the speedboat racer, and the fox hunter ride for the thrill that comes only from danger . . . and for every person who seeks fear in the real or personal sense, millions seek it vicariously, in the theatre and in the cinema.

>ALFRED HITCHCOCK, *ibid.*

It is my hope that the day may not be far off when the Court will go further and eliminate all political censorship of motion pictures so the screen will enjoy the same freedom of expression as the press under our constitution.

>ERIC JOHNSTON, president, Motion Picture Association of America, on U.S. Supreme Court ruling that states may not censor films as "immoral" or "inciting to crime," news summaries of Jan. 19, 1954.

The only secret knowledge we have is know-how and you can't break up know-how by court order.

>HERBERT KALMUS, engineer who developed Technicolor for Hollywood, reply to a 1949 decree that his process should not constitute a monopoly; comment recalled on his death, *New York Herald Tribune,* July 12, 1963.

When I was nine I was the Demon King in *Cinderella* and it appears to have launched me on a long and happy life of being a monster.

>BORIS KARLOFF, *Sunday Times,* London, July 28, 1957.

That was my one big Hollywood hit, but, in a way, it hurt my picture career. After that, I was typecast as a lion, and there just weren't many *parts* for lions.

>BERT LAHR, on his *Wizard of Oz* role, *New Yorker,* Jan. 26, 1963.

If you are joking me, I will get up immediately and kill you wherever you are.

>ANNA MAGNANI, on learning from a reporter's phone call that she had been awarded an Oscar for best performance by an actress, March 22, 1956.

Hollywood continued to furnish the heroes and heroines of our time. The ubiquitous cinema screen projected their images throughout the world. Sex is the ersatz, or substitute, religion of the 20th century. These were its priests and priestesses. They were the American Dream, soon to be in technicolor—a Dream in terms of material satisfactions and sensual love, whose requisite happy ending was always a long drawn-out embrace.

> MALCOLM MUGGERIDGE, "The Titans: United States of America," BBC-TV, Jan. 16, 1962.

Hollywood money isn't money. It's congealed snow. . . .

> DOROTHY PARKER, on Hollywood as provider for the artist, *Paris Review*, Summer, 1956.

If you're going to write, don't pretend to write down. It's going to be the best you can do, and it's the fact that it's the best you can do that kills you. . . .

> DOROTHY PARKER, *ibid*.

There are lots of people in this country who can't shake off the idea that Pat O'Brien is a priest who has a parish in Pasadena and who coaches the Notre Dame football team on the side.

> ROBERT PRESTON, on type-casting, *New York World-Telegram & Sun*, Feb. 6, 1958.

I was a 14-year-old boy for 30 years.

> MICKEY ROONEY, on his film roles, *New York Journal-American*, April 15, 1958.

It's confusing. I've had so many wives and so many children I don't know which house to go to first on Christmas.

> MICKEY ROONEY, on his five marriages, *New York Post*, Nov. 13, 1960.

We never make sport of religion, politics, race or mothers. A mother never gets hit with a custard pie. Mothers-in-law—yes. But mothers—never.

> MACK SENNETT, pioneer director-producer, on his slapstick school of comedy, *New York Times*, Nov. 6, 1960.

412

She was "discovered" for movies in the drug store, sitting at the soda fountain. Thousands of girls have since sat at drug store fountains drinking sodas and waiting to be discovered. They have only got fat from the sodas.

> SIDNEY SKOLSKY, on the discovery of Lana Turner, *New York Post*, Jan. 12, 1958.

Now I've laid me down to die,
I pray my neighbors not to pry
Too deeply into sins that I,
Not only cannot here deny,
But much enjoyed as life flew by.

> PRESTON STURGES, stage and screen writer, epitaph quoted in obituary, *New York Times*, Aug. 7, 1959.

I was the first of the Hollywood stars to have a baby. After that, it became an epidemic.

> GLORIA SWANSON, ABC-TV, Oct. 1, 1958.

I class myself with Rin Tin Tin. At the end of the Depression, people were perhaps looking for something to cheer them up. They fell in love with a dog, and with a little girl. . . . I think it won't happen again.

> SHIRLEY TEMPLE, on her success as a child star, *New York Post*, Sept. 13, 1956.

But her friends stand by her: when she prematurely published the claim that a certain actress was pregnant, the actress's husband hastened to prove her correct.

> TIME, Nov. 24, 1961, on influence of columnist Louella Parsons.

. . . An actor is never so great as when he reminds you of an animal—falling like a cat, lying like a dog, moving like a fox.

> FRANÇOIS TRUFFAUT, producer, *New Yorker*, Feb. 20, 1960.

413

Theater

. . . The Jukes family of journalists who bring to the theater nothing but their own hopelessness, recklessness and despair.
> MAXWELL ANDERSON, on theatrical critics, *Saturday Evening Post,* April 13, 1957.

America is not playwright-conscious. There are still hordes of theatre-goers who say in all innocence, "I love to go see Lynn Fontanne. She always says such witty things."
> ROBERT ANDERSON, on the playwright in the modern theater, *New York Herald Tribune,* Aug. 5, 1956.

. . . For those who are aware that such creatures as playwrights exist, he is usually thought of as a slightly benighted child of nature who somehow or other did it all on a ouija board.
> ROBERT ANDERSON, *ibid.*

The clamoring for novelty in the method of telling a story is as though we were suddenly to say, "I'm tired of faces with two eyes and nose and a mouth." What we want, I think, is not faces with three eyes, but more beautiful, strong, truthful, wise, humorous faces with the usual complement of eyes, noses, and mouths.
> ROBERT ANDERSON, *ibid.*

The mission of the playwright . . . as I see it, is to look in his heart and write, to write of whatever concerns him at the moment; to write with passion and conviction. Of course the measure of the man will be the measure of the play.
> ROBERT ANDERSON, *Theatre Arts,* March, 1958.

414

Good plays drive bad playgoers crazy.
>BROOKS ATKINSON, *Theatre Arts*, Aug., 1956.

Nobody can be exactly like me. Sometimes even I have trouble doing it.
>TALLULAH BANKHEAD, news summaries of Jan. 1, 1951.

If you really want to help the American theatre, don't be an actress, darling. Be an audience.
>TALLULAH BANKHEAD, news summaries of Dec. 31, 1952.

Dahling Congressman Boykin: 10 a.m. is an unprecedented time for a child of the grease paint to cope with the sandman.
>TALLULAH BANKHEAD, response to invitation to speak at a campaign meeting for a civic auditorium for Washington, Jan. 15, 1955.

I never let them cough. They wouldn't dare.
>ETHEL BARRYMORE, on control of audiences during tense moments, *New York Post*, June 7, 1956.

For an actress to be a success she must have the face of Venus, the brains of Minerva, the grace of Terpsichore, the memory of Macaulay, the figure of Juno, and the hide of a rhinoceros.
>ETHEL BARRYMORE, in *The Theatre in the Fifties* by George Jean Nathan, Knopf, 1953.

Be daring, be different, be impractical; be anything that will assert integrity of purpose and imaginative vision against the play-it-safers, the creatures of the commonplace, the slaves of the ordinary. Routines have their purposes, but the merely routine is the hidden enemy of high art.
>CECIL BEATON, manifesto for theatrical designers, "The Secret of How to Startle," *Theatre Arts*, May, 1957.

I have the *worst* ear for criticism: even when I have created a stage set I like, I *always* hear the woman in the back of the Dress Circle who says she doesn't like blue.
>CECIL BEATON, BBC-TV, Feb. 18, 1962.

They live as if every moment were their next.
> SAMUEL BECKETT, instructions for characterization in one of his plays, *Vogue*, Oct. 15, 1958.

Call Me Madam *
> IRVING BERLIN, title of 1950 Broadway musical inspired by appointment of Mrs. Perle Mesta as U.S. Ambassador to Luxemburg.

The hostess with the mostest on the ball . . .
> IRVING BERLIN, opening line of hit song from *Call Me Madam*, ibid.

Actors should be overheard, not listened to, and the audience is fifty percent of the performance.
> SHIRLEY BOOTH, guiding rules for successful stage career, news summaries of Dec. 13, 1954.

It's the way to get over a deep inferiority complex, being onstage; you become another person and shed your own frightened personality.
> SHIRLEY BOOTH, *New York Journal-American*, Oct. 30, 1956.

I am just a nice, clean-cut, Mongolian boy.
> YUL BRYNNER, self-description, *New York Post*, Sept. 24, 1956.

When I am dead and buried, on my tombstone I would like to have it written, "I have arrived." Because when you feel that you have arrived, you are dead.
> YUL BRYNNER, *New York Post*, Sept. 30, 1956.

When you're a blonde, people sort of lean forward when you ask them a question. They take your arm to keep you from falling into an open manhole. But when you're a brunette . . . you're just one of the bunch.
> CAROL CHANNING, on her role in *Gentlemen Prefer Blondes*, news reports of Dec. 30, 1954.

---

* Reported *Time*, May 4, 1953: " 'Call me Madam,' said Frances Perkins, the first woman cabinet member, on her first day in office [1933]—and gave herself a title she has regretted ever since."

An artist carries on throughout his life a mysterious, uninterrupted conversation with his public.
    MAURICE CHEVALIER, *Holiday*, Sept., 1956.

They try to be clevah instead of watching me being clevah.
    NOEL COWARD, on talkative theater-goers, *New York Mirror*, Nov. 27, 1957.

In London, theatre-goers expect to laugh; in Paris, they wait grimly for proof that they should.
    ROBERT DHERY, French actor-producer, *Look*, March 4, 1958.

My greatest trouble is getting the curtain up and down.
    T. S. ELIOT, on writing plays, *Time*, March 6, 1950.

A play should give you something to think about. When I see a play and understand it the first time, then I know it can't be much good.
    T. S. ELIOT, *New York Post*, Sept. 22, 1963.

We read the lines so that people can hear and understand them; we move about the stage without bumping into the furniture or each other.
    LYNN FONTANNE, defining the art of acting, news reports of Oct. 31, 1954.

. . . Now that I had born the baby, I could not stand doctors and nurses hanging over it, cuddling and cooing at it. After so long living with my child, I felt lonely and empty. Post-natal blues.
    KETTI FRINGS, on dramatizing *Look Homeward, Angel*, *New York Mirror*, Dec. 5, 1957.

. . . Life itself is the real and most miraculous miracle of all. If one had never before seen a human hand and were suddenly presented for the first time with this strange and wonderful thing, what a miracle, what a magnificently shocking and inexplicable and mysterious thing it would be. In my plays I want to look at life—at the commonplace of existence—as if we had just turned a corner and run into it for the first time.
    CHRISTOPHER FRY, *Time*, Nov. 20, 1950.

Comedy is an escape, not from truth but from despair: a narrow escape into faith. It believes in a universal cause for delight, even though knowledge of the cause is always twitched away from under us . . . In tragedy every moment is eternity; in comedy, eternity is a moment . . .
    CHRISTOPHER FRY, *ibid.*

You are never so *alone* as when you are ill on stage. The most nightmarish feeling in the world is suddenly to feel like throwing up in front of 4,000 people.
    JUDY GARLAND, *Life*, June 2, 1961.

Men who love humanity have all dreamed at least once during their lives of bringing all their fellow men together in a state of carefree happiness. And only the world of the theatre ever really succeeds in doing this. For a minute or perhaps two—and this is a long time—the theatre makes man better and happier on this earth. That is why I love the theatre.
    JEAN-JACQUES GAUTIER, theater critic for *Le Figaro*, "A Thousand-and-One First Nights," *Réalités*, Jan., 1958.

. . . There is almost collusion between the stage and the audience. Everything goes. Everything carries. A magic fluid seems to be circulating. The actors have stage presence. Their characters really exist. The play has depth.
    JEAN-JACQUES GAUTIER, *ibid.*

I got all the schooling any actress needs. That is, I learned to write enough to sign contracts.
    HERMIONE GINGOLD, *Look*, Oct. 4, 1955.

Charity in the theatre begins and ends with those who have a play opening within a week of one's own.
    MOSS HART, *Act One*, Random House, 1961.

You need three things in the theatre—the play, the actors and the audience, and each must give something.
    KENNETH HAIGH, *Theatre Arts*, July, 1958.

Good actors are good because of the things they can tell us without talking. When they are talking, they are the servants of the dramatist. It is what they can show the audience when they are not talking that reveals the fine actor.
> SIR CEDRIC HARDWICKE, *Theatre Arts,* Feb., 1958.

It has always amused me to hear playwrights say that a good play should be actor-proof. I have never heard of a composer saying that his work is pianist-proof.
> SIR CEDRIC HARDWICKE, *ibid.*

An actress's life is so transitory—suddenly you're a building.
> HELEN HAYES, on learning that a Broadway theater was being named in her honor, news reports of Nov. 9, 1955.

In the theatre, I was brought up in the tradition of service. The audience pays its money and you are expected to give your best performance—both on and off the stage.
> HELEN HAYES, *New York Daily Mirror,* Nov. 9, 1956.

A low trick I hate to stoop to is tying and untying my shoelaces. It seems to fascinate audiences . . . probably because so many women in the audience have their shoes off, or wish they did.
> EDWARD EVERETT HORTON, on scene-stealing, news summaries of Dec. 14, 1954.

Playing Shakespeare is so tiring. You never get a chance to sit down unless you're a King.
> JOSEPHINE HULL, *Time,* Nov. 16, 1953.

It has taken me many years of living to realize the fears in us all, the fears in the most seemingly brave, the bravery in the most seemingly frightened.
> WILLIAM INGE, on his Broadway play, *The Dark at the Top of the Stairs, Time,* Dec. 16, 1957.

Theatre is not literature, propaganda or philosophy . . . It is simply what cannot be expressed by any other means . . . a complexity of words,

419

movements, gestures that convey a vision of the world unexpressible in any other way.

> Eugene Ionesco, Roumanian playwright, *New York Times*, Jan. 5, 1958.

In New York people don't go to the theatre—they go to see hits.

> Louis Jourdan, quoted by Art Buchwald, *New York Herald Tribune Syndicate.*

Wherever it came from, the musical came with its hair mussed and with an innocent, indolent, irreverent look on its bright, bland face. It has an air about it of having strolled in from the street with a few tricks up its sleeve, and if everybody would relax, please, it would do its best to pass the time whimsically. Harpo Marx looks like a musical comedy.

> Walter Kerr, theater critic, *New York Herald Tribune*, Sept. 1, 1963.

When somebody says they're writing something with you in mind, that's the end. I want them to write with Katharine Cornell or Helen Hayes in mind and then let me have a go at it.

> Beatrice Lillie, *Theatre Arts*, March, 1956.

Public life with all its attendant censure has no horrors for the man who . . . has once been taken naked over the live coals by a group of professional theatre critics. It is the quickest way I know to acquire a spiritual elephant hide.

> Clare Boothe Luce, *Newsweek*, Jan. 24, 1955.

On the whole, this production is a sustained insult to the critical sense, and yet a genuine delight to those amiable qualities that thrive best when the critical sense is out to lunch.

> Donald Malcolm, *New Yorker*, Nov. 28, 1959, reviewing off-Broadway operatic-parody, *Little Mary Sunshine*.

Intramural strife, a euphemism for backstage bickering and brawling, is a commonplace in the theatre, thanks to the neuroses of its inmates and the tooth-and-claw tactics they employ to maintain a queasy professional status variously achieved through self-denial, industry and witchcraft.

> Richard Maney, Broadway press agent, "No Feuds Like Show Feuds," *New York Times*, March 26, 1961.

Words can be deceitful, but pantomime necessarily is simple, clear and direct.

> MARCEL MARCEAU, *Theatre Arts*, March, 1958.

The theme is the theme of humiliation, which is the square root of sin, as opposed to the freedom from humiliation, and love, which is the square root of wonderful.

> CARSON McCULLERS, *New York Herald Tribune*, Oct. 27, 1957 on her play, *The Square Root of Wonderful*.

She's o.k. if you like talent.

> ETHEL MERMAN, on Mary Martin, *Theatre Arts*, Sept. 1958.

It is when life creates a new play that the theatre moves its limbs and wakens from its mesmerized fixation on ordinary reality; when the present is caught and made historic.

> ARTHUR MILLER, "The Shadows of the Gods: A Critical View of the American Theatre," *Harper's*, Aug., 1958.

The structure of a play is always the story of how the birds came home to roost.

> ARTHUR MILLER, *ibid.*

Predictions of greatness in the world of show business are usually, to borrow a few similes from the world of plant life, as sweet as the pomegranate and as impassioned as the orchid; as perishable as the crocus, as sticky as the fly trap and as common as the dandelion. Now and then the predictions are fulfilled, thereby endowing the forecaster with the reputation of a seer.

> GILBERT MILLSTEIN, *Collier's*, July 22, 1955.

In the theatre, a hero is one who believes that all women are ladies, a villain one who believes that all ladies are women.

> GEORGE JEAN NATHAN, *New York Times*, Nov. 5, 1950.

Impersonal criticism . . . is like an impersonal fist fight or an impersonal marriage, and as successful.

> GEORGE JEAN NATHAN, *The World of George Jean Nathan*, edited by Charles Angoff, Knopf, 1952.

421

Bosh sprinkled with mystic cologne.
> GEORGE JEAN NATHAN, on *The Cocktail Party* by T. S. Eliot, *ibid.*

So long as there is one pretty girl left on the stage, the professional under-
takers may hold up their burial of the theatre.
> GEORGE JEAN NATHAN, *Theatre Arts*, July, 1958.

You know, acting makes you feel like a burglar sometimes—taking all that
money for all that fun.
> PAT O'BRIEN, *New York Journal-American*, Dec. 6, 1961.

When you're a young man, Macbeth is a character part. When you're
older, it's a straight part.
> SIR LAURENCE OLIVIER, on playing Macbeth at 30 and at 48, *Theatre
> Arts*, May 1, 1958.

Take some wood and canvas and nails and things. Build yourself a theatre,
a stage, light it, learn about it. When you've done that you will probably
know how to write a play.
> EUGENE O'NEILL, on how to be a playwright, *The Tempering of
> Eugene O'Neill* by Doris M. Alexander, Harcourt, Brace & World,
> 1962.

We tore them up, bit by bit, together. . . . It was awful, it was like tearing up children.
> MRS. EUGENE O'NEILL, on helping her husband destroy his unfinished
> plays before his death, *New York Times*, Nov. 4, 1956.

Sweden did this for O'Neill, not America. America was not a damn bit interested, excuse my language.
> MRS. EUGENE O'NEILL, on revival of interest in O'Neill's works, *ibid.*

Here the theatregoer is anxious to be surprised. He can take anything in
his stride. At home, in London . . . the theatre is something you do after
dinner, and use it as a sort of pleasant indigestion pill.
> JOHN OSBORNE, *Newsweek*, Feb. 24, 1958.*

---

* John Osborne became known as one of the theater's "angry young men" of the
1950's and '60's. According to *The Beat Generation and the Angry Young Man,*

It is as if you had to devise a whole banquet out of rice pudding and stewed pears.

> J. B. PRIESTLEY, on difficulty of writing realistic plays on contemporary English, *The Art of the Dramatist*, Heinemann Publishers, London, 1957.

A playwright must be his own audience. A novelist may lose his readers for a few pages; a playwright never dares lose his audience for a minute. In point of fact, I have to please myself, constantly.

> TERENCE RATTIGAN, *New York Journal-American*, Oct. 29, 1956.

Every playwright ought to try acting just as every public prosecutor should spend some weeks in jail to find out what he is meting out to others.

> ERICH MARIA REMARQUE, *New York Herald Tribune*, Oct. 24, 1957.

Two thousand dear ladies. All very careful and diplomatic with one another. Ever so sweet and catty, you know. I can hear that sweet-and-catty sound through the curtain while the house lights are still on. They all applaud with their gloves on, never too hard or too much. They're busier watching each other than the show.

> CYRIL RITCHARD, on matinee audiences, *Holiday*, Sept., 1960.

An excellent play . . . but I have no feeling of reality about it. It had no more to do with me than the man in the moon.

> ELEANOR ROOSEVELT, on seeing *Sunrise at Campobello*, play about her family, *Theatre Arts*, April, 1958.

I'll match my flops with anybody's but I wouldn't have missed 'em. Flops are a part of life's menu and I've never been a girl to miss out on any of the courses.

> ROSALIND RUSSELL, *New York Herald Tribune*, April 11, 1957.

. . . Behave as citizens not only of your profession but of the full world in which you live. Be indignant with injustice, be gracious with success,

edited by Gene Feldman and Max Gartenberg, Citadel Press, 1958, "The term derives from the title *Angry Young Man* by Leslie Paul. The irony is that Paul's memoir deals with a different brand of angry young man, that of the 20's and 30's seeking to create a better world through leftist good causes. If the angry young men of the 50's have any attitude in common it is that they all reject the 'good cause' per se."

be courageous with failure, be patient with opportunity, and be resolute with faith and honor.
> DORE SCHARY, address to American Academy of Dramatic Arts, *Atlantic*, Oct., 1959.

Mr. [Monty] Woolley reduced the nurse in *The Man Who Came to Dinner* to the potency of a pound of wet Kleenex. It was probably the best thing that had happened to the art of the insult since the Medicis stopped talking in the 16th century.
> RICHARD SEVERO, *New York Herald Tribune*, May 7, 1963.

He [Monty Woolley] wore his beard with the aplomb of a Madison Ave. Santa Claus.
> RICHARD SEVERO, *ibid.*

. . . General consultant to mankind.
> GEORGE BERNARD SHAW, self-description quoted in reports of his death, Nov. 1, 1950.

The utmost I can bear for myself in my best days is that I was one of the hundred best playwrights in the world, which is hardly a supreme distinction.
> GEORGE BERNARD SHAW, letter to W. D. Chase, Flint, Mich., president of the Shaw Society in U.S., recalled in reports of Shaw's death, *ibid.*

A drama critic is a man who leaves no turn unstoned.
> GEORGE BERNARD SHAW, *New York Times*, Nov. 5, 1950.

Go on writing plays, my boy. One of these days one of these London producers will go into his office and say to his secretary, "Is there a play from Shaw this morning?" and when she says, "No," he will say, "Well, then, we'll have to start on the rubbish." And that's your chance, my boy.
> GEORGE BERNARD SHAW, advice quoted by William Douglas Home, author of *The Reluctant Debutante* and other plays, *New York Times*, Oct. 7, 1956.

424

I have to keep ripping off my trousers at odd times between scenes.
> HIRAM SHERMAN, on his dual role as master-of-ceremonies and actor in an unprecedented Shakespearian evening in the White House, *New York Times*, Oct. 5, 1961.

It's as though some poor devil were to set out for a large dinner party with the knowledge that the following morning he would be hearing exactly what each of the other guests thought of him.
> CORNELIA OTIS SKINNER, on opening night reviews, *The Ape in Me*, Houghton Mifflin, 1959.

We are a nation that has always gone in for the loud laugh, the wow, the belly laugh and the dozen other labels for the roll-'em-in-the-aisles gagerissimo. This is the kind of laugh that delights actors, directors, and producers, but dismays writers of comedy because it is the laugh that often dies in the lobby. The appreciative smile, the chuckle, the soundless mirth, so important to the success of comedy, cannot be understood unless one sits among the audience and feels the warmth created by the quality of laughter that the audience takes home with it.
> JAMES THURBER, "The Quality of Mirth," *New York Times*, Feb. 21, 1960.

. . . A British comedienne whose appearance suggests an overstuffed electric chair.
> TIME, Feb. 2, 1962, on actress Margaret Rutherford.

Her writhing stare could reduce a rabid dog to foaming jelly.
> TIME, May 24, 1963, again commenting on Margaret Rutherford.

A good many inconveniences attend playgoing in any large city, but the greatest of them is usually the play itself.
> KENNETH TYNAN, British drama critic, *New York Herald Tribune*, Feb. 17, 1957.

The sheer complexity of writing a play always has dazzled me. In an effort to understand it, I became a critic.
> KENNETH TYNAN, *New York Mirror*, June 6, 1963.

By increasing the size of the keyhole, today's playwrights are in danger of doing away with the door.

> PETER USTINOV, *Christian Science Monitor*, Nov. 14, 1962.

Playwrights are like men who have been dining a month in an Indian restaurant. After eating curry night after night, they deny the existence of asparagus.

> PETER USTINOV, *ibid.*

Every actor in his heart believes everything bad that's printed about him.

> ORSON WELLES, news reports of Jan. 13, 1956.

Many plays—certainly mine—are like blank checks. The actors and directors put their own signatures on them.

> THORNTON WILDER, *New York Mirror*, July 13, 1956.

A dramatist is one who believes that the pure event, an action involving human beings, is more arresting than any comment that can be made upon it. On the stage it is always *now;* the personages are standing on that razor-edge, between the past and the future, which is the essential character of conscious being; the words are rising to their lips in immediate spontaneity . . . The theatre is supremely fitted to say: "Behold! These things are."

> THORNTON WILDER, *Writers at Work*, Viking, 1958.

The unencumbered stage encourages the truth operative in everyone. The less seen, the more heard. The eye is the enemy of the ear in real drama.

> THORNTON WILDER, *New York Times*, Nov. 6, 1961.

I am not interested in the ephemeral—such subjects as the adulteries of dentists. I am interested in those things that repeat and repeat and repeat in the lives of the millions.

> THORNTON WILDER, *ibid.*

Some mystery should be left in the revelation of character in a play, just as a great deal of mystery is always left in the revelation of character in life, even in one's own character to himself.

> TENNESSEE WILLIAMS, stage directions for *Cat On A Hot Tin Roof*, New Directions, 1955.

426

I don't believe in villains or heroes, only in right or wrong ways that individuals are taken, not by choice, but by necessity or by certain still uncomprehended influences in themselves, their circumstances and their antecedents.

TENNESSEE WILLIAMS, *New York Post*, March 17, 1957.

If the writing is honest it cannot be separated from the man who wrote it. It isn't so much his mirror as it is the distillation, the essence, of what is strangest and purest in his nature, whether that be gentleness or anger, serenity or torment, light or dark. This makes it deeper than the surface likeness of a mirror and that much more truthful.

TENNESSEE WILLIAMS, preface to William Inge's play, *The Dark at the Top of the Stairs*, Random House, 1958.

Every now and then, when you're on stage, you hear the best sound a player can hear. It's a sound you can't get in movies or in television. It is the sound of a wonderful, deep silence that means you've hit them where they live.

SHELLEY WINTERS, *Theatre Arts*, June, 1956.

Has anybody ever seen a dramatic critic in the daytime? Of course not. They come out after dark, up to no good.

P. G. WODEHOUSE, *New York Mirror*, May 27, 1955.

There is no more offensive act of theatrical rudeness than coming late to a performance.

MAURICE ZOLOTOW, *Theatre Arts*, Feb., 1958.

Music and the Dance

No good opera plot can be sensible, for people do not sing when they are feeling sensible.
> W. H. AUDEN, author and poet, *Time*, Dec. 29, 1961.

One of the current hazards of organ-building is that after you've designed and placed an organ as well as you possibly can, some well-meaning lady is able to ruin the whole thing by donating memorial carpeting to the church.
> DR. ROBERT BAKER, organist, Fifth Avenue Presbyterian Church, in interview in *The New Yorker*, Dec. 23, 1961.

If you are happy you can always learn to dance.
> BALINESE SAYING quoted by Santha Rama Rau in *East of Home*, Harper & Row, 1950.

Competitions are for horses, not artists.
> BÉLA BARTÓK, composer, *Saturday Review*, Aug. 25, 1962.

Its members are quite hopeless—drooling, driveling, doleful, depressing, dropsical drips.
> SIR THOMAS BEECHAM, conductor, on music critics, news summaries of Feb. 13, 1954.

If an opera cannot be played by an organ-grinder—as Puccini's and Verdi's melodies were played—then that opera is not going to achieve immortality.
> SIR THOMAS BEECHAM, news summaries of May 21, 1955.

428

Most of them sound like they live on seaweed.
> SIR THOMAS BEECHAM, on sopranos, *Newsweek*, April 30, 1956.

Movie music is noise. It's even more painful than my sciatica.
> SIR THOMAS BEECHAM, *Time*, Feb. 24, 1958.

A pretty one will distract the other musicians, and an ugly one will distract me.
> SIR THOMAS BEECHAM, on the prospect of hiring a woman musician, *New York Post*, May 8, 1959.

Composers should write tunes that chauffeurs and errand boys can whistle.
> SIR THOMAS BEECHAM, quoted in report of his death at 81, *New York Times*, March 9, 1961.

That which penetrates the ear with facility and quits the memory with difficulty.
> SIR THOMAS BEECHAM, on good music, *ibid.*

Any great work of art is great because it creates a special world of its own. It revives and readapts time and space, and the measure of its success is the extent to which it makes you an inhabitant of that world—the extent to which it invites you in and lets you breathe its strange, special air.
> LEONARD BERNSTEIN, "What Makes Opera Grand?" *Vogue*, Dec., 1958.

The opera always loses money. That's as it should be. Opera has no business making money.
> RUDOLF BING, general manager, Metropolitan Opera, *New York Times*, Nov. 15, 1959.

Do, do things, act. Make a list of the music you love, then learn it by heart. And when you are writing music of your own, write it as you hear it inside and never strain to avoid the obvious. The person who does that is living outside life.
> NADIA BOULANGER, internationally known as "the most influential teacher of the 20th century," *Life*, July 21, 1958.

429

The cello is like a beautiful woman who has not grown older, but younger with time, more slender, more supple, more graceful.

PABLO CASALS, *Time*, April 29, 1957.

It is no part of the functions of orchestral hall managers to tell me when I should cough. Anybody who wants to collect British seat money in the British winter must put up with the British cough.

PERCY CATER, music critic of London *Daily Mail*, on "coughing in-structions" inserted in programs at Royal Festival Hall, *Newsweek*, Feb. 18, 1963.

I think that long after the people have forgotten who won the Tchaikovsky competition they will remember that an American won it. This is impor-tant.

VAN CLIBURN, on returning to the U.S. from International Piano Fes-tival in Moscow, *New York Post*, May 16, 1958.

Only paper flowers are afraid of the rain. We are not afraid of the noble rain of criticism because with it will flourish the magnificent garden of music.

KONSTANTIN DANKEVICH, one of five Soviet composers entertained by Music Critics Circle of New York, *New York Times*, Nov. 19, 1959.

What we provide is an atmosphere. It's a kind of orchestrated pulse which works on people in a subliminal way. Under its influence I've seen shy debs and severe dowagers kick off their shoes and raise some wholesome hell.

MEYER DAVIS, society orchestra leader, *Saturday Evening Post*, April 20, 1963.

A good education is usually harmful to a dancer. A good calf is better than a good head.

AGNES DE MILLE, news summaries of Feb. 1, 1954.

Stretching about me was the beloved floor, the classic empty floor. It waited for the blow, for the caress, answering the striking as a musical instrument answers the players. I put my hot and readied foot on the wood and felt the power up my leg and in my ready back. I felt with my toes and my

strong instep and my heel that supported my spine and my lifted head—
and from the heel I pushed. The floor pushed back and the instep held like
a wing and I suspended in the air and my arms were released: my throat
and my back ached again with the good pain of supporting, and my body
was strong enough and held.

> AGNES DE MILLE, on the sensation of dancing, recounted in her auto-
> biographical *And Promenade Home*, Atlantic–Little, Brown, 1958.

The universe lies before you on the floor, in the air, in the mysterious
bodies of your dancers, in your mind. From this voyage no one returns
poor or weary.

> AGNES DE MILLE, *To A Young Dancer*, Atlantic–Little, Brown, 1962.

Modern dancers give a sinister portent about our times. The dancers don't
even look at one another. They are just a lot of isolated individuals jiggling
in a kind of self-hypnosis and dancing with others only to remind themselves that we are not completely alone in this world.

> AGNES DE MILLE, *New York Times*, June 10, 1963.

There is a natural hootchy-kootchy motion to a goldfish . . .

> WALT DISNEY, chief exponent of animated cartoons, on a ballet of fish
> for *Fantasia*, quoted in *Profile of America*, Crowell, 1954.

You cannot create genius. All you can do is nurture it.

> NINETTE DE VALOIS, director, Royal Ballet, *Time*, Sept. 26, 1960.

Playing "bop" is like playing Scrabble with all the vowels missing.

> DUKE ELLINGTON, orchestra leader, *Look*, Aug. 10, 1954.

It's like an act of murder; you play with intent to commit something.

> DUKE ELLINGTON, on playing jazz, *New York Herald Tribune*, July
> 9, 1961.

As a student of American culture, I am willing to argue . . . that the
Twist is a valid manifestation of the Age of Anxiety; an outward mani-

431

festation of the anguish, frustration, and uncertainty of the 1960's; an effort to release some of the tension which, if suppressed and buried, could warp and destroy.

> MARSHALL FISHWICK, Professor of American Studies, Washington and Lee University, *Saturday Review*, March 3, 1962.

Miss Farrell has a voice like some unparalleled phenomenon of nature. She is to singers what Niagara is to waterfalls.

> ALFRED FRANKENSTEIN, music critic, *San Francisco Chronicle*, on American soprano Eileen Farrell, *Newsweek*, Sept. 22, 1958.

A nation creates music—the composer only arranges it.

> MIKHAIL GLINKA, Russian composer, *Theatre Arts*, June, 1958.

If a guy's got it, let him give it. I'm selling music, not prejudice.

> BENNY GOODMAN, first conductor to integrate Negroes into a big-time band, *Saturday Evening Post*, Dec. 18, 1954.

You do what you do because you must do it at that instant in time. If it lives, it is because posterity demands it.

> MARTHA GRAHAM, on her choreography, *Newsweek*, April 7, 1958

Nowhere else in the world has such an audience survived. It is one of the great charms of New York that at the Met one may still see bejeweled Grandes Dames, rouged like crazy, wearing what at first appear to be black fur stoles, but then turn out to be their enervated sons slung across their mamas' magnificent shoulders; one may still see Elderly Patricians hanging from boxes by the heels, with their opera glasses pointing like guns right *down* the décolletage of a huge soprano; one may still see swarms of Liveried Chauffeurs waiting to escort their Employers to their cars, to place fur wraps about their aged shanks, to touch their caps respectfully at the words, "Home, James, and don't spare the Rolls."

> TYRONE GUTHRIE, "The 'Grand' Opera Behind Grand Opera," *New York Times*, Jan. 5, 1958.

I hand him a lyric and get out of his way.

> OSCAR HAMMERSTEIN II, on his partnership with Richard Rodgers, news summaries of May 12, 1955.

432

I occasionally play works by contemporary composers and for two reasons. First to discourage the composer from writing any more and secondly to remind myself how much I appreciate Beethoven.

> JASCHA HEIFETZ, violinist, *Life*, July 28, 1961.

Miss Truman is a unique American phenomenon with a pleasant voice of little size and fair quality. . . . There are few moments during her recital when one can relax and feel confident that she will make her goal, which is the end of the song.

> PAUL HUME, music critic, *Washington Post*, whose review of a concert by Margaret Truman drew a wrathful letter from her father, *Time*, Dec. 18, 1950.

I have read your lousy review of Margaret's concert. I've come to the conclusion that you are an "eight ulcer man on four ulcer pay." . . . Some day I hope to meet you. When that happens you'll need a new nose, a lot of beefsteak for black eyes, and perhaps a supporter below.

> PRESIDENT TRUMAN's reply to Mr. Hume,* *ibid.*

From the number of self-taught courses in music, one might guess that a substantial number of Americans no longer laugh when their friends sit down at the piano. Of course, it may be they are laughing all the harder . . .

> JOHN W. C. JOHNSTONE, professor of sociology, University of Chicago, *New York Times*, May 20, 1963.

We listen too much to the telephone and we listen too little to nature. The wind is one of my sounds. A lonely sound, perhaps, but soothing. Everybody should have his personal sounds to listen for—sounds that will make him exhilarated and alive, or quiet and calm. . . . As a matter of fact, one of the greatest sounds of them all—and to me it is a sound—is utter, complete silence.

> ANDRÉ KOSTELANETZ, conductor, *New York Journal-American*, Feb. 8, 1955.

---

* In the ensuing national furor, only critic Hume's voice was calm: "I can only say that a man suffering the loss of a close friend [press secretary Charles G. Ross] and carrying the terrible burden of the present world crisis ought to be indulged in an occasional outburst of temper."

Genius is an overused word. The world has known only about a half dozen geniuses. I have achieved only a medium approach to my ideal in music. I got only fairly near.

> Fritz Kreisler, on eve of 80th birthday, news summaries of Feb. 2, 1955.

Art is a complex riddle of life. You can't define it, the complexity of things Every day the artist is a different man. He may be better or worse. If he tries to tell you what he is, he isn't being honest. For he doesn't know himself. I have never even been able to say if I did or didn't play well.

> Fritz Kreisler, *ibid*.

I never practice; I always play.

> Wanda Landowska, on her mastery of the harpsichord, *Time*, Dec. 1, 1952.

You have always given me more than I gave to you. . . . You were the wings on which I soared.

> Lotte Lehmann, to her farewell concert audience in Town Hall, New York, *Life*, March 5, 1951.

It was like a Japanese ballplayer being invited to play first base for the Yankees.

> George London, first American to sing *Boris Godunov* in Russia, *Time*, Sept. 26, 1960.

Regard your voice as capital in the bank. When you go to sing, do not draw on your bank account. Sing on your interest and your voice will last.

> Lauritz Melchior, news reports of April 1, 1956.

To play great music, you must keep your eyes on a distant star.

> Yehudi Menuhin, *Reader's Digest*, Dec., 1953.

If you think you've hit a false note, sing loud. When in doubt, sing loud.

> Robert Merrill, *Saturday Evening Post*, Oct. 26, 1957.

434

Singers' husbands! Find me stones heavy enough to place around their necks and drown them all! In all my 35 years of managing artists, I never quite got used to the sharp little men who tell me where Madame is to be booked, what fee she is to be paid, who is to sing with her and what the critics will have to write. Somewhere in the brain of every prima donna there is a deep craving for security and comfort, linked with a fear of old age. This causes her to pick a man who is prepared to act as a permanent wet nurse.

> ANDRÉ MERTENS, Columbia Artists Manager, *Time*, Aug. 1, 1960.

Keep it simple, keep it sexy, keep it sad.

> MITCH MILLER (Mitchell William Miller), producer of "pop" records, *Time*, Feb. 23, 1950.

Not an audience but a habit.

> GIAN-CARLO MENOTTI, on the Metropolitan Opera, *Time*, May 1, 1950.

. . . Melody is a form of remembrance. . . . It must have a quality of inevitability in our ears.

> GIAN-CARLO MENOTTI, *ibid.*

Any subject is good for opera if the composer feels it so intently he must sing it out.

> GIAN-CARLO MENOTTI, *ibid.*

I never use a score when conducting my orchestra. . . . Does a lion tamer enter a cage with a book on how to tame a lion?

> DIMITRI MITROPOLOUS, news summaries of Jan. 22, 1951.

I live with music like a monk who prays every moment, including the night when he gets up to say *Ave Maria*. It is no more or no less. Simply utter devotion. The utmost devotion.

> DIMITRI MITROPOLOUS, news reports of Feb. 19, 1956.

Success can corrupt; usefulness can only exalt.

> DIMITRI MITROPOLOUS, *Hi-Fi Music at Home*, May–June, 1956.

435

. . . *La Sonnambula* is dull enough to send the most athletic sleepwalker back to bed.

> NEWSWEEK, March 4, 1963, reviewing Bellini's opera.

I think I'd take more pride in it had it been written under more romantic, more patriotic circumstances. Had I sat down in the midst of the bombings and dashed it off in defiance to the world, perhaps. But I did no such thing. In April of 1939 my publisher said, "Ross, there's a song doing very well in the States called 'God Bless America.' Think you can do one like it?" I sat down and wrote, *There'll Always Be An England.*

> Ross PARKER, composer and comedian, on his best-known song, *New York Mirror*, April 22, 1959.

If I was a good trumpet player I wouldn't be here. I got desperate. I hadda look for a job. I went in the union business.

> JAMES C. PETRILLO, president, American Federation of Musicians, *New York Times*, June 14, 1956.

Any song that moves you to joy or tears has greatness. Everything in life should be enjoyed for what it is.

> MARGUERITE PIAZZA, Metropolitan Opera star, news reports of Jan. 19, 1955.

. . . Jazz may be thought of as a current that bubbled forth from a spring in the slums of New Orleans to become the main stream of the twentieth century.

> HENRY PLEASANTS, critic, news summaries of Dec. 30, 1955.

My sole inspiration is a telephone call from a producer.

> COLE PORTER, news summaries of Feb. 28, 1955.

His personal blues are now finished. No more the problems of Beale Street. No more the irritations of Memphis. No more the vexation of the St. Louis woman. No more the cynical *Love, Oh Love, Oh Careless Love.*

> ADAM CLAYTON POWELL, JR., U.S. Congressman and Pastor, Abyssinian Baptist Church of Harlem, funeral tribute to "the father of the blues," W. C. Handy, *New York Times*, April 3, 1958.

It wasn't a man singing a song. It was a man singing his autobiography.
> Tom Prideaux, entertainment editor, *Life*, May 3, 1963, on Irving Berlin singing his song *There's No Business Like Show Business*.

I cannot tell you how much I love to play for people. Would you believe it—sometimes when I sit down to practice and there is no one else in the room, I have to stifle an impulse to ring for the elevator man and offer him money to come in and hear me.
> Artur Rubenstein, *Holiday*, May, 1963.

The notes I handle no better than many pianists. But the pauses between the notes—ah, that is where the art resides!
> Artur Schnabel, pianist and composer, *Chicago Daily News*, June 11, 1958.

. . . Dance is the only art of which we ourselves are the stuff of which it is made.
> Ted Shawn, veteran leader in ballet theater, *Time*, July 25, 1955.

A creative artist works on his next composition because he was not satisfied with his previous one. When he loses a critical attitude toward his own work he ceases to be an artist.
> Dmitri Shostakovich, Soviet composer, *New York Times*, Oct. 25, 1959.

To listen is an effort, and just to hear is no merit. A duck hears also.
> Igor Stravinsky, news summaries of June 24, 1957.

The real composer thinks about his work the whole time; he is not always conscious of this, but he is aware of it later when he suddenly knows what he will do.
> Igor Stravinsky, *Saturday Review*, Nov. 9, 1957.

Conductors must give unmistakable and suggestive signals to the orchestra —not choreography to the audience.
> George Szell, conductor, Cleveland Orchestra, *Newsweek*, Jan. 28, 1963.

Music is indivisible. The dualism of feeling and thinking must be resolved to a state of unity in which one thinks with the heart and feels with the brain.

> GEORGE SZELL, *Time*, Feb. 22, 1963.

On the dance floor, a tight tangle of people shuddered and shook through a series of hip-tossing, pelvis-thrusting, arm-swinging gyrations that go by the name of "The Twist."

> TIME, Oct. 20, 1961, on a dance sensation originating at the Peppermint Lounge, New York City.

After I die I shall return to earth as the doorkeeper of a bordello and I won't let a one of you in.

> ARTURO TOSCANINI, threat to an orchestra that displeased him, recalled in reports of his death at 89, Jan. 17, 1957.

I don't give a damn about *The Missouri Waltz* but I can't say it out loud because it's the song of Missouri. It's as bad as *The Star-Spangled Banner* so far as music is concerned.

> HARRY S. TRUMAN, *Time*, Feb. 10, 1958.

Tenors are noble, pure and heroic and get the soprano, if she has not tragically expired before the final curtain. But baritones are born villains in opera. Always the heavy and never the hero—that's me.

> LEONARD WARREN, American baritone, *New York World-Telegram and Sun*, March 13, 1957.

I think we as a whole—speaking for my race—I think we are all gifted. That is our inheritance, fun, pleasure, laughter, and song.

> ETHEL WATERS, Negro singer, CBS-TV, Jan. 8, 1954.

Art

Being present at your own exhibit is like being called out of rank during an Army physical inspection. It's embarrassing.

LUDWIG BEMELMANS, *Time*, March 31, 1952.

I wonder whether art has a higher function than to make me feel, appreciate, and enjoy natural objects for their art value? So, as I walk in the garden, I look at the flowers and shrubs and trees and discover in them an exquisiteness of contour, a vitality of edge or a vigor of spring as well as an infinite variety of color that no artifact I have seen in the last sixty years can rival. . . . Each day, as I look, I wonder where my eyes were yesterday.

BERNARD BERENSON, *Time*, April 25, 1955.

When I am finishing a picture I hold some God-made object up to it—a rock, a flower, the branch of a tree or my hand—as a kind of final test. If the painting stands up beside a thing man cannot make, the painting is authentic. If there's a clash between the two, it is bad art.

MARC CHAGALL, *Saturday Evening Post*, Dec. 2, 1962.

Without tradition, art is a flock of sheep without a shepherd. Without innovation, it is a corpse.

WINSTON CHURCHILL, address to Royal Academy of Arts, *Time*, May 11, 1953.

I have a feeling that people who go in for involved, unexpected superoriginal—if I may coin that word—forms of art ought to have credentials.*

WINSTON CHURCHILL, *New York Times*, May 1, 1954.

---

* An American opinion on abstract art was voiced by cartoonist Al Capp (*National Observer*, July 1, 1963): "A product of the untalented, sold by the unprincipled to the utterly bewildered."

An artist cannot speak about his art any more than a plant can discuss horticulture.

> JEAN COCTEAU, *Newsweek*, May 16, 1955.

Art produces ugly things which frequently become beautiful with time. Fashion, on the other hand, produces beautiful things which always become ugly with time.

> JEAN COCTEAU, *New York World-Telegram & Sun*, Aug. 21, 1960.

There is only one difference between a madman and me. I am not mad.

> SALVADOR DALI, *American*, July, 1956.

Compared to Velasquez I am nothing, but compared to contemporary painters, I am the most big genius of modern time . . . but modesty is not my speciality.

> SALVADOR DALI, *New York Herald Tribune*, Jan. 13, 1960.

Unless a picture shocks, it is nothing.

> MARCEL DUCHAMP, *Life*, Jan. 2, 1950.

It is amazing how English women of no uncertain age fancy themselves dressed as Venus.

> SIR JACOB EPSTEIN, on décolletage preferred for portraits, *Epstein, An Autobiography*, Dutton, 1955.

A wife, a lover, can perhaps never see what the artist sees . . . They rarely ever do. Perhaps a really mediocre artist has more chance of success in this respect.

> SIR JACOB EPSTEIN, *ibid.*

Since nudes in all countries and centuries possess standard equipment, it's difficult to say precisely why the pictures at the Brooklyn Museum right now are so thoroughly American.

> EMILY GENAUER, art critic, on historical survey of the nude in American painting, *New York Herald Tribune*, Oct. 10, 1961.

440

All I wanted was to connect my moods with those of Paris. Beauty pains, and when it pained most, I shot.
> ERNST HAAS, photographer, "The Glow of Paris," *Life*, Aug. 1, 1955.

New artists must break a hole in the subconscious and go fishing there.
> ROBERT BEVERLY HALE, on rationale of his school of bold, blot-like painting, *Time*, April 11, 1960.

My aim in painting has always been the most exact transcription possible of my most intimate impression of nature.
> EDWARD HOPPER, American realist, *Life*, April 17, 1950.

There is no need for alarm; the monster is amenable and responds to kindness.
> AUGUSTUS JOHN, self-description, news summaries of April 25, 1954.

Art does not reproduce the visible; rather, it makes visible.
> PAUL KLEE, "creative credo" quoted in *The Inward Vision*, Harry N. Abrams, 1959.

I am the most curious of all to see what will be the next thing that I do.
> JACQUES LIPCHITZ, sculptor, news summaries of May 24, 1954.

Some pictures are in the gallery because they belong to humanity and others because they belong to the United States.
> ANDRÉ MALRAUX, France's minister of culture, on visiting the National Gallery of Art, in Washington, *New York Herald Tribune*, May 12, 1962.

There has been talk of the risks this painting took by leaving the Louvre. . . . But the risks taken by the boys who landed one day in Normandy— to say nothing of those who had preceded them 25 years before—were much more certain. To the humblest among them, who may be listening to me now, I want to say, without raising my voice, that the masterpiece to which you are paying historic homage this evening, Mr. President, is a painting which he has saved.

> ANDRÉ MALRAUX, reply to toast by President Kennedy at Washington dinner marking the showing of *Mona Lisa* in U.S., Jan. 8, 1963.

You study, you learn, but you guard the original naïveté. It has to be within you, as desire for drink is within the drunkard or love is within the lover.

> HENRI MATISSE, *Time*, June 26, 1950.

There is nothing more difficult for a truly creative painter than to paint a rose, because before he can do so he has first to forget all the roses that were ever painted.

> HENRI MATISSE, comment recalled in obituaries reporting his death, news reports of Nov. 5, 1954.

I offer you, with greatest humility, this chapel which I consider the master-piece of my life, despite its imperfections, and I hope that those who visit it will be purified and solaced.

> HENRI MATISSE, quoted at a requiem mass in the chapel he designed for Dominican Order at Nice, news reports of Nov. 9, 1954.

That's rather a lot of money for a single gentleman to get.

> SOMERSET MAUGHAM, on learning that his art collection sold at auction for $1,466,864, *New York Times*, April 11, 1962.

I've helped some people.

> ANNA MARY MOSES' ("Grandma" Moses) reply, at 93, when asked of what she was proudest in her life, news summaries of Jan. 2, 1954.

Paintin's not important. The important thing is keepin' busy. If you know somethin' well, you can always paint it . . . [but] people would be better off buyin' chickens.

> "GRANDMA" MOSES, *Life*, Sept. 19, 1960.

Her face is like a wise Pekingese that has seen everything from a box by the bed, her bare arms are filled with spent cartridges of old age, and she is packaged in fateful red, as if she has just received the final invitation.

> NEWSWEEK, July 22, 1963, on René Bouché's painting of "social mix-master" Elsa Maxwell.

442

When one starts from a portrait and seeks by successive eliminations to find pure form . . . one inevitably ends up with an egg. Similarly, by starting from an egg and following the opposite course, one can arrive at a portrait.

PABLO PICASSO, *Look*, June 6, 1956.

If only we could pull out our brain and use only our eyes.

PABLO PICASSO, on painting objectively, *Saturday Review*, Sept. 1, 1956.

It's true. Matisse is dead now, and I must paint for both of us.

PABLO PICASSO, *ibid*.

Ah, good taste! What a dreadful thing! Taste is the enemy of creativeness.

PABLO PICASSO, *Quote*, March 24, 1957.

To draw, you must close your eyes and sing.

PABLO PICASSO, NBC-TV, Sept. 15, 1957.

Art is a lie that makes us realize the truth.

PABLO PICASSO, *Quote*, Sept. 21, 1958.

[It will] bridge the gap of lost time which the brain takes to make the hand do its bidding.

PABLO PICASSO, announcing his invention of a keyboard-machine to paint pictures, *New York Herald Tribune*, April 30, 1963.

The French look exactly like French, the faces of Dutchmen are Dutch. Danes look like Danes and Egyptians look very Canalish. Americans have a sad countenance. They probably look like this because they developed catarrh when they landed on Plymouth Rock.

SIR ALFRED RICHARDSON, president, Royal Academy of Art, Sept. 17, 1956.

In them one can see the spontaneous—and often aesthetic—expression of a people reflected, not in a gilt-framed drawing room mirror, but in an

443

honest glass held up to the face of a nation. Here can be seen not only the face but the heart of the generations who preceded us.

> WINTHROP ROCKEFELLER on exhibit of American folk art at U.S. Embassy, London, Jan., 1962.

In the springtime of America's cultural life its itinerant folk artists took to the road to record the life and times of a people. Perhaps never again will we have an artistic record created in such direct and unassuming terms.

> WINTHROP ROCKEFELLER, *ibid.*

For me, painting is a way to forget life. It is a cry in the night, a strangled laugh.

> GEORGES ROUAULT, French modernist, *Look*, April 15, 1958.

The tendency to make the capital a catch-all for a variety of monuments to honor the immortals, the not-so-immortals, the greats, the near-greats, and the not-so-greats must stop. We must be on our guard lest the nation's capital come to resemble an unplanned cemetery.

> SENATOR HUGH SCOTT, *New York Times*, Sept. 11, 1960.

I picked him up in a gutter, and saved him for France.

> MADAME LUCIE UTRILLO, on her husband, Maurice Utrillo, recalled in obituaries, Nov. 6, 1955.

All the really good ideas I ever had came to me while I was milking a cow.

> GRANT WOOD, news summaries of March 1, 1954.

Architecture

Billowing in plaster dust, probing, chipping, gouging with blunt instrument to find and pull out old building entrails, remodeling goes on all the time, but only as building's stepchild and architecture's bastard.
> ARCHITECTURAL FORUM, Jan., 1960, on remodeling, "The Art That Science Forgot."

Built originally round a small open courtyard, it had grown with the centuries till it lay like a long, grey, sleeping lizard, clutching two other courtyards and a cloister garth between its claws. In winter, the cold cut into you like a knife. The pale light crept in through deep-silled, leaded windows and was frozen immediately into the same wan blue as the whitewashed walls. You might have been standing in the heart of an iceberg, so strange it was, so silent, so austere.
> MONICA BALDWIN, describing Belgian convent in which she was a nun for 27 years, *I Leap Over the Wall*, Holt, Rinehart and Winston, 1950.

It is a library with living rooms attached.
> BERNARD BERENSON, art critic and collector, on his villa in Italy, *Time*, April 25, 1955.

This House regrets the recent erection of buildings of a skyscraper type in the Metropolis from the aesthetic and aeronautical point of view.
> LORD BRABAZON OF TARA, asking House of Lords to censure construction work in London, particularly "the new Hilton Hotel that will be looking very intimately down into the backyard of Buckingham Palace," *The Times*, London, Feb. 23, 1962.

It makes Westminster Abbey look like a country church . . .
> LORD BRABAZON OF TARA, on London's 34-story Vickers building, *ibid.*

They do everything to ruin the charm of the present and make cheap the glories of the past . . . for no reason that I can see except the satisfaction of calling those who disagree with them "squares." My Lords, the British "square" has a noble history in our life and I would rather be a British "square" than one of these irregular polygons.
> LORD BRABAZON OF TARA, *ibid.**

The Solomon R. Guggenheim Museum . . . is a war between architecture and painting in which both come out badly maimed.
> JOHN CANADAY, art critic, *New York Times*, Oct. 21, 1959, on opening of Fifth Avenue museum designed by Frank Lloyd Wright.

We shape our buildings; thereafter they shape us.
> WINSTON CHURCHILL, *Time*, Sept. 12, 1960.

The outside is really "desert sand." The columns and trim are white, but that's all. I am really amazed. Why isn't the White House white? What can I tell the sidewalk superintendents?
> DEWEY D'AGOSTINO, Trenton, N.J., contractor, on being awarded a contract to paint the White House, *New York Herald Tribune*, Sept. 30, 1960.

The automobile has not merely taken over the street, it has dissolved the living tissue of the city. Its appetite for space is absolutely insatiable; moving and parked, it devours urban land, leaving the buildings as mere islands of habitable space in a sea of dangerous and ugly traffic. . . . Gas-filled, noisy and hazardous, our streets have become the most inhumane landscape in the world.
> JAMES MARSTON FITCH, professor of architecture, Columbia University, *New York Times*, May 1, 1960.

Round 1902 all that was most ponderous in Victorian architecture, all that was most ostentatious in the Edwardian era, joined hands to provide a monumental journey's end for railway travellers. These fantastic mau-

---

* Said Lord Conesford, replying to the opposition: "A skyscraper can be a splendid thing. It can enrich even London."

soleums erected in the cast-iron jaws of the steam-and-smoke-belching stations are our ponderous inheritance.

> PATIENCE GRAY, on "station hotels" of Britain, *The Observer*, London, Jan. 18, 1959.

When we started the UN we were not trying to make a monument. We were building a workshop—a workshop for world peace. And we tried to make it the best damn workshop we could.

> WALLACE HARRISON, chief architect of UN building, *Time*, Sept. 22, 1952.

. . . the Hilton is layed out with a competence that would make a computer blush.

> ADA LOUISE HUXTABLE, on opening of New York Hilton at Rockefeller Center, *New York Times*, June 30, 1963.

. . . superfluous curtains that needlessly cover glass would give Salome a lifetime supply of veils.

> ADA LOUISE HUXTABLE, *ibid*.

This is a sad day. In terms of beauty New York is not a great city. In terms of activity it is an epic city. We need to keep buildings which are an expression of that epic quality.

> NORMAN JAFFEE, architect, on the beginning of demolition of Pennsylvania Station described by *Newsweek*, Nov. 11, 1963, as "the 53-year-old cathedral of arrival and departure designed by Stanford White in the neo-classic grandeur of the early 20th century." *

I know that the White House was designed by Hoban, a noted Irish-American architect, and I have no doubt that he believed by incorporating several features of the Dublin style he would make it more home-like

---

* Of Penn Station's passing a *New York Times* editorial, Oct. 30, 1963, observed: "Any city gets what it admires, will pay for, and, ultimately, deserves. Even when we had Penn Station, we couldn't afford to keep it clean. We want and deserve tin-can architecture in a tin-horn culture. And we will probably be judged not by the monuments we build but by those we have destroyed."

for any President of Irish descent. It was a long wait, but I appreciate his efforts.

> PRESIDENT KENNEDY, addressing Irish Parliament, Dublin, assembled in a Georgian mansion that was once the seat of Fitzgerald clan, *New York Times*, June 29, 1963.

Architecture is a cultural instrument. Man wants to express something that he sees in his mind or feels in his soul, but few men get the chance—especially college students. But every time a college student walks past a really urgent, expressive piece of architecture that belongs to his college, it can help reassure him that he does have that mind, does have that soul.

> LOUIS I. KUHN, first American architect to achieve fame for college buildings, *Fortune*, May, 1963.

The styles of Louis XIV, XV, XVI, or Gothic, are to architecture what a feather is on a woman's head.

> LE CORBUSIER, *Time*, May 5, 1961.

I prefer drawing to talking. Drawing is faster, and allows less room for lies.

> LE CORBUSIER, *ibid*.

I venture to predict that long after the public has wearied of Frank Lloyd Wright's inverted oatmeal dish and silo with their awkward cantilevering, their jaundiced skin and the ingenious spiral ramp leading down past the abstractions which mirror the tortured maladjustments of our time, the Metropolitan will still wear well.

> ROBERT MOSES, New York park commissioner, defending Metropolitan Museum of Art against its new neighbor, the Wright-designed Guggenheim Museum, *New York Times*, May 21, 1959.

The [New York] skyscrapers began to rise again, fraily massive, elegantly utilitarian, images in their grace, audacity and inconclusiveness, of the whole character of the people who produced them.

> MALCOLM MUGGERIDGE, *The Titans: United States of America*, BBC-TV, Jan. 16, 1962.

The typical nineteenth-century character of many aspects of its monumental design—the fine, foolish mixture of mythology and great men in

its sculptured details, its confident, unorthodox use of classical motifs—
has lost its simple, period naïveté for a kind of hard, grotesque vulgarity.
What was charming in the original became pretentious in the copy. Time
and grime will soften it, but never restore its authenticity.

> New York Times, April 12, 1962, on replacement of U.S. Capitol's
> sandstone front with a vast new expanse of gleaming marble.

The surroundings householders crave are glorified autobiographies ghost-
written by willing architects and interior designers who, like their clients,
want to show off.

> T. H. Robsjohn-Gibbings, "Robsjohn-Gibbings Names The Biggest
> Bore," *Town & Country*, Jan., 1961.

Always design a thing by considering it in its next larger context—a chair
in a room, a room in a house, a house in an environment, an environment
in a city plan.

> Eliel Saarinen, Finnish architect, quoted by his son, Eero Saarinen,
> *Time*, July 2, 1956.

We live in the time of the colossal upright oblong. We are meeting in the
city where the skyscraper was born.

> Carl Sandburg, opening words of an address for Chicago Dynamic
> Committee, *Life*, Nov. 4, 1957.

The emotion that possessed me was one of great elation, that my life's wish
had been granted; but with it came a strange humility, the awful feeling
that the finger had pointed at me; and that I was not worthy or able.

> Sir Basil Spence, on learning that he had won architectural design
> competition for Coventry Cathedral, *Phoenix At Coventry*, Harper
> & Row, 1962.

A chair is a very difficult object. A skyscraper is almost easier. That is why
Chippendale is famous.

> Mies van der Rohe, *Time*, Feb. 18, 1957.

Less is more.

> Mies van der Rohe, on restraint in design, *New York Herald Tribune*,
> June 28, 1959.

I doubt if there is anything in the world uglier than a midwestern city.
> Frank Lloyd Wright, address in Evanston, Ill., news reports of Aug. 8, 1954.

Clear out eight hundred thousand people and preserve it as a museum piece.
> Frank Lloyd Wright, a suggestion for disposal of Boston, *New York Times*, Nov. 27, 1955.

New York: Prison towers and modern posters for soap and whisky. Pittsburgh: Abandon it.
> Frank Lloyd Wright, *ibid.*

If you're going to have centralization, why not have it!
> Frank Lloyd Wright, announcing plans for a 510-story office building for Chicago's Loop, news summaries of Sept. 10, 1956.

Early in life I had to choose between honest arrogance and hypocritical humility. I chose honest arrogance and have seen no occasion to change.
> Frank Lloyd Wright, statement recalled in obituaries reporting his death at 89, April 9, 1959.

Give me the luxuries of life and I will willingly do without the necessities.
> Frank Lloyd Wright, *ibid.*

A shadow falls; I feel coming on me a strange disease—humility.
> Frank Lloyd Wright, on accepting Gold Medal Award of National Institute of Arts and Letters, *ibid.*

Fashion

My grandfather, Frank Lloyd Wright, wore a red sash on his wedding night. That is glamour!

> Anne Baxter, actress, *Time*, May 5, 1952.

I love luxury. And luxury lies not in richness and ornateness but in the absence of vulgarity. Vulgarity is the ugliest word in our language. I stay in the game to fight it.

> Gabrielle Chanel, Parisian designer and perfumer, *Life*, Aug. 19, 1957.

Fashion is made to become unfashionable.

> Gabrielle Chanel, *ibid.*

Once *Vogue* showed two or three dresses for stout women, but we were so shaken by the experience we haven't repeated it in 57 years.

> Edna Woolman Chase, for nearly 60 years editor of *Vogue*, writing in her autobiography, *Always In Vogue*, Doubleday, 1954.

Fashion can be bought. Style one must possess. I have seen a Texas cowboy swing himself into his saddle with more real elegance, more style, than many gentlemen on the hunting field.

> Edna Woolman Chase, *ibid.*

[It is] a lightning-quick epidemic which forces different and antagonistic persons all to obey the same mysterious order, to submit themselves to new habits which overturn their old ways of life, up to the moment when a new order arrives and obliges them to turn their coat once more.

> Jean Cocteau, description of fashion, *Paris Arts*, Aug., 1956.

. . . A lot of life is sitting and an evening dress should sit prettily. Entrances and exits are a matter of minutes, but sitting goes on for hours.
> GLADYS COOPER, on ideal evening dress, *Vogue*, April 1, 1956.

When I was six I made my mother a little hat—out of her new blouse.
> LILLY DACHÉ, designer, on start of her career, news summaries of Dec. 3, 1954.

Glamour is what makes a man ask for your telephone number. But it also is what makes a woman ask for the name of your dressmaker.
> LILLY DACHÉ, *Woman's Home Companion*, July, 1955.

. . . Chinchilla is said to be more chic than mink though personally it reminds me of unborn burlap.
> PATRICK DENNIS (Edward Everett Tanner), novelist, *Life*, Dec. 7, 1962.

My dream is to save them from nature.
> CHRISTIAN DIOR, on desire to make all women look beautiful, *Collier's*, June 10, 1955.

Women are most fascinating between the age of 35 and 40 after they have won a few races and know how to pace themselves. Since few women ever pass 40, maximum fascination can continue indefinitely.
> CHRISTIAN DIOR, *ibid*.

To manufacture emotion a man must have a working agreement with madness.
> CHRISTIAN DIOR, *ibid*.

A woman who doesn't wear lipstick feels undressed in public. Unless she works on a farm.
> MAX FACTOR, cosmetics executive, *Time*, June 16, 1958.

If you adore her, you must adorn her. There lies the essence of a happy marriage.
> ANNE FOGARTY, designer, *Wife Dressing*, Messner, 1959.

You just put the minimum of beads on the maximum of chassis.
> EDITH HEAD, on dressing actress Juliet Prowse, *Saturday Evening Post*, Nov. 30, 1963.

Go to Kansas, go to Iowa. Walk the streets of Amarillo, read the papers in Salt Lake City. You'll find plenty of rimless people out there—rimless and happy. They wouldn't be found dead wearing intellectual specs.
> MIKE JULIAN, advertising consultant to Better Vision Institute, on enduring popularity of rimless spectacles, *New Yorker*, Feb. 20, 1960.

Poor Englishwomen! . . . When it comes to their clothes—well, the French reaction is a shrug, the Italian reaction a spreading of the hands and a lifting of the eyes and the American reaction simply one of amused contempt.
> JAMES LAVER, of the staff of Victoria and Albert Museum, London, reporting an improvement in English styles, "Chic-ness Crosses the Channel," *New York Times*, Nov. 24, 1963.

Seventh Avenue is the hard heave of a push boy rolling his clean dress racks down the middle of a dirty, littered street, the graceful pause of a model in a smoke-filled showroom packed with buyers. It is the hullabaloo of the fittings, the cacophony of luncheon shoptalk, the horns of traffic-maddened drivers.
> LIFE, "Seventh Rules Nation's Style," Oct. 3, 1960.

Seventh Avenue's working population is all caught up in the frenzied, never-finished business of supplying new clothes for the American woman. The haughty Paris houses may often pioneer the new styles, but it is Seventh Avenue that translates them into wearable—and buyable —reality for the United States.
> LIFE, *ibid.*

I've had my best times when trailing a Mainbocher evening gown across a sawdust floor. I've always loved high style in low company.
> ANITA LOOS, novelist, *New York Times*, March 28, 1961.

I got a coat lined with hamster. You couldn't do that kind of thing in America. All the Boy Scouts would go on strike.
> SUZY PARKER, actress and model, *Newsweek*, Feb. 18, 1963.

453

To call a fashion wearable is the kiss of death. No new fashion worth its salt is ever wearable.

> EUGENIA SHEPPARD, *New York Herald Tribune*, Jan. 13, 1960.

Our strapless bras have all seemed to lead a vicious life of their own. Amenable as they looked when the salesgirl showed them to us in the store, they have hated us from the very start. It has been a pitched battle between us, usually won by the strapless bra.

> EUGENIA SHEPPARD, *New York Herald Tribune*, May 5, 1961.

Except when it comes to bravery, we are a nation of mice. We dress and behave with timid circumspection. Good taste is the worst vice ever invented.

> EDITH SITWELL, interview on eve of her 75th birthday, *New York Times*, Sept. 7, 1962.

A hat is a flag—a shield—a bit of armor—and the badge of femininity. A hat is the difference between wearing clothes and wearing a costume; it's the difference between being dressed—and being dressed up; it's the difference between looking adequate and looking your best. A hat is to be stylish in—to glow under—to flirt beneath—to make others seem jealous over—and to make all men feel masculine about. A piece of magic is a hat.

> MARTHA SLITER, writer quoted by Millinery Institute, *Advertising Age*, April 13, 1959.

Elegance is good taste *plus* a dash of daring.

> CARMEL SNOW, for many years editor of *Harper's Bazaar*, in her autobiography, *The World of Carmel Snow*, McGraw-Hill, 1962.

The first thing the first couple did after committing the first sin was to get dressed. Thus Adam and Eve started the world of fashion, and styles have been changing ever since.

> TIME, Nov. 8, 1963, fashion survey entitled "Gilding the Lily."

Mink is for football games . . . Please. Out in the fresh air, sit in it, eat hot dogs in it, anything. But not evening, not elegance, I beg of you.

> VALENTINA, fashion designer, *Ladies' Home Journal*, March, 1958.

454

I adore that pink! It's the navy blue of India!

> DIANA VREELAND, *Vogue* editor, in praise of bright pink silk, *New York Times*, March 28, 1962.

The only real elegance is in the mind; if you've got that, the rest really comes from it.

> DIANA VREELAND, on becoming *Vogue's* editor-in-chief, *Newsweek*, Dec. 10, 1962.

The time was right for her, no doubt about that. We wanted to grow up. She came along, and suddenly we forgot about *the American girl*—that improbably golden never-never child who roved through the world's imagination with a tennis racket, an unmarred make-up, and some spotty phrase-book French—and fell in love instead with *the American woman*, a creature possessed of thoughtful responsibility, a healthy predilection for the good and the beautiful and the expensive, and a gift for moving through the world aware of its difficulties, its possibilities, its large and small joys. . . . If, at her birthday dinner, corn on the cob is served, she will eat it without thought that in her pleasure a little lipstick may smear.

> VOGUE, July, 1963, on Jacqueline Kennedy.

Food and Drink

Souffle is more important than you think. If men ate souffle before meetings, life could be much different.

> JACQUES BAEYENS, French Consul General in New York, *New York Journal-American*, May 7, 1958.

The real, native South Seas food is lousy. You can't eat it.

> "TRADER VIC" BERGERON, owner-operator of numerous South Seas restaurants in the U.S., *Newsweek*, April 21, 1958.

The powder is mixed with water and tastes exactly like powder mixed with water.

> ART BUCHWALD, columnist, on liquid diet fad, *New York Herald Tribune*, Dec. 29, 1960.

I am such a great connoisseur that I can tell the difference between the tang of the Beaverbrook *Daily Express* and the mellow flavor of *The Times*.

> LORD CHAMPION, claiming that the English habit of wrapping fish and chips in newspapers flavors the taste, *New York Times*, July 14, 1963.

My good health is due to a soup made of white doves. It is simply wonderful as a tonic.

> MADAME CHIANG KAI-SHEK, *Time*, Feb. 27, 1956.

Always remember, that I have taken more out of alcohol than alcohol has taken out of me.

> WINSTON CHURCHILL, quoted in the autobiographical *By Quentin Reynolds*, McGraw-Hill, 1963.

456

No government could survive without champagne. Champagne in the throat of our diplomatic people is like oil in the wheels of an engine.
> JOSEPH DARGENT, French vintner, *New York Herald Tribune*, July 21, 1955.

Cheese—milk's leap toward immortality.
> CLIFTON FADIMAN, *Any Number Can Play*, World Publishing Co., 1957.

The bagel, an unsweetened doughnut with rigor mortis. . . .
> BEATRICE AND IRA FREEMAN, "About: Bagels," *New York Times*, May 22, 1960.

Coffee in England is just toasted milk.
> CHRISTOPHER FRY, playwright, *New York Post*, Nov. 29, 1962.

A gourmet is just a glutton with brains.
> PHILLIP W. HABERMAN, JR., "How To Be A Calorie Chiseler," *Vogue*, Jan. 15, 1961.

In shape, it is perfectly elliptical. In texture, it is smooth and lustrous. In color, it ranges from pale alabaster to warm terra cotta. And in taste, it outstrips all the lush pomegranates that Swinburne was so fond of sinking his lyrical teeth into.
> SYDNEY HARRIS, "Tribute to An Egg," *Majority of One*, Houghton Mifflin, 1957.

I've run more risk eating my way across the country than in all my driving.
> DUNCAN HINES, on his guides to good restaurants, May 27, 1956.

Cookbooks are not just for cooking. . . . Cookbooks are for inspiration, for lifting the spirit and freeing the mind, for brightening your outlook as well as your parties and table conversation . . . for the understanding of people and places, for the revelation of the past and for the interpretation of the present . . . for culture, education, for inviting the soul, reviving memories, reliving experiences. Cookbooks, like poetry, are for the intensification of precious moments. Where, except in cookbooks and in lyrics,

457

does one find so much emotion distilled, charted and recollected in tranquility?

HOUSE BEAUTIFUL, Feb., 1957, "How, Where and Why to Read a Cookbook."

Condiments are like old friends—highly thought of, but often taken for granted.

MARILYN KAYTOR, food editor, "Condiments: the Tastemakers," *Look*, Jan. 29, 1963.

People sometimes praise a restaurant by saying it makes them feel at home. . . . I don't want to feel at home in a restaurant. I want to feel that I'm having a night out.

ALVIN KERR, "Specialités de la Maison," *Gourmet*, Oct., 1960.

In America, even your menus have the gift of language. . . . "The Chef's own Vienna Roast. A hearty, rich meat loaf, gently seasoned to perfection and served in a creamy nest of mashed farm potatoes and strictly fresh garden vegetables." Of course, what you get is cole slaw and a slab of meat, but that doesn't matter because the menu has already started your juices going. Oh, those menus. In America, they are poetry.

LAURIE LEE, British author, *Newsweek*, Oct. 24, 1960.

The day has the color and the sound of winter. Thoughts turn to chowder. . . . Chowder breathes reassurance. It steams consolation.

CLEMENTINE PADDLEFORD, food editor, *New York Herald Tribune*, Oct. 19, 1961.

. . . It is dazzling to discover smorgasbord at a South Carolina inn or a Caesar salad in Arkansas. Surely, we think, such internationalism is a good sign, rather like the Daughters of the American Revolution voting for an increase in foreign aid.

ELEANOR PERENYI, "Whatever Happened to American Cooking?" *Saturday Evening Post*, June 15, 1963.

Few things are more revolting than the spectacle of a normally reasonable father and husband gowned in one of those hot, massive aprons inscribed with disgustingly corny legends, presiding over a noisome brazier as he destroys huge hunks of good meat and fills the neighborhood with greasy, acrid smoke: a Boy Scout with five o'clock shadow.

> Donald Rogers, business columnist, "Cookout's Got to Go," *New York Herald Tribune*, July 21, 1961.

A wife who is obliged to shop with the utmost of care and thrift throughout the rest of the year is, in summer, constrained to watch her husband demand the choicest, thickest, juiciest pieces of good red beef so that he might, on weekends, destroy them over an unmanageable charcoal fire and then try to take the curse off with anointments of home-brewed barbecue sauce representing as horrid a concoction to come out of a pot since Macbeth's witches gave up cooking.

> Donald Rogers, *ibid.*

I could have done with some strong whisky but . . . all I got was dry sherry. It was but the first of many such drinks, as I found that Anglican clergy favor it above all others.

> Sir Basil Spence, architect, on learning that he had won design competition for Coventry Cathedral, *Phoenix at Coventry*, Harper & Row, 1962.

. . . What is sauce for the goose may be sauce for the gander but is not necessarily sauce for the chicken, the duck, the turkey or the guinea hen.

> Alice B. Toklas, *The Alice B. Toklas Cook Book*, Harper & Row, 1954.

I think if I were a woman I'd wear coffee as a perfume.

> John van Druten, *Think*, Feb., 1963.

Cooking is like love. It should be entered into with abandon or not at all.

> Harriet Van Horne, *Vogue*, Oct. 15, 1956.

Sports

When I was 40, my doctor advised me that a man in his forties shouldn't play tennis. I heeded his advice carefully and could hardly wait until I reached 50 to start again.

> Hugo Black, Associate Justice, U.S. Supreme Court, *Think*, Feb., 1963.

. . . When you tell the story of this year's American League race . . . you go with a little thing called money, because money gets the job done better than all the pride and guts and whatever it is they talk about when an athlete does well.

> Jimmy Breslin, columnist, on importance of World Series winnings, "The Other Check," *New York Herald Tribune*, July 26, 1963.

You gotta be a man to play baseball for a living but you gotta have a lot of little boy in you, too.

> Roy Campanella of the Brooklyn Dodgers, *New York Journal-American*, April 12, 1957.

I'm not the greatest; I'm the double greatest. Not only do I knock 'em out, I pick the round. . . .

> Cassius Clay, world's heavyweight boxing champion contender, *New York Times*, Dec. 9, 1962.

When you investigate the nether world of fish as I did, you find the flashing green and blue and turquoise and emerald surroundings they live in a tremendous busy-mess. While I watched, a group of pirate fish—a fish that looks as if it had been painted by Dufy—swam by with brisk determination as if they were late to a Parent-Teacher meeting and were

460

determined to raise hell about the new school board. Five seconds later a swarm of grunts, a yellow fish of great charm and staggering numbers, headed due East as if they were old grads going to the Yale-Harvard game. Then a solitary grouper flashed by for a luncheon date with a blonde he knew. They all seemed to be going somewhere and they knew the quickest route where the traffic is lightest. . . . Then a few seconds later the mood in this watery world changed utterly. There were a thousand or so fish just sitting around looking at each other, nobody going anywhere. It was a Sunday afternoon in the park.

> JOHN CROSBY, columnist, on skin-diving in the Bahamas, *New York Herald Tribune*, Nov. 27, 1957.

A ball player's got to be kept hungry to become a big-leaguer. That's why no boy from a rich family ever made the big leagues.

> JOE DI MAGGIO, *New York Times*, April 30, 1961.

I am still a victim of chess. It has all the beauty of art—and much more. It cannot be commercialized. Chess is much purer than art in its social position.

> MARCEL DUCHAMP, recalling his decision in 1920's to give up art for chess, *Time*, March 10, 1952.

To me, the sea is like a person—like a child that I've known a long time. It sounds crazy, I know, but when I swim in the sea I talk to it. I never feel alone when I'm out there.

> GERTRUDE EDERLE, 30 years after becoming the first woman to swim English Channel, *New York Post*, Sept. 5, 1956.

I'll be around as long as the horses think I'm smarter than they are.

> JAMES E. "SUNNY JIM" FITZSIMMONS, at 83 the trainer who had saddled more winners than anyone in American turf history, *New York Times*, June 22, 1958.

There are two groups in racing whose rights should be considered. There are people who furnish the actors for the show, the owners with the costly stables. And there is the public that furnishes the money. Both of them got to lose, no chance in the world to break even.

> JAMES E. ("SUNNY JIM") FITZSIMMONS, *New York Herald Tribune*, April 14, 1963.

461

I've liked the losing horses too. I treat 'em all like kids in an orphan home
—with kindness and firmness.

> James E. ("Sunny Jim") Fitzsimmons, *Newsweek*, June 17, 1963.

It can be set down in four words: the best of everything. The best hay,
oats and water.

> James E. ("Sunny Jim") Fitzsimmons, on training winners, *Life*,
> June 28, 1963.

I occasionally get birthday cards from fans. But it's often the same message:
they hope it's my last.

> Al Forman, National League umpire, *Time*, Aug. 25, 1961.

He has short reddish hair, a face as innocent as milk, and a build like a
chocolate eclair.

> William Barry Furlong, sportswriter, describing Jack Nicklaus,
> winner at 22 of U.S. Open golf championship, *New York Times*,
> Sept. 1, 1963.

Steel is a man's weapon. It has always been the great equalizer. Little men
have brought big men crashing like storm-stricken oaks by sliding six
inches of it gently into their bodies. Speed and guile offset brawn and
size; trickery can take the measure of knowledge.

> Paul Gallico, "Gentle Art of Swordplay," *Sports Illustrated*, Sept.
> 20, 1954.

Pro football is like nuclear warfare. There are no winners, only survivors.

> Frank Gifford, New York Giants halfback for eight years, *Sports
> Illustrated*, July 4, 1960.

In a way an umpire is like a woman. He makes quick decisions, never re-
verses them and doesn't think you're safe when you're out.

> Larry Goetz, umpire, news summaries of April 17, 1955.

Men like to win; but women hate to lose. The difference can be summed
up in one word: bridgemanship.

> Charles Goren, bridge authority, *McCall's*, Aug., 1961.

462

. . . One of the greatest educational swindles ever perpetrated on American youth.

> WHITNEY GRISWOLD, president, Yale University, on athletic scholarships, *New York Times*, April 20, 1963.

The fundamental difference between intercollegiate and professional athletics is that in college the players are supposed to be students first and foremost. This does not mean that they should all be Phi Beta Kappas or physics majors, but neither should they be subnormal students majoring in ping-pong.

> REV. THEODORE HESBURGH, president, University of Notre Dame, *Sports Illustrated*, Sept. 27, 1954.

The rigid volunteer rules of right and wrong in sports are second only to religious faith in moral training. . . .

> HERBERT HOOVER, *Sports Illustrated*, July 8, 1957.

If you watch a game, it's fun. If you play it, it's recreation. If you work at it, it's golf.

> BOB HOPE, *Reader's Digest*, Oct., 1958.

Any ballplayer that don't sign autographs for little kids ain't an American. He's a Communist.

> ROGERS HORNSBY, National League batting champion of St. Louis Cardinals, *Saturday Evening Post*, June 15, 1963.

Eighty percent of big-league ballplayers go out to the race track today. Sneak around in sunglasses. Other 20 percent ain't that holy. Just can't find anybody who'll give 'em free tickets.

> ROGERS HORNSBY, *ibid*.

A major league baseball team is a collection of 25 youngish men who have made the major leagues and discovered that in spite of it, life remains distressingly short of ideal. A bad knee still throbs before a rainstorm. Too much beer still makes for an unpleasant fullness. Girls still insist on tiresome preliminaries. And now there is a wife who gets headaches or a baby who has colic.

> ROGER KAHN, "Intellectuals and Ballplayers," *The American Scholar*, Nov. 3, 1957.

Football is violence and cold weather and sex and college rye. Horse racing is animated roulette. Boxing is smoky halls and kidneys battered until they bleed. Tennis and golf are best played, not watched. Basketball, hockey and track meets are action heaped upon action, climax upon climax, until the onlooker's responses become deadened. Baseball is for the leisurely afternoons of summer and for the unchanging dreams.

> ROGER KAHN, *ibid.*

Football today is far too much a sport for the few who can play it well; the rest of us, and too many of our children, get our exercise from climbing up the seats in stadiums, or from walking across the room to turn on our television sets. And this is true for one sport after another, all across the board.

> PRESIDENT KENNEDY, address at National Football Foundation dinner, Dec. 5, 1961.

Rodeoing is about the only sport you can't fix. You'd have to talk to the bulls and horses, and they wouldn't understand you.

> BILL LUNDERMAN, holder of title "All-Around Cowboy of the U.S.," news summaries of March 8, 1954.

I swim down through liquid green heavens, down through the poem of the sea. Down to delicate castles of convoluted corals, pale fish and rainbow-hued fish, fishes supple and rigid, festoons of fish, festooning of coral, festoons of the reefs.

> CLARE BOOTHE LUCE, on skin-diving, *Sports Illustrated*, Aug. 11, 1958.

I have always adhered to two principles. The first one is to train hard and get into the best possible physical condition. The second is to forget all about the other fellow until you face him in the ring and the bell sounds for the fight.

> ROCKY MARCIANO, world heavyweight boxing champion, news reports of Sept. 2, 1955.

San Francisco has been saying for decades that it is big league. In its secret heart it has never been quite sure. These days it is.

> CHARLES McCABE, sports columnist, on transfer of Giants from New York to San Francisco, *New York Herald Tribune*, May 24, 1958.

464

In this game, you have to be a finisher. I call it "finishing," and you don't learn it in Miss Hewitt's school for young ladies.

> ARCHIE MOORE, light-heavyweight boxing champion, on his penchant for putting away an opponent at first opportunity, *New Yorker*, Nov. 11, 1961.

It's necessary to relax your muscles when you can. Relaxing your brain is fatal.

> STIRLING MOSS, British racing-car driver, *Newsweek*, May 16, 1955.

For the hunter—not the game hog or the despoiler—hunts memories and time past, as well as a brace of birds. He hunts his own simpler self. The self that knows the difference between a white oak and a black oak, between hickory and butternut, between hare and rabbit. The self that knows the whirr of a partridge, the hoarse call of a cock pheasant, the rasping bark of a fox. The self that can, on occasion, put up a bird and merely stand and watch in admiration, though the game bag is still empty.

> NEW YORK TIMES, Nov. 3, 1957, editorial entitled "Open Season."

Meat hunting is a vanished necessity, the professional hunter virtually a thing of the past. But man and the open hills and fields persist, and open season is an excuse for them to renew their acquaintance. Even the hunter does not live by meat alone.

> NEW YORK TIMES, *ibid*.

If I know I make this much trouble, I never climb Everest.

> TENSING NORKAY, Sherpa guide who was member of expedition to Mount Everest, on attempt to secure a passport to U.S., news summaries of March 29, 1954.

The art of running the mile consists, in essence, of reaching the threshold of unconsciousness at the instant of breasting the tape.

> PAUL O'NEIL, *Sports Illustrated*, Aug. 16, 1955.

. . . sport is [also] working its changes on them and the atmosphere in which they live. A banker rounding a buoy, a stenographer on horseback, a mechanic in a duck blind can all savor—even in the age of the desk, the lathe, the tractor and the split-level-with-mortgage—that expansiveness of spirit, that sense of uniqueness, which have always been the hall-marks of a full and satisfying life.

> PAUL O'NEIL, "Nobody Falls Asleep on Sunday Afternoon," *Sports Illustrated*, Aug. 20, 1956.

The reason the Yankees never lay an egg is because they don't operate on chicken feed.

> DAN PARKER, columnist, *Sports Illustrated*, April 7, 1958

He had splendid conformation—broad shoulders, white hair, and erect carriage—and was beautifully turned out in an ensemble of rich brown. One was inclined to hope he would, in the end, award first prize to him-self.

> RED SMITH, columnist, description of a judge at a dog show, *Newsweek*, April 21, 1958.

. . . Ray Robinson, a brooding genius, a darkly dedicated soul who walks in lonely majesty, a prophet without honor, an artist whom nobody, but nobody, understands.

> RED SMITH, on boxing's Sugar Ray Robinson, *ibid*.

The baseball mind is a jewel in the strict sense—that is to say, a stone of special value, rare beauty, and extreme hardness. Cut, polished and fixed in the Tiffany setting of a club owner's skull, it resists change as a diamond resists erosion.

> RED SMITH, *New York Herald Tribune*, Aug. 7, 1961.

Here is no sentiment, no contest, no grandeur, no economics. From the sanctity of this occupation, a man may emerge refreshed and in control of his own soul. He is not idle. He is fishing, alone with himself in dignity and peace. It seems a very precious thing to me.

> JOHN STEINBECK, "Of Fish and Fishermen," *Sports Illustrated*, Oct. 4, 1954.

You done splendid.

> CASEY STENGEL, accolade reserved for best players, *Casey Stengel: His Half-Century in Baseball*, by Frank Graham, Jr., John Day, 1958.

466

Wall Street bankers supposedly back the Yankees; Smith College girls approve of them. God, Brooks Brothers and United States Steel are believed to be solidly in the Yankees' corner. . . . The efficiently triumphant Yankee machine is a great institution, but, as they say, who can fall in love with U.S. Steel?

> GAY TALESE, "There Are Fans—and Yankee Fans," *New York Times,* June 29, 1958.

His legs are buckled into clumsy shin guards; his face is hidden by the metal grille of a heavy mask. . . . His chest is covered with a corrugated protective pad, and his big mitt is thrust out as if to fend off destruction . . . his field of vision gives him his own special view of the vast ballpark. In a sense, the game belongs to him. He is the catcher.

> TIME, the role of catcher in baseball, Aug. 8, 1955.

Ideally, the umpire should combine the integrity of a Supreme Court justice, the physical agility of an acrobat, the endurance of Job and the imperturbability of Buddha.

> TIME, Aug. 25, 1961, on "The Villains in Blue."

It's a lot tougher to be a football coach than a President. You've got four years as a President, and they guard you. A coach doesn't have anyone to protect him when things go wrong.

> HARRY TRUMAN, *Sports Illustrated,* March 17, 1958.

I do not think that winning is the most important thing. I think winning is the only thing.

> BILL VEECK, president, Chicago White Sox, quoted in *The Management Evolution,* American Management Association, 1963.

467

Source Index

475

Subject Index